Preventive Justice

OXFORD MONOGRAPHS ON CRIMINAL LAW AND JUSTICE

Series Editor: Professor Andrew Ashworth, Vinerian Professor of Law at All Souls College, Oxford.

This series aims to cover all aspects of criminal law and procedure including criminal evidence. The scope of this series is wide, encompassing both practical and theoretical works.

OTHER TITLES IN THIS SERIES

Abuse of Process and Judicial Stays of Criminal Proceedings
Andrew LT Choo

A Philosophy of Evidence Law
Justice in the Search for Truth
Hock Lai Ho

The Criminal Justice System and Healthcare
Edited by Charles A Erin and Suzanne Ost

Rethinking Imprisonment
Richard Lippke

Killing in Self-Defence
Fiona Leverick

Delayed Prosecution for Childhood Sexual Abuse
Penney Lewis

Lying, Cheating, and Stealing
A Moral Theory of White Collar Crime
Stuart P Green

Defining Crimes
The Special Part of Criminal Law
Edited by Anthony Duff and Stuart P Green

Criminal Responsibility
Victor Tadros

Proportionate Sentencing
Exploring the Principles
Andrew von Hirsch and Andrew Ashworth

Appraising Strict Liability
Edited by Andrew Simester

Excusing Crime
Jeremy Horder

Preventive Justice

Andrew Ashworth and Lucia Zedner

OXFORD
UNIVERSITY PRESS

OXFORD
UNIVERSITY PRESS

Great Clarendon Street, Oxford, OX2 6DP,
United Kingdom

Oxford University Press is a department of the University of Oxford.
It furthers the University's objective of excellence in research, scholarship,
and education by publishing worldwide. Oxford is a registered trade mark of
Oxford University Press in the UK and in certain other countries

First Edition published in 2014

Impression: 1

Published in the United States of America by Oxford University Press
198 Madison Avenue, New York, NY 10016, United States of America

British Library Cataloguing in Publication Data
Data available

Library of Congress Control Number: 2014934471

ISBN 978–0–19–871252–7

Printed and bound in Great Britain by
CPI Group (UK) Ltd, Croydon, CR0 4YY

Acknowledgements

In November 2009 we were fortunate enough to secure a very generous grant from the Arts and Humanities Research Council for a three-year project on preventive justice (Application ID: AH/H015655/1). This project arose out of our separate and joint researches in several fields, including security and terrorism (LZ) and criminal law and human rights (AA), and out of our teaching. Whenever the question of justifying a punishment or sentence came up, we would reach for well-known writings in the philosophy of punishment. But whenever the question of justifying a preventive measure came up, we were faced with a normative void and no corpus of writings on which to draw. Yet many preventive measures are no less intrusive, no less liberty-restricting, than many punishments. So we set out to examine the state's use of preventive techniques that involve coercion, particularly those entailing loss of liberty, and to consider what principles and values should guide and limit these laws and measures.

In carrying out the project we were assisted by two outstanding post-doctoral researchers. Dr Patrick Tomlin was appointed from August 2010, and worked with us until he took up a Lectureship at the University of Reading in January 2012. Dr Ambrose Lee was then appointed, and he worked with us until he took up a Leverhulme Early Career Fellowship, to work on a research project entitled Internal Constraints to Coercive Harm Prevention at the Centre for Criminology in the University of Oxford, in May 2013. We are immensely grateful to both of them for their intellectual and organizational contributions to the project.

Part of our endeavour was to invite a range of scholars from law, criminal justice, criminology, political theory, and philosophy to enrich our study by writing essays on topics related to preventive justice, and coming to Oxford to debate the issues. We held two seminars at All Souls College, Oxford, the first in September 2011 and the second in January 2012. Papers were given at the first seminar by Markus Dubber, Antony Duff, Bernard Harcourt, Doug Husak, Pat O'Malley, Carol Steiker, and Victor Tadros; and at the second seminar by Petter Asp, David Dyzenhaus, Klaus Günther, Matt Matravers, Jim Nickel, Peter Ramsay, and Fred Schauer. We are grateful to all these scholars for their willingness to engage with the project, and for writing up their papers for publication in *Prevention and the Limits of the Criminal Law* (edited by A. Ashworth, L. Zedner and P. Tomlin, Oxford University Press, 2013). We are also grateful to the other scholars who attended the seminars and participated in the discussions, particularly to James Edwards, Cecile Fabre, Murray Hunt, Nicola Lacey, Ian Loader, Laurence Lustgarten, Andreas von Hirsch, and Shlomit Wallerstein, all of whom acted as respondents to the papers.

In addition, several Swedish colleagues—Petter Asp, Magnus Ulvang, Sandra Friberg, Iain Cameron, and Erick Svensson—kindly read large parts of the manuscript and came to Oxford in April 2013 for a one day seminar to discuss their responses to our work. The book is undoubtedly better for their insightful comments and constructive criticisms, and we are truly indebted to them. We also thank Mary Bosworth and Ana Aliverti for their detailed comments on Chapter 10 and Jill Peay for her helpful comments on Chapter 9.

We also held a fourth seminar, in which we drew together a range of practitioners and policy makers whose work brings them into contact with issues of preventive justice. The seminar was held at the British Academy in June 2013, and we benefitted immensely from the discussions. We are grateful to all those who attended, and particularly to Keir Hopley (Ministry of Justice), Shami Chakrabarti (Liberty), Stan Gilmour (South-East Counter-Terrorism Unit), Jon Collins (Police Foundation), Neil Stevenson (Ministry of Justice), and Nick Armstrong (Matrix Chambers), each of whom acted as a commentator.

We were also fortunate to receive invitations to participate in seminars related to our work. Larry Alexander invited us to a seminar on preventive detention at the School of Law, University of San Diego, in April 2011. We participated in the 'Anti-Terror Laws and Preventive Justice Postgraduate Workshop' hosted by the Gilbert + Tobin Centre of Public Law, Faculty of Law, University of New South Wales, and held at the Centre for Criminology, University of Oxford, in December 2011. We are grateful to the organizers: George Williams, Andrew Linch, Fergal Davies, and Kieran Hardy. Finally, we were greatly flattered and assisted by Antony Duff's offer to arrange a seminar on our work at the Robina Institute of Criminal Law and Criminal Justice at the University of Minnesota. Antony Duff and his team organized the event, in September 2012. Papers were given by Susan Dimock, David Cole, Kim Ferzan, Allegra McLeod, and Stuart Green; and the commentators were Alice Ristroph, Alec Walen, Sharon Dolovich, Malcolm Thorburn, Claire Finkelstein, and David Sklansky. Once again, we are indebted to them all for their comments and suggestions.

We are also indebted to All Souls College, Corpus Christi College, the Centre for Criminology, and the Faculty of Law at the University of Oxford, and to the British Academy for providing support and for hosting our various endeavours. Material in three of the chapters has appeared in an earlier form elsewhere. Chapter 3 is based on Andrew Ashworth, 'Negotiating the Fundamental Right to Personal Liberty' (2014) 16 *Otago Law Review* (forthcoming); Chapter 5 is based on Andrew Ashworth and Lucia Zedner 'Prevention and Criminalization: Justifications and Limits', (2012) 15 *New Criminal Law Review* 542–571; and Chapter 6 draws upon Lucia Zedner, 'Erring on the Side of Safety: Risk Assessment, Expert Knowledge, and the Criminal Court', in I Dennis and GR Sullivan (eds.), *Seeking Security: Pre-Empting the Commission of Criminal Harms* (Oxford: Hart Publishing, 2012), 221–41.

In the production of this book we have been aided by the research assistance of Paolo Ronchi, and at Oxford University Press by the continued support and encouragement of Alex Flach, Natasha Flemming, Briony Ryles, Stacey Prigent, Catherine Bailey, Paul Nash, and Caroline Quinnell. We are sincerely grateful to them all.

AA and LZ

December 2013

Table of Contents

Table of Cases

ECHR

United Kingdom

United States of America

Canada

Australia

UN Commission on Human Rights

Table of Legislation

United States of America

Australia

Sweden

List of Abbreviations

ARAI	Actuarial Risk Assessment Instrument
ASBO	Anti-Social Behaviour Order
BPA	Border Policing Command
CBO	Criminal Behaviour Order
CDA	Contagious Diseases Acts
CJA	Criminal Justice Act 2003
CMPs	closed material proceedings
CTO	Community Treatment Order
DOLS	deprivation of liberty safeguards
DSPD	Dangerous and Severe Personality Disorder
ECHR	European Convention on Human Rights
ECtHR	European Court of Human Rights
EEA	European Economic Area
Eurosur	European Border Surveillance System
FNP	foreign national prisoner
IPNA	Injunction to Prevent Nuisance and Annoyance
IPP	Imprisonment for Public Protection
IRA	Irish Republican Army
IRC	Immigration Removal Centre
JCHR	Joint Committee on Human Rights
LASPO	Legal Aid, Sentencing and Punishment of Offenders Act 2012
MAPPA	Multi-Agency Public Protection Arrangements
MHT	Mental Health Tribunal
MoU	Memorandum of Understanding
NCA	National Crime Agency
NOID	Notification of Infectious Diseases
NOMS	National Offender Management Service
OASys	Offender Assessment System
PNR	Passenger Name Records
PTA	Prevention of Terrorism Act 2005

SCPO	Serious Crime Prevention Order
SIAC	Special Immigration Appeals Commission
SOPO	Sexual Offences Prevention Order
STHFs	Short-Term Holding Facilities
TPIM	Terrorism Prevention and Investigation Measure
UKBA	United Kingdom Border Agency
UNCRPD	UN Convention on the Rights of Persons with Disability 2006

1

Introduction: The State and Coercive Preventive Measures

1.1 The Study

This book is the product of a three-year study of what we chose to call 'preventive justice'. The principal objective is to develop an account of the principles and values that should guide and limit the state's use of preventive techniques that involve coercion. Although there is an extensive literature on the rationales for and limitations on state punishment, there has been relatively little systematic exploration or analysis of the corresponding rationales, scope, and principled limits of coercive preventive techniques. Preventive endeavours are ubiquitous, but they have yet to be mapped, analysed, or rationalized. Our aim in this book is to reassess the foundations for the range of coercive measures that states now take in the name of prevention. The focus of the study is on the law of England and Wales, under the European Convention on Human Rights (ECHR), but comparisons with other jurisdictions (for example, the United States, Germany, Sweden, and Australia) are made from time to time. Rather than adopting an explicitly comparative approach, we have used comparative materials in order to assist our examination of the principled limits of coercive preventive measures.

We begin, in Section 1.2, with a brief survey of the terrain of the study. The range of coercive preventive measures is wide, and we have selected for analysis a number of measures that are conspicuous and contentious, and which also give an impression of the variety of situations in which state coercion may be used for ostensibly preventive ends. Different spheres of prevention could have been examined—for example, environmental policy or financial regulation—but we decided to focus mainly on the core issue of preventing physical harm to individuals, especially where deprivation of liberty is used for this purpose. We then turn, in Section 1.3, to examine the role of the state in preventing harm: this takes the discussion into the realms of political philosophy, and into engagement with the so-called right to security. On the basis of this groundwork, Section 1.4 examines the concept of preventive justice, and also the concept of coercion. Section 1.5 discusses the historical context for the study.

This leads into two definitional sections of this opening chapter. Section 1.6 examines the definition of a punitive measure, the rationales for punishment, and the reasons for ensuring that certain safeguards and procedural protections are in place. These features of punitive measures having been explored, Section 1.7 then examines the same features of coercive preventive measures—how should such a measure be defined, what rationales support such measures, and are there convincing reasons for insisting that certain procedural protections and safeguards should be in place? The concluding Section 1.8 charts the course of the chapters that follow.

1.2 The Terrain

Preventive measures taken by the state in order to reduce risks to harm are legion. Many of them, such as those involving situational crime prevention, social crime prevention, and even the most common forms of surveillance, do not involve (direct) coercion and therefore lie beyond the scope of the present study. Our concern lies with preventive measures that involve some element of coercion or loss of liberty, whether minor or substantial.[1] Even confining our study to coercive preventive measures, there is a wide range of possible topics to be examined. In order to orientate the theoretical discussion that follows, we outline the seven forms of coercive preventive measure that are to be our focus, all potentially involving loss of liberty:

(1) preventive powers in policing and criminal procedure;
(2) civil preventive orders;
(3) preventive criminal offences;
(4) preventive sentences;
(5) preventive counterterrorism measures;
(6) preventive aspects of public health law; and
(7) preventive aspects of immigration law.

Later chapters explore the justification for these preventive powers and the appropriate limits on their form and extent. In the paragraphs that follow here, we briefly describe those coercive measures so as to provide a context for the discussion in the remainder of this chapter.

(1) *Preventive powers in policing and criminal procedure*: we focus on three controversial types of coercive police power. First, there is the power to stop and search people on the street. Second, the power of arrest is sometimes exercised for preventive purposes. And third, the power of the police to contain or 'kettle' people for several hours in order to prevent major disorder has proved a contentious tactic, and we seek to raise questions about its justification and limits. We then go on to examine a

---

[1] The concept of coercion, so obviously important in this connection, is discussed in Section 1.3.

much-used coercive power in criminal procedure, that of pre-trial detention. The ECHR (like many similar documents internationally) declares the right to liberty of the person, but allows for exceptions, one of which is the detention pending trial of persons charged with an offence. We examine the various reasons that have been accepted as providing a justification for this deprivation of liberty—preventing the defendant from absconding, preventing interference with witnesses, preventing harm to the defendant, and (most controversially) preventing the commission of offences. In Chapter 3 we discuss whether, and to what extent, each of these reasons should be capable of outweighing the presumption of innocence and the general right to liberty of the person.

(2) *Civil preventive orders*: the law of England and Wales has a long history of preventive orders, going back to before 1361 in respect of the power to bind a person over to keep the peace.[2] Since the mid-1990s, it has seen the rapid development of a legal form known as the civil preventive order. These are essentially two-step orders: the first step is the making of a preventive order according to civil procedure, prohibiting a person from doing certain acts or going to certain places; the second step is that a person who breaches any of the conditions of such an order without reasonable excuse commits a serious criminal offence, usually punishable by up to five years' imprisonment. More than a dozen types of civil preventive order have been created in England and Wales, ranging from the well-known Anti-Social Behaviour Order (ASBO) to Serious Crime Prevention Orders, Risk of Sexual Harm Orders and Terrorism Prevention and Investigation Measures (TPIMs). In Chapter 4 we scrutinize the justifications for such measures, and propose limitations to which they should be subjected.

(3) *Preventive criminal offences*: prevention forms part of the rationale for most criminal offences,[3] but there are some groups of offences for which the preventive rationale is heightened. We focus on four forms of criminal offence: *inchoate offences*, particularly the crimes of attempt and conspiracy; *substantive offences defined in an inchoate mode*, in respect of which the form of definition prohibits not the causing of a prohibited harm but the doing of acts with intent to cause such a harm, thereby criminalizing conduct at a similar stage to an inchoate offence; *preparatory or pre-inchoate offences*, which include crimes of possession and of membership of a prohibited organization, which may be criminalized without the need for proof of an intent to cause harm; and offences of *risk-creation*, which might include offences such as drunk-driving and speeding, as well as offences involving the breach of health and

---

[2] In this year the Justices of the Peace Act 1361 put some of the common law powers in statutory form: see Law Commission of England and Wales, 'Binding Over', *Law Com No. 222* (1994).

[3] As Nils Jareborg has observed: 'It comes in on the level of criminalization. The very point of threatening with punishment would be lost if one did not presuppose that the threat has some preventive effect.' N Jareborg, *Essays in Criminal Law*, ed. (Sweden: Iustus Forlag, 1988).

safety regulations. In Chapter 5 we demonstrate the respects in which these offences depart from standard criminal law doctrines, explore the justifications for these departures, and propose a principled approach to limitations on such uses of the criminal law.

(4) *Preventive sentences*: as with criminal offences, prevention forms part of the rationale for most sentences. However, there are some forms of sentence which are explicitly conceived as preventive measures involving deprivation of liberty. The most conspicuous are mandatory or mandatory minimum sentences and extended determinate sentences for those who commit certain offences persistently, and the indeterminate preventive detention of so-called 'dangerous' offenders, although there has been an abiding difficulty in defining and identifying such offenders. In Chapter 7 we examine the justifications for measures of this kind, and propose a principled approach to the problems they are designed to tackle.

(5) *Preventive counterterrorism measures*: perhaps the most draconian and burgeoning preventive laws are those presented as countering the potentially catastrophic harms inflicted by terrorist attack. Within the criminal law these include specific terrorism offences of possession, preparatory offences, crimes of publication and dissemination of inflammatory material, and offences of association with and support for terrorist organizations. Counterterrorist procedural powers include special powers of stop and search and of detention in a police station. Outside the criminal process, the development of counterterrorist civil preventive orders—notably Control Orders and their replacement TPIMs—the use of security-cleared special advocates and closed material proceedings together constitute substantial departures from ordinary procedures and established norms. The justifications for these and related powers will be explored in Chapter 8, and suggestions made for the imposition of principled restraints on their use.

(6) *Preventive aspects of public health law*: among the various compulsory measures in public health law are three that involve deprivation of liberty. First, there are powers to impose isolation or quarantine on persons who have or might have a contagious disease. Second, there are powers to detain mentally disordered persons as civil patients. And third, there are powers to detain convicted offenders who are mentally disordered. The justifications for these powers are scrutinized in Chapter 9.

(7) *Preventive aspects of immigration law*: compulsory powers to detain people are also a prominent feature of the law relating to immigration and asylum. There are, for example, powers to detain those whose application for asylum has been rejected and other intending or illegal immigrants. Other important aspects of immigration control include the policing of entry at, and often well beyond, the border; the enactment of immigration offences; the detention of foreign national prisoners in prison beyond the term of their sentence with a view to deportation; and the provision of short-term holding cells, immigration removal centres, and pre-departure accommodation. These measures are designed to identify illegal immigrants and failed asylum seekers in order to prevent their entry into the UK or to secure

their removal and return to their country of origin. In Chapter 10 we examine the preventive justifications offered for these measures and propose principled restrictions on their use.

1.3 'Preventive Justice' and 'Coercive Preventive Measures'

Before going much further, we should reflect on the key terms used in the study—'preventive' and 'justice', as combined in the concept of 'preventive justice' and '*coercive* preventive measures'. In their common usage the terms 'preventive' and 'prevention' rarely bear the apparently uncompromising meaning of totally eliminating harmful behaviour. It would be rare indeed for anyone advocating a preventive measure to believe, or to be understood as claiming, that the realistic objective of the measure was to prevent *all* harms of a particular kind. The more accurate term 'reductivism' has been coined,[4] in recognition of the fact that 'prevention' ought strictly to be confined to the meaning of 'preventing all instances of *x*'. However, reductivism is an ugly term that has not passed into common usage; we will, therefore, persist with the more normal term 'prevention', while recognizing that it bears an attenuated meaning such as *the significant reduction of (potentially) harmful behaviour*, or *the reduction of (potentially) harmful behaviour to a tolerable level*. Whichever of those attenuated meanings is chosen, we are left with the problem of determining what degree of reduction of harms is required, which must depend on what are thought to be socially acceptable levels of risk. Such calculations, weighing the predicted level of harmful outcomes against the curtailment of liberty involved in the preventive measure, are illustrated by decisions about the appropriate speed limits for particular roads. There is no set form of calculus for such decisions, and when Bentham stated confidently that any punishment greater or lesser than that indicated by the principle of utility would be 'so much misery run to waste', he was assuming far greater precision than is attainable in practice.[5] For the present, we can say that the terms 'preventive' and 'prevention' are uncertain in respect of the degree of reduction of harm envisaged, and that this uncertainty must be kept firmly in view in discussions below. The same analysis applies to a range of other terms that are often used as synonyms for, or close approximations to, prevention. Thus,

---

[4] By Nigel Walker in his many writings (eg N Walker, *Sentencing in a Rational Society* (Harmondsworth: Allen Lane, 1972), 18).

[5] J Bentham, *The Works of Jeremy Bentham*, ed. J Bowring (Edinburgh: William Tait, 1838–43), vol. 1 *Principles of Penal Law*, part ii, Ch. V; see also J Bentham, *An Introduction to Principles of Morals and Legislation* (Oxford: Blackwell, 1967; 1789), Ch. XV, 2: 'if the punishment be less than what is suitable to that degree, it will be *inefficacious*; it will be so much thrown away: if it be more, as far as the difference extends, it will be *needless*; it will therefore be thrown away also in that case'.

security, public safety, public protection, and social defence—to take but four of the prominent synonyms in contemporary debate—all share the element of uncertainty just identified in the concept of prevention. When applied to particular strategies or policy proposals, it will be rare that they can truly be interpreted as calling for the total elimination of harm from a given source. Usually, they are calling for a reduction in harm; a reduction of an unspecified degree.

As for the term 'justice', it is used here in two senses. The first is a formal sense, bearing the same general meaning as in the phrases 'criminal justice system' and 'civil justice system', to convey that it is part of an official framework of measures aimed at dealing with certain issues. Unlike criminal justice or civil justice, of course, preventive justice does not refer to an established system or even an acknowledged, coherent domain of legal enterprise. So, in part, recourse to the term preventive justice seeks to draw attention to the extent and nature of preventive endeavour, whether it takes place within the criminal justice system or within adjacent fields such as security, public health, and immigration. The second sense is substantive. We do not claim that preventive justice is part of a wider theory of social justice, enabling its general aims and limiting principles to be deduced from a master theory. We are cautious about the claims of grand theory, divorced from specific laws and substantive practices, measures, and institutions. Rather, the chapters of the book work towards the articulation of a set of values capable of generating both justifications for preventive measures and limiting principles that might be applied to concrete matters of lawmaking, policy, and practice. This set of values recognizes the state's duty to protect (discussed in Section 1.4), but also the state's duty to respect individuals as autonomous beings—which means, among other things, respect for rights, the maintenance of rule-of-law values, the avoidance of arbitrariness, and kindred principles. We argue the case for these principles in the various chapters, and then bring them together in Chapter 11.

The book is concerned with preventive measures that are coercive: non-coercive preventive measures, such as situational crime prevention, social crime prevention, rehabilitation, and a whole range of medical measures, are left in the background. But why do we place the emphasis on coercion, and wherein resides the element of coercion? The law uses coercion when it prescribes a sanction that is intended to impose sufficient pressure on a person to force or make that person act in a certain way.[6] The use of coercion stands contrary to a basic respect for the autonomy of individuals—whether it involves physical coercion, for example detention, or merely amounts to rational compulsion (a threat to bring about some other significant disadvantage to the person if compliance is not forthcoming).[7] These forms of coercion therefore involve the authorized deprivation of basic rights, and are consequently in need of moral and political justification. The roots of this

---

[6] G Lamond, 'The Coerciveness of Law', *Oxford Journal of Legal Studies* 20 (2000), 39.
[7] Lamond, 'The Coerciveness of Law' (n 6), 49.

justification may be found in the harm that the coercion is designed to avert or minimize, but, as we shall see in later chapters, there may be different ways in which one can justify particular coercive preventive measures. However, it is important to point out that coercion, rather like security, can be viewed from a subjective or objective point of view. There may be situations in which an individual feels coerced (ie feels that his or her options are so few and unattractive that a particular course of action must be taken) and where it was not the law's intention to coerce the individual. Our focus here is on purposively coercive measures, while bearing in mind the reality that coercive effects may be experienced in other situations.

1.4 The State's Duty to Prevent Harm

Before we can begin the task of trying to formulate a conceptual framework for preventive justice, we need to address the prior question of what founds the state's duty to prevent harm. The duty of the state to punish crime has been much explored, and the case for its exclusive right to do so has been stoutly defended.[8] The role of the state in preventing harm and ensuring security is more complex because it is neither exclusive nor so well defined. Understanding what underpins the state's preventive function requires close attention to fundamental questions about the relationship between state and citizen, the role and remit of the state, and the obligations of citizens.

Classical liberal conceptions of the relationship between state and citizen focus upon the obligations owed to the state by citizens and to citizens by the state. The citizen's obligation to obey the law is explained variously by reference to tacit consent to its authority; fair play to other citizens; submitting to reciprocal burdens when accepting the benefit of the services and protection provided by the state; or the consequentialist ground that, absent obedience to the law, the result would be chaos or a return to a Hobbesian state of nature.[9] What the state owes to citizens in return is less well defined, but seems always to include a duty to provide protection from the hazards and threats that they would otherwise face.[10] Thus, in exchange for the promise of the security of their persons and property, citizens agree to

---

[8] A Harel, 'Why Only the State May Inflict Criminal Sanctions: The Case against Privately Inflicted Sanctions', *Legal Theory* 14 (2008), 113–33; M Thorburn, 'Reinventing the Nightwatchman State', *University of Toronto Law Journal* 60 (2010), 425–43.

[9] For further analysis, see, eg, D Knowles, *Political Obligation: A Critical Introduction* (Abingdon: Routledge, 2010).

[10] A Ryan, 'Hobbes' Political Philosophy', in T Sorell (ed.), *The Cambridge Companion to Hobbes* (Cambridge: Cambridge University Press, 2011), 208–45; 228–99. See also K Günther, 'Responsibility to Protect and Preventive Justice', in A Ashworth, L Zedner, and P Tomlin (eds.), *Prevention and the Limits of the Criminal Law* (Oxford: Oxford University Press, 2013), 69–90.

renounce the right to self-government and to submit to the state's coercive force. As Hobbes observed in *Leviathan*: 'The very end for which this renouncing, and transferring of right is introduced, is nothing else but the security of a man's person.'[11] It follows that the state's primary task and indeed its very *raison d'être* is to secure for its citizens the conditions of order and security that are prerequisites of freedom. Accordingly, Hobbes characterized the duty of the state as follows: 'The office of the Sovereign, (be it a Monarch, or an Assembly,) consists in the end, for which he was trusted with Sovereign Power, namely the procuration of the *safety of the people*.'[12] Several things follow from this characterization of the state's primary function. First, the protective or preventive function is written into the very fabric of state authority and imposes upon the state a duty to promulgate laws and pursue policies in order to provide security for its citizens. Second, citizens owe a *prima facie* duty to the state and to one another to abide by law and to accept state coercion as the necessary price of peace and good order. Third, the state retains the prerogative of exercising executive powers in conditions of emergency outside the normal legal and constitutional limits placed on it.[13] The absolute necessity of the prerogative is a central theme in classical political theory (found in the writings of Locke, Montesquieu, Hume, Rousseau, and Adam Smith among others) and it points to the centrality of security to the liberal conception of the state.

Unsurprisingly, this prerogative power has been much debated in recent years, not least because it underpins executive action in situations of emergency and permits the exercise of extraordinary powers in the name of security.[14] If the duty to protect is not to give the state a *carte blanche* to exercise coercive powers in pursuit of its preventive function, closer consideration needs to be given to the question of what limits should apply, irrespective of the imminence or magnitude of the risk faced. In matters of everyday prevention, some limits are to be found in constitutional requirements of a liberal state first suggested by Locke, such as the system of checks and balances furnished by the separation of legislature, executive, and judiciary.[15] Other central requirements are the universal fair application of laws

---

[11] T Hobbes, *Leviathan* (Oxford: Oxford University Press, 2008;1651), Ch. XIII.

[12] Hobbes, *Leviathan* (n 11), Ch. XXX 'Of the Office of the Sovereign Representative'.

[13] J Dunn, *The Political Thought of John Locke* (Cambridge: Cambridge University Press, 1969), 150.

[14] D Dyzenhaus, 'The Permanence of the Temporary: Can Emergency Powers Be Normalized?', in R Daniels, P Macklem, and K Roach (eds.), *The Security of Freedom: Essays on Canada's Anti-Terrorism Bill* (Toronto: Toronto University Press, 2001), 21–37; B Ackerman, 'The Emergency Constitution', *Yale Law Journal* 113(5) (2004), 1029–91; L Tribe and P Gudridge, 'The Anti-Emergency Constitution', *Yale Law Journal* 113(8), 1801–70; D Cole, 'The Priority of Morality: The Emergency Constitution's Blind Spot', *Yale Law Journal* 113(8), 1753–800; O Gross and F Ní Aoláin, *Law in Times of Crisis: Emergency Powers in Theory and Practice* (Cambridge: Cambridge University Press, 2006); M Neocleous, *Critique of Security* (Edinburgh: Edinburgh University Press, 2008), 39–75.

[15] J Locke, *Two Treatises of Government* (Cambridge: Cambridge University Press, 1988;1690), Ch. IX 'Of the Ends of Political Society and Government'.

that are clear, intelligible, widely and well publicized; implemented by an impartial and independent judiciary; and backed up by powers of enforcement that are no more extensive than those required to secure order and prevent crime. It is in conditions of emergency, where exceptional powers are sought by governments, that the question of what limiting requirements should apply is most fiercely contested, as we shall see in Chapter 8. But our concern is also with those preventive measures that are widespread in non-emergency conditions, and with their justifications and proper limits.

The core duty to protect sets its own limit on the proper role and scope of the state in those liberal theories that espouse a minimalist or laissez-faire conception of government. In such accounts, the scope of legitimate state authority barely extends beyond the provision of security. Adam Smith, for example, in the first of his *Lectures on Jurisprudence*, argued that: the 'security of the people...that is, the preventing all crimes and disturbances which may interrupt the intercourse or destroy the peace of the society by any violent attacks' is best achieved through the implementation and enforcement of laws—as he went on to expound: 'the best means of bringing about this desirable end is the rigorous, severe, and exemplary execution of laws properly formed for the prevention of crimes and establishing the peace of the state'.[16] In Smith's account, a central element of the legal system is thus its preventive function. Indeed, the provision of security was among the few core functions that Smith acknowledged were more appropriately performed by the state than by the market. As we shall see, later libertarians like Robert Nozick read this to mean that the proper role of the state should be limited to that of 'night-watchman' or provider of security, and be no more extensive than this preventive function.[17] On this reading, the goal of prevention becomes not only an authorization for, and but also a limit on, the state's exercise of coercive powers.

Bolder claims have also been made for prevention. Thus, Sir William Blackstone wrote that 'preventive justice is, upon every principle of reason, of humanity, and of sound policy, preferable in all respects to punishing justice'.[18] Henry Fielding somewhat extravagantly claimed that 'it is better to prevent even one man from being a rogue than apprehending and bringing forty to justice'.[19] A much broader social notion of prevention was central to the agenda of nineteenth-century

---

[16] A Smith, *Lectures on Jurisprudence* (Oxford: Oxford University Press, 1978; 1763), 331; see also F Schauer, 'The Ubiquity of Prevention', in A Ashworth, L Zedner, and P Tomlin (eds.), *Prevention and the Limits of the Criminal Law* (Oxford: Oxford University Press, 2013), 10–22.

[17] R Nozick, *Anarchy, State and Utopia* (Oxford: Blackwell, 1974).

[18] W Blackstone, *Commentaries on the Laws of England in Four Books* (London: Routledge, 2001; 1753), Book IV, Ch. XVIII, 251.

[19] For this quotation and related discussion, see L Zedner, 'Policing before and after the Police: The Historical Antecedents of Contemporary Crime Control', *British Journal of Criminology* 46(1) (2006), 78–96; 85–6.

reformers such as Sir Edwin Chadwick, who saw the essence of preventive work in alleviating and regulating the conditions of the poor, and regarded this as a precondition of the imposition of strong punishments.[20] More will be said in Chapter 2 about how and in what ways developing conceptions of the state's preventive function informed the development of early policing and criminal justice. This is by no means only a matter of historical interest. The place of preventive endeavour among the very foundations of state authority is one of the key questions of contemporary political theory. It is also central to contemporary legal theory, in that we cannot properly understand what obligations citizens owe to each other and to the state until we establish what the role of the state itself entails. Even if there were agreement that the state has a fundamental duty to prevent harm and ensure security, there remain questions about the extent of that duty (as we saw in Section 1.3, when discussing the concept of prevention), and about the measures it may properly use in furtherance of that duty. Thus, a major theme here is the search for principled limits on the state's discharge of its duty to protect people from harm resulting from human actions. We will suggest that these limits derive from the state's duty of justice and its duty to respect the autonomy of those to whom its laws apply.

1.5   The Rise of the Preventive State?

It has been variously claimed that recent years have seen a 'preventive turn',[21] that this is part of a 'new penology',[22] or, more broadly, of the 'risk society',[23] now taking the form of an overriding concern for the management of uncertainty.[24] Others argue that the paradigm of governmental social control has shifted from solving and punishing crimes that have been committed, to identifying 'dangerous' people and depriving them of their liberty before they can do harm.[25] Some

---

[20] E Chadwick, 'Preventive Police', *London Review* 1 (1829), 252–308.

[21] G Hughes, *Understanding Crime Prevention: Social Control, Risk and Late Modernity* (Buckingham: Open University Press, 1998); A Edwards and G Hughes, 'The Preventive Turn and the Promotion of Safer Communities in England and Wales', in A Crawford (ed.), *Crime Prevention Policies in Comparative Perspective* (Cullompton: Willan Publishing, 2009), 62–85.

[22] M Feeley and J Simon, 'The New Penology: Notes on the Emerging Strategy of Corrections and Its Implications', *Criminology* 30(4) (1992), 449–74; although see J Simon, 'Reversal of Fortune: The Resurgence of Individual Risk Assessment in Criminal Justice', *Annual Review of Law and Social Science* 1 (2005), 397–421.

[23] U Beck, *The Risk Society; Towards a New Modernity* (London: Sage Publications, 1992).

[24] R Ericson, *Crime in an Insecure World* (Cambridge: Polity, 2007), Ch. 6.

[25] E Janus, 'The Preventive State, Terrorists and Sexual Predators: Countering the Threat of a New Outsider Jurisprudence', *Criminal Law Bulletin* 40 (2004), 576; 576. See also J McCulloch and B Carlton, 'Pre-empting Justice: Suppression of Financing of Terrorism and the "War on Terror"', *Current Issues in Criminal Justice* 17(3) (2006), 397–412.

commentators suggest that there has been a significant break with the past in terms of governmental concerns and policies, and that a new social and conceptual framework is needed to understand and to interpret changing phenomena.[26] In Chapter 2 we show that governmental concern about the prevention of harm is certainly not a new phenomenon; on the contrary, prevention motivated the very founding of the modern criminal justice system. To determine whether the discontinuities now outstrip the continuities is not the objective: our claim is solely that prevention is a major feature of contemporary social policies in many Western countries and that, because of its prominence and its implications for liberty, its foundations and manifestations call for close normative study.

Although we are not seeking to make a historical claim, we take seriously the observation made by Steiker, in her trailblazing 1998 article 'The Limits of the Preventive State', that the preventive powers of the state demand closer attention. Whereas the limits of the 'punitive state' have been explored extensively, Steiker observes:

Courts and commentators have had much less to say about the related topic of the limits of the state not as punisher (and thus necessarily as investigator and adjudicator of criminal acts) but rather as preventer of crime and disorder generally. Indeed, courts and commentators have not yet even recognized this topic as a distinct phenomenon either doctrinally or conceptually. Of course, one way to prevent crime is to punish criminals, thereby incapacitating (and perhaps even rehabilitating) them during the period of their incarceration, deterring the specific individuals involved from further criminality, and deterring others by example. But punishment is not the only, the most common, or the most effective means of crime prevention. The state can also attempt to identify and neutralize dangerous individuals before they commit crimes by restricting their liberty in various ways. In pursuing this goal, the state often will expand the functions of the institutions primarily involved in the criminal justice system – namely, the police and the prison. But other analogous institutions, such as the juvenile justice system and the civil commitment process, are also sometimes tools of, to coin another phrase, 'the preventive state'.[27]

Where supposedly preventive measures are found to be punitive, the usual 'criminal justice' protections should apply. The greater difficulty arises in respect of preventive measures that are not found to be punitive. These tend to be regarded as 'merely' preventive and as less in need of justification or limiting principles, despite the fact that such measures may impose heavy burdens. In Steiker's view, the tendency to downplay preventive measures arises also because courts and commentators 'do not tend to see the various preventive policies and practices . . . as part of a unified

---

[26] M Feeley and J Simon, 'Actuarial Justice: The Emerging New Criminal Law', in D Nelken (ed.), *The Futures of Criminology* (London: Sage, 1994), 173–201.

[27] C Steiker, 'The Limits of the Preventive State', *Journal of Criminal Law and Criminology* 88 (1998), 771–808; 774.

problem'.[28] The failure to draw connections among preventive endeavours has the consequence that 'each individual preventive practice has been treated *sui generis* rather than as a facet of a larger question in need of a more general conceptual framework'.[29] Our enumeration of some of the preventive endeavours now in use (see Section 1.2) underlines the importance of this observation. Recognizing the similarities and connections between these diverse measures would enable parallels to be drawn and similar principles to be deployed; the dangers known to attend one measure might be avoided; and appropriate limits might be set in the formulation of new measures. The tracing of similarities and correspondences need not be confined to explicitly preventive orders: it can productively be extended to identify and target other manifestations of the preventive state irrespective of the labels formally used. In short, the task ahead is to identify instances of coercive power exercised by the state in the name of prevention and to identify when, where, and how the exercise of those powers should be subject to limiting principles or otherwise constrained. The challenges thrown up by Steiker have been the subject of a small but growing literature on the jurisprudence of the 'preventive state'.[30] Others have called for a 'jurisprudence of dangerousness' or 'jurisprudence of security',[31] which likewise identifies the need to address the justifications for and limits to preventive endeavour. Some scholars have taken up the challenge to engage in more extended analysis of particular measures or discrete substantive domains: notable work has been undertaken on self-evidently preventive endeavours such as the extension of inchoate criminal liability,[32] civil preventive orders,[33] and

---

[28]   Steiker, 'The Limits of the Preventive State' (n 27), 778.

[29]   Steiker, 'The Limits of the Preventive State', 778.

[30]   See, for example, E Janus, 'The Preventive State, Terrorists and Sexual Predators: Countering the Threat of a New Outsider Jurisprudence', *Criminal Law Bulletin* 40, 576; E Janus, *Failure to Protect: America's Sexual Predator Laws and the Rise of the Preventive State* (Ithaca: Cornell University Press, 2006); S Krasmann, 'The Enemy on the Border: Critique of a Programme in Favour of a Preventive State', *Punishment and Society* 9(3) (2007), 301–18; T Tulich, 'A View inside the Preventive State: Reflections on a Decade of Anti-Terror Law', *Griffith Law Review* 21(1) (2012), 209.

[31]   For example, C Slobogin, 'A Jurisprudence of Dangerousness', *Northwestern University Law Review* 98 (2003), 1–62 and L Farmer, 'The Jurisprudence of Security: The Police Power and the Criminal Law' in MD Dubber and M Valverde (eds.), *The New Police Science: the Police Power in Domestic and International Perspective* (Stanford CA: Stanford University Press, 2006), 145–67.

[32]   For example, L Alexander and KK Ferzan, 'Danger: The Ethics of Preemptive Action', *Ohio State Journal of Criminal Law* 9(2) (2012), 637–67; KK Ferzan, 'Inchoate Crimes at the Prevention/Punishment Divide', *San Diego Law Review* 48(4) (2011), 1273–97; AP Simester, 'Prophylactic Crimes', in GR Sullivan and I Dennis (eds.), *Seeking Security: Pre-Empting the Commission of Criminal Harms* (Oxford: Hart Publishing, 2012), 59–78; P Ramsay, 'Democratic Limits to Preventive Criminal Law', in A Ashworth, L Zedner, and P Tomlin (eds.), *Prevention and the Limits of the Criminal Law* (Oxford: Oxford University Press, 2013), 214–34.

[33]   For example, A Ashworth and L Zedner, 'Preventive Orders: A Problem of Under-Criminalization?', in RA Duff et al. (eds.), *The Boundaries of the Criminal Law* (Oxford: Oxford University Press, 2010); AP Simester and A von Hirsch, 'Regulating Offensive Conduct

preventive detention.[34] What is as yet missing is any sustained and systematic analysis of the gamut of preventive endeavours of the sort that we undertake in this book. We make no claim that our exercise is exhaustive; rather we hope that by mapping out and examining the broad array of preventive endeavour it will be possible to see the connections and commonalities that might underpin a larger articulation of preventive justice.

In what follows, we engage critically with a wide variety of preventive endeavours that have become prominent in recent years—three examples are civil preventive orders (Chapter 4), counterterrorist measures (Chapter 8), and immigration laws (Chapter 10)—as well as with more long-standing sites of preventive measures such as policing and criminal procedure (Chapter 3), public health law (Chapter 9), and the preventive detention of the dangerous (Chapter 7). We will argue that the preventive endeavour is manifest and problematic in its two broad forms—its use as a rationale for extending the boundaries of the criminal law, and its use as a rationale for developing various coercive measures designed to sit outside or alongside the criminal process and thereby to avoid the procedural safeguards attached to that process. One obvious point is that the politics of the preventive has a strong element of irresistibility built into it, since it generally appears perverse to argue against a preventive measure. Who could be against the prevention of harm? The political force behind terms such as prevention, security, public protection, and public safety is practically very powerful, not least because the critics of any such measure can be portrayed as courting insecurity and jeopardizing public safety. In Section 1.7 and in subsequent chapters, we set out to provide some more stable indicators of what should, and what should not, be taken as justifications for coercive preventive measures involving deprivation of liberty.

1.6 Punitive Measures: Rationales and Safeguards

One of the motivating thoughts behind our work is the contrast between the extensive research and writing on 'theories of punishment' and the virtual absence of equivalent normative debate about preventive measures. Theories of punishment

---

through Two-Step Prohibitions', in A von Hirsch and AP Simester (eds.), *Incivilities: Regulating Offensive Behaviour* (Oxford: Hart Publishing, 2006), 173–94; P Ramsay, 'The Theory of Vulnerable Autonomy and the Legitimacy of Civil Preventative Orders', in B McSherry, A Norrie, and S Bronitt (eds.), *Regulating Deviance: The Redirection of Criminalisation and the Futures of Criminal Law* (Oxford: Hart Publishing, 2009), 109–39.

[34] For example, RL Lippke, 'No Easy Way Out: Dangerous Offenders and Preventive Detention', *Law and Philosophy* 27(4) (2008), 383–414; D Husak, 'Lifting the Cloak: Preventive Detention as Punishment', *San Diego Law Review* 48 (2011), 1173–204; A Walen, 'A Punitive Precondition for Preventive Detention: Lost Status as a Foundation for a Lost Immunity', *San Diego Law Review* 48 (2011), 1229–72.

have generated much discussion through the centuries, and it is possible to identify a prevailing approach to the definition of punishment, a set of rationales for punishment, a standard set of procedural rights available to persons charged with offences that can lead to conviction and punishment, statistics about the imposition of punishment in given jurisdictions, research into the impacts of punishment on offenders and others, and so forth. But when we turn to preventive measures, most of these features are missing. Little has been written about the definition of, or rationales for, preventive measures; no standard set of procedural rights available to persons subjected to coercive preventive measures exists; statistics are not gathered routinely on all such measures; and research is also patchy. In this section of the chapter we examine the relevant contours of normative theorizing about punitive measures, and in Section 1.7 we go on to demonstrate the problems involved in constructing a corresponding theoretical framework for coercive preventive measures.

The discussion here will focus on three aspects: (1) the definition of a punitive measure; (2) rationales for imposing punitive measures; and (3) the procedural safeguards that ought to be available to persons charged with criminal offences and thus liable to punishment. In criminal law, and in human rights law, there is a close interaction between (3) and (1), in the sense that definitional conclusions under (1) determine the applicability of the safeguards under (3) and may therefore be influenced by these practical consequences. Some examples from European human rights law will therefore be cited in the discussion that follows, but the focus will be on identifying theoretically sound accounts of (1), (2), and (3).

(1) Definition of a punitive measure: the two key elements that mark out a measure as punitive are (a) the censure of an offender for an offence, and (b) the intentional imposition of hard treatment on the offender for the offence. The first element insists that punishment is a censuring institution, a point not brought out in some definitions or quasi-definitions.[35] It is the offender who is being censured, but inherent in this exercise is the communication of that censure to the victim (if any) and to the public at large. The second element specifies that a punitive measure must involve some coercive response rather than a mere verbal reprimand,[36] and the term 'hard treatment' is intended to convey that the response must be coercive but need not involve physical pain.[37]

---

[35] HLA Hart's five-part definition is probably the best known, HLA Hart, *Punishment and Responsibility*, ed. J Gardner (Oxford: Oxford University Press, 2008), 4–5, but it does not mention censure or any equivalent concept in relation to (a). Cf. A von Hirsch and A Ashworth, *Proportionate Sentencing: Exploring the Principles* (Oxford: Oxford University Press, 2005), 17.

[36] For the meaning of 'coercion' in this context, see the discussion in Section 1.3.

[37] Cf. Hart, who referred to 'pain or other consequences normally considered unpleasant': Hart, *Punishment and Responsibility* (n 35), 4; and RA Duff, who states that 'punishment is, typically, something intended to be burdensome or painful, imposed on a (supposed)

It is evident that some preventive measures might satisfy a definition of punishment with these two elements. One example would be the crime of attempts, and other inchoate or pre-inchoate offences. Some would argue that such offences are primarily preventive. Even if that were so (see Chapter 5), they result in conviction and hard treatment, and therefore should also be classified as punitive measures. Since they are criminal offences, this hardly seems controversial. A more intricate example might be an order for the confiscation of assets. Most legal systems have some such provisions, either for drug-trafficking offenders or more generally, and they are often rationalized on preventive grounds—reducing the risk of the offenders returning to their illegal activities, and deterring others by taking away the profits of crime.[38] In order to examine the justifications for and proper limitations on preventive measures, we first need to settle the definitional question of what distinguishes predominantly preventive measures from punitive measures. How should the confiscation order be classified? In the leading case of *Welch v United Kingdom*,[39] the applicant challenged an order confiscating his assets under the Drug Trafficking Act 1986, an order that was retrospective because the legislation permitted that. He claimed that it was a penalty and therefore argued that to give it retrospective application would violate Article 7 of the ECHR, which prohibits retrospective increases in punishment. The government argued that the order was not a penalty, since it was partly confiscatory (to remove illegal profits) and partly preventive (by preventing the future use of the money in the drug trade), and that since it was a preventive rather than a punitive measure there was nothing to impede it from operating retrospectively. The Court reviewed all the elements of the order—including the discretion of the judge to take account of the culpability of the offender in fixing the amount, the 'sweeping' statutory assumptions about the illegal provenance of the money, and the judge's specification of a period of imprisonment for default—and concluded that 'when considered together [they] provide a strong indication of *inter alia* a regime of punishment'.[40] Thus, the Court regarded its task as one of determining the substance rather than the form of the measure. It considered what the government stated to be the measure's purpose (prevention) but held that, even if that was its purpose, its substance and

---

offender for a (supposed) offence by someone who (supposedly) has authority to do so' and is 'typically intended to express or communicate censure': RA Duff, *Punishment, Communication and Community* (Oxford: Oxford University Press, 2001), xiv–xv; J Tasioulas, 'Punishment and Repentance', *Philosophy* 81 (2006), 279; 284, referring to 'hard treatment' that is 'intended to communicate to the wrong-doer justified censure for their wrong-doing'.

[38] There is, of course, the independent rationale of depriving an offender of the profits of offending, since and insofar as those profits derive from wrongdoing.

[39] (1995) 20 EHRR 247.

[40] (1995) 20 EHRR 247, para. 33. See further B Emmerson, A Ashworth, and A Macdonald, *Human Rights and Criminal Justice* 3rd edn (London: Sweet & Maxwell, 2012), Ch. 16.

effects were punitive to a significant extent. So, since the measure had these charac-teristics, it should be classified as a penalty and could not be allowed to operate retrospectively.[41]

This was a determination within a given legal regime. If we were instead to apply the two definitional elements of a punitive measure set out above, we might also conclude that the confiscation order did impose censure on the offender for the offence, and that it did constitute hard treatment—both based on the element of fault involved, the significant sums confiscated, and the term of imprisonment specified in default. However, we should note two further features of the European Court's approach to this case. First and foremost, the Court implicitly denies that the crucial argument is whether a measure is preventive or not. Even if there is a distinction between punitive and preventive measures, it is not relevant here. Thus, there are measures (such as the confiscation order) that are preventive in purpose but substantially punitive in nature or effect, which we may term punitive-preventive measures. Then there are measures that are preventive in purpose and not signifi-cantly punitive in nature and effect, and they may be classified as predominantly preventive measures. The key question is whether the measure is punitive: it may also be preventive in its purpose, but the classification (in order to determine what safeguards are applicable) depends on whether it is punitive in substance. This leads into the second point about the Court's judgment: it seemed to be accepted on all sides that, if a measure is classified as predominantly preventive, it can operate retrospectively. None of the extra safeguards applicable to criminal charges and punishments would apply if the measure were held to be predominantly preventive, as distinct from punitive-preventive. We will return, in Section 1.7, to the question of safeguards attaching to predominantly preventive coercive measures.

One further example may be helpful. What if a legal system were to create a form of preventive detention, to take effect after an offender has served a prison sentence for the offence and to authorize further indefinite detention on grounds of danger-ousness? This was similar to the position in Germany until a few years ago. The German courts held that this was a preventive measure, not a form of punishment, and therefore that it could be applied retrospectively. In *M v Germany*[42] the European Court of Human Rights (ECtHR) reached the opposite conclusion. The argument of the German government was that the measure was preventive in purpose. The conclusion of the Court was that, accepting that this was its purpose, the reality of the measure was punitive—the detention took place within ordinary prisons (albeit in separate wings), the regime differed only in minor respects from a sentence of imprisonment, and special psychological treatment of a kind

---

[41] This should not be taken to indicate that all forms of confiscation are punitive. The confiscation of explosives, guns, or counterfeit money may not have the features described above, and may be predominantly preventive.

[42] (2010) 51 EHRR 976.

required for persons held indefinitely for preventive reasons was not provided.[43] Both this judgment and that in *Welch*, referred to above, show the European Court adopting what it calls an 'autonomous meaning' of a key concept—here 'penalty' or punishment—as a way of preventing the subversion of the ECHR. If the Convention provides safeguards for persons subjected to measures that are punitive, it would be subversive of the Convention if states were able to avoid those safeguards simply by labelling a measure as preventive.

(2) Rationales for imposing punitive measures: punishment involves both censure and hard treatment, as we have seen. The latter entails a deprivation of rights that people normally have (right to property, right to freedom of movement, right to liberty), and therefore requires justification. The first line of justification must be for the criminal law itself: certain wrongs are so serious that they should be condemned as criminal and should be able to result in punishment. This is not the place to attempt a full theory of criminalization, but in general it may be said that, to warrant criminalization, the conduct should amount to a moral wrong, should be (potentially) harmful and should be brought about culpably, and that there must not be strong countervailing considerations such as the creation of unwelcome social consequences, the curtailment of important rights, and so forth.[44] Assuming that a given criminal offence is justifiable (and, as we will see in later chapters, notably Chapter 5, many current offences do not satisfy the standard criteria for criminalization), we move to the second line of justification—the justification for punishment.

Many of the familiar rationales for punishment are preventive.[45] Deterrence is one prominent rationale, which may take the form of general deterrence (deterring others from future offences) or of individual or special deterrence (deterring this offender from future offences). The distinctive method of deterrence is to induce fear through the threat of punishment; its aim is to prevent offences from being committed. Incapacitation is another prominent rationale, which takes the form of measures designed to remove a person's capability or opportunity for committing offences (for example, by removal of a driving licence, by curfew, or by imprisonment). The distinctive method of incapacitation is the removal of capacity or opportunity for offending; its aim is to prevent offences from being committed. A third rationale is rehabilitation, taking the form of programmes designed to persuade offenders that offending is wrong or to tackle the perceived causes of offending behaviour, for example through alcohol- or drug-treatment programmes. The distinctive method of rehabilitation is to alter an offender's value-system or at least to alter an offender's response to certain types of situation or stimulus; its aim is

---

[43] (2010) 51 EHRR 976 at [127]–[129].

[44] A Simester and A von Hirsch, *Crimes, Harms and Wrongs: On the Principles of Criminalization* (Oxford: Hart Publishing, 2011), Chs 2 and 11; D Husak, *Overcriminalization: The Limits of the Criminal Law* (Oxford: Oxford University Press, 2008), Chs 2 and 3.

[45] Schauer, 'The Ubiquity of Prevention' (n 16), 12–15.

to prevent offences from being committed. Each of these three rationales, therefore, has the objective of prevention. The differences lie in their methods of trying to achieve the objective.

What about the retributive rationale for punishment? There are some purists who argue that punishment is the appropriate social response to crimes, and that there is no need to seek any further justification. Wrongdoers deserve to suffer.[46] More common among contemporary 'desert' theorists, however, is a position that recognizes desert as an integral part of everyday judgments of praise and blame, transfers that to the institution of punishment as a form of official censure of offenders, but rests the justification for hard treatment on the need for underlying deterrence.[47] In other words, contemporary desert theory has retributive roots and requires punishments to be proportionate, but nevertheless insists that without the element of hard treatment (rather than, simply, the solemn condemnation of wrongdoers) there would inevitably be too much crime. Thus, prevention underpins most forms of modern desert theory,[48] just as it is the animating purpose of deterrent, incapacitative, and rehabilitative rationales.

There appears to be broad acceptance, even among those who are not wholly wedded to retributivism or desert theory, that in principle the punishment for an offence should not be disproportionate to the seriousness of the crime(s) committed (in terms of culpability and wrongdoing).[49] But where a measure is preventive, a rather different logic seems to be entailed—that the type and quantum of the measure imposed must be those judged necessary to bring about a significant reduction in the risk of future harm, irrespective of whether those measures are proportionate to any past or present conduct of the subject. This logic creates a tension when applied to the preventive rationales for punishment: if rehabilitation is the chosen rationale, the logic indicates that the restrictions imposed on the subject must be sufficient in intensity and duration to enable the rehabilitative treatment to be concluded successfully; if deterrence is the chosen rationale, the restrictions must be sufficient to deter the subject from causing harm (individual deterrence) or to deter others from following his bad example (general deterrence); and if incapacitation is the chosen rationale, the measures taken against the subject must be kept in place for so long as is necessary for the protection of the public. In retributive or

---

[46] eg MS Moore, 'The Moral Worth of Retribution', in A von Hirsch, A Ashworth, and J Roberts (eds.), *Principled Sentencing: Readings on Theory and Policy* 3rd edn (Oxford: Hart Publishing, 2009), 110–14.

[47] eg Von Hirsch and Ashworth, *Proportionate Sentencing: Exploring the Principles* (n 35).

[48] For a different view, which cannot be discussed here, see Tasioulas, 'Punishment and Repentance', (n 26).

[49] For non-retributive theories making a similar point, see N Lacey, *State Punishment: Political Principles and Community Values* (London: Routledge, 1988), 194; J Braithwaite and P Pettit, *Not Just Deserts: A Republican Theory of Justice* (Oxford: Oxford University Press, 1990), Ch. 6, 9.

desert theory the hard treatment and deprivations must be proportionate to past offending, out of respect for the subject as a responsible agent, and the role of prevention is merely to supply an underlying deterrence. Thus there is a distinct tension between preventive logic, according to which the hard treatment and deprivations must be sufficient to bring about a significant reduction in the antici-pated risk of future harm (which means concluding a course of treatment or a detention thought necessary for public protection even if that goes beyond the proportionate sentence), and the principle of proportionality of sentence. This tension is increased when a concept of proportionality is invoked as part of the preventive logic, eg by prescribing that preventive measures must be proportionate to the risk (taking account of the magnitude of the risk and the seriousness of the harm-to-be-avoided).[50] That usage will not be adopted here, since the central concept of proportionality relates punishment to the seriousness of the offending; a rather different relationship. So, to summarize: where the rationale is desert, the punishment must censure the subject in a way and to an extent that respects his or her responsible agency, and the role of prevention is to supply underlying deterrence whereas the choice or quantum of the sanction should be governed by proportionality considerations. Where prevention is the rationale its logic applies without respect for whether the subject is a responsible agent or not, since the purpose is to obtain the optimal preventive outcome.

(3) Procedural safeguards: the imposition of censure and hard treatment is so significant that it should not take place unless the individual involved has had the benefit of various safeguards and protections. Censure and hard treatment not only involve the state depriving an individual of what are normally regarded as funda-mental rights, but they do so within the framework of proceedings that are public and condemnatory. For these reasons it is normal for declarations of human rights and constitutional rights to provide additional safeguards, over and above those available for civil proceedings, for any person charged with a criminal offence. In the ECHR, for example, these rights include the presumption of innocence, the prohibition of retrospective criminal laws and retrospective increases in penalties, the right to legal representation, the right to confrontation of witnesses, and the right to an interpreter. As was apparent from (1) above, a large part of the significance of the definition of 'penalty' or 'punishment' resides in its implication for consequential rights. Thus, the cases of *Welch v United Kingdom*[51] and *M v Germany*[52] were fought so hard because of the respective governments' desire that the measures should have retrospective application. The finding that both measures

---

[50] See, eg, C Steiker, 'Proportionality as a Limit on Preventive Justice: Promises and Pitfalls', in A Ashworth, L Zedner, and P Tomlin (eds.), *Prevention and the Limits of the Criminal Law* (Oxford: Oxford University Press, 2013), 194–213.

[51] Ericson, *Crime in an Insecure World* (n 24).

[52] *M v Germany* (2010) 51 EHRR 976 (n 42).

fell within the definition of punishment ruled that out, because the principle of non-retrospectivity applies to punitive measures. However, the cluster of additional rights applicable to persons charged with a criminal offence and/or subjected to a penalty is so powerful that governments may be tempted to devise measures falling just outside the relevant definitions. As noted above, the ECtHR has developed its doctrine of the 'autonomous meaning' of key terms in order to ensure that there is no unfair manipulation of the boundaries, and that if a measure has the substance of a criminal charge or of a penalty it will be treated as such, despite a different domestic classification or label. In effect, this gives institutional expression to the definition of a punitive measure with which this section began.

1.7 Preventive Measures: Rationales and Safeguards

In an attempt to follow an approximately parallel structure to the discussion of punitive measures in Section 1.6, we deal here with (1) the definition of a coercive preventive measure; (2) rationales for imposing coercive punitive measures; and (3) the procedural safeguards that ought to be available to persons liable to be subjected to, or actually subjected to, coercive preventive measures. The paths are much less well trodden, and many of the arguments will be developed further in later chapters of the book.

(1) The definition of a coercive preventive measure: a measure is preventive if it is created in order to avert, or reduce the frequency or impact of, behaviour that is believed to present an unacceptable risk of harm. It is coercive if it involves state-imposed restrictions on liberty of action, backed by a coercive response, or the threat of a coercive response, to the restricted individual.[53] This fairly simple definition of a coercive preventive measure can be adapted easily to measures of public safety, public protection, security, social defence, and other broadly synonymous purposes. As noted in Section 1.2, prevention and these related purposes can also be pursued by methods not involving this kind of direct coercion of the individual, such as situational crime prevention (through the design of buildings, transport systems, and other public facilities in such a way as to reduce the risk of crime and/or harm) and social crime prevention (through schemes aimed at engaging people in recreational or community-orientated activities intended to turn them away from committing crimes and/or causing harm). Neither situational nor social crime prevention typically involves the coercion of individuals, whereas our focus here is on preventive measures that involve coercion.

---

[53] For the concept of coercion, see the discussion in Section 1.3.

It will be evident that most criminal offences satisfy the definition of a coercive preventive measure, as already suggested. Indeed, the element of prevention is integral to the justification for the criminal law, as we have argued elsewhere:[54] 'the "backward-looking" justification for making these wrongs punishable must imply a "forward-looking" concern that fewer such wrongs should occur in the future'. In Section 1.2, four groups of specifically preventive crimes were identified—inchoate offences, substantive offences defined in an inchoate mode, preparatory or pre-inchoate offences, and offences of risk-creation. These, clearly, are coercive preventive measures that also satisfy the definition of a punitive measure offered in Section 1.6. However, there is also a wide range of coercive preventive measures that do not, or at least do not always or uncontentiously, qualify as punitive measures too. For example, the quarantining or isolation of people with contagious diseases, the revocation of the driving licence of a person suffering from a particular illness, and the hospitalization of some mentally disordered persons are all coercive preventive measures but not punitive. On the other hand, pre-trial detention, immigration detention, and civil preventive orders are all coercive preventive measures that lie on, or close to, the boundaries of punitive measures. Their categorization, and its implications, will be the subject of further discussion in the relevant chapters below.

(2) Rationales for imposing coercive preventive measures: the general rationale for imposing a coercive preventive measure is the prevention of harm (or, as approximate synonyms, the enhancement of security, public safety, or public protection), and not the censure of the person subjected to the measure. In terms of justifications for measures that restrict an individual's rights, however, a much stronger rationale is required for a preventive measure that is coercive than for one that imposes no coercion. If the coercion takes the form of a restriction on liberty this may involve an incursion into freedom of movement. More significantly, if the coercive measure involves detention, this strikes at a basic human right (the right to liberty of the person)—albeit one with exceptions, in all systems of rights[55]—and therefore calls for a strong and convincing justification.

In Section 1.4 we argued that the state has a general duty to seek to protect its citizens from harm, but we must now begin to develop the details of this proposition. In order to prevent what types or levels of harm might it be justifiable to impose *coercive* measures on certain people? What degree of risk of harm should be

---

[54] A Ashworth and L Zedner, 'Just Prevention and the Limits of the Criminal Law', in RA Duff and SP Green (eds.), *Philosophical Foundations of the Criminal Law* (Oxford: Oxford University Press, 2011), 279–303; 281.

[55] eg ECHR, Article 5, which declares the right to liberty of the person and then enumerates six categories of exception; and the International Covenant on Civil and Political Rights, Article 9, which declares the right to liberty but provides for (unspecified) exceptions established by law.

required before coercive measures can be justified? The most persuasive answer to the first question would be that, in principle, the use of coercive measures should be restricted to the prevention of serious physical (violent or sexual) harms, since those are the most serious harms,[56] and particularly where the coercive measures involve a deprivation of liberty. Thus, if the proposal is for the detention of persons with contagious diseases or for the detention of mentally disordered persons, the harm to be prevented must be a major physical harm rather than a minor disease or, say, the risk of financial misdealings.

Turning to the second question, it should surely be necessary to show that the serious harm is more likely than not to occur, if it is being sought to justify a deprivation of liberty. Research continues to show that predictions of serious harm are more frequently wrong than right.[57] The fallibility of these predictions is so well established that even the current British coalition government admitted, in relation to the former sentence of imprisonment for public protection (IPP), that 'the limitations of our ability to predict future serious offending... [call] into question the whole basis on which many offenders are sentenced to IPPs'.[58] Now it is true that the qualifying conditions for the IPP sentence were much broader than those for some other forms of preventive or protective sentences, including the sentences that have now replaced IPP in English law.[59] However, the general sentiment of the British government's statement would be widely shared by many of those conversant with the research on the prediction of seriously harmful incidents. Continuing controversy over the reliability of Actuarial Risk Assessment Instruments raises serious questions about the justifiability of basing extended, and particularly indefinite, detention on data derived from risk-assessment tools. However, some of the harms done by these people are likely to be at a highly serious level (eg homicide), raising the question whether a low probability of a very serious harm should be accepted as an adequate rationale. That question will be discussed further in Chapters 6 and 7.

One further step must be taken here, and that is to consider a narrowing of the group of risk-bearing people eligible for a form of preventive detention. It can be argued that, once a person has committed a serious sexual or violent offence, that person has lost the right to be treated as 'free from harmful intentions'. Thus, Floud

---

[56] A von Hirsch and N Jareborg, 'Gauging Criminal Harm: A Living-Standard Analysis', *Oxford Journal of Legal Studies* 11 (1991), 1–38; 1.

[57] See, eg, Simon, 'Reversal of Fortune: The Resurgence of Individual Risk Assessment in Criminal Justice' (n 22); B Harcourt, *Against Prediction: Profiling, Policing, and Punishing in an Actuarial Age* (Chicago: University of Chicago Press, 2007); J Skeem and J Monahan, 'Current Directions in Violence Risk Assessment', *Current Directions in Psychological Science* 21(1) (2011), 38–42.

[58] Ministry of Justice, *Breaking the Cycle: Effective Punishment, Rehabilitation and Sentencing of Offender Cm 7972* (London: Ministry of Justice, 2010), para. 186.

[59] Legal Aid, Sentencing and Punishment of Offenders Act 2012, introducing a revised 'extended sentence' and an 'automatic life sentence' for qualifying offenders.

and Young argued for a 'just redistribution of risk' between people who have demonstrated their capacity to perpetrate serious wrongs, and their potential future victims.[60] While other members of society should be presumed harmless, unless and until it is proved otherwise,[61] those who have previously committed such a serious crime can properly be made subject to restrictions, so as to reduce the risks to potential victims.[62] This approach assigns less weight to the proposed detainee's right to liberty of the person and right to be presumed innocent than to the possible victim's rights to security of the person, and it does so on the basis of a prior conviction for a serious offence. Taking a less expansive view, Bottoms and Brownsword have argued that such an incursion into individual liberty can only be justified by evidence that the offender presents a 'vivid danger' of further serious offending,[63] and von Hirsch and Ashworth have argued that such a departure from the principle of proportionality can only be justified if maintaining that principle would inevitably result in evil consequences of such exceptional magnitude as to warrant deviating from the normal constraint.[64] It is doubtful whether the potential victim's right not to be injured should be allowed to defeat the offender's right not to be punished more than is proportionate to the crime(s) committed: the victim does indeed have a right against a potential attacker not to be subjected to an infringement of personal security, but the degree to which that should affect the state's responsibility towards the offender not to impose a disproportionate sentence remains debatable.[65] Moreover, it is not clear whether the same or similar reasoning would apply to a person who has previously perpetrated a serious harm which did not result in a criminal conviction, perhaps because the perpetrator was mentally disordered or because the harm derived from the communication of a contagious disease.

(3) Procedural safeguards: in Section 1.6(3) above we saw that measures that satisfy the definition of punishment (because they involve the censure of an offender for an offence and the imposition of hard treatment) bring in their train a cluster of extra safeguards, which are thought appropriate in order to protect innocent persons from

---

[60] J Floud and W Young, *Dangerousness and Criminal Justice* (London: Heinemann, 1981).

[61] Controversial in this respect are those measures in English law that treat people as dangerous before or without conviction, such as TPIMs, sexual offences prevention orders, and other preventive orders. For discussion, particularly of the question how the presumption of freedom from harmful intentions can be rebutted, see Ch. 4.

[62] Somewhat similar arguments can be found in RA Duff, 'Dangerousness and Citizenship', in A Ashworth and M Wasik (eds.), *Fundamentals of Sentencing Theory* (Oxford: Clarendon, 1998), 141–64 and in Walen, 'A Punitive Precondition for Preventive Detention: Lost Status as a Foundation for a Lost Immunity' (n 34).

[63] AE Bottoms and R Brownsword, 'Dangerousness and Rights', in JW Hinton (ed.), *Dangerousness: Problems of Assessment and Prediction* (London: George Allen and Unwin, 1983), 233–7.

[64] A von Hirsch and A Ashworth, *Proportionate Sentencing* (n 35), 52–3.

[65] See further von Hirsch and Ashworth, *Proportionate Sentencing* (n 35), 51–61, and the discussion in Ch. 7.

the public censure and punitive response. We now move to the question of the safeguards available where a coercive preventive measure does not satisfy the definition of a punishment. Do these 'predominantly preventive' measures fall into a black hole, with no presumption of innocence, no principle of non-retrospectivity, no right to confront witnesses, and so on? Or do other, different arguments support the invocation of all or some of these safeguards? One possible approach starts from the fact that most of the coercive measures mentioned in Section 1.7(1) involve a deprivation of one of the most basic rights, ie the right to personal liberty. It can be argued that no person should be liable to lose that basic right without special safeguards being in place. The process whereby the right to liberty is taken away as a preventive measure is not at all like ordinary civil processes, since they can only result in an order to pay damages or an order of specific performance, and cannot of themselves lead to loss of personal liberty. So, the question is whether the possibility of being deprived of the fundamental right to personal liberty should be regarded as sufficient to call for greater safeguards than are applicable to ordinary civil proceedings.

Such a course of reasoning is familiar in the law. Thus, in a leading civil case the Court of Appeal held that 'the very elements of gravity [arising in the particular case] become a part of the whole range of circumstances that have to be weighed in the scale when deciding as to the balance of probabilities'.[66] More explicitly, in a case in the House of Lords, Lord Steyn held that what he termed 'the heightened civil standard of proof' ought to be applied in view of 'the seriousness of the matters involved', and Lord Hope added that the 'serious consequences for the person' indicated that a standard close to that in criminal cases would be appropriate.[67] These statements suggest that the potential consequences of a particular civil decision may be such that, although the proceedings remain civil and therefore the criminal law safeguards do not apply, the ordinary civil procedures should be adapted in response to the seriousness of the special consequences. This is fairly straightforward where the key issue is the standard of proof to be attained, since a heightened civil standard (close to that in criminal cases) is simply an appropriate development of an existing doctrine. What this line of argument does not address is whether all or any of the other safeguards applicable in criminal cases ought to apply here. One example is the privilege against self-incrimination and its companion, the so-called right of silence. These are often said to derive from the presumption of innocence,[68] and so some may wish to argue that insofar as the presumption of

---

[66] Per Morris LJ in *Hornal v Neuberger Products* [1957] 1 QB 247, at 266.

[67] *Clingham v Royal Borough of Kensington and Chelsea; R. v Crown Court at Manchester, ex parte McCann* [2002] UKHL 39, at [37] per Lord Steyn and at [84] per Lord Hope. For discussion of the authorities, see Cross and Tapper's *Law of Evidence*, 12th edn by C Tapper (Oxford: Oxford University Press, 2010), 154–61.

[68] For discussion, see A Ashworth and M Redmayne, *The Criminal Process* 4th edn (Oxford: Oxford University Press, 2010), 145–55; JD Jackson and SJ Summers, *The Internationalisation of Criminal Evidence* (Cambridge: Cambridge University Press, 2012), Ch. 8.

innocence applies to coercive preventive measures affecting liberty, these allied doctrines should also apply. Rather different would be the prohibition of retrospective criminal laws and retrospective increases in sentence. This has nothing to do with the presumption of innocence, and everything to do with the law as a guide to conduct. As Fuller observed half a century ago:

> Taken by itself... a retroactive law is truly a monstrosity. Law has to do with the governance of human conduct by rules. To speak of governing or directing conduct today by rules that will be enacted tomorrow is to talk in blank prose . . . The reason the retrospective criminal statute is so universally condemned does not arise merely from the fact that in criminal litigation the stakes are high. It arises also—and chiefly—because of all branches of law, the criminal law is the most obviously and directly concerned with shaping and controlling human conduct.[69]

Fuller was certainly right to single out the criminal law for its role of controlling conduct, although he might have given greater emphasis to the techniques of censure and punishment and their intended effect on the individuals subjected to them. But some coercive preventive measures are also intended to control conduct—a clear example would be civil preventive orders (Chapter 4)—and they are cases in which 'the stakes are high' too: thus, there are two reasons in favour of prohibiting some coercive preventive measures from operating retrospectively.[70] A similar argument might apply in favour of allowing legal representation and indeed requiring public funding for some such representation, and for some other defence rights.[71] These arguments will be followed through in the relevant chapters. The importance of the present discussion is to establish that there is a separate stream of justification for procedural safeguards, apart from that depending on the criminal law, and that this flows from the fundamental nature of the rights at stake when the imposition of some coercive preventive orders is being proposed, most especially the right to liberty of the person.

1.8 Conclusions

In this opening chapter our objective has been to establish the terminology that will be used throughout the book, to discuss the justifications for the state's duty to protect citizens and to provide security through preventive measures, and to explore

---

[69] LL Fuller, *The Morality of Law* (New Haven: Yale University Press, 1964), 53–9.

[70] For a case in which different and less satisfactory reasons were held not to prevent a civil preventive order from operating retrospectively, see the decision of the English Court of Appeal in *Field and Young* [2003] 1 WLR 882.

[71] For discussion of whether the presumption of innocence should apply to preventive measures, see KK Ferzan, 'Preventive Justice and the Presumption of Innocence', *Criminal Law and Philosophy* (forthcoming).

the differences between measures that are punitive and measures that are predominantly preventive. In developing those ideas we have begun to confront the question of appropriate safeguards for persons subjected to preventive measures. We will continue to develop these ideas throughout the book, and will also begin to build the foundations for a set of principles to restrain the pursuit of prevention through coercive state measures, particularly those involving loss of liberty.

2

The Historical Origins of the Preventive State

'[F]or sure it is much better to prevent even one man from being a rogue than apprehending and bringing forty to justice'[1]

In the previous chapter, we noted the common contention that a shift of emphasis from punishment to prevention is occurring. Demands for public protection, the influence of a precautionary approach, and legal powers and measures with which to prevent harms are all prominent features of contemporary criminal justice. As we will discuss further in Chapter 5, criminal liability has been extended back in time by the expansion of inchoate liability in criminal law, by the enactment of preparatory crimes and possession offences, as well as crimes of endangerment, association, and risk-taking. These changes are explained variously by reference to the rise of the 'risk society', the emergence of actuarial justice, and the new penology[2]—poorly chosen though that last term may turn out to be. Less attention has been paid to the historical antecedents of present developments and this oversight has led to claims that preventive endeavour is a new phenomenon or constitutes a paradigm shift from punishment to prevention.[3] Observers have asked 'why did "crime prevention" develop so late?'[4] This chapter asks whether in fact it did, by tracing the longer history of preventive endeavour back to the early establishment of the police in the late eighteenth and early nineteenth centuries. This was an important period during

---

[1] H Fielding, *An Account of the Origin and Effects of a Police Set on Foot by His Grace the Duke of Newcastle, in the Year 1753* (London: A Millar, 1758); quoted in E Chadwick, 'Preventive Police', *London Review* 1 (1829), 252–308; 280.

[2] P O'Malley (ed.), *Crime and the Risk Society* (Aldershot: Ashgate, 1998); M Feeley and J Simon, 'Actuarial Justice: The Emerging New Criminal Law', in D Nelken (ed.), *The Futures of Criminology* (London: Sage, 1994), 173–201.

[3] A Edwards and G Hughes, 'The Preventive Turn and the Promotion of Safer Communities in England and Wales', in A Crawford (ed.), *Crime Prevention Policies in Comparative Perspective* (Cullompton: Willan Publishing, 2009), 62–85; R Ericson, *Crime in an Insecure World* (Cambridge: Polity, 2007).

[4] P O'Malley and S Hutchinson, 'Reinventing Prevention: Why Did "Crime Prevention" Develop So Late?', *British Journal of Criminology* 47(3) (2007), 373–89. Though see M Neocleous, 'Theoretical Foundations of the "New Police Science"', in MD Dubber and M Valverde (eds.), *The New Police Science: The Police Power in Domestic and International Governance* (Stanford: Stanford University Press, 2006), 17–41; 29.

which the very scope and purpose of the modern criminal justice state were subject to intense deliberation.[5] As this chapter will reveal, in its formative years criminal justice was decidedly more preventive than punitive in orientation. So the question is less 'why did crime prevention develop so late?' than 'why did prevention not persist more robustly nor shape more determinedly the subsequent two centuries of criminal justice history such that prevention now appears to be a new direction?'[6]

Exploring the origins of penal ideas, practices, and policies, particularly those said to be novel or paradigm-changing, is a useful antidote to the brevity of collective memory. As Garland observes: 'Every new policy reinvents its own forerunners, sometimes with interesting results, and it may be possible to learn more about the present by examining its newly apparent ancestors.'[7] Historical enquiry reveals that the largely post hoc orientation of policing and criminal justice over the past 200 years was in no way predetermined. Nor, of course, was it exclusively post hoc. Although the strong, overarching preventive rationale that informed the founding of key criminal justice institutions such as the police waned, further preventive innovations over the nineteenth and twentieth centuries provoked renewed debate about the state's preventive powers.

Earlier debates about the rationales for and limits to the state's preventive function are not merely a matter of historical interest; they speak directly to present dilemmas about the proliferation of preventive measures in and outside the criminal law. Criminal justice institutions and practices rely heavily on claims of custom and convention to justify their existence. Likewise in criminal law, the historical weight of precedent has a powerful legitimating and justificatory role. Yet, as Dubber and Farmer observe, '[t]he critical, as opposed to the legitimating, potential of criminal law historiography has yet to be fully realized'.[8] Revisiting historical deliberations about the place of preventive measures within criminal justice reveals that questions about what the state may do to prevent criminal harms are far from new.

2.1 Prevention and the Criminal Law

Though its origins are uncertain, the term 'preventive justice' can be traced back at least as far as the eighteenth century. In his *Commentaries on the Laws of England*,

---

[5] N Rafter, 'Origins of Criminology', in M Bosworth and C Hoyle (eds.), *What Is Criminology?* (Oxford: Oxford University Press, 2011), 143–56.

[6] Garland describes the development of the modern criminal justice system as an 'epistemological break' with its preventive origins. D Garland, 'Ideas, Institutions and Situational Crime Prevention', in A von Hirsch, D Garland, and A Wakefield (eds.), *Ethical and Social Perspectives on Situational Crime Prevention* (Oxford: Hart Publishing, 2000), 1–16; 1.

[7] D Garland, 'The Limits of the Sovereign State: Strategies of Crime Control in Contemporary Society', *British Journal of Criminology* 36(4) (1996), 445–71; 464.

[8] MD Dubber and L Farmer (eds.), *Modern Histories of Crime and Punishment* (Stanford: Stanford University Press, 2007), 8.

Blackstone gave the term a central role by arguing that, 'preventive justice is, upon every principle of reason, of humanity, and of sound policy, preferable in all respects to punishing justice'.[9] For Blackstone, '[t]his preventive justice consists in obliging those persons whom there is a probable ground to suspect of future misbehaviour to stipulate with and to give full assurance to the public that such offence as is apprehended shall not happen, by finding pledges or securities for keeping the peace, or for their good behaviour'.[10] Blackstone also identified a preventive aspect to punishment itself, observing: 'if we consider all human punishments in a large and extended view, we shall find them all rather calculated to prevent future crimes than to expiate the past'.[11] This emphasis on the preventive aspect of punishment calls into question the preventive/punitive dichotomy that modern observers are perhaps too quick to assume. That said, Blackstone does distinguish between punishment and those measures which are 'merely for prevention, without any crime actually committed by the party, but arising only from a probable suspicion that some crime is intended or likely to happen; and consequently it is not meant as any degree of punishment, unless perhaps for a man's imprudence in giving just ground of apprehension'.[12] The acknowledgement that 'man's imprudence' may provide grounds for punishment ahead of time foreshadows the later development of pre-inchoate liability and risk-based offences. However, individual responsibility figures less prominently in Blackstone's conception of preventive justice than does his designation of certain groups as inherently suspect. Thus, Blackstone contends that:

[a] justice may bind over all night-walkers; eaves-droppers; such as keep suspicious company, or are reported to be pilferers or robbers; such as sleep in the day and wake in the night; common drunkards; whore-masters; the putative fathers of bastards; cheats; idle vagabonds; and other persons whose misbehaviour may reasonably bring them within the general words of the statutes as persons not of good fame: an expression, it must be owned, of so great a latitude as to leave much to be determined by the discretion of the magistrate himself.[13]

Blackstone's acknowledgement that the class of 'persons not of good fame' is so general as to give undue scope for discretion seems to overlook the considerable scope for interpretation entailed by the other suspect categories that he enumerates. If Blackstone appears only partially alert to the problem of designating entire categories as suspicious, he was certainly alive to the problem of determining what suffices to ground liability for future risks. He suggested:

---

[9] W Blackstone, *Commentaries on the Laws of England in Four Books* (London: Routledge, 2001, 1753), 4th Book 'Public Wrongs',Ch. XVIII 'Of the Means of Preventing Offences', 251. See also discussion in MD Dubber, 'Preventive Justice: The Quest for Principle', in A Ashworth, L Zedner, and P Tomlin (eds.), *Prevention and the Limits of the Criminal Law* (Oxford: Oxford University Press, 2013), 47–68; 52–4.

[10] Blackstone, *Commentaries on the Laws of England in Four Books* (n 9).

[11] Blackstone, *Commentaries on the Laws of England in Four Books*, 252.

[12] Blackstone, *Commentaries on the Laws of England in Four Books*, 252.

[13] Blackstone, *Commentaries on the Laws of England in Four Books*, 256.

A recognizance for good behaviour may be forfeited by all the same means as one for the security of the peace may be; and also by some others. As, by going armed with unusual attendance, to the terror of the people; by speaking words tending to sedition; or by committing any of those acts of misbehaviour which the recognizance was intended to prevent. But not by barely giving fresh cause of suspicion of that which perhaps may never actually happen. For though it is just to compel suspected persons to give security to the public against misbehaviour that is apprehended; yet it would be hard, upon such suspicion, without the proof of any actual crime, to punish them by a forfeiture of their recognizance.[14]

In this, Blackstone plainly identifies the difficulty of deciding which conduct justifiably attracts preventive intervention and where the grounds for intervention, if made in respect of that 'which perhaps may never actually happen', may prove unwarranted.[15]

Reading Blackstone's analysis of preventive justice, it is evident that crime prevention rested on the assumption that it was possible to identify potential wrongdoers not so much by their choices or actions but rather by who they were or appeared to be. All towns were required to establish a Watch, to which all householders were periodically required to contribute their services, and whose principal function was to patrol the streets to maintain order by arresting designated categories of person.[16] In London, watchmen were authorized to arrest 'all night walkers, malefactors, rogues, vagabonds and other disorderly persons whom they shall find disturbing the publick peace, or shall have just cause to suspect of any evil designs'.[17] Although suspicious activity attracted attention, surveillance focused mainly upon particular populations who were deemed innately suspicious.

The modern conception of the individual as a rational decision-maker who could be deterred by the presence of the Watch appears to have been less salient in the eighteenth century. Lacey observes that 'a vision of the human subject as a rational actor capable, therefore, of being deterred by a systematic and well publicised system of criminal law proscriptions and sanctions' was absent from Blackstone's *Commentaries*.[18] She traces a gradual and uneven development from reliance upon character to attribution of responsibility in criminal law: a shift closely related to the advance of its preventive function. Only those deemed capable of rational deliberation, and who might therefore be held to account for their decisions, could justifiably be subject to a regime designed to prevent them from proceeding

[14] Blackstone, *Commentaries on the Laws of England in Four Books*, 257.

[15] Blackstone, *Commentaries on the Laws of England in Four Books*, 257.

[16] E Reynolds, *Before the Bobbies: The Night Watch and Police Reform in Metropolitan London 1720–1830* (Palo Alto, CA: Stanford University Press, 1998); L Zedner, 'Policing before and after the Police: The Historical Antecedents of Contemporary Crime Control', *British Journal of Criminology* 46(1) (2006), 78–96.

[17] 10 Geo. II. c. 22 cited in P Rawlings, 'Policing before the Police', in T Newburn (ed.), *Handbook of Policing* (Cullompton, Devon: Willan Publishing, 2003), 41–65; 45.

[18] N Lacey, 'In Search of the Responsible Subject: History, Philosophy and Social Sciences in Criminal Law Theory', *Modern Law Review* 64(3) (2001), 350–71; 360.

with the commission of a crime.[19] The development of the preventive aspect of the criminal law arguably relied, therefore, not only upon the capacity of the state to identify prospective wrongdoing ahead of its commission, but also upon the emergence of a fully fledged conception of responsibility.

If the rise of responsibility was a prerequisite of the preventive ambit of criminal law, another central element of early preventive endeavour was reform of the criminal code itself. As the Scottish magistrate Patrick Colquhoun observed, '[t]owards accomplishing the desirable object of perfection in a criminal code, every wise Legislature will have it in contemplation rather to prevent than to punish crimes'.[20] The infamous 'Bloody Code' relied upon the preventive logic of general deterrence by making hundreds of crimes capital offences. Increasingly widespread revulsion against such ready recourse to execution led reformers to advocate the promotion of certainty in the criminal law as an important means of reducing reliance upon capital punishment. Campaigners drew heavily on comparison with neighbouring countries whose 'security did not proceed from severer punishments for in very few Countries are they more sanguinary than in England. It is to be attributed to a more correct and energetic system of Police.'[21] Certainty and effective enforcement of the criminal law was favoured over the wide-ranging brutality of the Bloody Code and the vagaries of judicial discretion that were so much a characteristic of eighteenth-century criminal justice.[22] The role of judicial discretion in undermining certainty, and thus the authority of criminal law, was the subject of bitter attack by Bentham. In his famous polemic *Truth versus Ashurst* (written in 1792 but only published in 1823), Bentham savaged 'judge-made law' as so capricious and unpredictable that it was impossible for an individual to know how to conduct himself. He branded the exercise of judicial discretion over crime as 'dog-law':

It is the judges (as we have seen) that make the common law. Do you know how they make it? Just as a man makes laws for his dog. When your dog does anything you want to break him of, you wait till he does it, and then beat him for it. This is the way you make laws for your dog: and this is the way the judges make law for you and me. They won't tell a man beforehand what it is he *should not do* - they won't so much as allow of his being told: they lie by till he has done something which they say he should not *have done*, and then they hang him for it.[23]

---

[19] Lacey, 'In Search of the Responsible Subject' (n 18), 366.
[20] P Colquhoun, *Treatise on the Police of the Metropolis* (London: H. Fry, 1796), 32.
[21] Colquhoun, *Treatise on the Police of the Metropolis* (n 20), 94.
[22] JA Beattie, *Crime and the Courts in England 1660–1800* (Oxford: Oxford University Press, 1986); P King, *Crime, Justice and Discretion in England 1740–1820* (Oxford: Oxford University Press, 2000).
[23] 'Truth versus Ashurst or Law as it is' in J Bentham, *The Works of Jeremy Bentham*, ed. J Bowring (Edinburgh: William Tait, 1838–43), 233–7; 235.

The clear message of Bentham's attack is that if law is to inform rational deliberation it must do so in advance. Certainty in the criminal law was essential to provide fair warning and to place 'utmost limits' on its capacity to infringe the freedom of the individual unwarrantedly. Consolidation of the criminal code would improve confidence in the criminal law and make it possible to implement a more parsimonious system of penalties.

For all these reasons, Sir Robert Peel (Home Secretary 1822–1830), well known as the architect of the modern police, also devoted himself to reform of the criminal law. He successfully introduced four Acts between 1827 and 1830 that sought to consolidate and, with less success, to reduce the severity of the criminal law.[24] In similar vein, Sir Edwin Chadwick, social reformer and later the chief architect of Poor Law reform, insisted: 'Nor, in plain truth, will the utmost severity to offenders be justifiable, unless we take every possible means of preventing the offence.'[25] This view echoed a growing sense that resort to capital punishment—which by the early nineteenth century was far more extensively available and more frequently imposed than liberal public opinion found tolerable—could not be justified where the state failed in its duty to forewarn citizens, to remove temptations, and take measures to prevent crime (see discussion in Chapter 1). The preventive impulse was fed, therefore, not only by the desire to prevent the harms entailed by crime but also by the strong sense that the brutality of capital punishment could be justified only if all efforts had first been made to avert the commission of capital offences. It is against this background of legal reform that one should set the establishment of the police and, with it, the founding institutions of the modern criminal justice system.

2.2 The Preventive Principle and the Good of Security

Today's criminal justice estate is such a vast and entrenched edifice that it is difficult to conceive that it might have taken other forms or that it might have pursued its goals in quite different ways. Garland identifies 'an emphatically *preventative* form of regulation' as 'the path not taken'[26] by early criminal justice institutions that instead adopted predominantly prosecutorial and punitive responses to crime. Yet, in the late eighteenth century, it was far from self-evident that the criminal justice system would develop as it did. The founding orientation focused on pre-empting offending at source by reducing opportunities and temptations to crime. In public debates about the establishment of a formal police force, it was assumed that its role should

---

[24] JA Sharpe, *Judicial Punishment in England* (London: Faber & Faber, 1990), 47.

[25] Chadwick, 'Preventive Police' (n 1), 307.

[26] D Garland, *The Culture of Control: Crime and Social Order in Contemporary Society* (Oxford: Oxford University Press, 2001), 30. Author's emphasis.

be primarily preventive. In its early years, the modern prison was also ascribed a principally reformative rather than punitive function.[27] The eighteenth-century magistrate and social reformer, Sir John Fielding, can justifiably be credited with conceiving the preventive model of criminal justice. He saw 'prevention as being a matter of both pro-active surveillance and deterrence through effective detection'.[28] Fielding's 1755 *Plan for Preventing Robberies* proposed that magistrates should employ professional runners to seek out criminals and bring them to justice.[29] He secured funding from the public purse for the 'Bow-Street runners', attached to the Bow-Street Magistrates' Court; laid the groundwork for modern criminal procedure; and helped to establish the first recognizably modern courts—a monumental series of endeavours that played a crucial role in establishing criminal justice as a branch of 'public justice'.[30]

Yet, it is Colquhoun's *Treatise on the Police of the Metropolis*,[31] which is now more usually regarded as one of the founding documents of the criminal justice system, not least because it makes a comprehensive and persuasive case for the institution of the modern police. Colquhoun's writings also set out a sophisticated case for the primacy of prevention over punishment.[32] This early prioritizing of prevention relied upon acceptance of crime as normal social fact of everyday life more than two centuries before Felson coined the term.[33] Garland notes that 'Colquhoun's *Treatise* sets out an analysis of crime and a programme for its prevention that are remarkably similar to the thinking which has recently re-emerged in official circles'.[34] And yet the historical circumstances and triggers for reform were very different to those that motivate the preventive impulse today. The growth of trade, transport, and rapid urbanization created the conditions of overcrowding, social dislocation, and rising crime, particularly in London, that prompted demands for more effective

---

[27] M Ignatieff, *A Just Measure of Pain: The Penitentiary in the Industrial Revolution 1750–1850* (London: Macmillan, 1978); M Foucault, *Discipline and Punish: The Birth of the Prison* (Harmondsworth, Middlesex: Peregrine, 1979).

[28] J Styles, 'The Emergence of the Police', *British Journal of Criminology* 27(1) (1987), 15–22; 17.

[29] J Fielding, *A Plan for Preventing Robberies within Twenty Miles of London with an Account of the Rise and Establishment of the Real Thieftakers* (London: A Millar, 1755).

[30] JM Beattie, 'Sir John Fielding and Public Justice: The Bow Street Magistrates' Court, 1754–1780', *Law and History Review* 25(1) (2007), 61–100.

[31] Colquhoun, *Treatise on the Police of the Metropolis* (n 20).

[32] As several commentators have observed—see: M Neocleous, 'Social Police and the Mechanisms of Prevention: Patrick Colquhoun and the Condition of Poverty', *British Journal of Criminology* 40(4) (2000), 710–26; F Dodsworth, 'Police and the Prevention of Crime: Commerce, Temptation and the Corruption of the Body Politic, from Fielding to Colquhoun', *British Journal of Criminology* 47(3) (2007), 439–54.

[33] M Felson, *Crime and Everyday Life* 3rd edn (London: Sage, 2002).

[34] Garland, 'The Limits of the Sovereign State: Strategies of Crime Control in Contemporary Society' (n 7), 464.

prevention. Colquhoun was a realist and he observed that especially among the 'lower orders' and the 'indigent', faced with the temptations of urban life:

> it will not altogether be possible, amid the various opposite attractions of pleasure and pain, to reduce the tumultuous activity of mankind to absolute regularity - We can only hope for a considerable reduction of the evils that exist.[35]

Colquhoun's observations of the growth of petty crime, pilfering, prostitution, and social disorder in metropolitan London prompted him to argue that 'the fundamental principle of good legislation is rather to prevent crimes than to punish'.[36] In this he was undoubtedly influenced by Jeremy Bentham's argument that all punishment was a necessary evil, that it was justified only insofar as was necessary for crime prevention, and that preventive measures were to be preferred over punishment.[37] In eighteenth-century England, criminal law was largely post-hoc, uncertain in its terms, severe in its application, and unsupported by strong preventive elements. Together, these failings were identified as a primary cause of the social disorder and criminality that blighted life in late eighteenth-century London. Colquhoun argued: '[t]o establish a System calculated to prevent criminals from returning to their evil practices after punishment is the very essence of good Police; but notwithstanding its importance to the Community, no measures have ever yet been adopted, calculated to attain so desirable an object'.[38] Accordingly, he suggested that '[i]n developing the causes which have produced that want of security, which it is believed prevails in no other civilised country in so great a degree as in England, it will be necessary to examine how far the System of Criminal Jurisprudence has been, hitherto, applicable to the prevention of crimes'.[39] Arguably his most important and enduring achievement was the founding of a river police whose continual presence on the Thames was designed to deter thefts of cargo from boats, wharves, and dockyards. Inaugurated with private funding in 1798, the Thames River Police were so successful in preventing theft that it was adopted as a public agency two years later and, as such, set the precedent for the later establishment of the Metropolitan Police.

A close reading of Colquhoun's work reveals an interpretive hazard for the modern reader: the very terms 'prevention', 'preventive principle', and 'preventive policing' are deployed to connote activities that extend well beyond the prevention of particular crimes. Colquhoun's *Treatise on the Police of the Metropolis* articulates a conception of preventive endeavour that goes far beyond the realm of crime control

---

[35] Colquhoun, *Treatise on the Police of the Metropolis* (n 20).

[36] Colquhoun, *Treatise*, 72. J McMullen, 'The Arresting Eye: Discourse, Surveillance and Disciplinary Administration in Early English Police Thinking', *Social and Legal Studies* 7(1) (1998), 97–128.

[37] For discussion see P O'Malley, 'Jeremy Bentham', *University of Sydney Law School, Legal Studies Papers* 09/10 September (2009), 5.

[38] Colquhoun, *Treatise* (n 20), 433.   [39] Colquhoun, *Treatise*, 3.

or the maintenance of public order to encompass, for example, regulations relating to 'markets, hackney-coach stands, paving, cleansing, lighting, watching, marking streets, and numbering houses'.[40] Innumerable regulations relating to every aspect of urban economic and social life, planning, and the administration of poor relief were rationalized on preventive grounds. So too was the regulation of 'Public Houses, Tea-Gardens, Theatres, and other places of Public Amusement; indecent Publications; Ballad-Singers—Female Prostitution—Servants out of Place—The Lottery; Gaming—Indigence, and various other causes'.[41] In short, the scope of preventive endeavour went much further than that which is now contemplated under the heading of crime prevention to encompass a broad range of social policies and regulatory endeavours. Moreover, it is clear that this programme of policing and regulation was considered inseparable from a larger still preventive programme that encompassed education, upbringing, employment, and social morals.

Jeremy Bentham[42] likewise envisaged that the preventive function of government should extend beyond the enactment and enforcement of criminal laws—the 'direct methods of preventing offence'[43]—to include 'indirect or preventive legislation' which might provide 'a train of legislative proceedings for the prevention of offences'.[44] The indirect means considered by Bentham (though he was careful not directly to endorse them)[45] included the regulation of weapons and poisons and the practice of stamping goods to prevent fraud. One of his most controversial proposals was to implement more widely the practice common among sailors of 'printing their family and Christian names upon their wrists, in well-formed and indelible characters' (or, in modern parlance, tattooing) as a means of personal identification.[46] Bentham suggested that, if it were universally adopted, tattooing 'would be a

[40] Colquhoun, *Treatise*, 594.   [41] Colquhoun, *Treatise*, 617.

[42] Bentham was also a friend and collaborator of Colquhoun and had a well-documented influence upon his thinking. Dodsworth, 'Police and the Prevention of Crime: Commerce, Temptation and the Corruption of the Body Politic, from Fielding to Colquhoun', (n 32).

[43] Bentham, *The Works of Jeremy Bentham.Principles of Penal Law*, Ch. II 'Of Direct Methods of Preventing Offences'.

[44] According to Engelmann, it appears first to have been published in 1789 as a chapter in *An Introduction to the Principles of Morals and Legislation* (SG Engelmann, '"Indirect Legislation": Bentham's Liberal Government', *Polity* 35 (2003), 369–88; 372. Engelmann suggests that Bentham's conception of indirect legislation was really an essay on crime prevention, and this is evidenced by the fact that it was subsequently published under the title 'Of Indirect Means of Preventing Crimes' in *vol. 1 Principles of Morals and Legislation, Fragment on Government, Civil Code, Penal Law*.

[45] Bentham insisted 'the object in view is, not to propose the adoption of any given measure, but solely to exhibit it to the view, and recommend it to the attention, of those who may be able to judge of its fitness'.

[46] SG Engelmann, '"Indirect Legislation": Bentham's Liberal Government', *Polity* 35 (2003), 369–88. Bentham, *The Works of Jeremy Bentham. Principles of the Civil Code*, Part III: 'Of Indirect Means of Preventing Crimes', Ch. XII '*To facilitate the Recognition and the Finding of Individuals*'.

new spring for morality, a new source of power for the laws, an almost infallible precaution against a multitude of offences'.[47] Against the anticipated criticism that such measures would be 'favourable to tyranny', he argued that, far from being erosive of individual liberties, tattooing would instead be 'favourable to personal liberty, by permitting relaxations in the rigour of proceedings. Imprisonment, having for its only object the detention of individuals, might become rare, when they were held as it were by an invisible chain.'[48]

This placing of prevention at the heart of the protection of liberty lay at the core of one of Bentham's most important works, *Principles of the Civil Code*, in which he developed the concept of security and stressed the vital role of law in promoting 'security of expectations' into the future.[49] For Bentham, liberty could be exercised and lasting choices made only in the context of a legal system that, by minimizing adverse contingencies, creates such stability that individuals can formulate goals and make decisions in the reasonable expectation that they will be fulfilled. In his later, magisterial, but unfinished, work, *Constitutional Code*, Bentham went so far as to propose the establishment of a 'Preventive Services Ministry', whose function would be 'the prevention of delinquency and calamity'. The proposed Preventive Services Minister was to be charged with implementing legislation to tackle flood prevention, precautions against fire, safety regulations in mines and factories, prevention of contagious diseases through vaccination, and the regulation of drugs.[50] Here too, prevention of crime was scarcely differentiated from the prevention of the other hazards and 'calamities' of nineteenth-century life.

Bentham's influence on social thought and the subsequent development of government is well documented. Many of the grandest, most ambitious projects of state-building in nineteenth-century Britain can be understood principally as Benthamite endeavours in security. Quite apart from Bentham's well-documented plans for the reform of prisons,[51] his proposals for urban planning, provision of sewerage, safe water supplies, tackling of disease and promotion of social health, and the establishment of elementary education were all motivated in significant degree by the need to tackle the problems of crime and social disorder that blighted urban life. O'Malley and Hutchinson thus argue: 'it is not at all the case that risk-based prevention is new. To the contrary, the nineteenth century was the site of some of the most spectacular governmental projects in urban security,

---

[47] Bentham, *The Works of Jeremy Bentham* (n 46).

[48] Bentham, *The Works of Jeremy Bentham*.

[49] Bentham, *The Works of Jeremy Bentham. Principles of the Civil Code*. Part 1, Chapter 7 'Of Security'. See discussion in J Dinwiddy, *Bentham* (Oxford: Oxford University Press, 1989), 96.

[50] J Bentham, *Constitutional Code* (London: Robert Heward, 1830). See discussion in Dinwiddy, *Bentham* (n 49), 97.

[51] J Semple, *Bentham's Prison: A Study of the Panopticon Penitentiary* (Oxford: Oxford University Press, 1993).

environmental design, and risk reduction.'[52] Nor were these projects temporally limited to preventing immediate harms. As Dubber observes, in respect of police regulations to prevent fire, 'The idea was to prevent the exigency. And so the possibility of an exigency became the justification for police power actions, rather than the exigency itself.'[53] In short, the establishment of laws, institutions, and regulatory measures designed to anticipate threats to safety, welfare, and social order was a central motivating force of early nineteenth-century state-building.

2.3 The Founding of the Preventive Police

Arguably the most important institutional edifice of early preventive endeavour was the founding of the modern police force. Although the police is now taken for granted as the cornerstone of modern criminal justice, its establishment should not be regarded as a foregone conclusion. In the late eighteenth and early nineteenth century, a deep-seated suspicion, and quintessentially English, fear prevailed concerning the extension of state power that the establishment of a preventive police force would involve. Debates about the possible form and function of the police were peppered with references to France, a feared enemy and a country whose perceived deployment of the police as agents of state espionage against its citizens epitomized the threat of a police state. A British House of Commons enquiry sat for a full three years to consider the possibility of reform, including the introduction of a formal police force, and it concluded that:[54]

though their property may occasionally be invaded, or their lives endangered by the hands of wicked and desperate individuals, yet the institutions of the country being sound, its laws well administered, and justice executed against offenders, no greater safeguards can be obtained, without sacrificing all those rights which society was instituted to preserve.[55]

This hostile conclusion was reached not because the committee failed to appreciate the desirability of prevention but because it found it impossible to envisage a preventive system that did not entail an excessive extension of state power:

---

[52] O'Malley and Hutchinson, 'Reinventing Prevention: Why Did "Crime Prevention" Develop So Late?' (n 4), 375.

[53] MD Dubber, *The Police Power: Patriarchy and the Foundations of American Government* (New York: Columbia University Press, 2005), 118.

[54] House of Commons, *The Third Report from the Select Committee on the Police of the Metropolis* (London: House of Commons, 1818).

[55] House of Commons, *The Third Report* (n 54), 32. This conclusion was later to be subject to savage critique by Sir Edwin Chadwick who observed that it was based on no more than 'vague generalities as their conclusions from three years enquiries'. Chadwick, 'Preventive Police' (n 1), 256.

It is no doubt true, that to prevent crime is better than to punish it: but the difficulty is not in the end but the means, and though your committee could imagine a system of police that might arrive at the object sought for, yet in a free country, or even in one where any unrestrained intercourse of society is admitted, such a system would of necessity be odious and repulsive, and one which no government would be able to carry into execution . . . the very proposal would be rejected with abhorrence; it would be a plan which would make every servant of every house a spy upon the actions of his master, and all classes spies upon each other.[56]

The fear that to establish a police force was inconsistent with individual liberty and even 'Englishness' was no less evident in the House of Commons Select Committee Fourth Report of 1822, which concluded:

It is difficult to reconcile an effective system of police, with that perfect freedom of action and exemption from interference, which are the great privileges and blessings of society in this country; and your Committee think that the forfeiture or curtailment of such advantages would be too great a sacrifice for improvements in police, or facilities in detection of crime, however desirable in themselves if abstractedly considered.[57]

Continuing disquiet about state interference in civil liberties constituted a powerful inhibition on attempts to institute a formal police. Yet, the pressure to secure public order and to prevent crime in a rapidly industrializing and urbanizing society did not abate. A recurrent theme in contemporary political discourse was dispute about how a formal police force was to be conceived, what powers it should have, and what goals or purposes it should pursue. The matter was fiercely debated on many occasions in Parliament, as it was in wider society. Sir Robert Peel's early attempts to persuade Parliament of the virtues of a 'preventive police' had a decidedly defensive air: 'God forbid that he should mean to countenance a system of espionage; but a vigorous preventive police, consistent with the free principles, of our free constitution, was an object which he did not despair of seeing accomplished.'[58] The reference here to espionage was a direct rejection of the powers of surveillance in the Continental model of policing exemplified in the public mind by the French police.[59]

Throughout the 1820s, Parliament kept returning to the question of whether it was possible to conceive of a model of preventive policing that would not erode the liberty of citizens unduly. For example, in 1826 John Lockhart, MP for Oxford, tried to argue 'that we ought not to have an unconstitutional or preventive police, such as they had on the continent; but a strong protective police was a useful

---

[56] House of Commons, *The Third Report*, 32.

[57] Cited in Chadwick, 'Preventive Police' (n 1), 257.

[58] HC Deb 4 June 1822 vol. 7 cc790–805, 804.

[59] Dubber, *The Police Power: Patriarchy and the Foundations of American Government* (n 53), Ch. 3.

body'.[60] All the while Peel remained dogged in his insistence that the detection and prevention of crime were 'objects of such deep importance, not merely as they regard the security of individual property, but also as they regard the morals and habits of the entire population'.[61] Only in 1828 did Peel finally succeed in setting up a Select Committee whose ultimate recommendation that a centralized police force be established proved to be decisive. Even at this late stage, the orientation of the proposed police remained decidedly preventive. Alderman Waithman MP insisted: 'Let the committee . . . recollect, that they would do no good by multiplying the number of committals. Their main object ought to be the prevention of crime, and not the punishment of it.'[62]

The priority of a preventive system of crime control was also a preoccupation of one of the leading social reformers of the day, Sir Edwin Chadwick, who lent his considerable weight to the cause by publishing an article entitled 'A Preventive Police' in which he insisted that 'the introduction of a preventive system of police has become absolutely necessary'.[63] Chadwick elaborated his conception of police at great length arguing: 'A good police would be one well-organised body of men acting upon a system of precautions, to prevent crimes and public calamities; to preserve public peace and order.'[64] Chadwick was motivated by the pursuit of security and also by his abhorrence of the ready resort to capital punishment as a primary means of crime control: 'The acknowledged inefficacy of severity of punishment, has directed attention to the possibility of obtaining the aid of another set of remedies in such precautionary measures as it would be the province of a body of men, like that we have described, to execute.'[65] Precaution, as an integral aspect of the preventive ideal, had earlier been anticipated by Colquhoun, but a more expansive notion of prevention in which the moral responsibility rested as much with prospective victims as it is did with potential offenders was gaining importance. Chadwick insisted:

A good preventive police would, under a thousand circumstances, interpose in behalf of the public, and by authority or admonition prevent temptation from the incautious exposure of property. Caution in this respect should be enforced upon every individual as a high moral duty. No man should be permitted wantonly to neglect due precautions with respect even to his own property, since the loss which occurs in consequence of such neglect contributes to the formation of a predatory habit, by which others of the community may suffer.[66]

[60] HC Deb 9 March 1826 vol. 14 cc1214–44, 1241.
[61] HC Deb 28 February 1828 vol. 18 cc784–816, 798.
[62] HC Deb 28 February 1828 vol. 18 cc784–816, 813.
[63] Chadwick, 'Preventive Police' (n 1), 252.
[64] Chadwick, 'Preventive Police', 252.
[65] Chadwick, 'Preventive Police', 252–3.
[66] Chadwick, 'Preventive Police', 272.

In this conception of prevention, an important role was assigned to victims who were encouraged and expected to take suitable precautions. Property thefts would continue 'unless they are prevented by the alarm and precaution of the owners, or by the increase of danger from the adoption of some measures of a preventive nature by a police'.[67] Such measures were to include intelligence sharing, warnings, registers of stolen goods and of offenders, and free information-sharing Gazettes. Together, '[t]he primary effects of these measures would be prevention, by giving warning to those interested, by exciting their attention to all suspicious persons or circumstances' and in so doing 'serve to promote habits of caution in the public'.[68] Another important aspect of 'the preventive principle of police' was the separation of police and judicial functions. As early as 1796, Colquhoun had insisted: 'It is thus by giving Police its true and genuine character, and divesting it of those judicial functions which are the province of Magistrates alone, that a proper line will be drawn between *Prevention,* and those proceedings which lead to *Punishment* after an offence is actually committed.'[69] Separation of police and judicial functions came to be akey distinction between the British system of criminal justice and its continental inquisitorial counterpart.

Only in 1829, against considerable opposition, even from within his own Tory Party, did Peel finally succeed in securing the passage of the Metropolitan Police Act which founded the Metropolitan Police.[70] This development owed much to the success of those who promoted the preventive police in persuading themselves and others that its establishment was consistent with the legitimate exercise of state power. That prevention was to be the core function of the newly founded police is clear in the direction issued by the first Commissioner of the Metropolitan Police in 1829, Sir Richard Mayne:

The primary object of an efficient police is the prevention of crime: the next that of detection and punishment of offenders if crime is committed. To these ends all the efforts of police must be directed. The protection of life and property, the preservation of public tranquillity, and the absence of crime, will alone prove whether those efforts have been successful and whether the objects for which the police were appointed have been attained.[71]

This direction is still quoted today by the Metropolitan Police as its founding purpose.[72] Yet the largely regulatory and social aspect of prevention, so clearly articulated by early advocates, was undermined by its implementation in practice.

---

[67] Chadwick, 'Preventive Police', 275.   [68] Chadwick, 'Preventive Police', 282.

[69] Colquhoun, *Treatise* (n 20), 619.

[70] Thorburn notes that Canada created its own police forces around the same time—Toronto in 1829, Halifax in 1864, and Montreal in 1865. In the US, Boston established a police force in 1836, Chicago in 1837, and New York in 1845. M Thorburn, 'Reinventing the Nightwatchman State', *University of Toronto Law Journal* 60 (2010), 425–43.

[71] See <http://content.met.police.uk/Site/historypolicing>.

[72] See for example —<http://content.met.police.uk/Site/historypolicing>.

Part of the problem was that the preventive rationale came to be articulated in sweeping provisions such as s. 7 of the Metropolitan Police Act 1829 that empowered a police constable to apprehend 'all loose, idle and disorderly Persons whom he shall find disturbing the public Peace, or whom he shall have just Cause to suspect of any evil Designs, and all Persons whom he shall find between sunset and the Hour of Eight in the Forenoon lying in any Highway, Yard, or other Place, or loitering therein, and not giving a satisfactory Account of themselves'.[73] Legal provisions such as this targeted the homeless and designated them as *prima facie* suspicious on little more ground than that they were too poor to find shelter. It is perhaps not surprising that throughout the middle years of the nineteenth century the police came to be regarded with deep hostility, not least by the primary subjects of policing, the poor of the metropolis.

The subsequent development of the police and of the criminal justice system away from its preventive origins and toward a more formal prosecutorial model was influenced in part by the professionalization of lawyers over the course of the nineteenth century. Crawford and Evans observe: 'despite the explicit emphasis on prevention within Peel's vision of policing, the subsequent organizational history of the British police saw the increasing marginalization of crime prevention as an object of police activity and as a focus of governmental attention'.[74] By the mid-nineteenth century, the very idea of 'preventive policing' had largely passed out of favour in favour of a prosecutorial and punishment oriented criminal justice system, albeit one in which due process protections were much more developed.

Any proposal that preventive policing should be revived aroused considerable suspicion. This became a live issue when the ending of transportation to Australia in 1868 generated the pressing problem of what to do with those 'habitual' criminals who could no longer be sent to the colonies. Instead, they were now subject to lengthy periods of penal servitude in Britain but the issue of how to deal with ex-convicts, or 'ticket-of-leave men', on their release remained. The mooted revival of preventive policing in the form of police supervision and surveillance of ex-convicts met with fierce opposition as being 'anti-constitutional', not least because it was deemed to undermine the presumption of innocence and likely to be arbitrary in application. Once again, proposals for police supervision were likened to instituting state espionage, an undertaking inconsistent with the now established role of the

---

[73] Provision to stop, search, and arrest anyone suspected of loitering originated in the 1824 Vagrancy Act. It was seen as a key element in the legal provision for the prevention of crime but was opposed by many of the public against whom it was deployed. Its use became controversial again in the late twentieth century: in 1981, misuse of this historic provision (which had become known as the 'sus' law) resulted in race riots in many UK cities.

[74] A Crawford and K Evans, 'Crime Prevention and Community Safety', in M Maguire, R Morgan, and R Reiner (eds.), *The Oxford Handbook of Criminology* (Oxford: Oxford University Press, 2012), 769–805; 770.

police as handmaiden to the criminal justice system.[75] Despite fierce debate, the countervailing view that 'innocent men' had nothing to fear prevailed and the Habitual Criminals Act was passed in 1869. Most controversially, it included a provision that shifted the burden of proof by requiring ex-prisoners to demonstrate that they obtained their livelihood by honest means. The numbers who came under police supervision quickly exceeded the capacity of the police to keep track of them and the police were soon accused of failing to supervise effectively. Reform of its provisions by the Prevention of Crimes Act 1871 shifted the burden of proof back to the prosecution, and gave them greater discretion to determine which offenders should be subject to surveillance, but subjected those who were targeted to tighter supervision. In practice, however, the unwillingness of the police to undertake surveillance, combined with the enormous difficulty of tracking offenders in the growing metropolises, made the task of police supervision almost impossible.

2.4 Justifying and Limiting Prevention: Mill and the Harm Principle

The considerable unease about the revival of preventive policing evident in these debates can only properly be understood in the context of larger political deliberation about the legitimate extent of state preventive powers. An important subject for deliberation among contemporary political theorists was the legitimate scope of and limitations upon the state's power over its citizens. Arguably none were more influential than the writings of John Stuart Mill. For Mill, interference in individual liberty was justified only where an action 'violates a distinct and assignable obligation' to others or where 'there is a definite risk of damage, either to an individual or to the public'.[76] Mill recognized both the obligation upon government to prevent crime and the risks inherent in its exercise of its preventive function, as is evident in these observations:

It is one of the undisputed functions of government to take precautions against crime before it has been committed, as well as to detect and punish it afterwards. The preventive function of government, however, is far more liable to be abused, to the prejudice of liberty, than the punitory function; for there is hardly any part of the legitimate freedom of action of a human being that would not admit of being represented, and fairly too, as increasing the facilities for some form or other of delinquency.[77]

---

[75] L Radzinowicz and R Hood, *The Emergence of Penal Policy in Victorian and Edwardian England* (Oxford: Oxford University Press, 1986), 247.

[76] JS Mill, *On Liberty* (Harmondsworth, Middlesex: Penguin, 1979; 1859), 149.

[77] Mill, *On Liberty* (n 76), 165.

A key question for Mill, therefore, was to ascertain 'the proper limits of what may be called the functions of the police; how far liberty may legitimately be invaded for the prevention of crime'.[78] Mill's deliberations on this question were enormously influential not only in Britain but also in Europe and North America.[79] One of Mill's most enduring legacies is his articulation of the harm principle as a guide to the exercise of state power, namely: 'That the only purpose for which power can be rightfully exercised over any member of a civilized community, against his will, is to prevent harm to others.'[80] And yet, as many commentators have since acknowledged, the harm principle provides a necessary but hardly a sufficient justification for the deprivation of liberty and it can be read to justify as well as to limit state interference.[81] It thus arguably raises as many questions about the legitimate scope of state preventive power as it purports to answer.

Mill might have done more to flesh out the harm principle and to subject it to limiting considerations. Further insight into his views can be found his response to the Contagious Diseases Acts (CDA). Passed in the 1860s, these Acts provided for the compulsory medical inspection of alleged prostitutes in port and garrison towns and the forced detention and treatment of those found to be diseased in so-called lock hospitals. The 1866 Act established a special medical police force to patrol these towns which was empowered to require suspected prostitutes to undergo regular forced inspections for up to one year and the 1869 Act required prostitutes to carry official registration cards. The Acts provoked considerable political opposition from early feminists, not least the redoubtable Josephine Butler, who objected to the fact that they licensed degrading and discriminatory treatment of already disadvantaged women. Despite the fact that the CDA were undoubtedly preventive in intent and, as such, arguably fell squarely within the scope of the harm principle, Mill became a prominent critic. Accepting that the Acts were aimed at the prevention of a grave harm, he nonetheless objected on grounds of 'legislative intent' and 'distribution of liberty' to argue that, if Parliament had really intended to protect against disease, the provisions within the CDA would have applied to men as well as women.[82]

---

[78] Mill, *On Liberty*, 165.

[79] Indeed, some commentators consider that Mill self-consciously saw himself as contributing to European public opinion. N Urbinati and A Zakaras, 'Introduction', in N Urbinati and A Zakaras (eds.), *J.S. Mill's Political Thought: A Bicentennial Reassessment* (Cambridge: Cambridge University Press, 2007), 1–7.

[80] Mill, *On Liberty* (n 76), 68.

[81] WE Parmet, 'J.S. Mill and the American Law of Quarantine', *Public Health Ethics* 1(3) (2008), 210–22; 213. J Waldron, 'Mill on Liberty and the Contagious Diseases Act', in N Urbinati and A Zakaras (eds.), *J.S. Mill's Political Thought: A Bicentennial Reassessment* (Cambridge: Cambridge University Press, 2007), 11–42, 17; B Harcourt, 'The Collapse of the Harm Principle', *The Journal of Criminal Law and Criminology* 90(1) (1999), 109–94.

[82] See Mill's lengthy testimony to the *Royal Commission of 1870, on the Administration and Operation of the Contagious Diseases Acts of 1866 and 1869.* <http://oll.libertyfund.org/?option=com_staticxt&staticfile=show.php%3Ftitle=255&chapter=21693&layout=html&Itemid=27>.

Appearing before the 1870 Royal Commission which enquired into the legislation, Mill argued:

I do not consider it justifiable on principle, because it appears to me to be opposed to one of the greatest principles of legislation, the security of personal liberty. It appears to me that legislation of this sort takes away that security, almost entirely from a particular class of women intentionally, but incidentally and unintentionally, one may say, from all women whatever... We ought not to give powers liable to very great abuse, and easily abused, and then presume that those powers will not be abused.

Although the prevention of harm provided clear grounds for medical intervention, the forcible detention of women was fiercely contested as overly coercive and unfair. Between 1870 and 1885, 17,365 petitions against the CDA bearing 2,606,429 signatures were presented to the House of Commons, and more than 900 meetings were held.[83] Only in 1886 were the Acts finally repealed. The affair provides a powerful illustration of the readiness and the capacity of the Victorian state to enact and enforce extremely intrusive measures in the name of prevention and the difficulty thereafter, even for those as intellectually powerful and eloquent as Mill, to press home the case for restraint.

2.5 The Institution of Preventive Detention

The problem of preventing crime and limiting recidivism remained a live issue throughout the nineteenth century. As we have seen, attempts to institute preventive regimes for ex-convicts were heavily criticized in the second half of the century.[84] By 1910 the experiment in preventive policing through the supervision of ex-convicts was finally abandoned. Its demise can be attributed partly to the impossibility of keeping track of ex-offenders, who simply disappeared from view in teeming conurbations, partly to a reluctance to depart from fundamental principles of justice (not least the presumption of innocence), and partly to an continuing suspicion of 'the tyranny of police surveillance'.[85]

Later attempts to institute regimes of preventive detention did not fare much better. A Report from the Departmental Committee on Prisons (1898) pressed for a

---

See also the discussion in Waldron, 'Mill on Liberty and the Contagious Diseases Act' (n 81), 32 ff.

[83] EM Sigworth and TJ Wyke, 'A Study of Victorian Prostitution and Venereal Disease', in M Vicnius (ed.), *Suffer and Be Still: Women in the Victorian Age* (London: Methuen & Co Ltd, 1980), 77–99; 77.

[84] See analysis in L Radzinowicz, *A History of English Criminal Law and Its Administration from 1750. Vol. 3* (London: Steven & Sons Limited, 1956), 46 ff.

[85] A Rutherford, 'Boundaries of English Penal Police', *Oxford Journal of Legal Studies* 8(1) (1988), 132–41; 133.

more reformative role for prisons to combat the rising prison population. Repeated attempts by the Home Office to institute powers of preventive detention for 'habitual' offenders were subject to severe criticism and energetically resisted, by notable figures such as Hilaire Belloc among others, on the grounds that the proposed provisions were too wide-ranging, liable to be imposed upon persistent petty rather than dangerous offenders, and likely to result in disproportionate penalties. The Prevention of Crimes Act, finally passed in 1908, created the first system of preventive detention in Britain and it permitted those designated as habitual offenders (ie who had been convicted on indictment on at least three previous occasions) to be sentenced to an indeterminate term up to a maximum of ten years. After an initial period of penal servitude, convicts were subject to an indefinite period of imprisonment at hard labour 'for the protection of the public'. Release was at the discretion of an Advisory Board and those who were released before the end of their term remained under supervision for the remainder of the sentence.[86]

In theory, convicts held under preventive detention were to enjoy less rigorous conditions and be subject to 'disciplinary and reformatory influences' during the supposedly preventive part of their sentence. In 1910, however, the then Home Secretary Winston Churchill observed that 'it ought not to be imagined by the courts or by the public, that a period of prolonged confinement amongst the worst of men within the walls of a prison ... is not, whatever name it may be called by, a most serious addition to any other punishment'.[87] Churchill concluded that 'preventive detention is penal servitude in all essentials, but it soothes the conscience of judges and of public and there is a very grave danger that the administration of the law should under softer names assume in fact a more severe character'.[88] He proposed that instead of merely requiring three previous convictions, preventive detention should be limited to those who had served three previous sentences of 18 months or more and could be shown to be a danger to society. He warned that if the scope of the regime were not substantially limited by administrative means, he would subject it to drastic legislative amendment. The consequence was a very significant reduction from 177 sentences of preventive detention in 1910 to 53 in the following year. Although attempts were made to revive preventive detention after the First World War, during the 1920s only on average 31 sentences of preventive detention were passed each year.

Oddly, despite earlier opposition and criticisms, provisions for post-custodial supervision proved to be more enduring. In 1911, release on licence, which

---

[86] The provision thus prefigured later developments in provision for preventive sentencing and parole—see further Ch. 7.

[87] Quoted in Radzinowicz, *A History of English Criminal Law and Its Administration from 1750. Vol. 3* (n 84), 279.   [88] Radzinowicz, *A History*, 283.

combined the provision of 'after-care' with surveillance and control, was extended to apply to all convicts released from sentences of penal servitude.[89] This development should be seen in the context of the larger transition to more individualized techniques of prevention that were influenced by the rise of medical and welfare professions who identified the 'feeble-minded', 'habitual inebriates', women, and children as problem populations and as suitable subjects, therefore, of preventive intervention.[90] The targeting of those 'degenerates' deemed to threaten social order was fuelled by ascendant theories of social Darwinism, the teachings of the eugenics movement, fears about the effects of urban degeneration, and wider concern about the decline of Britain's imperial status. By contrast to the continental focus of Lombrosian positivism on physical degeneracy,[91] British eugenicists focused more upon mental inheritance as a cause of crime. Preventing the transmission of mental infirmity and tackling the causes of the mental disorder that was thought to explain much criminal behaviour were primary objects of the many specialized reformatories which were founded in the early decades of the twentieth century.[92] Another important and lasting provision of the Prevention of Crimes Act 1908 was the establishment of borstals or reformatory institutions for young offenders.

It is clear that much of the debate around the legitimacy of identifying habitual offenders and of instituting variant forms of preventive detention centred upon the severity and intrusiveness of measures whose primary justification was preventive rather than punitive.[93] Many of these institutions were located outside the criminal justice system and were ostensibly reformatory and therapeutic, which may have mitigated concerns about the authoritarian nature of their provision and the lengthy deprivations of liberty imposed upon those incarcerated. Another important factor was the emergence of 'new liberalism' in the early years of the twentieth century.[94] By striking contrast to classical liberalism, which had regarded threats to liberty as mainly coming from the exercise of coercion by the state, new liberalism promoted the idea that active government was a better guardian of liberty and that collectivist provision was a better guarantee of welfare than laissez-faire. The substantial body of reforms undertaken by Lloyd George's Liberal government of 1906–1914 was a vital precursor to the later development of social security and signalled the birth of

---

[89] D Garland, *Punishment and Welfare: A History of Penal Strategies* (London: Gower, 1985), 20.

[90] Garland, *Punishment and Welfare* (n 89). L Zedner, *Women, Crime, and Custody in Victorian England* (Oxford: Oxford University Press, 1991). V Bailey, *Delinquency and Citizenship: Reclaiming the Young Offender 1914–1948* (Oxford: Oxford University Press, 1987).

[91] Rafter, 'Origins of Criminology' (n 5).

[92] Garland, *Punishment and Welfare: A History of Penal Strategies* (n 89), Ch. 8.

[93] Rutherford, 'Boundaries of English Penal Police' (n 85), 137–8.

[94] M Freeden, *The New Liberalism: An Ideology of Social Reform* (Oxford: Oxford University Press, 1978).

the welfare state,[95] a monumental development that had profound implications for the preventive endeavour writ large.

2.6 Prevention in the Twentieth Century

The story of prevention for much of the twentieth century is bound up with the development of welfarism, and the faith in scientific progress and the ameliorative potential of intervention upon which it was based.[96] For example, in the 1920s and 1930s, the development of psychiatric and psychological theories of crime had a considerable influence on moves to identify pathological tendencies in deprived families and to target intervention at vulnerable youngsters well ahead of any wrongdoing.[97] In the 1930s, the ecological approach of the Chicago School informed developments in community crime prevention, urban planning, and environmental design.[98] In the post-war period, the range of intellectual and scientific influences on preventive endeavour has been similarly diverse. For example, developmental crime prevention draws upon epidemiology to identify biological, psychological, and social childhood risk factors and to target pre-emptively those shown to be most closely correlated with the subsequent development of delinquency.[99] Sociological approaches have informed community-based crime prevention strategies that seek to alter the social conditions and institutional arrangements deemed to conduce to offending, for example by making interventions in relation to family, peers, clubs, and organizations.[100] A common facet of community crime prevention is the adoption of multi-agency or partnership approaches that seek to maximize preventive effects by bringing together criminal justice and other agencies in co-operative endeavour.[101]

---

[95] RM Titmuss, *Essays on the Welfare State* (London: Allen & Unwin, 1958).

[96] Hughes goes so far as to identify 'the rise of medico-welfare professions in the early twentieth century as preventive agencies' and to describe 'rehabilitation as "prevention"'. G Hughes, *Understanding Crime Prevention: Social Control, Risk and Late Modernity* (Buckingham: Open University Press, 1998), 43.

[97] Hughes, *Understanding Crime Prevention* (n 96), 43–5. See also B Harcourt, 'Punitive Preventive Justice: A Critique', in A Ashworth, L Zedner, and P Tomlin (eds.), *Prevention and the Limits of the Criminal Law* (Oxford: Oxford University Press, 2013), 232–72; 256–7.

[98] D Downes and P Rock, *Understanding Deviance* 6th edn (Oxford: Oxford University Press, 2011), Ch. 3 'The University of Chicago Sociology Department'.

[99] DP Farrington, 'Developmental Criminology and Risk-Focused Prevention', in M Maguire, R Morgan, and R Reiner (eds.), *The Oxford Handbook of Criminology* 3rd edn (Oxford: Oxford University Press, 2002), 657–701.

[100] A Crawford, *Crime Prevention and Community Safety: Politics, Policies, and Practices* (London: Longman, 1998).

[101] A Crawford, 'The Partnership Approach to Community Crime Prevention: Corporatism at the Local Level?', *Social and Legal Studies* (1994), 497–518.

Since the 1970s, economics and, particularly, rational choice theory has been highly influential in the development of crime control.[102] It has resulted, for example, in the rise of situational crime prevention—an approach that sees crime primarily in terms of costs to be reduced, criminal justice as an expensive and ineffective machinery for cost-reduction, and prevention as a more efficient means of control.[103] Situational crime prevention is predicated upon the assumption that humans act rationally and that utility maximization is common to us all. This thus constitutes a sharp move away from moral and social understandings of crime as product of pathology or delinquency to posit that crime is simply rational where the expected rewards of criminal conduct are higher than the anticipated costs (of detection, censure, and sanction).

Economic analysis also has clear implications for crime prevention. Felson and Clarke, for example, argue: 'social prevention implies improving people, which we regard as a goal almost sure to produce frustration'.[104] Instead, new strategies drawing upon rational choice theory alter the opportunity structures of offending and thereby seek to raise the marginal costs of offending. By so doing they aim to create sufficient disincentives to inhibit much criminal activity. The resulting focus is on small-scale, practical alterations, for example by target-hardening locations or objects vulnerable to crime; by increasing surveillance, enhancing lighting, and encouraging the public to act as 'capable guardians'; and by reducing the anticipated benefits of crime or by removing the objects of crime altogether (coinless public telephone boxes for example). Environmental criminology, routine activity theory, and crime pattern theory stress the crime-preventive effects of minor, mundane changes to the environment that have the combined effect of reducing vulnerable targets and increasing forms of natural surveillance in an economic manner.[105] The cost-driven aspect of economic analysis also led to the promotion of risk assessment and the rise of actuarial justice aimed at identifying and neutralizing risky populations ahead of wrongdoing.[106] The neo-liberal politics of the Thatcher era also

---

[102] Perhaps the seminal text is G Becker, 'Crime and Punishment: An Economic Approach', *The Journal of Political Economy* 76(2) (1968), 169–217.

[103] RV Clarke, 'Situational Crime Prevention', in M Tonry and N Morris (eds.), *Crime and Justice: An Annual Review of Research* 19 (Chicago: University of Chicago, 1995), 91–150.

[104] M Felson and RV Clarke, 'The Ethics of Situational Crime Prevention', in G Newman and R Clarke (eds.), *Rational Choice and Situational Crime Prevention* (Aldershot: Dartmouth, 1997), 197–218; 205.

[105] M Felson and RV Clarke, *Opportunity Makes the Thief: Practical Theory for Crime Prevention. Police Research Series No. 98* (London: Home Office, 1998); L Zedner, 'Opportunity Makes the Thief-Taker: The Influence of Economic Analysis on Crime Control', in T Newburn and P Rock (eds.), *The Politics of Crime Control* (Oxford: Oxford University Press, 2006).

[106] Feeley and Simon, 'Actuarial Justice: The Emerging New Criminal Law' (n 2); M Feeley, 'Actuarial Justice and the Modern State', in G Bruinsma, H Elffers, and J De Keijser (eds.), *Punishment, Places, and Perpetrators: Developments in Criminology and Criminal Justice Research* (Devon, Cullompton: Willan Publishing, 2004), 62–77.

drew upon economic theory to institute a managerialist agenda for crime prevention that focused upon efficient disposal of limited resources, an administrative role
for criminological research, and an emphasis on effectiveness and economy.[107]

2.7 Conclusions

The preventive powers of the modern criminal law[108] are grounded upon the
assumption that it is possible to inhibit would-be harm-doers before they cause the
prohibited harm. And it is this preventive impulse that underpins liability for
possession, preparatory, and inchoate offences. The preventive aspect of the criminal law is therefore predicated upon the existence of a police whose function it is
not only to investigate and secure evidence regarding consummate or completed
crimes but also to act in advance of their commission. Today, the preventive role of
the police is wide-ranging: compiling registers of those known to be persistent
offenders; gaining intelligence about would-be offenders, their whereabouts, pro-
clivities, and temptations; observing suspicious and risky behaviour; and engaging in
surveillance are essential prerequisites to inchoate liability. Without them the
preventive aspect of the criminal law would be little more than an empty threat.
It follows that the establishment of the 'preventive police' in the early nineteenth
century was a necessary precursor to the development of the state's preventive
capacity and to the evolution of the preventive aspect of the criminal law.

  This chapter has also suggested that claims that prevention constitutes a new
departure or paradigm shift are, at best, only partially true since today's preventive
endeavours have clear precursors in the eighteenth- and nineteenth-century origins
of the criminal justice system and preventive aims have informed many developments in the twentieth century. The claim that prevention was 'the path not
taken'[109] underplays the degree to which criminal justice institutions were predicated upon and continued to have an important preventive element. The early
emphasis on crime prevention, on the identification of suspicious characters and on
the preventive aspects of policing, never entirely disappeared from the practice of
crime control and it is arguable that modern actuarial techniques constitute something of a resurgence of much earlier assumptions about the power of the state to
identify, categorize, and apprehend would-be offenders. For all their claims of
scientific rigour and statistical validity, modern actuarial categories of suspicion

---

[107] See discussion in Garland, *The Culture of Control: Crime and Social Order in Contemporary
Society* (n 26), 188–92.
[108] A Ashworth and L Zedner, 'Prevention and Criminalization: Justifications and Limits',
New Criminal Law Review 15(4) (2012), 542–71.
[109] Garland, *The Culture of Control: Crime and Social Order in Contemporary Society* (n 26), 30.

bear a striking resemblance to the preventive measures taken against supposedly suspicious populations by our historical forebears.

It is fair to say that, during the latter half of the nineteenth century, the criminal justice system substantially retreated from ideas of preventive policing in favour of a more narrowly construed and largely (though, of course, not exclusively) retrospective system of prosecution and punishment. This retreat owed much to the powerful debates and philosophical deliberations about the appropriate limits to the exercise of state power; to widespread public resistance to overly extensive police powers; and to the refinement of due process protections. Together, these furnished a powerful brake on the pursuit of prevention. Later chapters will demonstrate the extent to which similar arguments and similar fears have played a role in contemporary developments in prevention. In the remainder of the book we explore significant recent developments in state preventive endeavour in the light of this longer history and seek to delineate principles by which it might be subject to restraint.

3

Prevention, Policing, and Criminal Procedure

In this chapter we move from historical examination of prevention as a central motivating force behind the very establishment of the modern criminal justice system to examine its role in present-day policing and procedure. As we saw in the previous chapter, the origins of policing had a strong preventive orientation. The founding aim of the police, announced in a speech by Sir Richard Mayne in 1829, was that 'the primary object of an efficient police is the prevention of crime; the next that of detection and punishment of offenders if crime is committed'.[1] This is still cited by the Metropolitan Police today.[2] Although that original commitment to preventive policing came to be largely overlaid in the nineteenth century by a post hoc orientation committed to reactive investigation, case building, and prosecution, clear preventive and deterrent elements remained. The tension between these two approaches is exemplified by the difference between intelligence gathering and obtaining evidence about specific offences that will be admissible in court and which grounds the case for the prosecution. Security-oriented policing that seeks to produce actionable intelligence is different from and often incompatible with the production of admissible evidence and the requirements of due process. The vulnerability of the pre-trial process to the imperatives of security is particularly acute where the risks are most grave, and Chapter 8 will examine the particular pressures that apply in respect of counterterrorism. But the impulse to prevent crime comes not only from the gravest risks but also from larger political pressures to protect the public, as well as the proliferation of new technologies. These security technologies include CCTV cameras, satellite tracking, data mining and retention, and new developments in biometrics such as iris scans and DNA profiling. Technological developments facilitate low-cost mass surveillance which allows for the effective observation, screening, risk-profiling, categorization, and tracking of offenders.[3] They also effect changes in the ways in which preventive endeavours are pursued and alter the nature and orientation of policing even with respect to

---

[1] See <http://content.met.police.uk/Site/historypolicing>.
[2] See <http://content.met.police.uk/Site/historypolicing>.
[3] See, eg, KF Aas, H Oppen Gundhus, and H Mork Lomell (eds.), *Technologies of (In) Security: The Surveillance of Everyday Life* (London: Routledge, 2008).

core functions within the criminal process. In what follows we examine how some of the most important police powers are exercised within this larger political and technological context.

Numerous police powers and pre-trial processes come within the ambit of this study, being coercive measures introduced or used for the purpose of preventing harm. Although the details of these powers and procedures differ from country to country, there is a widespread recognition that the state's law enforcement officers must be given some coercive powers if they are to carry out their task of preventing harm. The corollary is that the individuals subjected to those powers lose some of their rights, usually temporarily but often in circumstances that can cause great anxiety. As we shall see, most of these coercive powers are supposed to be exercised only in situations of 'necessity', and in that way it may be argued that they should be regarded as a regrettable but essential element in the democratic compromise whereby citizens yield up some liberty to the state in exchange for protection from harm. However, that may be to move too quickly; we must first examine the rights at stake, and scrutinize any purported justifications for whittling them down.

Among the police powers that can be rationalized, partly at least, on preventive grounds are temporary containment (often known as 'kettling'), powers to exclude certain categories of people from certain areas or to disperse them, powers to reroute processions and to relocate static demonstrations, stop-and-search powers, the power to arrest suspected offenders, detention for questioning, and remand in police custody. Within criminal procedure the principal power that can be rationalized on preventive grounds is that of remand in custody pending and during trial, a particularly intrusive power which can lead to detention in prison for months. In this chapter we select for close attention three of these powers—stop-and-search, temporary containment, and remand in custody pending trial—and we refer more briefly to the other police powers. First, however, we describe the issues of principle which provide the context in which the three powers will be examined.

3.1 Pre-Trial Preventive Measures: Some Issues of Principle

Two widely recognized fundamental rights provide the analytical framework for the discussions in this chapter. The first is the right to liberty of the person, which is a central feature of most statements of human rights or constitutional rights. Thus, Article 5 of the ECHR declares that 'everyone has the right to liberty and security of person'.[4] It goes on to state: 'No one shall be deprived of his liberty save in the

---

[4] See also the International Covenant on Civil and Political Rights, Art. 9.1.

following cases and in accordance with a procedure prescribed by law'—a formulation which indicates that the list of exceptions is exhaustive, and that there must be a legal framework for any proposed exception, in order to prevent arbitrariness. The exception that most concerns us here is exception (c): 'the lawful arrest or detention of a person effected for the purpose of bringing him before the competent legal authority on reasonable suspicion of having committed an offence'. However, it should be noted that this exception, and the other five, relate to cases where there is a 'deprivation of liberty'. If a particular set of circumstances is held not to amount to a 'deprivation of liberty', then there is no need to seek an exception in order to justify it. However, as a matter of principle any coercive restraint on an individual's liberty requires a justification that is consistent with respect for that person as a rational, autonomous agent, although the strongest justifications must of course be required for any deprivation of liberty.

The second right that is essential to the framework of this chapter is the presumption of innocence, which, again, is recognized in all declarations of human rights and constitutional rights.[5] This states that every person should be treated as innocent until and unless charged and convicted of a crime, thereby respecting each individual's status as an autonomous responsible agent.[6] Two exceptional cases do not challenge this general proposition: thus, the quarantining of those with dangerous infectious diseases may be compatible with it inasmuch as the confined person, although perfectly responsible, would otherwise be unable to control their communication of the infection (see Section 9.2); and the detention of mentally disordered persons adjudged to be dangerous may be compatible with it insofar as the persons concerned are not responsible agents (see Section 9.3). Beyond those exceptions, however, the presumption of innocence should be respected as a defining feature of the proper relationship between the state and individuals.[7]

Another way of phrasing this key liberal principle is that the state should presume each person to be harmless, and that therefore it is in principle wrong to take coercive measures against people for preventive reasons unless there are very strong justifications for doing so:

---

[5] See, eg, International Convention on Civil and Political Rights, Art. 14.2; European Convention on Human Rights, Art. 6.2; Constitution of the United States of America, 5th and 14th Amendments.

[6] RA Duff, 'Pre-Trial Detention and the Presumption of Innocence', in A Ashworth, L Zedner, and P Tomlin (eds.), *Prevention and the Limits of the Criminal Law* (Oxford: Oxford University Press, 2013), 115–32; 119–20; A Walen, 'A Punitive Precondition for Preventive Detention: Lost Status as a Foundation for a Lost Immunity', *San Diego Law Review* 48 (2011), 1229–72; 1229.

[7] For further discussion of the presumption of innocence in this connection, see KK Ferzan, 'Preventive Justice and the Presumption of Innocence', *Criminal Law and Philosophy* (forthcoming), and other essays in this special issue.

The crucial objection is that such measures would entail abrogating the right to be presumed harmless which, like the right to be presumed innocent, is fundamental to a free society . . . These are not absolute rights: legally sane and innocent persons may be detained or otherwise prevented from doing harm they are suspected of intending to do; but infringements (e.g. police powers of arrest) are hedged about with restrictions and safeguards and in the end only wrongful actions can lead to just forfeiture of these rights, as is generally well understood in respect of the presumption of innocence.[8]

We will have occasion below to question the latter parts of this quotation, and to ask whether the various police powers are infringements that can be justified, in their present or any other form. But the presumption of harmlessness is an implication of the presumption of innocence, ensuring that its spirit is honoured whenever the state takes coercive powers against individuals, and especially where deprivation of liberty is at stake. This is consistent with proper respect for each individual's status as a responsible agent, one of the values underlying the presumption of innocence.

Neither the right to liberty of the person nor the presumption of innocence is absolute. Indeed, one of the important tasks of this chapter is to explore and to test the boundaries of these rights. Clearly, a deprivation of liberty requires stronger justification than a mere restriction on liberty, for example. The justifications will be assessed in the context of the state's obligation to provide security for its citizens. As argued in Section 1.4, we can posit a democratic compromise in which individuals give up a portion of their liberty in exchange for the state's protection from harm. Many details of this compromise remain to be worked out, and in this chapter we examine the extent to which the right to personal liberty and the presumption of innocence should be treated as limits on the state's pursuit of the goal of protecting people from harm.

3.2 Stop-and-Search Powers

The power of law enforcement officers to stop and search persons and vehicles may be supported on either of two grounds—that it may assist in the investigation of crimes that have already taken place, and that it may help to prevent future crimes from taking place. In English law there is a wide power of this kind, but it is subject to the limitation that the officer must have 'reasonable grounds for suspecting that he will find stolen or prohibited articles', the latter referring to drugs and also to knives and other weapons.[9] The relevant Code of Practice acknowledges that such stops constitute 'an intrusion on liberty',[10] and draws attention to the

---

[8]   J Floud and W Young, *Dangerousness and Criminal Justice* (London: Heinemann, 1981), 44.
[9]   Police and Criminal Evidence Act 1984, s. 1(3).
[10] Police and Criminal Evidence Act *Code of Practice* (2011), para. 1.2.

anti-discrimination provisions in the Equality Act 2010.[11] Unfortunately, there are also some powers of stop-and-search that do not require reasonable suspicion of the individual or vehicle searched, and these give cause for concern.[12] A prominent example of this is the power provided by s. 60 of the Criminal Justice and Public Order Act 1994, which enables stop-and-search (for a period of up to 24 hours) in a particular locality where a senior police officer reasonably believes that 'incidents involving serious violence may take place', or that persons are carrying weapons or other dangerous instruments.[13] While the general authorization requires reasonable belief, the actual stop-and-search does not require reasonable suspicion—a regrettable departure from principle.

Two further examples may be found in the Terrorism Act 2000. One, which is still in force, is the power to stop, examine, and if necessary detain port and airport travellers.[14] No ground for suspicion is required. The second example was the power to search people without the need for reasonable suspicion where the police decided that it was 'expedient for the prevention of acts of terrorism' to designate an area for this purpose.[15] The designation had to be authorized by a senior police officer and confirmed by the Secretary of State; the authorization was limited to a police force area; and the authorization was limited to 28 days, although it could be renewed on application. In fact the police secured rolling authorizations for the whole of London for several years. This was called into question in the *Gillan* case, which raises several points of principle.

An arms fair was being held in the London docklands. The police, using their power to stop and search anyone without the need for reasonable suspicion,[16] stopped Gillan, who was riding his bicycle in the direction of the arms fair in order to join a demonstration, and also Quinton, who was walking towards the demonstration in her capacity as a journalist and who was taking photographs. Each of them was stopped for around 20 minutes and searched. Subsequently, they brought actions against the police for judicial review. The House of Lords held that there was no violation of the appellants' rights under the ECHR.[17] There was then an application to the ECtHR, which held that the applicants' Convention

---

[11] This is a response to concern about the abnormally high rate of stops of people from ethnic minorities: see Ministry of Justice, *Statistics on Race and the Criminal Justice System 2010* (2010) which shows that black people were stopped seven times as frequently, per head of population, and Asian people twice as frequently as white people.

[12] Suspicionless searches are confined to cases of 'special needs' in the United States: see C Steiker, 'The Limits of the Preventive State', *Journal of Criminal Law and Criminology* 88 (1998), 771–808; 793.

[13] Criminal Justice and Public Order Act 1994, s. 60, as amended by s. 8 of the Knives Act 1997 and s. 87 of the Serious Crime Act 2007.

[14] Terrorism Act 2000, Schedule 7.

[15] See further Ch. 8 on anti-terrorism powers under s. 44 of the Terrorism Act 2000.

[16] Terrorism Act 2000, ss. 44–5.

[17] *R. (Gillan) v Commissioner of Police for the Metropolis* [2006] 2 AC 307.

rights had been violated.[18] We focus here on two points of principle—whether the stop-and-search violated the right to privacy, and whether the stop-and-search amounted to a deprivation of liberty.

First, did these searches engage the Article 8(1) right to respect for private life, or did they involve only a degree of intrusion that fell below the level of seriousness needed to engage that right? The ECtHR pointed out that the relevant Code of Practice stated that the police officer 'may place his or her hand inside the searched person's pockets, feel around and inside his or her collars, socks and shoes and search the person's hair', as well as turning out the contents of any bag carried by that person.[19] All these searches take place in public, with the result that items are exposed to the gaze of other people. Although there is a question of degree involved here, the ECtHR rightly concluded that 'the use of the coercive powers conferred by the legislation to require an individual to submit to a detailed search of his person, his clothing and his personal belongings amounts to a clear interference with the right to respect for private life'.[20]

Second, did the stop-and-search involve a breach of the right to liberty of the person? Lord Bingham, in the House of Lords, decided that the appellants were merely 'detained in the sense of being kept from proceeding or kept waiting',[21] and thus that Article 5 was not engaged because this was a mere restriction of liberty. Without determining the question finally (in view of its decision on Article 8), the ECtHR indicated its disagreement with that assessment, stating that during the period of 20–30 minutes:

the applicants were entirely deprived of any freedom of movement. They were obliged to remain where they were and submit to the search and if they had refused they would have been liable to arrest, detention at a police station and criminal charges. This element of coercion is indicative of a deprivation of liberty within the meaning of Art. 5(1).[22]

For the ECtHR, it was the coercive umbrella sitting over the whole stop-and-search process that led to its classification as a deprivation, rather than a mere restriction, of liberty. This suggests that a relatively brief detention may still amount to a 'deprivation of liberty' for this purpose. On this view, Lord Bingham placed his emphasis on the wrong element, making too much of the brief duration and too little of the coercive legislative framework.

A similar issue came before the Supreme Court of Canada in *Grant*,[23] and the Court held that the key question was whether a reasonable person would have

---

[18]   *Gillan and Quinton v United Kingdom* (2010) 51 EHRR 1105.

[19]   *Gillan and Quinton v United Kingdom* (2010) 51 EHRR 1105, [62].

[20]   *Gillan and Quinton v United Kingdom* (2010) 51 EHRR 1105, [63].

[21]   *R. (Gillan) v Commissioner of Police for the Metropolis* [2006] 2 AC 307, [25].

[22]   *R. (Gillan) v Commissioner of Police for the Metropolis* [2006] 2 AC 307, [57] referring to *Foka v Turkey*, App. No. 28940/95, judgment of 24 June 2008, [74]–[79].

[23]   [2009] 2 SCR 353, per McLachlin CJ and Charron J. The stop in this case lasted only 3–4 minutes.

concluded that in the circumstances he or she had no choice but to comply.[24] This approach means that, when the police officers stood in the street blocking G's way, G was effectively deprived of his liberty and therefore should have been accorded all the rights of an arrestee, whereas if it had been found that he was voluntarily 'helping the police with their enquiries', as the police claimed, he would not be treated as having lost his liberty and therefore would not have those rights.[25] Given the extent to which the police (certainly in the UK) prefer to use informal persuasion rather than formal powers, this line of authority would have considerable practical implications.

Let us now review the justifications for stop-and-search powers. There is a strong instrumental argument that some such powers are necessary if the state is adequately to perform its role of preventing harm. However, random searching is likely to be inefficient (in terms of results) and socially divisive (insofar as stereotypes are used to select people for search), and so is unlikely to be the most productive law enforcement policy. Moreover, randomly searching people would involve a large number of incursions on liberty. So, the normative justification for this 'intrusion on liberty'[26] must depend on the requirement of 'reasonable grounds', a concept so uncertain that it might itself fail the 'quality of law' test under the ECHR.[27] How might the crucial test be rendered less vague? The English approach is to use a Code of Practice, which specifies that the suspicion must have an objective basis in fact, information, or intelligence that links this individual to the kind of article for which the search is made, or may be based on the person's behaviour.[28] However, in practice it is likely that the police will often use the power on the basis of their 'hunch' about a particular person or vehicle, and will then hope to find a suitable justification retrospectively.[29]

The power to stop and search is a coercive power, largely because there is the 'background coercion' of a probable arrest if the individual refuses to comply. Even if one disagrees with the ECtHR's *Gillan* ruling that it involves a deprivation of liberty, it is undoubtedly true that it involves a *prima facie* violation of a person's right to respect for private life. The powers under s.44 of the Terrorism Act 2000 were used disproportionately against members of ethnic minorities, and also in situations far removed from terrorism, most notoriously against a heckler at a Labour Party

---

[24] [2009] 2 SCR 353 at [44].

[25] For discussion, see J Gans et al., *Criminal Process and Human Rights* (Sydney: Federation Press, 2011), 108–9 and Ch. 4 generally.

[26] See n 10 and accompanying text.

[27] Cf. *O'Hara v United Kingdom* (2002) 34 EHRR 812, where the ECtHR held that the facts raising suspicion need not be of the level required to institute a prosecution, let alone to justify conviction. The Court added that the police may properly act on information received, if it was honestly thought to furnish reasonable grounds for arrest and questioning.

[28] Police and Criminal Evidence Act *Code of Practice A* (2011), para. 2.2.

[29] For a review of relevant empirical evidence, see A Sanders, R Young, and M Burton, *Criminal Justice* 4th edn (Oxford: Oxford University Press, 2010), Ch. 2.

conference, leading the Joint Committee on Human Rights to make the (rather obvious but sadly necessary) recommendation that 'counter-terrorism powers should not be used against peaceful protesters'.[30] In 2010, the incoming government set up a review of counterterrorism powers that specifically included stop-and-search in the wake of the Strasbourg judgment in *Gillan and Quinton*. The review was critical of the unduly wide use of the s. 44 power, of the disproportionate impact on minorities, and of the ineffectiveness of the power in terms of yielding terrorism-related convictions.[31] The report set out options for change, and these have led to the provisions in the Protection of Freedoms Act 2012.

Essentially, the new legislation abolishes the original ss. 44–47 of the Terrorism Act 2000 and replaces them with a revised provision (s. 47A) that allows a senior police officer to designate an area if he reasonably believes that an act of terrorism will take place and that it is necessary to authorize searches, and once that power of designation is exercised that authorizes a constable to stop and search a vehicle or a pedestrian without a requirement for reasonable suspicion.[32] While the authorization power appears compliant with the *Gillan and Quinton* judgment, the actual stop-and-search power appears not to be.[33] That provision is supported by a Code of Practice that urges constables not to use this power if they have reasonable suspicion (but instead to use the powers under s. 43 or 43A), reminds them that a search can only be carried out to look for an item that connects the vehicle or person with terrorism, advises them that there should be some behaviour, clothing, bag, or other item that indicates the appropriateness of a search, reminds them of their duty to inform the person why the stop-and-search is being carried out, and so forth.[34] These paragraphs of the Code of Practice provide greater detail than those in the previous Code, but they still fall short of full compliance with the judgment in *Gillan and Quinton*. In the absence of a requirement of reasonable suspicion, the Code merely provides 'indicators' for selecting an individual or vehicle for a search—failing to provide guidance that adequately reduces the 'arbitrariness' that was the concern of the Strasbourg Court.[35]

---

[30] Joint Committee on Human Rights, *Demonstrating Respect for Rights? A Human Rights Approach to Policing Protest* (HC 320-1, 2009), [93].

[31] Home Office, *Review of Counter-Terrorism and Security Powers* Cm 8004 (2011).

[32] Protection of Freedoms Act 2012, ss. 59–62.

[33] This unsatisfactory approach may also be found in s. 60 of the Criminal Justice and Public Order Act 1994: see n 13.

[34] Home Office, *Code of Practice (England, Wales and Scotland) for the Exercise of Stop and Search Powers under Section 43 and 43a of the Terrorism Act 2000, and the Authorisation and Exercise of Stop and Search Powers Relating to Section 47a and Schedule 6b to the Terrorism Act 2000* (2012), para. 4.9.

[35] For fuller argument, see E Cape, 'The Counter-Terrorism Provisions of the Protection of Freedoms Act 2012: Preventing Misuse or a Case of Smoke and Mirrors?', *Criminal Law Review* (2013), 385–99, 385; J Ip, 'The Reform of Counterterrorism Stop and Search after Gillan v United Kingdom', *Human Rights Law Review* 13(4) (2013).

Since 'none of the many thousand searches [under the Terrorism Act] has ever resulted in a conviction of a terrorist offence', the main instrumental argument for these powers seems unsustainable.[36] Moreover, the use of the power of stop-and-search without reasonable suspicion declined steeply after the *Gillan* judgments and appears to have ceased entirely.[37] Whether the reassertion of the power to make a suspicionless search in the 2012 Act will lead to a revival remains to be seen. But, in principle, the stop-and-search power does involve a *prima facie* violation of an individual's rights; this violation can be justified if the police officer has 'reasonable grounds' (as further specified) to believe that the person has a prohibited article or an item intended for use in a terrorist offence; but any violation of rights must be the least restrictive appropriate use of coercion in order to determine whether the person has a prohibited article; and there must be effective powers of accountability and review. Probably the most pressing practical problem is to specify what the crucial concept of 'reasonable suspicion' includes and excludes. Given the need for a stop-and-search power, this is a pressing problem not only of principle but also of practice. Indeed, a recent report of Her Majesty's Inspectorate of Constabulary revealed loose habits in the use of this power, insufficient training of officers, and inadequate supervision.[38] Its recommendations—of better specification of appropriate reasons for making a stop (emphasizing priority crimes, rather than low-level street possession of drugs) and of more respectful procedures—chime well with the argument here.

3.3 Police Containment

In what circumstances, if any, can the police contain people within a small area, stopping them from leaving that area in order to prevent serious disorder? In recent decades the police in various countries, including Germany and the UK, have used containment (usually known as 'kettling') in order to manage major public demonstrations, by confining a number of demonstrators within a relatively small area for a few hours in the hope of preventing a volatile situation from turning into significant disorder. The police in Germany have also used a form of pre-emptive arrest and detention of persons in order to prevent the imminent commission of an offence. The police in both Germany and England and Wales also have the corresponding power to exclude people from a specified area. These forms of preventive policing

---

[36] Lord Carlile, *Report on the Operation in 2008 of the Terrorism Act 2000* (2009), para. 148.

[37] Home Office, *Operation of Police Powers under the Terrorism Act* (HOSB 11/12, 2012), 41, records 102,504 in 2009/10; 9,744 in 2010/11; and none at all in 2011/12; see also Cape, 'The Counter-Terrorism Provisions of the Protection of Freedoms Act 2012: Preventing Misuse or a Case of Smoke and Mirrors?' (n 35), 395.

[38] Her Majesty's Inspectorate of Constabulary, *Stop and Search Powers: Are the Police Using Them Effectively and Fairly?* (London: HMSO, 2013), <http://www.hmic.gov.uk>.

raise serious questions about the right to personal liberty and the presumption of harmlessness, which we will explore in this section through the doctrines of European human rights law.

In *Austin and others v Commissioner of Police for the Metropolis*[39] some 2,000 people were 'kettled' or contained in a side street near Oxford Circus, in central London, during a demonstration against capitalism and globalization. The police stated that they feared a substantial breach of the peace if this action were not taken, and that this justified their actions at common law. The containment was maintained for seven hours; about 400 people were released in the meantime, but some members of the kettled group were violent and the police stated that this made it difficult to pursue a programme of phased release. Ms Austin, a peaceful demonstrator, was not allowed to leave; nor were the other three claimants, who were uninvolved members of the public who had been taking a short break from work when they were swept into the police cordon. They all sued the police for false imprisonment.

In the House of Lords the leading speech was given by Lord Hope, who identified the purpose of the police's actions as the crucial element in the case. The starting point is that Article 5 protects the right to liberty of the person, and that Article 5(1) sets out six sets of exceptional circumstances in which a person may properly be deprived of liberty. None of those exceptions applied in this case, but Lord Hope held that in determining whether there has been a 'deprivation of liberty' a court must take account of the whole situation. He stated that the police action 'must be resorted to in good faith and must be proportionate to the situation', but also went on to say that 'measures of crowd control that are undertaken in the interests of the community will not infringe the Article 5 rights of individual members of the crowd whose freedom of movement is restricted by them'.[40] This is problematic: references to 'the interests of the community' are inappropriate in this context, since Article 5 contains no exception for what is 'necessary in a democratic society' or for proportionality. What Lord Hope should have said is something along the lines of 'the rights of other people who might be affected by the dangerous behaviour that was anticipated'. The argument should not be skewed by any leverage falsely derived from the political irresistibility of 'community safety' or the like.

When the case came before the Grand Chamber of the ECtHR in *Austin and others v United Kingdom*,[41] it held by 14 votes to three that there was no deprivation of liberty in this case and therefore no violation of the right to liberty of the person guaranteed by Article 5. The Strasbourg majority started from the proposition that the Convention is a 'living instrument' which must be interpreted according to the exigencies of the time. This doctrine, which makes sporadic and unpredictable

---

[39] [2009] UKHL 5, on which see D Mead, 'Of Kettles, Cordons and Crowd Control', *European Human Rights Law Review* (2009), 376; R Glover, 'The Uncertain Blue Line—Police Cordons and the Common Law', *Criminal Law Review* (2012), 245.
[40] [2009] UKHL 5, [34].   [41] (2012) 55 EHRR 359.

appearances in the Court's jurisprudence, may have considerable merits; but one of those is not, surely, that it entitles the Court to ignore (rather than to depart from with reasons) its own recent judgments. Thus, as we saw above, in *Gillan and Quinton v United Kingdom*,[42] the Court held that a 20-minute police stop did amount to a 'deprivation of liberty' within Article 5(1) because 'the applicants were entirely deprived of any freedom of movement' and if they had tried to leave the place 'they would have been liable to arrest, detention at a police station and criminal charges. This element of coercion is indicative of a deprivation of liberty within the meaning of Art. 5(1).'[43] For the majority in *Austin* not even to mention this judgment, let alone to discuss its relevance to the issue at hand, is most unsatisfactory and surely not dictated by the 'living instrument' doctrine.

In the House of Lords, Lord Hope had rested much of his reasoning on the point that the police acted for the purpose of preserving public order and ensuring public safety. However, the Grand Chamber recognizes that a well-motivated purpose has not hitherto been considered sufficient to determine whether or not a person has been deprived of liberty.[44] Instead, the majority points to the recognized 'definition' of a deprivation of liberty[45] which refers, among other characteristics, to the 'type' and 'manner of implementation' of the measure in question. The majority treats this as the solution to the problem in this case: regard should be had to the 'specific context and circumstances' of the restrictions on liberty, particularly where the restrictions are 'unavoidable as a result of circumstances beyond the control of the authorities and are necessary to avert a real risk of serious injury or damage, and are kept to the minimum required for the purpose'.[46] In effect, therefore, the majority is arguing that the crucial point is not so much the degree of the restrictions, or the coercive threat that surrounds them, but rather what kinds of justification may be offered for them. This is unpersuasive: the issue of whether there is a deprivation of liberty should be distinguished from the issue of whether it is justified. In effect, the majority has smuggled the element of purpose back into its concept of 'deprivation of liberty' under the unconvincing guise of the 'type and manner of implementation' of the restrictive measure.

In the House of Lords, Lord Hope had pointed out that Articles 2 and 3 of the ECHR place positive obligations on the authorities to take preventive measures to protect individuals at risk of serious harm.[47] These are powerful elements in any case of this nature, but they should not be expanded unduly. Thus, the trial judge, Tugendhat J, had found that the police were acting in order to prevent 'damage to property, serious physical injury and even death'.[48] In the judgment of the Strasbourg majority this becomes diluted to 'serious injury or damage', which is

---

[42] (2010) 50 EHRR 1105; n 17 and accompanying text.
[43] (2010) 51 EHRR 1105, [57].   [44] (2012) 55 EHRR 359, [58].
[45] *Guzzardi v Italy* (1980) 3 EHRR 333.   [46] (2012) 55 EHRR 359, [59].
[47] [2009] UKHL 5, at [34].   [48] *Austin v United Kingdom* (2012) 55 EHRR 359, [26].

unsatisfactory because 'damage' falls below the death or injury against which Articles 2 and 3 are meant to protect. But if it were accepted, *pace* the majority here, that the 'kettling' did deprive the applicants of their liberty, could it not be said that there was a conflict between their Article 5 rights and the rights of other members of the public, other demonstrators, and police officers under Articles 2 and 3 not to be subjected to serious injury or even death?

If the majority had taken this argument seriously, then two further points should have been considered. One is that where rights conflict, the proper approach is not to reach for some nebulous 'balancing' but rather to pursue the policy of minimum deprivation. Thus, the approach should be to reduce each individual's right as little as possible, and to provide compensating or counterbalancing measures for any reduction that is thought unavoidable.[49] What this would mean in practice remains to be worked out. But, second, this whole line of argument can only be based on a finding that there were reasonable grounds for the police commander to believe that there was a real risk of serious injury or death. Otherwise, the mere assertion of the risk of serious injury becomes the simplest of ways to circumvent the protection of the right to personal liberty. As the Grand Chamber itself held in the anti-terrorism case of *A. v United Kingdom*, if detention does not fit within the confines of the exceptions enumerated in Article 5(1), 'it cannot be made to fit by an appeal to the need to balance the interests of the State against those of the detainee'.[50]

This brings the discussion to a matter touched on hardly at all in the majority's judgment. The focus of the application here is the right to personal liberty of four individuals. Article 5 is one of the more powerful provisions in the Convention— less fundamental than Articles 2 and 3, just considered, but plainly more powerful than many other Articles in the Convention, in the sense that Article 5 contains no override for the public interest, or for what is 'necessary in a democratic society' etc. One feature of the right to liberty of the person is that it is personal: it is each person's right, and no-one should be deprived of that right by proxy, as it were. This was recognized in the less demanding context of the rights to freedom of assembly and expression, in the decision that it was wrong to send a whole coach full of demonstrators (including the appellant) back to London when a few of the passengers were bent on unlawful activity but there was no evidence that the appellant was.[51] The police should start from the point of view of dealing with each person separately, even if operational problems render this difficult. It is doubtful whether this would justify the drawing of any distinctions between the four applicants in *Austin*, three of whom were uninvolved members of the public coincidentally

---

[49] Applying the framework laid down in *Doorson v Netherlands* (1996) 22 EHRR 330.

[50] (2009) 49 EHRR 625, [171]; see the earlier analysis of this proposition by D Meyerson, 'Why Courts Should Not Balance Rights', *Melbourne University Law Review* (2007), 873.

[51] *R. (Laporte) v Chief Constable of Gloucestershire* [2006] UKHL 55, per Lord Bingham at [55], applying Arts. 10 and 11 of the European Convention.

swept up into the police cordon and one who was a non-violent participant in the demonstration. The liberty of the non-violent people inside the cordon should have been a primary concern of the police and not a small matter easily overwhelmed by 'operational necessities'.

This leads on to the question of the compatibility of police tactics with human rights.[52] Recent police guidance on decision-making in general refers to the importance of preserving the human rights of all parties, while recognizing that officers may have to take decisions quickly in strained situations.[53] More specifically, the *Manual of Guidance on Keeping the Peace*[54] states that the police should start from a presumption in favour of peaceful assembly. Subsequently, it sets out three conditions under which the police may resort to 'kettling': good faith on the part of the police, proportionate to the situation making the measure necessary, and enforced for no longer than necessary. This is followed by a list of some 21 court decisions, including *Gillan and Quinton v United Kingdom* which, as stated above, stands for a very different proposition. However, it seems that the Manual is now broadly compatible with the judgment in *Austin v United Kingdom*, although 'proportionate to the situation' is much looser than even the majority's judgment, and should be replaced by the requirement that the measures taken are 'unavoidable as a result of circumstances beyond the control of the authorities and are necessary to avert a real risk of serious injury or damage, and are kept to the minimum required for the purpose'.[55]

The tactic of kettling may hold advantages for the police in their preventive role, since it may enable a relatively small number of officers to control a large and belligerent crowd. It could be argued that kettling is a preferable response to, for example, a baton charge by the police; but each of those responses has to be justified on its own terms, particularly if it affects uninvolved people. From the point of view of individuals subjected to it, kettling tends to be applied indiscriminately (so as to detain peaceful demonstrators and passers-by), it is disruptive of one's plans to a significant degree (because no-one can be sure of being released for several hours), and it can cause inconvenience and a risk to health and well-being (because of the absence of food, drink, medication, and toilet facilities). The reasoning of the House of Lords and of the majority of the Grand Chamber in *Austin*, in holding that there

[52] On which see, D Mead, *The New Law of Peaceful Protest* (Oxford: Hart Publishing, 2010), Ch. 7 and especially 349–56.

[53] Association of Chief Police Officers, *The National Decision Model* (2012).

[54] Association of Chief Police Officers, *Manual of Guidance on Keeping the Peace* (2010), paras. 2.79 and 2.80.

[55] *Austin v United Kingdom* (2012) 55 EHRR 359, [59]. This is reinforced by the judgment in *R. (Moos and McClure) v Commissioner of Police for the Metropolis* [2011] EWHC Admin 857: although it was reversed in the Court of Appeal at [2012] EWCA Civ 12, that court approved, at [95], the test of necessity propounded by the lower court and its statement that the test 'is met only in truly extreme and exceptional circumstances'.

was no deprivation of liberty on the facts, is monumentally unconvincing. It seems to be an example of result-pulled reasoning: because there may in exceptional cases be the need for emergency measures of detention, and this cannot be authorized by any of the enumerated exceptions to Art. 5(1) (which are exhaustive), therefore it is taken to be necessary to hold that 'kettling' does not amount to a deprivation of liberty if the police actions are to be approved.

In Germany there is a power to detain a person in order to prevent the imminent commission of an offence of considerable importance to the public.[56] English law has a power to exclude a person from a certain geographical area, that being the polar opposite of the power of containment.[57] The power is exercisable by a constable who has reasonable grounds for believing that members of the public have been intimidated, harassed, alarmed, or distressed at a particular place, and that anti-social behaviour there is a significant and persistent problem. The officer may designate the area as a dispersal zone, and anyone who disobeys the order by gathering there commits an offence; if a child under 16 disobeys the order, he or she may be escorted home. It will be noticed that this power is a restriction on liberty rather than a deprivation of liberty, except perhaps in the case of children under 16. The justifications for the power need not be so strong as for a deprivation of liberty, but the power certainly curtails freedom of movement and does so without the need for any suspicion that the particular individual has been involved in any intimidation, harassment, alarm, or distress. Knowingly breaching the order is an imprisonable offence, however, and this sanction seems disproportionate for simple disobedience of a police order.

The need for the police to have powers to deal with extreme public disorder that threatens life or serious injury must be recognized. But the argument here is that the justification for such powers must be confined as narrowly as possible, consistent with the right to personal liberty and the presumption of harmlessness. Thus, the use of any such power should be confined to 'truly extreme and exceptional circumstances',[58] and safeguards against arbitrariness should be put in place, since the individual swept up in such situations is virtually powerless. That is not how the relationship of the state and individual should be.

3.4 Pre-Trial Detention

We move now from the powers of the police to the powers of the courts. At first sight the power to remand a defendant in custody before and during the trial seems

---

[56] See the analysis in *Ostendorf v Germany*, judgment of 7 March 2013.

[57] Anti-Social Behaviour Act 2003, s. 30; a similar power exists in some parts of Germany, see *Ostendorf v Germany*, judgment of 7 March 2003, [32].

[58] See the quotation from the *Moos and McClure* case in n 55.

flatly inconsistent with both the presumption of innocence and the right to personal liberty, as outlined in Section 3.1. Can sufficiently robust justifications for this practice be found? The ECHR has, in Article 5(3), a rather convoluted paragraph which is intended to allow pre-trial detention subject to the right 'to trial within a reasonable time or to release pending trial', which may be 'conditioned by guarantees to appear for trial'.[59]

What is the practical context? If a case is not disposed of at the first court hearing (because the prosecution or defence or both are not ready to proceed), it will be adjourned until a later date. The question is whether the defendant should be released on bail, either conditionally or unconditionally, or should be remanded in custody for that period (pre-trial detention). In England, around one-third of defendants committed to the Crown Court for trial are remanded in custody at some stage.[60] In many cases the period before trial will be lengthy: in 2011 the average waiting time for trial in the Crown Court for persons remanded in custody was nine weeks; in 2009 some 28 per cent of remanded prisoners lost their liberty for between three and six months, and for a further 8 per cent it was longer than six months.[61] We can take it, therefore, that what we are discussing here may be, on average, around two months' deprivation of the liberty of a person who has not yet been tried for, let alone convicted of, the offence.

What is the purpose of this pre-trial detention? We may approach this question through the jurisprudence of the ECtHR, which has extrapolated from the poorly worded Article 5(3) so as to recognize four purposes as relevant.[62] The first is the purpose of ensuring that the defendant is present at the trial and does not abscond: thus, a significant issue should be the court's assessment of this defendant's risk of absconding. This purpose is closely connected to conceptions of the proper operation of the criminal justice system, which would be impaired if defendants were usually not present at their trial and thus not able to be subjected to a sentence in the event of their conviction.[63] However, the importance of the proper operation of the criminal justice system is presumably related to the importance of the proceedings in question, and therefore the probability of absconding rather than facing a trial for a small theft from a shop would be a weak justification for pre-trial

---

[59] 'Everyone arrested or detained in accordance with the provisions of paragraph 1.c of this article shall be brought promptly before a judge or other officer authorised by law to exercise judicial power and shall be entitled to trial within a reasonable time or to release pending trial. Release may be conditioned by guarantees to appear for trial.'

[60] Ministry of Justice, *Criminal Justice Statistics* (2012), table Q3.3.

[61] Prison Reform Trust, *Bromley Briefings Prison Factfile* (November 2012), 22; see also E Player et al., 'Remanded in Custody: An Analysis of Recent Trends in England and Wales', *Howard Journal of Criminal Justice* 49 (2010), 231; 237.

[62] For elaboration, see B Emmerson, A Ashworth, and A Macdonald, *Human Rights and Criminal Justice* 3rd edn (London: Sweet & Maxwell, 2012), Ch. 8.

[63] However, trial *in absentia* remains possible in certain circumstances: see Emmerson et al., *Human Rights and Criminal* Justice, 577–83.

detention, if compared with trial for a serious sexual or violent offence. A second purpose is the prevention of interference with witnesses or other attempts to interfere with the course of justice: where the court is presented with evidence that such interference is probable, this may justify deprivation of liberty. This purpose is independent of the seriousness of the crime charged, since the gravamen of the risk lies in the probable perversion of the process of justice itself. A third, relatively unusual, purpose is the preservation of public order—where the release of a particular person might lead to disorder or to attacks on that person. The strength of this purpose must derive from the nature and scale of the anticipated disorder or attack. In recent years, however, the predominant purpose of custodial remands appears to be a fourth one—the 'prevention of crime' or the 'risk of committing offences'.[64] In England and Wales this has arisen partly from the fear among victims that, if a person who has (allegedly) subjected them to harm is released on bail, the victimization might be repeated. In part it has arisen from general concern about the number of offences being committed by defendants who have been released on bail pending their trial.[65]

Each of these exceptions is put forward as a justification for infringing the two relevant rights, the presumption of innocence and the right to liberty of the person. As we saw in Section 3.1, the presumption of innocence means that a person should be treated as innocent until and unless there has been a finding of guilt; and this is broadened by the presumption of harmlessness, which, like the presumption of innocence itself, is underpinned by the principle of respect for each individual's status as a responsible agent. The right to liberty of the person is explicitly subject to exceptions, but these exceptions should be narrowly confined and regulated so as to avoid arbitrariness.

What form of reasoning can be used to reach an appropriate adjustment between the two rights—the presumption of innocence and the right to personal liberty—and the four 'public interest' exceptions outlined above? The ECtHR gives prominence to the presumption of innocence in its judgments on pre-trial detention, and then imposes procedural limitations on the use of the exceptions. In the first place, therefore, the judge:

having heard the accused himself, must examine all the facts arguing for and against the existence of a genuine requirement of public interest justifying, with due regard to the presumption of innocence, a departure from the rule of respect for the accused's liberty.[66]

The appearance of the opaque concept of 'public interest' in this much-repeated passage may be taken as a reference to the four exceptions set out above. The

[64] References to the commission of *further* offences should be avoided, insofar as they suggest (contrary to the presumption of innocence) that the defendant has committed the offence for which he is awaiting trial.

[65] For fuller discussion and references, see A Ashworth and M Redmayne, *The Criminal Process* 4th edn (Oxford: Oxford University Press, 2010), Ch. 8.

[66] *Caballero v United Kingdom* (2000) 30 EHRR 643, at 652.

Strasbourg jurisprudence goes on to insist on proper evidence and reasoning in relation to the four exceptions. Thus:

the danger of an accused's absconding cannot be gauged solely on the basis of the sentence risked. As far as the danger of re-offending is concerned, a reference to a person's antecedents cannot suffice to justify refusing release.[67]

The ECtHR has also insisted that, before depriving a person of liberty, courts must consider 'whether there [is] another way of safeguarding public security and preventing him from committing further offences'.[68] Further, in cases where a person is deprived of liberty before trial, the ECtHR has emphasized the need for 'special diligence' in avoiding delay.[69] These are all worthy principles: the insistence on case-specific evidence rather than stereotypical reasoning, the principle of the least restrictive appropriate alternative, and the principle of minimum deprivation of liberty. Nonetheless, we must return to the two fundamental rights and enquire whether they have been given sufficient emphasis.

First, is the presumption of innocence sufficiently influential here? Duff argues not:

It would be very odd to insist that the state may subject us to the kind of coercion that constitutes punishment for a past offence only given proof of guilt, but to argue that the state may legitimately subject us to pre-emptive coercion that aims to prevent future crimes without proof that we would, unless coerced, commit such crimes.[70]

This is not to deny that there may be circumstances in which the presumption may be overridden, but it indicates that there must be (predictive) evidence of at least the same level of persuasiveness for pre-trial detention as for conviction. This would indicate, in turn, that the ECtHR's insistence on case-specific evidence is a step in the right direction but still falls short of requiring a high standard of proof before an exception to the presumption of innocence is allowed. English law's requirement of 'substantial grounds for believing' that one of the reasons for defeating the presumption of release on bail applies approaches this high standard, but may not be applied with rigorous reference to the standard of proof.[71]

---

[67]   *Caballero v United Kingdom*, citing *Yagci and Sargin v Turkey* (1992) 20 EHRR 505, at [52], on the first point and *Muller v France*, judgment of 17 March 1997, at [44], on the second point.

[68]   *Jablonski v Poland* (2003) 36 EHRR 455, at [84]. This accords with the first part of rule 6 of the UN Standard Minimum Rules for Non-Custodial Measures (the Tokyo Rules): 'Pre-trial detention shall be used as a means of last resort in criminal proceedings', but less so with the opaque second part, 'with due regard for the investigation of the alleged offence and for the protection of society and the victim'. See <http://www.unodc.org/pdf/criminal_justice/ UN_Standard_Minimum_Rules_for_Non-custodial_Measures_Tokyo_Rules.pdf>.

[69]   eg *Punzelt v Czech Republic* (2001) 33 EHRR 1159, at [73].

[70]   Duff, 'Pre-Trial Detention and the Presumption of Innocence' (n 6), 120.

[71]   Bail Act 1976; for broader discussion, see Ashworth and Redmayne, *The Criminal Process* (n 65), Ch. 8.

Second, is the right to liberty of the person accorded sufficient emphasis? Documents such as the ECHR provide for exceptions, but it is important not to move towards those exceptions without a true assessment of the right to personal liberty itself. Imprisonment involves a whole host of material deprivations,[72] including extreme restrictions on freedom of movement; low levels of comfort and amenity; idleness, with few opportunities for paid labour; relative isolation from family members, friends and the wider community; significant loss of autonomy in everyday life; substantial loss of privacy; and exposure to risk of personal harm. Other pains of imprisonment—such as the consequential effect on partners and children—may be added. Moreover, in many countries (including England and Wales) remand prisoners tend to have the worst conditions available, in local prisons that are overcrowded and have few facilities.[73] The few privileges granted to remand prisoners cannot compensate for these pains of imprisonment, and indeed the suicide rate among remand prisoners is much higher than that among sentenced prisoners.[74] All these elements underline the need to take account not only of the terrible disruption of life resulting from pre-trial detention but also of the material pains it may inflict.

With the rationales and implications of these two fundamental rights in mind, we must ask whether, why, and to what extent the state bears a responsibility for the conduct of a person between the time of charge and the time of trial. Such a responsibility can certainly be asserted in cases where the risk of absconding or risk of interference with the course of justice is relied upon, since these reasons are related directly to the integrity of the criminal trial as a public means of calling the defendant to account. This does not necessarily establish that detention is justified, but that there is a pragmatic rationale for some kind of coercive restrictions on the defendant during that period, which should be the least restrictive alternative compatible with the relevant purpose. Another necessary step in the process of justification is empirical. If the court has reason to believe that the defendant presents a danger to a particular person or to the public at large, this amounts to a prediction that the defendant would commit one or more offences if released on bail. Yet, the grounds for and accuracy of such predictions have been little explored. Where the reason for restrictions or detention is the prevention of absconding or the prevention of interference with witnesses, there appear to be no empirical data

---

[72] This list is adapted from RL Lippke, 'No Easy Way Out: Dangerous Offenders and Preventive Detention', *Law and Philosophy* 27 (2008), 383, 408; see also RL Lippke, *Rethinking Imprisonment* (Oxford: Oxford University Press, 2007).

[73] Some 40 per cent of remand prisoners surveyed stated that they were not involved in any activities (work, education, etc.) at the time of the survey: HM Inspectorate of Prisons, *Remand Prisoners: A Thematic Review* (2012), para. 1.27.

[74] Remand prisoners account for 15 per cent of the prison population, but in 2011 they accounted for 35 per cent of 'self-inflicted deaths' and in 2010 for 50 per cent: Prison Reform Trust, *Bromley Briefings Prison Factfile* (n 61), 22.

which are general and useful, and so courts assess the risk on the basis of evidence relating to the particular defendant (eg previous incidents, threats made). However, when we turn to the prevention of offending, there is a manifest problem: none of the statistics relating to the risk of persons charged with particular offences committing crimes if allowed bail indicate that offending is more probable than not—even where the person has previous convictions.[75] Such low rates of prediction raise serious questions about the justification for relying on this 'prevention of crime' purpose; and, in the context of the presumption of innocence, it seems wrong that a probability of around 20–25 per cent should be thought sufficient to justify pre-trial detention. The position may be different if the defendant has previously committed offences while on bail; it may also be different if the defendant is charged with a serious offence and has a previous conviction for a similar level of offence, where the seriousness of the possible harm may be thought to make up for the low rate of prediction.[76]

If, provisionally and doubtfully, one assumes that these predictions can reach a satisfactory level of accuracy, the next step in the justificatory chain is the assumption that the state has a responsibility to prevent offences being committed by persons who are already formally 'in the system'. This crucial assumption has received hardly any analysis. The argument seems to be that, if a person has been charged with an offence, and if the court is unable to deal with the case straight away (which may be because the prosecution or defence or both are not yet ready to proceed), the state has a responsibility to ensure that there is no undue risk of offences being committed by this person during the period before trial. The proposition is straightforwardly protective. It is accepted that the state has a positive obligation to protect the lives and security of people within its boundaries, and a specific obligation to provide protection for individuals whose lives are under known threat.[77] The question is whether the state also has a wider responsibility for the conduct of persons who have been charged with an offence but not yet tried, a responsibility that it does not bear for the conduct of other citizens walking the streets (who might present no smaller risk of offending). How might such a responsibility be supported? One argument might be that the decision of a public prosecutor to charge a person with an offence tips the balance: a decision that there is a 'realistic prospect' of convicting the defendant might be regarded as quasi-judicial if taken by a public prosecutor as distinct from a police officer. One difficulty is that by the time of the first court hearing the prosecutor may not

---

[75] For discussion, see Ashworth and Redmayne, *The Criminal Process* (n 65), 246–7.

[76] See, eg, s. 25 of the Criminal Justice and Public Order Act 1994 (UK) (as amended). However, even if such remands are thought justifiable in cases of serious violence, the presumption of innocence should operate to disallow the placement of a burden of proof on the defendant.

[77] *Osman v United Kingdom* (1999) 29 EHRR 245, and subsequent decisions discussed in Emmerson, Ashworth, and Macdonald, *Human Rights and Criminal Justice* (n 62), Ch. 19B.

have complete evidence on all points necessary for the offence charged, and the court is unlikely to be in a position to require this. So, the first and other early remand hearings proceed inevitably on a lesser standard of evidence—and, largely, on trust of the prosecutor's professionalism.[78] This means that, even if reliance on the public prosecutor's quasi-judicial determination can be considered a strong enough basis for outweighing the presumption of innocence, that rationale cannot be applied to the first and other early remand hearings.

As the various arguments of principle fail, we come ever closer to Duff's conclusion that, if we are serious about the presumption of innocence, then custodial remands before trial in order to prevent the commission of offences are absolutely unacceptable, chiefly because they treat defendants as objects or risk-bearers rather than as responsible agents entitled to the presumption of harmlessness,[79] and that often they do so on inadequate evidence (which would not be sufficient to justify a conviction). To abandon most pre-trial detention would strike many people as strange and dangerous, but that may be because over many centuries people have been sensitized to the normalcy of detaining people between charge and trial. As Duff points out, there has been much opposition to the regime of 'detention without trial' for suspected international terrorists—admittedly without the prospect of trial—whereas the routine remand of unconvicted defendants in custody in their thousands evokes little public or political concern, despite the presumption of innocence.[80]

One significant difference is the presence of many guilty pleaders among those remanded in custody: in England and Wales around a half of all persons charged with offences indicate from an early stage their intention to plead guilty, and in this context it may be thought artificial to rely on the presumption of innocence as a reason against remanding them in custody. If it is right to assume that the early indication of a guilty plea amounts to a free admission in almost all cases (doubts might be harboured about some of those who later change their plea from not guilty to guilty), then this is tantamount to accepting that there is good reason to treat them as guilty. This would mean that, if their offending behaviour is such as would normally lead to a custodial sentence, little is lost by remanding those who plead guilty in custody pending their court hearing—or, at least, that issues about the presumption of innocence are of less pressing significance. This reasoning is strengthened by the recent legislative amendment in England prohibiting magistrates from remanding in custody when there is no real prospect of the person

---

[78] The English *Code for Crown Prosecutors* (2010), s. 5, recognizes this explicitly with a lesser 'threshold' test for early hearings involving people suspected of serious offences: see <http://www.cps.gov.uk>.

[79] RA Duff, *Trials and Punishments* (Cambridge: Cambridge University Press, 1986), 140; see also his recent restatement of his position Duff, 'Pre-Trial Detention and the Presumption of Innocence' (n 6).

[80] Duff, 'Pre-Trial Detention and the Presumption of Innocence', 115–17.

receiving a custodial sentence on conviction.[81] However, that desirable reform serves only to accentuate the position of those pleading not guilty who are remanded in custody: just under a quarter of all those remanded in custody in 2011–12 (including those pleading guilty) were acquitted at trial.[82] These fairly constant statistics, together with the pains of imprisonment, highlight the subjugation of the right to personal liberty in these custodial remands.[83]

What if one were to assert, as did the US Supreme Court, that pre-trial detention is 'essentially regulatory' and imposed in order to protect 'the safety of the community'?[84] It is certainly true that pre-trial detention does not satisfy the definition of punishment, since it is not imposed in response to conviction for an offence.[85] If pre-trial detention involves the curtailment of one person's rights in order to protect the wider community, then an analogy might be drawn with quarantine and the detention of the dangerous mentally disordered; it will be argued in Section 9.5 that, insofar as there is any justification for depriving them of liberty, this should be done in conditions that are non-punitive and as normal as possible. However, this does not resolve the questions about the foundations of the state responsibility for defendants' conduct between charge and trial. True, the remand proceedings give the state the *opportunity* (through the courts) to take some protective action, but are there strong enough reasons for thus overriding the right to personal liberty and the presumption of innocence? The assertions of the US Supreme Court that 'there is no doubt that preventing danger to the community is a legitimate regulatory goal' and that 'the Government's regulatory interest in community safety can, in appropriate circumstances, outweigh an individual's liberty interest' fail to take sufficiently seriously the presumption of innocence or the presumption of harmlessness.[86]

---

[81] Legal Aid, Sentencing and Punishment of Offenders Act 2012, Schedule 11, para. 8.

[82] Prison Reform Trust, *Bromley Briefings Prison Factfile* (n 61), 22; a further one-third were given non-custodial sentences, and whether these would all have received such a sentence if they had not been remanded in custody before trial remains for debate, on which see Ashworth and Redmayne, *The Criminal Process* 4th edn (n 65), 241–5.

[83] See RL Lippke, *The Ethics of Plea Bargaining* (Oxford: Oxford University Press, 2011), *passim* and, on innocent defendants, 82–4 and 212–16.

[84] *United States v Salerno and Cafaro* (1987) 481 US 739; see also *Hall* [2002] 3 SCR 309, where the Supreme Court of Canada held that it is not contrary to the Charter to deny bail if 'necessary in order to maintain confidence in the administration of justice'. Cf. the discussion of the nature of the power of pre-trial remand in the High Court of Australia in *Chu Kheng Lim v Minister for Immigration, Local Government and Ethnic Affairs* (1992) 176 CLR 1, 28, and the analysis by S Mcdonald, 'Involuntary Detention and the Separation of Judicial Power', *Federal Law Review* 35 (2007), 25, esp. 72.

[85] See the definition of punishment in Section 1.6.

[86] *United States v Salerno and Cafaro* (n 84), 747; see ML Corrado, 'Punishment and the Wild Beast of Prey: The Problem of Preventive Detention', *Journal of Criminal Law & Criminology* 86(3) (1996), 778–814.

For many years, the Irish courts maintained that the presumption of innocence should stand in the way of any pre-trial detention motivated by a desire to reduce offending by defendants granted bail, and indeed that to impose pre-trial detention was to treat the current charge as indicative of guilt.[87] The strongest reasons for pre-trial detention are the importance of ensuring that a defendant is called to account at a public trial (which would justify pre-trial detention if there were substantial grounds for believing that the defendant would abscond and this were the least restrictive means of securing the defendant's attendance at trial), and the importance of securing the integrity of the administration of criminal justice (which would justify pre-trial detention if there were substantial grounds for believing that the defendant would interfere with witnesses and this were the least restrictive means of ensuring that such interference did not occur). A further reason would be the protection of a particular person from harm, which would justify pre-trial detention if there were substantial grounds for believing that the defendant would do harm to that person unless detained. Apart from that, and for other exceptional categories, the argument relating to future offending in general seems weak, both in its rationale and in its evidential basis. Liberty would be sacrificed on the basis of ungrounded predictions. And the argument that the decision of a public prosecutor to charge the defendant makes his subsequent conduct the proper concern of the state seems to be simply inconsistent with the presumption of innocence. The conclusion must, therefore, be that there are not strong enough grounds for the pre-trial detention of defendants predicted as likely to commit offences, at least if they are not pleading guilty to offences for which imprisonment is to be expected.

3.5 Conclusions

The justification for the three measures examined in this chapter—the power to stop and search, the power of temporary containment, and the power to remand defendants in custody before and during trial—lies, ultimately and in general, in the prevention of harm. It is accepted that states have the obligation to put in place laws and enforcement machinery to fulfil this preventive function. Equally, it is accepted that individuals have certain rights, due to them as responsible agents. Two of those rights have been particularly relevant to the three measures assessed above: first, the right to personal liberty; and second, the presumption of innocence (or right to be treated as innocent unless and until proved guilty), which, we have argued, supports the wider right of every individual to be presumed harmless.

Each of the three measures is usually defended as necessary for proper law enforcement, ie necessary for carrying out the preventive obligations of the state.

---

[87] U ni Raifeartaigh, 'Reconciling Bail Law with the Presumption of Innocence', *Oxford Journal of Legal Studies* 17 (1997), 1.

We have accepted this in relation to the stop-and-search power and the power of temporary containment, but have raised serious doubts in relation to pre-trial detention. We have then gone on to argue for limitations to be placed on these powers, in a context where individual rights are also engaged. The following principles emerge from the analysis above:

(1) While the right to personal liberty and the presumption of innocence should be recognized as fundamental rights, there may be exceptional circumstances in which those rights may properly be curtailed or taken away in pursuit of the state's obligation to provide security; but any such curtailment must be the least restrictive appropriate alternative.

(2) Powers of 'stop and search' may be essential for law enforcement agents to carry out the state's obligation of prevention, but the power should be exercisable only on 'reasonable grounds', a crucial concept that should be rendered more certain by detailed guidance.

(3) Powers of containment (or 'kettling') should be exercised only in order to prevent imminent death or serious harm to people, which cannot be averted by any lesser means; the power should be exercised on a principle of necessity, so as to affect the minimum number of people for the minimum amount of time.

Pre-trial detention is a particularly severe negation of the right to liberty and the presumption of innocence, and therefore should be reserved for truly exceptional circumstances. Where there are substantial grounds for believing that a defendant will abscond before trial or will interfere with the course of justice, pre-trial detention is justifiable only if it is the least restrictive appropriate alternative. In principle there are insufficient reasons for the pre-trial detention of a defendant on the basis of the likelihood of committing offences if allowed liberty, unless specific threats have been made or the person has previously committed offences on bail.

4

Civil Preventive Orders

The criminal law is chiefly a censuring institution, but it also has the function of preventing certain harms and wrongs (see further Chapter 5). Because the criminal law is society's primary means of condemning conduct as wrong—with the stigma associated with a finding of guilt, the censure inherent in sentencing, and the hard treatment of punishment—it should generally be used as a last resort, and reserved for responding to major wrongs. Not only have states been urged to make greater use of administrative and regulatory systems for dealing with non-serious wrongs,[1] but some have made greater use of civil measures for dealing with harms and potential harms.

Our main concern in this chapter is with civil preventive orders which are coercive. In the UK these are typically civil orders prohibiting a person from doing certain specified acts, backed up with the threat of conviction and a sentence of up to five years' imprisonment if the individual does not comply with the terms of the order. Given the umbrella of coercion that thus surrounds civil preventive orders, there is a powerful argument that such orders should only be used to the extent that measures less intrusive on individual liberties have proved, or are likely to prove, ineffective. Thus, in a rights-respecting society there should be a strong preference for using situational crime prevention measures and social crime prevention measures. Although the standard terminology here refers to 'crime prevention', such measures are really about harm prevention and can therefore be fitted into the present context without difficulty. The argument here is that the state should give priority to situational and to social crime prevention techniques because they are less coercive, and should then prefer civil preventive measures to using the criminal law itself, which should be kept as a last resort for the most serious wrongs.

In Section 4.1, we list the civil preventive orders in English law and then describe the two-step method characteristic of this particular legal form, distinguishing them from some other kinds of preventive order. Section 4.2 examines the reasons for introducing civil preventive orders into English law, and Section 4.3 raises a number of objections to this legal form. The focus of Section 4.4 is on the formulation of restraining principles for civil preventive orders, based on the analysis in previous parts of the chapter.

---

[1] eg Council of Europe, *The Simplification of Criminal Justice* (Strasbourg: Council of Europe, 1988).

4.1 Civil Preventive Orders in English Law

For present purposes, what qualifies a civil preventive order as *civil* is that it can be made in respect of a person who has not been convicted of a criminal offence. Probably the longest-standing example of such a measure is the binding-over order: since at least 1361,[2] a magistrate has had the power to bind over to keep the peace any person before the court (whether as defendant, complainant, or witness) whom there is reason to believe may cause a breach of the peace.[3] The subject is bound over on a recognizance, a sum of money to be forfeited in the event of breach, but non-compliance does not of itself give rise to a conviction. The bind-over is thus at heart a preventive order, designed to control future conduct by ensuring that the person subject to the order keeps the peace.

Our primary interest in this chapter, however, is in a particular form of civil preventive order which originated in the late 1990s and has subsequently been developed into several varieties. The following are the main examples in English law:[4]

Anti-Social Behaviour Orders[5]
Non-Molestation Orders[6]
Exclusion from Licensed Premises Orders[7]
Football Spectator Banning Orders[8]
Travel Restriction Orders[9]
Sexual Offences Prevention Orders[10]
Foreign Travel Restriction Orders[11]
Risk of Sexual Harm Orders[12]
Drinking Banning Orders[13]
Serious Crime Prevention Orders[14]

---

[2] For discussion and references, see A Ashworth, 'Preventive Orders and the Rule of Law', in D Baker and J Horder (eds.), *The Sanctity of Life and the Criminal Law* (Cambridge: CUP, 2013), 45–68; P Ramsay, *The Insecurity State: Vulnerable Autonomy and the Right to Security in the Criminal Law* (Oxford: Oxford University Press, 2012), Ch. 8.

[3] In W Blackstone, *Commentaries on the Laws of England in Four Books* (London: Routledge, 2001;1753). Book 4, Ch. XVIII, Blackstone made it clear that the power to bind over was central to his conception of preventive justice.

[4] For other surveys of preventive orders, see K Gledhill, 'Preventive Sentences and Orders: The Challenges of Due Process', *Journal of Commonwealth Criminal Law* 1(1) (2011), 78–104; 92–8 (Commonwealth and US jurisdictions); JW Nickel, 'Restraining Orders, Liberty and Due Process', in A Ashworth, L Zedner, and P Tomlin (eds.), *Prevention and the Limits of the Criminal Law* (Oxford: Oxford University Press, 2013), 156–77.

[5] Crime and Disorder Act 1998, s. 1 (as amended).

[6] Family Law Act 1996, s. 42A.

[7] Licensed Premises (Exclusion of Certain Persons) Act 1980, s.1.

[8] Football Spectators Act 1989, s. 14A.

[9] Criminal Justice and Police Act 2001, s. 33.   [10] Sexual Offences Act 2003, s. 104.

[11] Sexual Offences Act 2003, s. 114.   [12] Sexual Offences Act 2003, s. 123.

[13] Violent Crime Reduction Act 2006, s. 1.   [14] Serious Crime Act 2007, s. 1.

Violent Offender Orders[15]
Terrorism Prevention and Investigation Measures[16]

Although the Anti-Social Behaviour Order (to be discussed in detail below) was the first civil preventive order to be enacted, there was a precedent in the Protection from Harassment Act 1997. Section 5 of that Act empowers a court to impose a restraining order containing prohibitions on action, for the protection of victims or other named persons from harassment or acts that will cause a fear of violence. Breach of the order without reasonable excuse constitutes an offence. However, this order is different from those listed above because the court's power only arises when it is sentencing a person convicted of harassment under either section 2 or section 4 of the Act. It is therefore a criminal preventive order, not a civil one.

Also distinct from the civil preventive order are the various orders for disqualification that may be made by a court.[17] The power to disqualify from driving arises only on conviction of particular offences, and courts have a duty to disqualify from driving those who commit certain serious offences, unless there are special reasons for not doing so.[18] Courts have a duty to disqualify certain serious sexual offenders from working with children, and a power to do so for lesser offences.[19] There is also a power to disqualify an offender from directing a company if he or she has been convicted of a relevant offence.[20] These powers are all contingent on the subject having been convicted of a given offence, and in that respect they differ from civil preventive orders. The powers of disqualification are generally rationalized, not as punishments, but as instruments of prevention. However, that raises a whole host of theoretical and practical problems, which cannot be explored fully here.[21] 'Collateral' measures they may be, but they impose an additional burden on someone already sentenced for the crime. On what grounds can this be justified? Can it be said that persons convicted of a relevant offence should find themselves open to a disqualification of any length or breadth? As von Hirsch and Wasik have argued, preventive measures tend to be premised on over-predictions of the likelihood of further offending and on the assumption that the subject cannot be trusted to comply with the general law and

---

[15] Criminal Justice and Immigration Act 2008, s. 98.

[16] Terrorism Prevention and Investigation Measures Act 2011.

[17] I Dennis, 'Security, Risk and Preventive Orders', in GR Sullivan and I Dennis (eds.), *Seeking Security: Pre-Empting the Commission of Criminal Harms* (Oxford: Hart Publishing, 2012), 169–92, discussing preventive orders generally and not confined to civil preventive orders.

[18] Road Traffic Offenders Act 1988, ss. 34–5.

[19] Criminal Justice and Court Services Act 2000, s. 26, and Safeguarding Vulnerable Groups Act 2006, s. 63.

[20] Company Directors Disqualification Act 1986, s. 2.

[21] For discussion in the US context, see GJ Chin, 'The New Civil Death: Rethinking Punishment in the Era of Mass Conviction', *University of Pennsylvania Law Review* 160 (2012), 1789–833.

needs this extra threat.[22] If orders for disqualification are to be justified, then the argument is strongest where an occupation or activity is one that is especially open to abuse that could cause substantial harm. Automatic disqualification is to be opposed on the ground that it treats the subject as a member of a group, rather than assessing the risk of harm individually. Any prohibition will curtail the subject's normal liberty of action. In principle, therefore, the disqualification should be no broader than is indicated by the previous offence(s), and should last no longer than is absolutely necessary—the length and breadth of disqualification should be rationally connected to the nature and degree of the anticipated risk.[23]

Having discussed criminal preventive orders, including orders for disqualification, we now return to civil preventive orders. These are constructed on a two-step legal model:[24] the order is civil in the sense that it may be made by a civil court, according to civil rules of evidence,[25] but breach of this civil order is a criminal offence. The best-known civil preventive order is the Anti-Social Behaviour Order (ASBO),[26] and this was the model for most of the other orders listed at the beginning of this section. The Crime and Disorder Act 1998 provided that an ASBO could be made where the court found that the defendant had acted in an anti-social manner, ie 'in a manner that caused or was likely to cause harassment, alarm or distress', and that an order was necessary to protect persons from further such behaviour. The court could then make an order 'which prohibits the defendant from doing anything described in the order' for the next two years. If, 'without reasonable excuse a person does anything which he is prohibited from doing by an anti-social behaviour order', he is liable to conviction and to a maximum punishment of five years' imprisonment. The ASBO (like other civil preventive orders) thus creates a set of prohibitions that apply only to the person subject to the order, or, as Leng, Taylor, and Wasik put it, an order that amounts to 'a form of personalized criminal law'.[27]

---

[22] A von Hirsch and M Wasik, 'Civil Disqualifications Attending Conviction: A Suggested Conceptual Framework', *Cambridge Law Journal* 56 (1997), 559; 607–11; see also RA Duff, 'Perversions and Subversions of Criminal Law', in RA Duff, et al. (eds.), *The Boundaries of the Criminal Law* (Oxford: Oxford University Press, 2010), 88–112; 110–11.

[23] Von Hirsch and Wasik, 'Civil Disqualifications Attending Conviction: A Suggested Conceptual Framework' (n 22).

[24] AP Simester and A von Hirsch, 'Regulating Offensive Conduct through Two-Step Prohibitions', in A von Hirsch and AP Simester (eds.), *Incivilities: Regulating Offensive Behaviour* (Oxford: Hart Publishing, 2006), 173–94.

[25] Except the standard of proof, which is equivalent to the criminal standard (beyond reasonable doubt): this was a compromise crafted by the House of Lords in *Clingham v Royal Borough of Kensington and Chelsea: R. (on behalf of McCann) v Crown Court at Manchester* [2003] 1 AC 787.

[26] Introduced under the Crime and Disorder Act 1998, and as amended.

[27] R Leng, R Taylor, and M Wasik, *Blackstone's Guide to the Crime and Disorder Act 1998* (London: Blackstone, 1998), 13; similarly Council Of Europe, *Report by the Commissioner for Human Rights on His Visit to the United Kingdom, 4–12 November 2004* (Strasbourg: Council of Europe, 2005), para. 110, stating that ASBOs resemble 'personalized penal codes, where

There is one significant exception to the particular two-step model just described. This is the TPIM, created in 2011 to replace the Control Orders used against suspected terrorists (see Section 8.3). A TPIM is imposed not by a civil court but by the Home Secretary, on the basis of a 'reasonable belief' that the subject is involved in terrorism and that it is necessary to protect the public from a risk of terrorism, and the TPIM is then reviewed by a court. If confirmed, the two-step features of the TPIM are similar to those of other civil preventive orders, with various prohibitions contained in the order and a criminal offence (with a maximum sentence of five years' imprisonment) for breach.

In Section 4.2 we discuss the origins and rationale of the ASBO, and in Section 4.3 we discuss the objections to two-step prohibitions. However, before doing so we must emphasize one feature of the civil preventive order not yet mentioned. This is that most of the orders may also be made after conviction, and are indeed often used in that way. Thus, they may be made by a civil court, or by a court sitting in its civil capacity (eg magistrates who are hearing an application for an ASBO or other civil preventive order), but they may also be made by a criminal court on conviction. Whichever approach is taken, the essential ingredients of the order are the same.

4.2 The Genesis and Rationale of the ASBO

The ASBO may fairly be regarded as the talisman of civil preventive orders. At the time of writing the Anti-social Behaviour, Crime and Policing Bill 2013 is progressing through Parliament, and that Bill would abolish the ASBO in favour of an Injunction to Prevent Nuisance and Annoyance and a Criminal Behaviour Order. These will be discussed at the start of Section 4.4. To trace the origins of the development which has led to these latest proposals, we examine briefly the history and rationale of the ASBO.[28]

When interest in tackling anti-social behaviour outside the criminal law began to develop in the mid-1990s, these measures were presented as essential sources of protection for citizens, as enhancing the quality of life (especially of those living in inner cities and in public housing) by imposing prohibitions on those that threaten it. But why did this particular concern result in the vigorous promotion of civil preventive measures in preference to resort to the criminal law? Several possible explanations present themselves, some more clearly persuasive than others. At the

---

noncriminal behaviour becomes criminal for individuals who have incurred the wrath of the community'.

[28] For full discussion, see E Burney, *Making People Behave: Anti-Social Behaviour, Politics and Policy* (Cullompton, Devon: Willan Publishing, 2005); Ramsay, *The Insecurity State: Vulnerable Autonomy and the Right to Security in the Criminal Law* (n 2).

more obviously defensible end of the explanatory spectrum sit a group of rationales that speak directly to the limits of the criminal law and, in particular, its limited capacity to tackle certain categories of harm or putative harm. Thus, one part of the explanation is *expansionist*: where the conduct in question, although actually or prospectively harmful or offensive, does not amount to a contravention of the existing criminal law (low-level anti-social behaviour is an obvious example here), preventive measures provide a means for state intervention without resort to criminalization. One of the reasons for introducing the ASBO was to expand the net of social control so as to deal with nuisance behaviour that is not an offence (perhaps because single incidents are not considered sufficiently serious) but where recurring acts significantly reduce the quality of life for those living in certain neighbourhoods—examples given at the time were noisy neighbours, youths hanging round on street corners, etc. A related motive was to ensure that victims' interests were given sufficient weight, particularly where their quality of life was blighted by cumulative, continuing low-level anti-social behaviour.[29] This said, in practice the ASBO has sometimes been used to prohibit conduct that is already a criminal offence, which is especially contentious when this use of the ASBO gives access to a higher maximum penalty on breach than would have been available for the offence itself.[30] This ambivalence of the ASBO, originally promoted as a protection against sub-criminal activities and subsequently used to prohibit the commission of criminal offences, flows largely from the disproportionately high maximum penalty for breach: five years' imprisonment.

A second and related impetus for resort to civil preventive measures was *pragmatic*. The criminal law and criminal process were said to be ill-equipped to deal with a course of conduct or series of omissions that either individually do not amount to a criminal offence (repeated acts of nuisance whether by act or omission) or, if they are crimes, would normally be prosecuted one by one, so that the court would not have a sense of the repetition and persistence of the nuisance. With its focus upon the individual offence, the criminal law is arguably ill-suited to the task of dealing with persistence.[31] Prosecuting a single crime (even when others are taken into consideration) may fail to address the aggregate impact or cumulative consequences over time of persistently harmful behaviour as well as the prospective risk of harm posed by the likelihood of its continuance.[32] Attempts have been made to capture courses of conduct within the definition of an offence, for example in respect of

---

[29] See S Bright and C Bakalis, 'Anti-Social Behaviour: Local Authority Responsibility and the Voice of the Victim', *Cambridge Law Journal* 62 (2003), 305–34.

[30] See eg *Boness* [2006] 1 Cr App R (S) 690; *Stevens* [2006] 2 Cr App R (S) 453, and the discussion by Ramsay, *The Insecurity State: Vulnerable Autonomy and the Right to Security in the Criminal Law* (n 2), 41–3.

[31] Labour Party, *A Quiet Life: Tough Action on Criminal Neighbours* (London: Labour Party, 1995).

[32] Labour Party, *A Quiet Life* (n 31).

stalking under the Protection from Harassment Act 1997, but these have been less than satisfactory.[33] Whether sentencing on the basis of a course of conduct (past or prospective) could be formulated in such a way as to resolve this difficulty without introducing a new problem of disproportionality to the present offence(s) remains doubtful at best.[34]

A third and distinct set of possible explanations for the state's resort to civil preventive measures is broadly *evidential*. In the 1990s there was concern that the hearsay rule meant that prosecutions could only be mounted if the alleged victim were willing to come to court and give evidence. In introducing the ASBO, the government envisaged that council officials would give evidence in the civil proceedings and so there would be no need for the alleged victim to come to court. Although the hearsay rule in criminal proceedings was relaxed in 2003, this use of 'professional witnesses' remains the normal approach, largely because of actual or anticipated witness intimidation. In respect of serious crime or terrorist activity, a further evidential problem is said to be the risk to the safety of intelligence personnel, to security operations, or to their informants (for example in the case of TPIMs).[35] Witness protection remains a significant issue across the criminal justice system, and in the Criminal Evidence (Witness Anonymity) Act 2008 a significant step was taken towards a new system that respects the rights of both defendants and (potential) witnesses.[36]

More amorphous is a fourth group of explanations that are broadly speaking *political*. Many countries, including England and Wales, have seen a strain of penal populism in government statements and in legislative initiatives that are often presented as measures of public protection. The political irresistibility of arguments based on harm prevention has been widely felt,[37] and undoubtedly the introduction of the ASBO is an example of this. Another political trend may be found in the state's desire to shift the 'prosecutorial' or policing burden on to other bodies or, at least partially, to divest itself of responsibility for crime control. This has been well captured by the responsibilization thesis originated by O'Malley and later developed

---

[33] C Wells, 'Stalking: The Criminal Response', *Criminal Law Review* (1997), 463–70.

[34] S Macdonald, 'The Principle of Composite Sentencing: Its Centrality to, and Implications for, the ASBO', *Criminal Law Review* (2006), 791.

[35] L Zedner, 'Preventive Justice or Pre-Punishment? The Case of Control Orders', *Current Legal Problems* 59 (2007), 174–203; 194, dealing with the predecessor of the TPIM, the Control Order. See also the discussion, in Chapter 8, of the inhibiting effect of the duty not to compromise the security operations of another nation with whom Britain has international co-operation in anti-terrorist matters.

[36] The 2008 Act was replaced and refined by provisions in the Coroners and Justice Act 2009: see D Ormerod, A Choo, and R Easter, 'The "Witness Anonymity" and "Investigation Anonymity" Provisions', *Criminal Law Review* (2010), 368.

[37] AE Bottoms, 'The Philosophy and Politics of Punishment and Sentencing', in C Clarkson and R Morgan (eds.), *The Politics of Sentencing Reform* (Oxford: Clarendon Press, 1995), 17–49; J Pratt, *Penal Populism* (London: Routledge, 2007).

by Garland.[38] Responsibilization refers to the state's recognition of the limits of its sovereign power to rule and consequent efforts to shift some of the responsibility for crime control onto individuals, families, communities, and other non-governmental organizations. So, for example, the Crime and Disorder Act 1998 shifted part of the burden of policing anti-social behaviour on to local authorities and housing associations (just as the same Act shifted part of the burden of dealing with young offenders to parents, through parenting orders and parenting contracts). Whereas in other spheres it is arguable that responsibilization tactics were an unproblematic instance of the larger phenomenon of 'governing at a distance' characteristic of Western neo-liberal market economies,[39] in respect of crime control it is arguable that the state devolved its powers with greater ambivalence. This ambivalence is evident when the two examples above relating to anti-social behaviour and youth offending are contrasted with the Home Secretary's power to impose TPIMs (and their predecessor, Control Orders). Far from responsibilizing others, this regime retains decision-making firmly in the hands of the executive and downgrades judicial scrutiny to post hoc ratification of executive decision-making. The political elements of the various measures are therefore complex in their motivations and their implications.

A further question (and perhaps an unanswerable one without further research) is how far the proliferation of civil preventive measures constitutes an instance of *policy transfer*. One possibility, suggested by Burney, is that the introduction of civil remedies to pursue crime prevention ends was a direct policy transfer from the United States where the use of civil measures (against gang members, young offenders, nuisance, public order, and drug- and alcohol-related offending) was well developed and closely observed by British politicians.[40] Quite another reading is that this is a domestic policy transfer from earlier civil injunctions and remedies to the ASBO and from the ASBO to all those civil preventive orders (Control Orders, Serious Crime Prevention Orders, and Violent Offender Orders, etc.) that followed in its wake. Such is the symbolic power of the ASBO that Serious Crime Prevention Orders were heralded in the press as 'Super ASBOs' and 'Gangster ASBOs'.[41] Macdonald, referring particularly to the ASBO and the Control Order, identifies not only a governmental willingness to circumvent the criminal law at the very time

[38] P O'Malley, 'Risk and Responsiblity', in A Barry, T Osborne, and N Rose (eds.), *Foucault and Political Reason: Liberalism, Neo-Liberalism and Rationalities of Government* (London: UCL Press, 1996), 189–207; 200; D Garland, *The Culture of Control: Crime and Social Order in Contemporary Society* (Oxford: Oxford University Press, 2001), 124–7.

[39] D Osborne and T Gaebler, *Reinventing Government: How the Entrepreneurial Spirit Is Transforming the Public Sector* (New York: Penguin, 1992).

[40] Burney, *Making People Behave: Anti-Social Behaviour, Politics and Policy*, (n 28), drawing on LG Mazerolle and J Roehl, *Civil Remedies and Crime Prevention* (Cullompton, Devon: Willan Publishing, 1998).

[41] 'Home Office reveals details of "super Asbos"', *The Guardian* (London, 17 January 2007).

when the number of criminal offences was rising rapidly, but also a corresponding insistence that the executive can be trusted to employ wide-ranging powers of this kind responsibly.[42]

Over the past decade the British state has energetically adopted civil preventive measures to tackle various forms of harm and wrongdoing, and has shown itself to be committed to ensuring that these measures are actually used.[43] When, for example, after its initial introduction under the Crime and Disorder Act 1998, the ASBO failed to capture the imagination of those expected to deploy it, the British government waged a concerted campaign to ensure that the ASBO was taken up and used by local authorities and housing associations as part of a larger initiative to tackle local nuisance and disorder.[44] The more serious the prospective harm, the greater the commitment to prevention. As the Home Office robustly asserted, in respect of Serious Crime Prevention Orders introduced by the Serious Crime Act 2007, 'we are looking to ensure that penalties have the maximum possible impact on preventing future harm from organised criminals'.[45] Maximizing the prevention of harm and protecting the public is a laudable and defensible role of the state. But if it goes hand in hand with provisions drafted so as to avoid traditional procedural safeguards, as will appear in Section 4.4, the scheme becomes markedly less laudable and less defensible. The numbers of civil preventive orders made in recent years are as follows:

Table 4.1. Most recent statistics on selected civil preventive orders[46]

Type of Order	Year	Number
Anti-Social Behaviour Order	2012	1,329
Non-Molestation Orders	2012	19,381
Football Spectator Banning Orders	2012	493
Sexual Offences Prevention Orders	2011/12	2,658
Foreign Travel Restriction Orders	2011/12	14
Serious Crime Prevention Orders	2011/12	63
Terrorism Prevention and Investigation Measures	2012	10

[42] S Macdonald, 'ASBOs and Control Orders: Two Recurring Themes, Two Apparent Contradictions', *Parliamentary Affairs* 60(4) (2007), 601–24.

[43] P Ramsay, 'The Theory of Vulnerable Autonomy and the Legitimacy of Civil Preventative Orders', in B McSherry, A Norrie, and S Bronitt (eds.), *Regulating Deviance: The Redirection of Criminalisation and the Futures of Criminal Law* (Oxford: Hart Publishing, 2009), 109–39.

[44] Burney, *Making People Behave: Anti-Social Behaviour, Politics and Policy* (n 28), 89 ff; A Crawford, 'Governing through Anti-Social Behaviour: Regulatory Challenges to Criminal Justice', *British Journal of Criminology* 49 (2009), 810–31; 813.

[45] Home Office, *New Powers against Organised and Financial Crime* Cm 6875 (London: HMSO, 2006), 11.

[46] For the sources of the statistics in Table 4.1, see Ministry of Justice, *Anti-Social Behaviour Order Statistics England and Wales 2012* (2013); Ministry of Justice, *Court Statistics* (2012);

Although figures are not readily available for all forms of civil preventive order, the statistics in Table 4.1 suggest that—apart from the long-standing usage of Non-Molestation Orders in the family courts—civil preventive orders are made in only a small proportion of cases going through the courts each year. Nonetheless, the issues of principle (discussed in Section 4.3) remain important, not least for those individuals subjected to them.

How, finally, can the rationale of the ASBO be summarized? In simple terms, nuisance behaviour by neighbours and teenagers in areas of dense housing was significantly affecting the residents' quality of life. Although some of the behaviour was criminal, there was pessimism about the criminal law's ability to deal with it satisfactorily—prosecutions for individual offences failed to convey the overall effect of the conduct, and victims and witnesses were afraid to give evidence for fear of further victimization. The remedy was to create a preventive order that was civil in nature (imposed according to civil rules of evidence) but which contained one or more prohibitions lasting at least two years. Breach of a prohibition was made a criminal offence carrying a maximum sentence of five years' imprisonment. This institutionalized the ambivalence referred to earlier—that a measure aimed chiefly at low-level misbehaviour often came to be used in respect of quite serious offending. Ramsay argues that the ASBO was rationalized 'in terms of the protection of the *right to security*, enjoyed because of the citizenry's *vulnerable autonomy*'.[47] Thus, by reference to the statements of government ministers at the time, he argues that 'liability to an ASBO arises when a person manifests a disposition that fails to reassure others about their future behaviour'.[48] This emphasis on the failure to reassure leads him to argue that the ASBO is premised on recognition that we all have a right to security, and that, because we are vulnerable as well as autonomous, we need the protection of the ASBO. Yet, the emphasis on the right to security may undermine reassurance, in that it 'serves to institutionalize insecurity, distrust and

Ministry Of Justice, *Multi-Agency Public Protection Arrangements, Annual Report 2011–12* (2012); Home Office, *Statistics on Football-Related Arrests and Banning Order, Season 2011–12* (2013); D Anderson, *Terrorism Prevention and Investigation in 2012: First Report of the Independent Review on the Operation of the Terrorism Prevention and Investigation Act 2011* (London: TSO, 2013).

[47] Ramsay, *The Insecurity State: Vulnerable Autonomy and the Right to Security in the Criminal Law* (n 2), 215 (italics in original).

[48] Ramsay, *The Insecurity State*, 28. Note that some preventive measures also appear to encompass a paternalist aim, in that they identify individuals who are at risk of offending and therefore in need of the protection that the order provides. For example, the Foreign Travel Order introduced by the Sexual Offences Act 2003 imposes travel restrictions upon those identified as being 'at risk' of travelling to jurisdictions where they may offend. The legitimating rationale thus becomes a twofold claim to protect both the public and the offender.

suspicion'.[49] Just as the perceived impotence of the criminal law led to promotion of the ASBO and other civil preventive orders, so the ASBO appears not to have produced the required reassurance in many cases.[50] Moreover, it is important to distinguish between the justifications for prevention arising from the demand for substantive protection to stop harms eventuating and those arising from subjective security or the so-called 'reassurance function'. While reassuring the public is an important role of the state, it is questionable whether reassurance alone is sufficient grounds for adverse interference in the lives of others. Waldron suggests not: 'no doubt the psychological reassurance that people derive from this is a consequential gain from the loss of liberty. But whether it is the sort of gain that should count morally is another question.'[51] It is one thing to recognize vulnerable authority and to call for reassurance, but it is quite another to use the reassurance function to support liberty-deprivation rather than reassurance policing[52] and other non-coercive means of community restoration.

4.3 Objections to Civil Preventive Orders

A number of objections can be raised against the legal form of the civil preventive order, some of which have already become apparent in the previous discussion. Here we examine six arguments of principle against civil preventive orders in their present form.

First, the legislation leaves courts with considerable discretion as to the prohibitions that may be imposed by civil preventive orders, despite their potential impact on liberty of action. The courts have attempted to regulate this by holding that the prohibitions taken as a whole must not be disproportionate to the aim being pursued: the number and the breadth of the prohibitions should not be too onerous, especially where they involve interference with a right such as the right to respect for private life.[53] All statutory provisions on civil preventive orders require the prohibitions set out in the order to be 'necessary' for the given purpose, such as for the purpose of protecting people from further anti-social acts from the defendant (the ASBO)[54] or for the purpose of protecting people from serious sexual harm

---

[49] Ramsay, *The Insecurity State* (n 2), 232.   [50] Ramsay, *The Insecurity State*, 227.

[51] J Waldron, 'Security and Liberty: The Image of Balance', *Journal of Political Philosophy* 11(2) (2003), 191–210; 209.

[52] *Policing and Society*, special issue, 'Reassurance and the New Community Policing', 16(2) (2006).

[53] See, eg, *Boness, Bebbington et al.* [2006] 1 Cr App R (S) 690; *H, Stevens and Lovegrove* [2006] 2 Cr App R (S) 453; Judicial Studies Board, *Anti-Social Behaviour Orders: A Guide for the Judiciary* 3rd edn (London, 2007).

[54] Crime and Disorder Act 1998, s. 1(6).

from the defendant (the Sexual Offences Prevention Order).[55] It is vital that these stipulations—understood as requiring any prohibition(s) to be the minimum necessary—be rigorously enforced. However, the impact of the requirement of necessity is diluted by the breadth of the concepts to which it is applied, such as 'harassment, alarm, or distress' in the ASBO or the wide definition of 'serious crime' provided for the Serious Crime Prevention Order.[56] Such terms push the boundaries of the certainty requirement that forms part of basic rule-of-law standards.[57]

Second, civil preventive orders have been interpreted as permitting courts to impose wide prohibitions that have the effect of closing off many otherwise lawful and harmless activities. Thus, the requirement of necessity is interpreted as justifying not only direct prohibitions on behaviour that instantiates the harm-to-be-prevented, but also prohibitions on behaviour that may or may not be a prelude to the harm-to-be-prevented, as it were prohibiting the person from putting himself or herself in a position in which the harm-to-be-prevented could be perpetrated.[58] An example is provided by the decision in *Lamb*,[59] where an ASBO was imposed on a man who had repeatedly sprayed graffiti on trains serving the Tyneside metro. The terms of the ASBO prohibited him from entering the whole Tyneside metro system (not merely from spraying graffiti), thereby banning him from using the metro to travel from one place to another. This prohibition was designed to stop him from putting himself in a position whereby he might be able to spray further graffiti.[60] It is objectionable on the ground that it was not the minimum prohibition necessary, and that it prohibited conduct that caused no harm to anyone. It is also objectionable because it does not leave its subject with a *locus penitentiae*, because the prohibition may bite at a much earlier point than the decision to commit the harm-to-be-prevented. As Duff has argued, a civil preventive order 'does not treat [its subject] as a responsible agent in relation to the harm-to-be-prevented', insofar as:

it simply excludes him from the context in which he might misbehave. We might be justified in excluding from an activity for which a licence is properly required someone who has shown that she cannot be trusted to engage in it safely or appropriately: we can ban unsafe or unfit drivers from driving, dishonest or incompetent doctors from practising medicine . . . But

---

[55] Sexual Offences Act 2003, s. 104(1).

[56] On which see Serious Crime Act 2007 (UK), Schedule 1, Part 1.

[57] See A Cornford, 'Criminalising Anti-Social Behaviour', *Criminal and Philosophy* 6 (2012), 1–19; 1.

[58] See S Hoffman and S Macdonald, 'Should ASBOs Be Civilized?', *Criminal Law Review* (2010), 457–73; 458– 9; Dennis, 'Security, Risk and Preventive Orders' (n 17), 174–6; and Nickel, 'Restraining Orders, Liberty and Due Process' (n 4), 161–4, on the potentially harsh impact of civil preventive orders on liberty.

[59] *Lamb* [2006] 2 Cr App R (S) 84.

[60] This general technique in framing broad prohibitions is commended to judges by the Judicial Studies Board (n 53).

exclusion from the housing estate on which one lived, or from a shopping mall, cannot be thus normatively rationalized as exclusion from a specialized or especially risky activity for which a licence is properly required; it is exclusion from a central aspect of normal life.[61]

Thus, the ASBO or other civil preventive order 'is imposed precisely to deny [the subject] the opportunity to decide for himself how to behave—which is to fail to treat him as a responsible agent'.[62] Duff's view is that the only justification for such prohibitions would be as proportionate punishments imposed by a criminal court for clear public wrongs.[63] This, presumably, would be his response to those who point out that a Sexual Offences Prevention Order would typically prohibit the subject from going within, say, 200 metres of a school or children's play area. Duff would argue that this should be framed as a criminal offence, and all the procedural safeguards should be available at the stage of establishing the prohibitions. To allow such prohibitions to be imposed in civil proceedings, on the basis of an assumption that the subject will go on to make wrong choices, is to subvert the criminal law. Moreover, to convict a person for breach of a civil preventive order on the basis of otherwise normal and lawful acts, which in themselves did not cause any 'harassment, alarm or distress' (or other harm-to-be-prevented), is simply to convict on the basis of defiance of a court order, and a dubiously broad one at that. As the Court of Appeal observed in *Lamb*, the breach of prohibition in that case 'did not impact on the public in any way'.[64]

The third objection is constitutional—that civil preventive orders involve too great a delegation of rule-making authority. In their analysis of two-step prohibitions, Simester and von Hirsch argue that criminal offences should normally be created as a result of the deliberations of a representative authority (ie the legislature), and that this principle is breached by civil preventive orders for which the court has the discretion to decide on the prohibitions that go into the order.[65] As they argue, the preventive order 'is a form of criminalization: an *ex ante* criminal prohibition, not an *ex post facto* criminal verdict'.[66] In conferring such wide powers

---

[61] Duff, 'Perversions and Subversions of Criminal Law' (n 22), 100; it should be noted that Lamb was excluded not only from the whole Tyneside metro system but also from Whitley Bay town centre.

[62] Duff, 'Perversions and Subversions of Criminal Law', 110; to similar effect, see A Simester and A von Hirsch, *Crimes, Harms and Wrongs: On the Principles of Criminalization* (Oxford: Hart Publishing, 2011), Ch. 4; cf. the arguments of V Tadros, 'Controlling Risk', in A Ashworth, L Zedner, and P Tomlin (eds.), *Prevention and the Limits of the Criminal Law* (Oxford: Oxford University Press, 2013), 133–55; 144–8.

[63] Tadros, 'Controlling Risk' (n 62), 110.

[64] *Lamb* [2006] 2 Cr App R (S) 84 (n 59); however, the Court reduced the sentence from 22 months' imprisonment to two months, ie still convicting and imprisoning the subject despite the absence of harm.

[65] Simester and von Hirsch, 'Regulating Offensive Conduct through Two-Step Prohibitions' (n 24), 180.

[66] Simester and von Hirsch, 'Regulating Offensive Conduct through Two-Step Prohibitions', 178.

on courts, Parliament has effectively delegated to courts the power to put together a list of specific prohibitions for this defendant (a personal criminal law), with a severe maximum penalty attached to any breach of the order. Parliament itself, then, has effectively breached the separation of powers by giving 'a wholly discretionary judgment of character and disposition' to the courts, which effectively 'collapses legislative and adjudicative functions into the executive function'.[67] Furthermore, the procedure for the making of a preventive order fails—certainly in practice—to afford the defendant a sufficient opportunity to contest the restrictions on liberty that the court intends to impose. This, added to the fact that there has been no discussion of these particular prohibitions by any organ of the representative democracy, demonstrates what a constitutional anomaly these orders are.

Fourth, there is a further constitutional objection, not spelt out by Simester and von Hirsch. This is that, even though Parliament has taken a considered decision to remove the sanction of imprisonment from a particular form of behaviour, a court may then prohibit such behaviour as a condition of an ASBO, with the result that a substantial sentence of imprisonment becomes available for breach of the prohibition. Thus, when in 1982 Parliament abolished imprisonment for the offences of begging and of soliciting for prostitution, it was clearly conscious of the fact that some people commit these offences repeatedly; evidently, it took the decision that, no matter how often the offences are repeated, the offender should not be liable to imprisonment.[68] Yet this democratic decision can now be subverted by a court if it decides to insert into a preventive order a prohibition on begging or on soliciting. It is doubtful whether the supervisory jurisdiction of the appellate courts over the lower courts constitutes a sufficient constraint on the considerable powers to criminalize and to punish that have thus been bestowed upon magistrates and judges in the name of prevention.[69] As noted earlier, this apparent legislative gift, if it is that, runs quite counter to another trend observable in respect of counterterrorist measures where, in the name of protecting the public from the risk of catastrophic harm, the executive has wrested power away from the judiciary. Thus, in the case of TPIMs (and formerly Control Orders) the judicial role has been reduced to post hoc

---

[67] Ramsay, *The Insecurity State: Vulnerable Autonomy and the Right to Security in the Criminal Law* (n 2), 224, developing Simester and von Hirsch, *Crimes, Harms and Wrongs: On the Principles of Criminalization* (n 62).

[68] Criminal Justice Act 1982, ss. 70 and 71; see E Burney, '"No Spitting": Regulation of Offensive Behaviour in England and Wales', in A von Hirsch and A Simester (eds.), *Incivilities* (Oxford: Hart Publishing, 2006), 195–218.

[69] There is also the related point that a court may, when sentencing for breach of a preventive order, impose a sentence higher than the maximum prison term set by the legislature for the criminal offence that the subject was prohibited by the order from committing. This has sometimes been rationalized in terms of adding a penalty for defiance of the court order. Cf. *H., Stevens and Lovegrove* [2006] 2 Cr App R (S) 453, with Macdonald, 'The Principle of Composite Sentencing: Its Centrality to, and Implications for, the ASBO' (n 34).

ratification of executive decision-making.[70] These two constitutional objections raise questions about the appropriate relationship between the legislature and the judiciary in this context: the scope of liberty-depriving measures should require a democratic mandate, and it is surely wrong for Parliament effectively to delegate the scope of criminal prohibitions to the courts.

Fifth, as has become evident, civil preventive orders give rise to considerable problems of proportionality. One such problem is the minimum period for which several forms of order must be in force: for example, a Travel Restriction Order must be in force for at least two years, and a Sexual Offences Prevention Order must be in force for at least five years, whereas a Drink Banning Order may be in force between six months and two years as specified by the court. Whatever the logic behind these different periods, they leave courts with relatively little opportunity to respond to the facts of the case. A significant proportionality problem is created by the maximum punishment for the offence of failing to comply with a civil preventive order: although this varies somewhat,[71] several such orders have a maximum of five years' imprisonment, including the ASBO and the Foreign Travel Restriction Order.[72] Five years' imprisonment is a substantial sentence—indeed, any sentence of imprisonment simply for defiance of a court order requires strong justification. The maximum is higher than that for assaulting a police officer, drunk-driving, or a racially aggravated assault, and on the same level as unlawful wounding and other serious offences. Yet, the prohibitions set under a civil preventive order may not be offences themselves: the ASBO, in particular, has always been available for conduct which does not amount to a criminal offence. It is difficult to justify the use of prison sentences for breach of prohibitions on sub-criminal conduct, and generally difficult to justify maximum sentences for breach as high as five years.

Sixth, and finally, the two-step structure of the civil preventive order has unfair procedural consequences. At the civil stage, when the content of the prohibitions is decided, civil rules of evidence apply, not the more demanding criminal rules. However, if the subject is charged with the offence of breaching the order, the criminal rules of procedure apply but there is little to decide: the offence is one of strict liability, with only the presence of a 'reasonable excuse' as an issue, and so in most cases the main question is one of sentence—with the swingeing maximum of five years' imprisonment. The House of Lords decided that the two steps in procedure are separate and therefore that the many extra safeguards that apply in criminal proceedings are not available at the first stage, since this is separate and

---

[70] See Section 8.4.

[71] For example, failure to comply with a drink banning order is a summary offence with a maximum of a level four fine (Violent Crime Reduction Act 2006, s. 6); failure to comply with a football banning order is a summary offence with a maximum sentence of six months' imprisonment.

[72] For the latter, see Sexual Offences Act 2003, s. 122.

civil.[73] There is a substantial argument that this ruling fails to take proper account of the concept of 'criminal charge' in the ECHR,[74] and even the House of Lords concluded that, at the civil stage, the standard of proof should be equivalent to the criminal standard because of the prospect of a substantial prison sentence at the second stage.[75] The objection, then, is that civil preventive orders are in reality so close to criminal offences (certainly in view of the possible consequences) that the subject ought to have access to the 'criminal' procedural rights at the first stage of the two-step process when the terms of the prohibitions are set.[76]

4.4 Law Reform and the ASBO

In Section 4.1 we listed a dozen forms of civil preventive order. Much of the ensuing discussion has focussed on the ASBO, the talisman of this legal form. But the ASBO will disappear with the enactment of the Anti-Social Behaviour, Crime and Policing Bill 2013, and will be replaced by two new measures, the Injunction to Prevent Nuisance and Annoyance (IPNA) and the Criminal Behaviour Order (CBO). The IPNA is a civil measure (with a power of arrest attached if there is a risk of violence or harm to others) to be enforced by the ordinary processes of contempt of court. A civil court will be able to make an IPNA if it is satisfied on a balance of probabilities that the subject has engaged in, or threatened, conduct capable of causing nuisance or annoyance to any person, and that an injunction is just and convenient for the purpose of preventing further such behaviour. It is apparent from this summary that the IPNA will be a considerable extension of the ASBO. The targeted behaviour is even less tightly defined than 'harassment, alarm or distress',[77] since the Bill refers to 'conduct capable of causing nuisance or annoyance to any person', an objective test that turns on the two very broad concepts of 'nuisance' and 'annoyance'. Further, making an IPNA does not have to be 'necessary', as with the ASBO, but only 'just and convenient', a very wide phrase. Moreover, the standard of proof is lowered, since the conduct giving rise to an ASBO must be proved to the criminal standard, effectively, whereas a balance of probabilities will suffice for the IPNA. The injunction may include prohibitions or 'require the respondent to do anything', a move to positive obligations without the provision of support for those subjected to them. And although breach of an IPNA will not amount to a criminal offence, it can result in imprisonment for contempt.

---

[73] *R. (McCann) v Crown Court at Manchester* [2003] 1 AC 787.
[74] Cf. A Ashworth, 'Social Control and Anti-Social Behaviour Order: The Subversion of Human Rights?', *Law Quarterly Review* 120 (2004), 263–91; Ramsay, *The Insecurity State: Vulnerable Autonomy and the Right to Security in the Criminal Law* (n 2), Ch. 6.
[75] *R. (McCann) v Crown Court at Manchester* [2003] 1 AC 787 (n 73).
[76] See also Nickel, 'Restraining Orders, Liberty and Due Process' (n 4), 173–4.
[77] See the criticisms of Cornford, 'Criminalising Anti-Social Behaviour' (n 57).

Given that some 57 per cent of ASBOs were breached, and some 53 per cent of those in breach were given a custodial sentence,[78] it is not clear how the civil courts will resist the pressure to impose many more prison sentences for contempt. Thus, the demise of the ASBO will give rise to deep misgivings, since rule-of-law standards are no more respected by its replacements.[79]

Turning to the CBO, this can only be made by a criminal court following conviction for an offence. The court must be satisfied that the offender has engaged in behaviour likely to cause harassment, alarm, or distress and that making the order will help in preventing further such behaviour. However, the order can include any prohibition or requirement with the purpose of preventing the offender from engaging in anti-social behaviour; and breach of a prohibition is an offence carrying a maximum penalty of five years' imprisonment. The standard of proof that the defendant has engaged in anti-social behaviour is the balance of probabilities, lower than that for the ASBO. There remains the question of whether there should be a minimum duration for the order (it is not clear why this should not be left to the court, as is its maximum duration).[80] There are some doubts about the need for the CBO, given the court's extensive sentencing powers (including community sentences, with their range of requirements), and given the possibility of seeking an IPNA from the civil courts. The substantial maximum penalty for breach of a CBO—five years' imprisonment—will ensure that it remains a thoroughly disproportionate order, likely to result in further custodial sentences simply for disobedience of a court order, and not necessarily for harmful behaviour.

4.5 Conclusions

The introduction of the IPNA and the CBO in place of the ASBO will be a significant step, taken in the name of prevention. But it will leave undisturbed the many civil preventive orders that follow the model of the ASBO, particularly the Sexual Offences Prevention Order (SOPO) and the Serious Crime Prevention Order (SCPO). These orders have not attracted the same degree of scholarly and public debate, even though they have similar structures to the ASBO and most of the same objections apply. What civil preventive orders have in common is that

---

[78] Ministry of Justice, *Anti-Social Behaviour Order Statistics England and Wales 2011* (London: Ministry of Justice).

[79] For critical reviews of the proposals in the 2013 Bill, see House of Commons Home Affairs Committee, *The Draft Anti-Social Behaviour Bill: Pre-Legislative Scrutiny* (London: House of Commons, 2013); Liberty, *Committee Stage Briefing on the Anti-Social Behaviour, Crime and Policing Bill in the House of Commons* (London: Liberty, 2013).

[80] A SOPO 'has effect for a fixed period (not less than 5 years) specified in the order or until further order': Sexual Offences Act 2003, s. 107(1)(b). Thus, there is a minimum but no maximum.

they are primarily concerned to remove or reduce the risk of the harm-to-be-prevented, by placing a kind of buffer zone or *cordon sanitaire* between the occurrence of that harm and the subject's activities and movements. This is how the SOPO is designed to operate: typically the subject may be prohibited from entering certain zones (such as those surrounding schools, children's playgrounds, swimming pools, etc.), on the basis that his presence within those zones presents a heightened and unacceptable risk of offending and a well-grounded fear that he might offend. This is not to accept Ramsay's construction of the rationale as applicable to the majority of civil preventive orders. He rightly says that, in relation to the ASBO, 'there is no control for hypersensitivity'.[81] But this subjective sense of insecurity does not form part of the legislative structure of other civil preventive orders: their rationale looks to an increased risk of offending, not to personal perceptions.[82] To take three examples, the SOPO may only be made if it is necessary 'for the purpose of protecting the public or any particular members of the public from serious sexual harm from the defendant'. A Football Banning Order prohibits the subject from attending football matches, on the basis that this would present an unacceptable risk of further football-related offences. A Foreign Travel Order prohibits the subject from travelling to certain named countries, 'for the purpose of protecting children generally or any child from serious sexual harm from the defendant outside the United Kingdom'. The preventive element in these orders is, therefore, that of excluding the subject from a geographical area, space, or context in which it is expected that the harm-to-be-prevented might be perpetrated. The objective risk that forms the foundation for the prohibition is assessed by the court on the basis of evidence about the subject's past activities, which will usually have involved the commission of criminal offences—only a previous conviction, caution, or insanity verdict will suffice as the basis for a SOPO, for example.[83] While the prohibitions in some civil preventive orders will ban the commission of particular types of criminal offence, the real preventive thrust of the orders is to establish this buffer zone or *cordon sanitaire*—another example would be a Non-Molestation Order, which typically excludes the subject from an area around the protected person's dwelling, not just from that dwelling—in order to reduce objective risk rather than subjective perceptions.

On the basis of this analysis, we propose some justifying and some restraining principles for civil preventive orders:

(1) It is a good reason in favour of creating an order that it establishes a buffer zone or *cordon sanitaire* by prohibiting the subject from engaging in a certain

---

[81] Ramsay, *The Insecurity State: Vulnerable Autonomy and the Right to Security in the Criminal Law* (n 2), 207.
[82] Cornford, 'Criminalising Anti-Social Behaviour' (n 57).
[83] Sexual Offences Act 2003, s. 106(6).

activity, and that the order is the minimum restriction necessary to significantly reduce the risk of a (serious) harm being perpetrated by the subject.

(2) In determining whether there are sufficient reasons for creating an order that
may restrict normal liberties and breach of which may lead to serious consequences such as imprisonment, the gravity of the harm-to-be-prevented,
and also the costs and risks of such a course should be taken into account.

(3) In principle, the least restrictive alternative that is likely to achieve an
acceptable level of prevention should be adopted.

In principle, this rationale for civil preventive orders can be supported by reference
to the state's duty to protect and to provide security. But it remains for debate
whether the rationale can support the civil preventive order as a legislative technique, given the six objections enumerated in Section 4.3. Assuming that there is a
good reason for preventing harms through prohibitions on movement that establish
a buffer zone or *cordon sanitaire*, are the various features of the civil preventive order
acceptable or are there good grounds for placing certain restraints on this method of
pursuing security?

The principal objection derives from the clash between the establishment of a
cordon sanitaire and the fundamental notion of respect for individuals as responsible
agents.[84] By prohibiting the subject from engaging in ordinary activities and going
to public places for normal or 'innocent' reasons, a civil preventive order is not only
placing a significant restraint on freedom of movement but also assuming that the
subject would otherwise be unable to resist taking the opportunity to perpetrate the
harm-to-be-prevented. Essentially—and provided that the particular order is tightly
drafted so as to impose only the minimum necessary ban[85]—the objective risk is
thought to be unacceptably great, and in order to supply effective protection it must
be possible for the police to intervene before either harm or reasonable fear of harm
is caused. The objection that these orders fail to treat the subject as a responsible
agent by denying him the liberty to decide whether or not to offend is countered by
reference to the subject's previous offending history, and the seriousness of the
harm-to-be-prevented. The SOPO is a civil preventive order (although sometimes

---

[84] See M Matravers, 'On Preventive Justice', in A Ashworth, L Zedner, and P Tomlin
(eds.), *Prevention and the Limits of the Criminal Law* (Oxford: Oxford University Press, 2013),
235–51.

[85] On this, see eg Hughes LJ in *Smith et al.* [2012] 1 Cr App R (S) 470, 480, in relation to
SOPOs that ban people who have committed child pornography offences from accessing the
internet at all: 'A blanket prohibition on computer use is impermissible. It is disproportionate
because it restricts the defendant in the use of what is nowadays an essential part of ordinary
living for a large proportion of the public . . .'. Hughes LJ went on to indicate a preference for
a ban on communicating with any child under 16 together with a requirement to keep a
readable record of internet use together with an obligation to submit it for inspection on
request. This approach creates a relatively narrow *cordon sanitaire* between general internet use
and the harm-to-be-prevented.

imposed by a criminal court on conviction), and it is always premised on a prior criminal history. Moreover, the objection based on the failure to treat the subject as a responsible agent is partly premised on related elements of civil preventive orders, such as the absence of criminal procedure, the fact that a court must merely be satisfied that the order is necessary for preventive purposes, and the high maximum penalty. Thus, it is not so much that there is a fundamental objection to the state taking preventive measures that place restrictions on individuals' normal liberty of action by foreclosing certain movements or activities. It is more that these preventive measures are accompanied by disproportionately severe sanctions without adequate procedural protections.

In order to resolve this issue, two alternative (or indeed complementary) approaches may be considered. The first is to turn civil preventive orders into sentences that can only be imposed on conviction. This is effectively what has been done by replacing the ASBO with the CBO, although it was argued above that this order has various unprincipled features (lower standard of proof, absence of necessity requirement, and the possibility of imposing positive obligations without support). Nonetheless, this 'criminal model' has the merit of ensuring that ordinary criminal procedure applies to the decision to impose the order and to determine its terms.[86] In principle, if the subject has violated the prohibition by breaching the *cordon sanitaire* but in circumstances that created no danger,[87] no custodial sentence should be imposed. The essence of this approach comes close to those preparatory and pre-inchoate offences that seek to penalize 'any act done with intent to' cause a certain harm, with the major difference that the present approach is a sentencing decision taken after conviction for a substantive offence. The possibility that the subject would have a change of heart and not complete the offence, or might not succumb to temptation, forms a similar objection to both legislative techniques, as we shall see in Chapter 5. To summarize, the following additional restraining principles are proposed:

(4) In principle, an order that includes prohibitions on activities and movements should only be instituted as part of criminal procedure, on sentence after conviction of an offence.

(5) The evidential basis for making such an order should be conduct that would lead a reasonable person to apprehend harm of a given kind; and conduct that actually caused harassment, alarm, or distress but would not have caused those reactions in a reasonable person should be insufficient, unless there is evidence that the victim was targeted because of an unusual sensitivity.

---

[86] See A Ashworth and L Zedner, 'Preventive Orders: A Problem of Under-Criminalization?', in RA Duff et al. (eds.), *The Boundaries of the Criminal Law* (Oxford: Oxford University Press, 2010), 59–87; 82 ff.

[87] As in *Lamb* (n 59), where Leveson LJ remarked that the breach 'did not impact on the public in any way'.

(6) There should be no minimum duration of such an order; the duration should be proportionate to the degree of risk presented.[88]

(7) There should be no disproportionate punishment for breach of such an order: a maximum of five years' imprisonment is inappropriately high, and an offender should not be sent to prison simply for disobeying a court order, particularly where such disobedience was not accompanied by any danger to anyone.

A second alternative would be to create an entirely civil or regulatory order, the kernel of which would be to impose restrictions on the subject's activities reinforced by either the civil law of contempt or a regulatory framework with relatively low penalties. The procedures would be civil, but the sanctions would be much lower. Excluding a person from part of a town, or from using the internet for certain purposes, or from areas round schools and children's playgrounds, could all be achieved by these means. A court might make an order on proof of previous behaviour on a balance of probabilities. In order to fulfil the protective rationale it might be wise to authorize a court to add a power of arrest to the order if that seems necessary. As stated above, one of the replacements for the ASBO is the civil IPNA, reinforced by the powers of contempt of court, which have a maximum sentence of two years' imprisonment, aspects of which were criticized in Section 4.4. A preferable alternative would be to constitute these orders as regulatory, or as summary criminal offences with a fine as the maximum penalty, given that the prohibited conduct lies some distance short of the harm-to-be-prevented:

(8) If the order is not one that can only be made after conviction, it should be a wholly civil or regulatory measure; as well as the lower standard of proof, it should also have lower penalties, in principle excluding imprisonment; for preventive purposes a court should be authorized to add a power of arrest if there is a risk of violence or other serious harm.

One largely missing element in the spheres of conduct currently covered by civil preventive orders is that of support. The civil preventive orders are chiefly prohibitory, and tend not to be underpinned by any formal framework of support for the person subject to the order. It might be thought that their preventive efficacy would be enhanced by the provision of support, perhaps through the probation service.

---

[88] Cf. C Steiker, 'Proportionality as a Limit on Preventive Justice: Promises and Pitfalls', in A Ashworth, L Zedner, and P Tomlin (eds.), *Prevention and the Limits of the Criminal Law* (Oxford: Oxford University Press, 2013), 194–213.

5

Preventive Offences in the Criminal Law: Rationales and Limits

The criminal law is a censuring institution: it identifies and condemns forms of conduct that can be considered as public wrongs, and provides for a public trial with procedural safeguards and then a response to those found guilty (punishment).[1] However, even the most retributively focused system of criminal law could hardly fail to have regard to the prevention of the wrongs for which it has decided to censure people. If a certain form of wrongdoing is judged serious enough to criminalize, it ought surely to follow that the state—as part of its duty of prevention, discussed in Section 1.4—should assume responsibility for taking steps to protect people from such wrongdoing and harm. This preventive task may justify the creation of laws to criminalize acts falling short of causing the actual harm. As Duff has argued, 'a law that condemned and punished actually harm-causing conduct as wrong, but was utterly silent on attempts to cause such harms, and on reckless risk-taking with respect to such harms, would speak with a strange moral voice'.[2] Criminalizing such conduct also involves punishing people for wrongs— wrongs done by threatening or risking harms—but, given their inchoate character, the appropriate scale of punishment would turn chiefly on the offender's culpability and on the harm intended or risked.

In this chapter we explore the principled limits on the appropriate use of the criminal law for these purposes, and we consider the extent to which other legal forms (such as regulation) may be more fitting where criminalization is not justifiable. Thus, Section 5.1 describes nine categories of criminal law: the first is primarily retributive and the remaining eight are primarily preventive. In Section 5.2 we consider the justificatory arguments that are claimed to support some or all of these categories of preventive offences. In Section 5.3 we move on to develop some restraining principles that ought to apply to preventive offences, principles relating to problems of remoteness and to rule-of-law standards. Section 5.4 briefly

---

[1] RA Duff, 'Perversions and Subversions of Criminal Law', in RA Duff, et al. (eds.), *The Boundaries of the Criminal Law* (Oxford: Oxford University Press, 2010), 88–112; 91.
[2] RA Duff, *Criminal Attempts* (Oxford: Oxford University Press, 1997), 134.

considers the use of regulatory mechanisms to deal with some of the unwanted conduct, and Section 5.5 concludes the chapter.

5.1 The Contours of Preventive Criminal Laws

We have already established that the censure of people for past wrongdoing and the prevention of future wrongdoing are core rationales for the criminal law and for its various offences. However, there are some offences that were created especially for preventive reasons, and that can be said to have a primarily preventive rationale. In this section we discuss the paradigm form of substantive criminal offences (harm plus culpability), and then contrast with it a whole range of offence-types which may be said to be primarily preventive. Considerable detail is necessary when describing the elements of these offences, so as to lay the ground for the discussions of rationales and of limiting principles in the following sections of the chapter.

(1) The 'harm plus culpability' model: this remains the paradigmatic form of the most serious criminal offences. Typically, offences such as murder, rape, and robbery are defined in this way. Thus, in the Model Penal Code the key elements of murder are causing the death of another human being intentionally, knowingly, or with a form of recklessness that manifests extreme indifference to the value of human life.[3] In English law the key elements of rape are the intentional sexual penetration of another without consent and without reasonable belief in consent.[4] This form of offence therefore criminalizes the causing of a particular harm, with a culpability requirement. The law declares such conduct to be criminal and attaches a maximum sentence to it. The purpose of such a law is not only to provide for the censure of those who commit the crime, but also to provide for a sentence to be imposed; and those elements are both backward-looking or retributive (in relation to the offence committed) and forward-looking or preventive (in relation to possible future offences). Enacting substantive offences in this form is therefore part of the state's general responsibility for the prevention of harm, as discussed in Section 1.4.

(2) General inchoate offences: most systems of criminal law have some general inchoate offences, as an element of the 'general part' of the criminal law. Thus, the Model Penal Code provides for three general inchoate offences—attempt, conspiracy, and solicitation. English law also has three general inchoate offences, but the third (incitement, equivalent to the American solicitation) has been replaced with the offence of encouraging or assisting crime.[5] The ambit of all three inchoate offences is controversial—for example, is it right to criminalize conduct as an attempt if the person has not yet reached the last act before committing the

---

[3] American Law Institute, *Model Penal Code* (1962), ss. 210.1 and 210.2.
[4] Sexual Offences Act 2003 (UK), s. 1.   [5] Serious Crime Act 2007, Part 2.

substantive offence?[6] Is it right to convict a person of an attempt or a conspiracy if the relevant substantive offence cannot possibly be committed by the chosen method?[7] Moreover, each inchoate offence criminalizes conduct at a different stage of preparation: the 'agreement' in conspiracy may occur before there is a 'more than merely preparatory' act (for the purposes of the law of attempts), and an act of assistance or encouragement may also precede an attempt. More will be said about the rationales for and limits upon inchoate offences later in the chapter. For the moment, we should emphasize that the primary rationale for these offences is preventive: inchoate offences are intended to penalize conduct prior to the causing of the wrong or harm, thus authorizing official intervention (and hence prevention) before the intended result occurs. The inchoate offences are not *solely* preventive, however, since it may be said that a person is sufficiently deserving of conviction if he or she intends to commit the substantive offence and has embarked on a course of conduct intended to lead to that; thus there is a retributive justification as well as the preventive rationale.[8] It can be said that the existence of the three general inchoate offences casts a preventive margin around the substantive criminal offences in category (1), automatically extending the ambit of the criminal sanction in that regard.

(3) Substantive offences defined in the inchoate mode: these are substantive offences defined in such a way as to penalize conduct before it reaches the stage of causing harm. Thus, the Model Penal Code defines bribery so as to include a person who offers or agrees to confer upon another, or solicits or agrees to accept from another, any pecuniary benefit.[9] Similarly, the English offence of fraud is defined in terms of making a false representation with intent to cause gain or loss.[10] It is characteristic of offences defined in this mode that no loss or gain need have occurred, no harm done. The effect of defining an offence in this way is that it occupies the existential space that the crime of attempt would otherwise have occupied. Yet, the general part of the criminal law also applies to these offences, with the result that the inchoate offences cast a wider preventive margin around the wrong already defined in the inchoate mode (thus criminalizing, for example, an attempt to offer a bribe,

---

[6] For divergent views see L Alexander and KK Ferzan, *Crime and Culpability: A Theory of Criminal Law* (Cambridge: Cambridge University Press, 2009), Ch. VI 'When are inchoate crimes culpable and why?' and D Ohana, 'Desert and Punishment for Acts Preparatory to the Commission of a Crime', *Canadian Journal of Law & Jurisprudence* 20 (2007), 113–42.

[7] Duff, *Criminal Attempts* (n 2), Ch. 3; A Ashworth and J Horder, *The Principles of Criminal Law* 7th edn (Oxford: Oxford University Press, 2013), 464–7.

[8] RA Duff, 'Risks, Culpability and Criminal Liability', in GR Sullivan and I Dennis (eds.), *Seeking Security: Pre-Empting the Commission of Criminal Harms* (Oxford: Hart Publishing, 2012), 121–42.

[9] American Law Institute, *Model Penal Code* (n 3), s. 240.1.

[10] Fraud Act 2006 (UK), s. 1; D Ormerod, 'Criminalising Lying?', *Criminal Law Review* (2007), 19.

or an attempt to make a false representation). There appears to be no particular convention that results in the drafting of some offences in the inchoate mode: it has been observed that the inchoate mode is more common among acquisitive offences,[11] although there are other crimes such as perjury[12] and administering a poison or noxious thing[13] that are drafted in the inchoate mode.

(4) Preparatory or pre-inchoate offences: offences aimed at purely preparatory conduct are becoming more prominent. In Britain, the Terrorism Act 2006 includes three examples of pre-inchoate criminalization: publishing a statement that is likely to be understood as a direct or indirect encouragement of terrorism, reckless as to whether such encouragement may take place (s. 1); disseminating a terrorist publication, reckless as to whether it directly or indirectly encourages terrorism (s. 2); and 'engag[ing] in any conduct in preparation for' giving effect to an intention to commit acts of terrorism or to assist another in doing so (s. 5). These offences are specific to terrorism, and are ad hoc extensions of the criminal law aimed at exerting a preventive effect, largely by authorizing police action at a relatively early stage.[14] Thus, they criminalize conduct before it reaches the stage of an attempt, and in some instances before the conduct amounts to the inchoate offence of encouraging or assisting crime. For example, the minimum conduct requirement for an attempt in English law is an act that is 'more than merely preparatory' to the commission of the substantive offence; yet the offence in section 5 of the Terrorism Act criminalizes conduct well before that stage. Whether sufficient justification has been provided for the criminal law's intervention at this earlier stage will be discussed in Section 5.2:[15] while many legal systems include some discrete offences of this kind, others have a general inchoate offence of 'preparation for crime'.[16] It should

---

[11] J Horder, 'Harmless Wrongdoing and the Anticipatory Perspective on Criminalisation', in GR Sullivan and I Dennis (eds.), *Seeking Security: Pre-Empting the Commission of Criminal Harms* (Oxford: Hart Publishing, 2012), 79–102; 93.

[12] Perjury Act 1911 (UK); American Law Institute, *Model Penal Code* (n 3), s. 241.1.

[13] Offences Against the Person Act 1861 (UK), s. 24 and s. 58.

[14] For discussion, see V Tadros, 'Justice and Terrorism', *New Criminal Law Review* 10(4) (2007), 658–89. On the use of preparatory offences to combat terrorism in Australia see, A Goldsmith, 'Preparation for Terrorism: Catastrophic Risk and Precautionary Criminal Law', in A Lynch, E Macdonald, and G Williams (eds.), *Law and Liberty in the War on Terror* (Annandale, NSW: The Federation Press, 2007), 59–74. On the use of preparatory offences beyond terrorism, see I Leader-Elliott, 'Framing Preparatory Inchoate Offences in the Criminal Code', *Criminal Law Journal* 35 (2011), 80–97.

[15] On this issue see, D Ohana, 'Responding to Acts Preparatory to the Commission of a Crime: Criminalization or Prevention', *Criminal Justice Ethics* Summer/Fall (2006), 23–39; Ohana, 'Desert and Punishment for Acts Preparatory to the Commission of a Crime' (n 6); B McSherry, 'Expanding the Boundaries of Inchoate Crimes: The Growing Reliance on Preparatory Offences', in B McSherry, A Norrie, and S Bronitt (eds.), *Regulating Deviance: The Redirection of Criminalisation and the Futures of Criminal Law* (Oxford: Hart Publishing, 2009), 141–64.

[16] See, eg, the Swedish Penal Code, Ch. 23.2.

not be thought that pre-inchoate offences are confined to anti-terrorist legislation.[17] For example, English law has an offence known as 'sexual grooming', which essentially penalizes a person who (having communicated with the child at least twice) meets or travels in order to meet the child for the purpose of committing a sexual offence.[18] The act of travelling is a neutral or innocent act in itself, but the adult's intention and the perceived need to intervene before an offence takes place are held to justify this early criminalization.

(5) *Crimes of possession*: there is a growing list of articles whose possession is criminalized. Different reasons may be advanced in support of different prohibitions: possession of explosives, nuclear materials, and automatic firearms is prohibited, with only limited exceptions, in order to protect public safety; possession of other firearms, knives, and offensive weapons is prohibited subject to various exceptions, again on a public safety rationale; possession of information likely to be useful to a person preparing an act of terrorism, and possession of any article giving rise to a reasonable suspicion that the possession is for a purpose connected with terrorism, are criminalized in order to prevent terrorism and to advance security;[19] possession of drugs is criminalized as part of the strategy to suppress the drugs trade; the possession of indecent images of children is criminalized to protect children from exploitation; and so on. Possession offences criminalize a state of affairs (not necessarily an act by the defendant), and by no means all of them require a further intent.[20] Offences of possessing a firearm, knife, or drugs— to take three examples—do not require proof of any further intent, and may therefore criminalize people who find themselves in a situation without fault.[21] The primary rationale of all these possession offences is preventive, though the precise wrongful harm to be prevented is not always identified in the definition of the offence.

---

[17] See further McSherry, 'Expanding the Boundaries of Inchoate Crimes: The Growing Reliance on Preparatory Offences' (n 15) and P Ramsay, *The Insecurity State: Vulnerable Autonomy and the Right to Security in the Criminal Law* (Oxford: Oxford University Press, 2012), 144–8.

[18] Sexual Offences Act 2003 (England and Wales), s. 15 (as amended); the offence is also committed if it is the child who travels to a planned meeting. See also P Asp, 'Preventionism and the Criminalization of Noncomsummate Offences', in A Ashworth, L Zedner, and P Tomlin (eds.), *Prevention and the Limits of the Criminal Law* (Oxford: Oxford University Press, 2013), 23–46; 27–9, and HM Lomell, 'Punishing the Uncommitted Crime: Prevention, Pre-Emption, Precaution and the Transformation of the Criminal Law', in B Hudson and S Ugelvik (eds.), *Justice and Security in the 21st Century: Risks, Rights and the Rule of Law* (London: Routledge, 2012), 83–100; 86–8.

[19] These two offences may be found in ss. 57–8 of the Terrorism Act 2000 (UK).

[20] A Ashworth, 'The Unfairness of Risk-Based Possession Offences', *Criminal Law and Philosophy* 5(3) (2011), 237–57; MD Dubber, 'The Possession Paradigm: The Special Part and the Police Model of the Criminal Process', in RA Duff and SP Green (eds.), *Defining Crimes: Essays on the Special Part of the Criminal Law* (Oxford: Oxford University Press, 2005), 91–118.

[21] For discussion, see A Ashworth, *Positive Obligations in the Criminal Law* (Oxford: Hart Publishing, 2013), Ch. 6.

(6) Crimes of membership: English law proscribes organizations that have among their objects the promotion or encouragement of terrorism. It is an offence to belong or to profess to belong to a proscribed organization.[22] The rationales are preventive, sending a signal of public condemnation of the aims and methods of certain groups, and enabling law enforcement officers to intervene before any harm is done or attempted, although Walker (referring to the almost 100-year proscription of the IRA) concludes that 'proscription has often been of marginal utility in combating political violence'.[23] Crimes of membership are status offences, in the sense that they do not criminalize an act or even participation in a crime: although they could be drafted so as to penalize the act of joining a proscribed organization, that act would still lie a considerable distance away from planning, preparing for, or attempting an act of terrorism.[24] Undoubtedly, it is easier for the prosecution to prove that a person belongs or professes to belong to an organization, than to prove that person's involvement in inchoate or preparatory criminal acts. However, membership offences remain difficult to reconcile with standard criminal law doctrine and its general requirement of an act. Some similar difficulties are to be found in offences of membership of a criminal organization: such offences generally require participation in a criminal group (as defined), knowing that it is a criminal group and reckless as to whether that participation will contribute to the occurrence of criminal activity. These are essentially status offences, but at least they contain a generalized requirement relating to criminal activity, although that may not require proof of actual involvement in preparatory or inchoate offences.[25]

(7) Crimes of failure to report: it is often said that crimes of omission require special justification, since there must be good reason to impose a positive duty to act. As one leading textbook puts it, 'standard legal doctrine stipulates that the behaviour requirement is a requirement of positive action by the defendant. Except occasionally, an omission will not do.'[26] However, exceptions to the 'standard legal

---

[22] Terrorism Act 2000 (UK), s. 11; on the operation of proscription, see C Walker, *Blackstone's Guide to the Anti-Terrorism Legislation* (Oxford: Oxford University Press, 2009), 33–55.

[23] Walker, *Blackstone's Guide to the Anti-Terrorism Legislation* (n 22), 53. Certain national separatist organizations are on the proscribed list in the UK, giving rise to checks that intrude into the everyday lives of members of the ethnic community from which the organization derives support: D Anderson, 'Shielding the Compass: How to Fight Terrorism without Defeating the Law', *European Human Rights Law Review* (2013), 233; 240.

[24] See K Roach, 'The World Wide Expansion of Anti-Terrorism Laws after 11 September 2001', *Studi Senesi* CXVI/III Serie, LIII-Fasc. 3 (2004), 487–527, and B McSherry, 'Terrorism Offences in the Criminal Code: Broadening the Boundaries of Australian Criminal Laws', *University of New South Wales Law Journal* 27 (2004), 354.

[25] Loughnan argues that the creation of these offences drew on the creation of terrorism offences of association, driven in part by the perceived difficulty of proving assistance or encouragement. A Loughnan, 'Legislation We Had to Have: The Crimes (Criminal Organisations Control) Act 2009 (NSW)', *Current Issues in Criminal Justice* 20 (2008–2009), 457–65.

[26] AP Simester et al., *Simester and Sullivan's Criminal Law* 4th edn (Oxford: Hart Publishing, 2010), 68.

doctrine' have been made on preventive grounds. Thus, English law has four classes of offences of 'failure to report,' where a duty to report is imposed on a person and failure to fulfil that duty is a criminal offence. The four offences are failure to report suspected money-laundering (regulated sector);[27] failure to report suspected financial offences related to terrorism (regulated sector);[28] failure to report suspected financial offences related to terrorism (general employment);[29] and failure to report information about act of terrorism, including both information about a future terrorist act and information relevant to the apprehension of a person who has committed a terrorist act.[30] These four offences have clear preventive rationales; although it may be questioned how widely the last-mentioned offence is known, and whether it is not sometimes used to put pressure on the friends and family of suspected terrorists to divulge information.[31] English law also has a 'failure to protect' offence: this goes further than requiring a person to report an act of violence in the home, and actually requires an adult member of a household to take reasonable steps to protect a child or vulnerable adult in that household from death or serious bodily harm.[32] Depending on the circumstances, the duty to protect may be satisfied by calling the emergency services, or it may require some physical intervention by the adult. The preventive rationale is clear: to stop violence against a young or vulnerable person in the household.

(8) Crimes of concrete endangerment: these are offences that criminalize the creation of a risk of harm to one or more others.[33] Some legal systems have a general endangerment offence: the Model Penal Code, for example, provides for an offence of 'recklessly engag[ing] in conduct which places or may place another person in danger of death or serious bodily injury',[34] and that may be supplemented by specific offences such as dangerous driving. English law has no general endangerment offence, but contains a range of specific endangerment offences such as dangerous driving and endangering the safety of rail passengers, together with a

---

[27] Proceeds of Crime Act 2002 (UK), ss. 330 and 331. For discussion of relevant English laws, see S Wallerstein, 'On the Legitimacy of Imposing Direct and Indirect Obligations to Disclose Information on Non-Suspects', in GR Sullivan and I Dennis (eds.), *Seeking Security* (Oxford: Hart Publishing, 2012), 37–58; for discussion of similar laws in the United States, see SG Thompson, 'The White-Collar Police Force: "Duty to Report" Statutes in Criminal Law Theory', *William and Mary Bill of Rights Journal* 11 (2002), 3.

[28] Terrorism Act 2000 (UK), s. 21A.   [29] Terrorism Act 2000, s. 19.

[30] Terrorism Act 2000, s. 38B.

[31] Ashworth, *Positive Obligations in the Criminal Law* (n 21), 58–65.

[32] For references, see Ashworth, *Positive Obligations in the Criminal Law*, 47–9.

[33] RA Duff, 'Criminalising Endangerment', in RA Duff and SP Green (eds.), *Defining Crimes: Essays on the Special Part of the Criminal Law* (Oxford: Oxford University Press, 2005), 43–64.

[34] American Law Institute, *Model Penal Code* (n 3), s. 211.2 has been adopted verbatim by two states, Pennsylvania and Vermont. At least 22 other US states have a generic reckless endangerment statute. P Westen, 'The Ontological Problem of "Risk" and "Endangerment" in Criminal Law', in RA Duff and SP Green (eds.), *Philosophical Foundations of Criminal Law* (Oxford: Oxford University Press, 2011), 304–27; 305.

number of offences that penalize the commission of an act of violence or damage to property reckless as to causing danger to life, or the safe operation of an aerodrome, or the safety of a ship or fixed platform.[35] These are termed offences of 'concrete' or explicit endangerment because they penalize the actual or likely endangerment of persons. The preventive rationale is evident, in that the offences penalize conduct prior to the causing of the harm, and this enables law enforcement agents to step in as they see danger unfolding, and before the harm-to-be-prevented has occurred. [36] In this sense the rationale for these offences is closely parallel to that for the inchoate offences.[37]

(9) Crimes of abstract endangerment: these offences do not require proof of actual or likely danger in the particular situation. They presume that a given activity creates an unacceptable risk of harm to persons, and therefore criminalize that activity. Underlying these offences is a judgement about the degree of risk that is unacceptable. Thus, exceeding the speed limit is a crime of abstract endangerment: speed limits are set for different stretches of road, and exceeding the selected limit is deemed to create an unacceptable risk of harm. The same applies to driving a motor vehicle after taking alcohol: the offence colloquially referred to as 'drunk driving' consists of driving with an alcohol concentration above the prescribed limit, that limit being deemed to be the level at which the risk of harm to others becomes unacceptable. Such offences are 'abstract' in the sense that proof that a particular piece of driving in excess of the speed limit created no danger, or that a particular driver's perceptions and control were unaffected by the excess alcohol, is irrelevant. Sentences for offences of abstract or implicit endangerment may be considerably lower than those for crimes of concrete endangerment (speeding typically results in a fine, with disqualification from driving for repeated offences), but sentences would be higher, the greater the deviation from the statutory limit.

We do not claim that categories (2) to (9) constitute an exhaustive list of the categories of predominantly preventive offences, but this taxonomy suffices to capture the main classes of preventive offence. One further category contains the offences of doing anything that the person has been prohibited from doing by a civil preventive order—in effect, breach of an Anti-Social Behaviour Order, Sexual Offences Prevention Order, Foreign Travel Order, etc.: these offences are discussed in Chapter 4 in the context of civil preventive orders.

---

[35] eg Criminal Damage Act 1971 (UK), s. 1(2)(b); Aviation Security Act 1982 (UK), s. 2; Aviation and Maritime Security Act 1990 (UK), s. 1 and s. 11.

[36] MD Dubber, *The Police Power: Patriarchy and the Foundations of American Government* (New York: Columbia University Press, 2005), Ch. 7, 'The Forgotten Power and the Problem of Legitimation'.

[37] See the development of this perspective by L Alexander and KK Ferzan, 'Risk and Inchoate Crimes: Retribution or Prevention?', in GR Sullivan and I Dennis (eds.), *Seeking Security* (Oxford: Hart Publishing, 2012), 103–20 and the response by Duff, 'Risks, Culpability and Criminal Liability' 121–42 in the same volume.

5.2 Justifying Preventive Offences

What justifications can be found for creating primarily preventive offences? In this section we consider four rationales for doing so—the harm principle; the 'morally wrongful conduct' approach; the 'failure to reassure' argument; and the 'reverse harm' thesis. Beginning with the best-known rationale, the so-called 'harm principle' of criminalization may be linked to the discussion in Section 1.4, where we argued that one of the state's core responsibilities is to prevent physical harm. As John Stuart Mill famously stated, 'the only purpose for which power can be rightfully exercised over any member of a civilized community, against his will, is to prevent harm to others'.[38] A more positive formulation of the harm principle is that of Feinberg:

It is always a good reason in support of penal legislation that it would probably be effective in preventing (eliminating, reducing) harm to persons other than the actor *and* there is probably no means that is equally effective at no greater cost to other values.[39]

The second part of this quotation suggests that a calculation of benefits and burdens is integral to the justification, and Feinberg is here drawing on the principle of the least restrictive appropriate alternative (to be discussed further below). The first part of the quotation leans heavily on the concept of harm to others. How robust is this as a justification for the kinds of criminal laws that are to be found in categories (2) to (9) above? Mill's caution about using prevention as a justification for state coercion was discussed in Section 2.4.[40]

Focusing on the justification for criminalization, Mill insisted that the harm in question could not be based on vague assertions of 'merely contingent or, as it may be called, constructive injury', which 'neither violates any specific duty to the public, nor occasions perceptible hurt to any assignable individual except himself'.[41] For Mill, the basis must be 'a definite damage, or a definite risk of damage, either to an individual or to the public', although it must be said that the broad reference to a 'risk of damage' could be said to undermine the sense of restraint implicit in Mill's harm principle. That principle was formulated in recognition of 'the right inherent in society to ward off crimes against itself by antecedent precautions'.[42] Although Mill ruled out paternalistic intervention in spheres of personal liberty, the harm principle seems to permit criminalization as soon as the conduct in question conduces to harm to others. For example, writing of drunkenness, Mill argued that 'the making himself drunk in a person whom drunkenness excites to do harm to others is a crime against others'.[43] Although Mill distinguished between 'acts injurious to

---

[38] JS Mill, *On Liberty* (Harmondsworth, Middlesex: Penguin, 1979; 1859).
[39] J Feinberg, *Harm to Others* (New York: Oxford University Press, 1984), 26.
[40] Mill, *On Liberty* (n 38), 106.   [41] Mill, *On Liberty*, 149.
[42] Mill, *On Liberty*, 167.   [43] Mill, *On Liberty*, 167.

others' that require 'moral reprobation' and those 'grave cases' that call for 'moral retribution and punishment',[44] it remains unclear precisely what types of harm he regarded as meriting criminalization.

A broad harm principle could supply a *prima facie* justification for almost all the criminal laws falling within categories (2) to (9), in the sense that each of them can be rationalized as preventing harm to others. Indeed, given the early intervention permitted by offences in categories (3) (substantive offences defined in the inchoate mode), (4) (preparatory and pre-inchoate offences), (5) (crimes of possession), (6) (crimes of membership), (8) (crimes of concrete endangerment), and (9) (crimes of abstract endangerment), the emphasis is clearly on prevention. It is fair to point out that both Mill and Feinberg require further tests to be fulfilled, however. Feinberg, for example, brings into the calculation such matters as the gravity of the harm-to-be-prevented, its degree of probability, and the social value of the (otherwise dangerous) conduct.[45] This indicates the centrality of utilitarian calculations to the question of criminalization, and thus underlines the relative bluntness of the harm principle itself. As Gray and Smith point out, when it comes to consequentialist calculations:

the maximizing momentum of utilitarianism re-enters Mill's doctrine, with results that must be troubling for any liberal. For, clearly enough, restraint of liberty that is felicifically optimal in terms of harm-prevention may, at the same time, be highly inequitable in terms of the resultant distribution of liberty.[46]

The problem, then, is that restrictions on liberty in pursuit of harm prevention are, in practice, liable to fall disproportionately on the few for the benefit of the many.[47]

However, for the moment we are considering the credentials of the harm principle as a justification for criminalizing offences in categories (2) to (9). It appears that it is more appropriate as a justificatory than a restraining principle; but that, given its breadth and indeterminacy;[48] it can at best be a necessary rather than a sufficient justification. This leaves many of the key questions about criminalization open to political debate. 'For any harm that is non-trivial, and where there is some realistic possibility that it may occur, everything becomes a question of valuation.'[49]

---

[44] Mill, *On Liberty* (n 38), 145.

[45] Feinberg, *Harm to Others* (n 39), Ch. 5.

[46] J Gray and GW Smith, 'Introduction', in J Gray and GW Smith (eds.), *On Liberty in Focus* (London: Routledge, 1991), 17.

[47] A similar point is made by J Waldron, 'Security and Liberty: The Image of Balance', *Journal of Political Philosophy* 11(2) (2003), 191–210; R Dworkin, 'Terror and the Attack on Civil Liberties', *The New York Review of Books* 50(17) (2003).

[48] See further B Harcourt, 'The Collapse of the Harm Principles', *Journal of Criminal Law and Criminology* 90 (1999), 109.

[49] P Ramsay, 'Democratic Limits to Preventive Criminal Law', in A Ashworth, L Zedner, and P Tomlin (eds.), *Prevention and the Limits of the Criminal Law* (Oxford: Oxford University Press, 2013), 214–34; 219; also Asp, 'Preventionism and the Criminalization of Noncomsummate Offences' (n 18), 29–31.

However, to the extent that serious physical harm or terrorism is the harm-to-be-prevented, this places a powerful value (freedom from the risk of serious harm, a narrow version of the right to security)[50] on one side of the consequentialist calculation. As these serious risks increase, so the case for pre-emptive offences of the kinds found in categories (2), (3), (4), (5), (6), and (9) is strengthened. As Simester argues, 'Waiting for those risks to crystallise, waiting until people are concretely endangered, is already too late.'[51] Indeed, some have claimed that additional protection from harm is engendered by the kinds of pre-emptive offence just mentioned: 'given the generation of some additional deterrent effect through their creation and enforcement, prohibitions on inchoate or risky conduct may help to reduce the occurrence of the relevant harm-doing'.[52]

This line of justification becomes acutely controversial when preparatory and pre-inchoate offences are introduced in order to forestall catastrophic harms. The UK's Independent Reviewer of Terrorism Legislation, David Anderson, argues, adopting a football analogy, that the main justification for offences in categories (4), (5), and (6) stems from the need to 'defend further up the field' against terrorist incidents. The foundation for this is 'the highly destructive potential of single, concentrated terrorist attacks; the dangers of allowing such a plot to run; and so the resulting need to intervene at an earlier stage'.[53] However, with offences of the breadth of those in category (4), for example, 'the potential for abuse is rarely absent'. Thus:

By seeking to extend the reach of the criminal law to people who are more and more on the margins, and to activities taking place earlier and earlier in the story, their shadow begins to loom over all manner of previously innocent interactions. The effects can, at worst, be horrifying for individuals and demoralizing for communities. A well-known example, though not a typical one, is of Rizwaan Sabir, the University of Nottingham student who in 2008 downloaded the Al-Qaida training manual from the US Justice Department website in order to research his choice of thesis, and found himself detained for several days at a police station, along with a university employee, on suspicion of the commission, preparation or instigation of acts of terrorism. He eventually won his action for false imprisonment.[54]

---

[50] L Lazarus, 'The Right to Security—Securing Rights or Securitizing Rights', in R Dickinson et al. (eds.), *Examining Critical Perspectives on Human Rights* (Cambridge: Cambridge University Press, 2012), 87–106.

[51] A point made *arguendo* by AP Simester, 'Prophylactic Crimes', in GR Sullivan and I Dennis (eds.), *Seeking Security: Pre-Empting the Commission of Criminal Harms* (Oxford: Hart Publishing, 2012), 59–78; 60.

[52] Horder, 'Harmless Wrongdoing and the Anticipatory Perspective on Criminalisation' (n 11), 84; see also 94.

[53] Anderson, 'Shielding the Compass: How to Fight Terrorism without Defeating the Law' (n 23), 237.

[54] Anderson, 'Shielding the Compass', 240.

Adjustments to the definition of terrorism are unlikely to resolve this problem, and in the Reviewer of Terrorism Legislation's view offences of this kind are necessary. His ultimate fall-back is that a robust constitutionalism involving a culture of executive restraint remains the most effective means of minimizing abuse of laws that, in his view, are required in order to 'defend further up the field' against this type of harm.

A narrower strand of justification than the harm principle may be found in the 'morally wrongful conduct approach' adopted by Simester and von Hirsch, namely that one necessary prerequisite of criminalization is that the conduct amounts to a moral wrong.[55] This does not imply that this is a sufficient condition; merely that it is a prerequisite, since there may be morally wrong conduct (eg forms of lying or sexual infidelity) which, for other reasons, should not be criminalized. Nor does this rule out the criminalization of what might be termed co-ordination offences, ie those offences necessary to regulate an activity such as driving, where the law must make certain determinations (eg that drivers should drive on the left) which then, through their instrumental value, impart moral force to related requirements.[56] However, before criminalization is justified, it must be clear that there are not strong countervailing considerations, such as the absence of harm, the creation of unwelcome social consequences, the curtailment of important rights, and so forth.[57] This demonstrates that, once again, consequentialist calculations are to be found at the heart of the criteria for criminalization. However, given the content and consequences of public censure and punishment—in terms of restrictions on, and even deprivations of, basic liberties—there is a strong case for restricting criminalization to moral wrongs of a sufficient level of seriousness. We will return, below, to the Simester–von Hirsch approach in the context of restrictions on criminalization.

A third strand of justification might be found in the 'failure to reassure' argument, advanced by Ramsay as part of a critique of preventive offences. Ramsay suggests that the essential rationale of such offences is that the defendant's conduct fails to reassure the court, and fellow citizens, that the defendant would not go on to commit the harm-to-be-prevented.[58] In other words, the offences are justified because they involve proof 'that the defendant's conduct gives good grounds for suspecting that the risk of some eventual wrongful harm has been increased by virtue of this person's actions or possessions'.[59] On this view, this failure to reassure

---

[55] A Simester and A von Hirsch, *Crimes, Harms and Wrongs: On the Principles of Criminalization* (Oxford: Hart Publishing, 2011), 22 and Ch. 2 *passim*.

[56] Simester and von Hirsch, *Crimes, Harms and Wrongs* (n 55), 27.

[57] For fuller exploration, see Simester and von Hirsch, *Crimes, Harms and Wrongs*, Ch. 11, and D Husak, *Overcriminalization: The Limits of the Criminal Law* (Oxford: Oxford University Press, 2008), Chs 2–3.

[58] Ramsay, 'Democratic Limits to Preventive Criminal Law' (n 49), 216–17; also Asp, 'Preventionism and the Criminalization of Noncomsummate Offences' (n 18), 29–31.

[59] Ramsay, 'Democratic Limits to Preventive Criminal Law', 217.

both the court and other citizens provides the grounds for maintaining such preventive offences in the criminal law.

However, Ramsay also points out that preparatory and possession offences tend to require considerable surveillance if they are to be enforced: 'the more the criminal law makes externally innocuous private activity into a penal wrong, the more surveillance of that activity is legitimated'.[60] He then argues that, if we take seriously the theory of representative democracy, it becomes difficult to support pre-emptive offences because they coerce the private sphere and thus undermine the very kind of liberty (of thought and expression) that is essential in a democracy. On the other hand, he argues that a liberal theory of the state may accept the need for pre-emptive offences to prevent conduct only remotely connected with the eventual harm (on the basis that this reassures people about their security), and that this is likely to weaken the protection of liberty and other rights.

Fourth, we come to the 'reverse harm' thesis advanced by Gardner and Shute:

It is no objection under the harm principle that a harmless action was criminalized, nor even that an action with no tendency to cause harm was criminalized. It is enough to meet the demands of the harm principle that, if the act were not criminalized, *that* would be harmful.[61]

On this view, the criminalization of conduct that may entail no harm, nor even raise the prospect of harm (such as some cases of bribery or fraud), can be justified on the grounds that not to criminalize harmless instances of such conduct would lead to significant harm if these were known not to be criminal offences liable to prosecution and punishment. To put it another way, even harmless conduct may be criminalized under the harm principle if criminalization diminishes its wider occurrence and if this wider occurrence would constitute a setback to the interests of others. In the view of its supporters, the 'reverse harm' thesis is an educative approach that underwrites 'a civilizing move away from a traditional "fire brigade" model of criminal law to a criminal law aimed at (so to speak) preventing fire breaking out in the first place'.[62]

Two problems arise, one empirical and one normative. First, a reading of the harm principle that says that 'if the action were not criminalized, *that* would be harmful' relies upon a counterfactual claim that can rarely be subject to empirical testing other than by means of a social experiment that would entail criminalizing or decriminalizing conduct simply to determine whether or not harm results. Only if the conduct has not been criminalized previously might it be possible to gather evidence of its efficacy, by enacting the law and monitoring its impact. Otherwise, it

---

[60] Ramsay, 'Democratic Limits to Preventive Criminal Law' (n 49), 219.

[61] J Gardner and S Shute, 'The Wrongness of Rape', in J Horder (ed.), *Oxford Essays in Jurisprudence* (Oxford: Oxford University Press, 2000), 193–217; 216.

[62] Horder, 'Harmless Wrongdoing and the Anticipatory Perspective on Criminalisation' (n 11), 79.

would be difficult to prove that the absence of criminalization resulted in a calculable setback to the interests of others. Such an experiment would be both politically implausible and morally indefensible, but without it an assertion of 'reverse harm' could surely not be verified. The poverty of evidence of the deterrent effect of criminal laws hardly allows us to be confident that harm would be sure to occur if certain conduct were not criminalized.[63]

A second difficulty with the 'reverse harm' thesis is that it travels a long way from the harm done by *this* person. If the individual is not to be treated merely as a means to the ends of others but as an end in her own right, it cannot be justifiable to impose public censure and punishment on her in order to prevent a harm that might (and in the absence of experimental decriminalization, it must surely remain 'might' rather than 'would') be done, were this particular conduct not to be a crime. Moreover, account must also be taken of the dangers to which intrusive state interference with individuals may give rise. Would it be justifiable to criminalize night clubs, on the grounds that they facilitate drug dealing or tend to be productive of casual sexual liaisons, single mothers, and delinquent children? Presumably the reply would be that harm (including 'reverse harm') is a necessary but not a sufficient condition of criminalization, and that in this instance there might be other social costs and consequences militating against criminalization. But this does not deal with the objection that, insofar as this extension of the harm principle relies upon a claim that the absence of a criminal law might lead other people to engage in conduct that constitutes a setback to the interests of others, it fails to acknowledge that the original actor may have too remote an involvement in the subsequent voluntary conduct of others (see principle (5) below). We therefore conclude that the 'reverse harm' thesis is not a persuasive argument for creating offences of types (2) to (9).

The two justificatory principles that emerge from this discussion are therefore:

(1) It is a necessary condition of criminalization that the harm principle is satisfied, and that causing or risking the harm amounts to a wrong.

(2) In determining whether there are sufficient reasons for criminalizing particular conduct on primarily preventive grounds, the costs and risks of criminalization should be taken into account, as well as the gravity of the harm that is sought to be prevented. In principle, the least restrictive approach that is likely to achieve an acceptable level of prevention should be adopted; and any probable and unwarranted erosion of the security of the individual from state interference should be avoided.

---

[63] eg A von Hirsch et al., *Criminal Deterrence and Sentence Severity: An Analysis of Recent Research* (Oxford: Hart Publishing, 1999); A Doob and C Webster, 'Sentence Severity and Crime: Accepting the Null Hypothesis', in M Tonry (ed.), *Crime and Justice. A Review of Research* 30 (Chicago: University of Chicago Press, 2003), 143–95; 143.

5.3 Restraining Principles for Preventive Offences

We now turn to consider the credentials of a number of principles that may properly operate to restrain the creation of, or restrict the ambit of, preventive offences of the kinds listed in Section 5.1. Two groups of restrictive doctrines will be discussed—first, those dealing with problems of remoteness, which will be divided into three separate enquiries; and second, rule-of-law principles—but we will begin with a cautionary note about criminal law as a double-edged sword.

A leading purpose of creating laws of types (2) to (9) is to improve the security of individuals from physical harm, usually by criminalizing conduct before any harm is actually caused. But such extensions of the criminal law, beyond the harm-plus-culpability model, often go so far as to criminalize relatively normal and harmless conduct, and thereby to extend into areas of individual liberty. Individuals are thus required 'to forego options that are themselves valuable', curtailing their liberty. It is therefore possible that 'the threat of criminal liability [for one of the offences (2) to (9)] could become as much a threat to the security of citizens as the harms they are designed to safeguard against'.[64]

Insofar as the justifications for enacting preventive offences hold good, those offences are likely to lead to enforcement mechanisms that are intrusive, since liability is likely to be grounded in a preparatory or pre-inchoate act or membership of an organization. Detecting these offences is likely to intrude on individual liberties, since some of the offences penalize neutral or normal acts done with a particular intent and this may require close surveillance of everyday life. Such surveillance and early intervention is likely to be based on stereotypes, characterized by discriminatory enforcement that will lead to a greater threat to the security of individuals of a certain background, and a lesser threat to white middle-class and middle-aged members of the community.[65] Thus, the concept of security can be employed on both sides of the debate: preventive offences may be justified by the increased security they bring to society generally, but they need to be restrained lest they reduce the security of certain individuals and groups within society.

(a) The problems of remoteness: Simester distinguishes three senses of 'remoteness': the requirement of a nexus between the prohibited conduct and the harm-to-be-prevented; the distance between the prohibited conduct and the harm-to-be-prevented; and the problem of imputation.[66] Taking the nexus requirement first, he argues that there must be a sufficient connection between the prohibited act (X) and the intent to cause the harm-to-be-prevented (Y). This does not mean that the prohibited act must be a non-innocent, or abnormal act. What it means is that a neutral or normal act (such as entering a museum) can only be prohibited if it is

---

[64] Simester, 'Prophylactic Crimes' (n 51), 61.   [65] See Section 3.2.
[66] Simester, 'Prophylactic Crimes' (n 51), 68.

proved to be done with the purpose of causing Y. This emphasis on purpose would rule out most of the forms of offence cited in category (4)—the offences in sections 1 and 2 of the Terrorism Act 2006 extend to recklessness and so would fail this remoteness test, whereas the offence in section 5 of the Terrorism Act 2006 satisfies the test by requiring an 'intention of committing acts of terrorism or assisting another to commit such acts'.

What is the significance of the distance between the prohibited conduct (X) and the harm-to-be-prevented (Y)? Simester argues that, even if a sufficient nexus between X and Y is established in the particular case, X may still be too distant from Y to justify criminal liability. There is a well-known debate about the stage at which liability for a criminal attempt should be fixed.[67] There is a whole spectrum of possible tests, from 'any overt act' as the least demanding, through the 'substantial step' test of the Model Penal Code and the 'more than merely preparatory' test of English law, to the most demanding test of the 'last act'. It is generally accepted that punishment for mere thoughts is objectionable, since it invades the individual's private world and allows liability to turn on ideas that the individual has not gone so far as to bring into the external world. Moreover, individuals should be treated as capable of changing their mind and conforming to the criminal law, 'because this is what it is to respect him as a responsible agent'.[68] This may be a sufficient reason for ruling out 'any overt act' as an appropriate test, and also some of the 'substantial steps' set out in the Model Penal Code which involve preparatory acts such as reconnoitring a location.[69] What is wrong with those tests is that they criminalize the individual as an attempter when the distance to the substantive offence is so great that a change of mind remains a possibility. There are cases of people getting to an advanced stage and then thinking better of the enterprise.[70] Some might take the view that this approach places undue emphasis on the individual's freedom as a moral agent, and insufficient emphasis on the fact that an intention to commit the harm-to-be-prevented has been formed. Additionally, if the law provides for a defence of voluntary abandonment, does that not show due respect for the possibility of a change of mind? The most appropriate approach is surely that, if the concept of attempt is retained (as it should be, since it resonates with popular understanding), then the individual's moral agency is sufficiently respected by a test that ensures that he or she can fairly be said to be 'in the process of' committing

[67] See, eg, C Clarkson, 'Attempt: The Conduct Element', *Oxford Journal of Legal Studies* 29 (2009), 25; Alexander and Ferzan, *Crime and Culpability: A Theory of Criminal Law* (n 6), Ch. 6; and A Ashworth, 'Attempts', in J Deigh and D Dolinko (eds.), *Oxford Handbook of Philosophy of Criminal Law* (Oxford: Oxford University Press, 2011), 125–46.

[68] Duff, *Criminal Attempts* (n 2), 389.

[69] American Law Institute, *Model Penal Code* (n 3), s. 5.01.

[70] See the case cited by Lomell, 'Punishing the Uncommitted Crime: Prevention, Pre-Emption, Precaution and the Transformation of the Criminal Law' (n 18), 96–7.

the substantive offence.[71] On this view, the 'any overt act', 'substantial step', and 'more than merely preparatory' tests are not only lacking in certainty and lacking sufficient connection with the concept of an attempt, but also so distant from the harm-to-be-prevented as to show insufficient respect for the individual as a moral agent.[72]

The next question is whether these strictures apply to other preventive offences such as those in categories (3) to (6). The important patterns of principled reasoning set out in the preceding paragraph seem to disappear when the discussion turns to preventive offences of preparation, membership and possession, despite the fact that these offences are much more distant from the actual causing of harm, and often do not require proof of any subjective element in relation to the potential ultimate harm.[73] The arguments from certainty and from respect for moral agency clearly apply here. Should we not reject crimes of preparation and possession as too distant from the substantive offence, particularly those that do not require a further intent?[74] In terms of Simester's second sense of remoteness, the distance between offences of possession and of preparation and the harm-to-be-prevented seems too great for liability under the harm principle. Consideration should therefore be given to re-structuring the preparatory offences in accordance with rule-of-law standards,[75] and to recasting possession offences as regulatory offences, eg breach of registration require-ments, unless a further intent to misuse the 'dangerous' article can be established.[76]

The third sense of remoteness is concerned with the problem of imputation. Where the prohibited act neither causes harm nor has any immediate tendency to cause harm (as with preparatory and possession offences) then further issues arise. These are what Simester and von Hirsch label 'prophylactic crimes'—those offences where 'the risk of ... harm does not arise straightforwardly from the prohibited act. It arises only after further human interventions, either by the original actor or by others.'[77] One problem with offences of this kind is whether the

---

[71] See Duff, *Criminal Attempts* (n 2), 58 and 390.

[72] See further Asp, 'Preventionism and the Criminalization of Noncomsummate Of-fences' (n 18); Alexander and Ferzan, 'Risk and Inchoate Crimes: Retribution or Prevention?' (n 37).

[73] Cf. the discussion of this aspect of the writings of Günther Jakobs by D Ohana, 'Trust, Distrust and Reassurance: Diversion and Preventive Orders through the Prism of *Feind-strafrecht*', *The Modern Law Review* 73(5) (2010), 721–51; 726.

[74] Cf. Ramsay's discussion of the issues at stake in P Ramsay, 'Preparation Offences, Security Interests and Political Freedom', in RA Duff et al. (eds.), *The Structures of the Criminal Law* (Oxford: Oxford University Press, 2012), 203–28.

[75] On which see Law Commission, *Conspiracy and Attempts* (Law Commission Consulta-tion Paper 183, 2007) and the comments by J Rogers, 'The Codification of Attempts and the Case for "Preparation"', *Criminal Law Review* (2007), 937.

[76] See Section 5.4, and also W Wilson, 'Participating in Crime: Some Thoughts on the Retribution/Prevention Dichotomy in Preparation for Crime and How to Deal with It', in A Reed and M Bohlander (eds.), *Participation in Crime* (Farnham: Ashgate, 2013), 115–41; 139.

[77] Simester and von Hirsch, *Crimes, Harms and Wrongs: On the Principles of Criminalization* (n 55), 79.

harm-to-be-prevented may fairly be imputed to the individual. It is one thing to hold someone to account for a harm that she has done or risked herself, or has induced another to commit or risk. It is another thing to hold an individual responsible for the possible future acts of herself or of a third party. To hold a person liable now for her possible future actions (ie without proof of an intention to do those actions), as may occur with some forms of pre-inchoate liability and possession offences, is objectionable in principle, because such a prediction 'denies my responsible agency by treating me as someone who cannot be trusted to guide his actions by the appropriate reasons'.[78] One key issue here, of course, is proof of intent: the practical argument that it is necessary to 'defend up the field' against terrorist acts in order to avert terrible consequences may be maintained,[79] but that would indicate that offences in categories (4), (5), and (6) should be confined to cases of intention.

To hold a person liable now for the possible future actions of others, as may occur with crimes of possession or of membership, is also objectionable in principle, unless the person is normatively involved in the other's actions (through facilitation, assistance, or encouragement), or unless that person has a particular duty with respect to the conduct of those others (eg her children). It is not enough that the intervention of a third party is foreseeable, unless there is a sufficient reason for the criminal law to recognize a duty to prevent or avert a foreseeable harm. Thus, the principle of fair imputation requires that the original actor has 'some form of normative involvement in [the other person's] subsequent choice',[80] a sufficient level of involvement to make it fair to regard the actor as endorsing the other's acts.

The following three restraining principles therefore emerge from the above analysis:

(3) In principle, a person may be held criminally liable for acts he or she has done, on the basis of what he or she may do at some time in the future, only if the person has declared an intent to do those further acts.

(4) The more remote the conduct criminalized is from the harm-to-be-prevented, and the less grave that harm, the weaker is the case for criminalization; but, if the process outlined in (2) above leads to a decision to criminalize, there is a compelling case for higher-level fault requirements such as intention and knowledge.

(5) In principle, a person may fairly be held liable for the future acts of others only if that person has a sufficient normative involvement in those acts (eg that he or she has encouraged, assisted, or facilitated), or where the acts of the

---

[78] RA Duff, *Answering for Crime: Responsibility and Liability in the Criminal Law* (Oxford: Hart Publishing, 2007), 165.

[79] See text at nn 53–4.

[80] Simester and von Hirsch, *Crimes, Harms and Wrongs: On the Principles of Criminalization* (n 55), 81.

other were foreseeable, with respect to which the person has an obligation to prevent a harm that might be caused by the other.

(b) Rule-of-law standards: further difficulties for the preventive offences arise from various rule-of-law standards. Three principal arguments concern us here. The first is that criminal laws should be drafted with as much certainty as possible, so as to clarify the boundaries of the criminal sanction, both for individuals and for courts. This is a major problem in the law of attempts itself, since the Model Penal Code uses the test of 'a substantial step' and English law requires a 'more than merely preparatory' act. Both of these tests suffer from a degree of uncertainty that the more extreme tests ('any overt act', 'last act') do not. Since maximum certainty forms part of the rule-of-law standards, it is important (as the English Law Commission proposed)[81] to establish a less ambiguous test for attempts and to develop a more principled offence of criminal preparation, supported by legislative examples (as are found in the Model Penal Code).

The second rule-of-law argument is that it is contrary to principle to provide for the criminalization and punishment of conduct that is significantly broader than the wrong it is aimed to prevent. The preparatory offence of encouraging terrorism, in category (4), is a prime example of this: the government stated that the purpose of the offence is to criminalize those who incite violence, and yet the offence is drafted so as to criminalize the making of any statement likely to be understood as indirect encouragement of terrorism.[82] Husak argues for a 'presumption against over-inclusive criminal laws', explaining that an over-inclusive law is one whose 'justificatory rationale applies to some but not all of the conduct it proscribes'.[83] Edwards argues that offences drafted in this way are objectionable as 'ouster offences', so named because they effectively oust the jurisdiction of the courts by excluding them from adjudicating on the true wrong.[84] Thus, the objection is that the conduct specified by the legislation is not its real target but only a proxy for it, or identified as a likely precursor to it, and thus that the offence is over-broad.

The third rule-of-law argument was developed by HLA Hart, who argued that it would be wrong to convict and punish anyone who had not been given 'a fair

---

[81] Law Commission, *Conspiracy and Attempts* (n 75), pts 15 and 16. But cf. J Horder, 'Criminal Attempt, the Rule of Law, and Accountability in Criminal Law', in L Zedner and JV Roberts (eds.), *Principles and Values in Criminal Law and Criminal Justice* (Oxford: Oxford University Press, 2012), 37–50.

[82] A Hunt, 'Criminal Prohibitions on Direct and Indirect Encouragement of Terrorism', *Criminal Law Review* (2007), 441–58. It should also be noted that the English definition of terrorism is broad and extends to damage to property: see Terrorism Act 2000, s. 1, discussed in Ch. 8, and by CAJ Coady, 'Terrorism and the Criminal Law', in RA Duff et al. (eds.), *The Constitution of the Criminal Law* (Oxford: Oxford University Press, 2012), 185–208.

[83] Husak, *Overcriminalization: The Limits of the Criminal Law* (n 57), 154.

[84] J Edwards, 'Justice Denied: The Criminal Law and the Ouster of the Criminal Courts', *Oxford Journal of Legal Studies* 30 (2010), 725.

opportunity' to exercise the capacity for 'doing what the law requires and abstaining from what it forbids'.[85] The principle of *mens rea* is therefore identified as central to fairness in the criminal law, requiring advertence by the defendant to the prohibited consequences and/or prohibited circumstances. The most important point is that, insofar as the criminal law only penalizes people who have had a fair opportunity to avoid contravening it, it then becomes 'a method of social control that maximizes individual freedom within the coercive framework of law'.[86] All of this is intimately connected with the idea of criminal law as a guide to action, and thus the principle of *mens rea* takes its place as one of the key requirements of the rule of law— alongside the requirements that the law be clear, stable, and not retroactive in its operation.[87] In this vein, Raz, following Hart and Hayek, has argued that:

Respecting human dignity entails treating humans as persons capable of planning and plotting their future. Thus, respecting people's dignity includes respecting their autonomy, their right to control their future.[88]

What is unfolding here is a demonstrable connection between culpability require-ments in criminal law and basic moral and political principles. The fundamental notion of human dignity entails respect for individuals as autonomous subjects, which in turn calls for recognition that people should be able to plan their lives in order to secure maximum freedom to pursue their interests. In order to facilitate this, the criminal law should operate so as to guide people away from certain courses of conduct, and should provide for the conviction only of persons who intend or knowingly risk the prohibited consequences. In other words, the principle of *mens rea* should be the general standard for criminal conviction for offences in categories (1) to (7) (although, as we shall see in the next paragraph, a different approach is appropriate for endangerment offences).

The following restraining principles emerge from the above analysis:

(6) All offences, including those enacted on a preventive rationale, ought to comply with rule-of-law values, such as maximum certainty of definition, fair warning, and fair labelling, so as clearly to identify the wrong that they penalize, for the purpose of guiding conduct and publicly evaluating the wrong done.

(7) All offences, including those enacted on a preventive rationale, should be so drafted as to require the court to adjudicate on the particular wrong targeted, and not on some broader conduct.

---

[85] HLA Hart, *Punishment and Responsibility*, ed. J Gardner (Oxford: Oxford University Press, 2008), 152.

[86] Hart, *Punishment and Responsibility*, 23; Hart developed the point further in HLA Hart, *The Morality of Criminal Law: Two Lectures* (Jerusalem: Hebrew University, 1965), arguing that in a system that dispenses with the principle of *mens rea* 'the occasions for official interferences with our lives and for compulsion will be vastly increased'.

[87] J Gardner, 'Introduction', part 5, in Hart, *Punishment and Responsibility* (n 85), 168.

[88] J Raz, 'The Rule of Law and Its Virtue', *Law Quarterly Review* 93 (1977), 195; 204; cf. also FA Hayek, *The Constitution of Liberty* (Chicago: Chicago University Press, 1960), 156–7.

(c) Endangerment offences: the discussion so far has been confined to preparatory or pre-emptive offences, and we now turn to endangerment offences of the kinds described in (8) and (9) above. Crimes of concrete or explicit endangerment penalize conduct that causes danger, such as dangerous driving or failure to ensure the health and safety of employees. In practice, many everyday activities give rise to some danger to others, for example, bumping into other pedestrians on the street, misjudging one's manoeuvres in a car, and lack of care at work. That does not mean, however, that there is sufficient reason for criminalizing them, since the criminal law is a censuring and coercive institution, and the stigma and loss of liberty of action that it may bring should be reserved for serious cases. This suggests that crimes of endangerment should be limited to cases of potentially serious harm.[89] As to the requisite probability of the harm occurring, it can be argued that criminal liability should require a significant risk of serious harm, but even this formulation is vague about the precise level of probability, and it will rarely be possible to give an accurate assessment of the probability of a given consequence (see further Chapter 6). Moreover, there is the further possibility that the creation of danger may be reasonable (if only in extreme circumstances, where a dangerous manoeuvre is undertaken because lives are thought to be at stake). The culpability requirement for offences of endangerment ought to be recklessness, or at least a form of negligence, and both of those standards include a reference to the reasonableness of the conduct. So, for criminalization, it should be required that the conduct should have been unreasonable in the circumstances, in the sense that the defendant failed to show appropriate concern for the interests of others.

Turning, second, to offences of abstract or implicit endangerment, these often have a different structure and raise different issues. They tend to be clear in what they prohibit: for example, driving at a speed in excess of the relevant limit, driving with a blood alcohol reading above a certain limit, or sexual activity with a child under a particular age. Such offences draw a firm line as a rough, practical way of reflecting the degree of danger typically created by behaviour, despite the knowledge that it is difficult to draw a legal line that tracks the moral distinction. Certain people may not be any more likely to drive dangerously with a blood alcohol reading just in excess of the permitted limit, and some young people may be sufficiently mature to give meaningful consent to sexual activity before they attain the legal age. Abstract or implicit endangerment offences of this kind incorporate a certain amount of overreach (that is, they penalize some instances where no danger is actually or likely to be caused), as the price of giving clear guidance to citizens

---

[89] Duff, 'Criminalising Endangerment' (n 33); cf. Husak, *Overcriminalization: The Limits of the Criminal Law* (n 57), 159, referring to a not insubstantial risk and Westen, 'The Ontological Problem of "Risk" and "Endangerment" in Criminal Law' (n 34); L Alexander and KK Ferzan, 'Danger: The Ethics of Preemptive Action', *Ohio State Journal of Criminal Law* 9(2) (2012), 637–67.

about the limits of permissible behaviour and thereby leaving more space for individual autonomy to flourish. They offer strong compliance with rule-of-law principles, unlike the uncertainties that would be created by offences with a flexible standard of 'driving at a dangerous speed' or 'having sex with a young person whose level of understanding was insufficient to grasp the significance of what was being done', but they do so at a cost. The difficult question is whether the injustice done to a minority of individuals by the use of a sharp line for general criminalization, mitigated by fair warning about that sharp line, is conclusively outweighed by the social benefits of large-scale harm prevention. One answer is that this may be acceptable so long as the penalties remain relatively low.

The following principles emerge from the above analysis of endangerment offences:

(8) Concrete or explicit endangerment should only be considered for criminalization where a significant risk of serious harm is created by a person's actions, and where those actions were unreasonable in the circumstances in the sense that they failed to show appropriate concern for the interests of others.

(9) Abstract or implicit endangerment may supply a good reason for an offence that specifies a precise limit for conduct of a potentially dangerous nature, but only if it focuses criminalization on those instances where there is a significant risk of serious harm and applies regulatory or administrative measures to deal with lesser risks of harm.

5.4 Regulation and the Criminal Law

Whereas the criminal law is a censuring institution, regulation has a less morally condemnatory tone. It is still concerned to prevent unwanted behaviour by attaching penalties to it, but without the weight of public censure for significant wrongs. Insofar as the principle of the least restrictive appropriate alternative forms part of the normative architecture of prevention—and we have argued that it should do so—consideration should be given to the use of regulation as a means of preventing relatively minor wrongs.[90] One key element of the systems of administrative or regulatory offences in many continental European jurisdictions is that the penalties are set at a low level. The purpose of these mechanisms is to subject those who commit minor infractions to a lower-level system of sanctions that is efficient enough to ensure no resulting loss of preventive efficacy. Thus, there should be, in principle, an initial decision about whether the conduct constitutes a serious wrong that merits criminalization, with public censure and sentencing to follow, or

---

[90] See H Quirk, T Seddon, and G Smith (eds.), *Regulation and Criminal Justice: Innovations in Policy and Research* (Cambridge: Cambridge University Press, 2010).

whether the conduct is a minor wrong that can properly be dealt with in this non-stigmatic way by a financial penalty. If the conduct falls into the latter category, a system such as Germany's *Ordnungswidrigkeiten*[91] would provide that (1) the decision to impose a sanction may be taken by law enforcement officials or administrators and (2) the financial penalty would not require court proceedings unless the subject wished to contest liability, in which case all the safeguards appropriate to criminal proceedings would be available.

In its 2010 Consultation Paper, the English Law Commission proposed that the use of the criminal law to reinforce regulatory systems in England and Wales should be reviewed.[92] It suggested that the 'choice between civil sanction or criminal penalty is determined in part by questions of degree',[93] and put its weight behind a wider use of regulatory sanctions such as informal and formal warnings, notices to desist, and financial penalties. The Law Commission went on to propose that harm done or risked should be regarded as serious enough to warrant criminalization if 'a) in some circumstances (not just extreme circumstances) an individual could justifiably be sent to prison for a first offence,' or 'b) an unlimited fine is necessary to address the seriousness of the wrongdoing in issue, and its consequences'.[94] This is a bold attempt to find criteria to determine the question of degree, but it may be suggested that criterion (a) is unlikely to be helpful. There is a group of offences for which English courts tend to reserve imprisonment for first offenders, but there is no unifying theme or principle applicable to these offences, and they are contestable.[95] However, this should not detract from the importance of the Law Commission's support for a more extensive regulatory field and a less extensive criminal law. So long as such a movement is not motivated chiefly by a desire for great speed and efficacy without reference to the need for public censure of serious wrongs,[96] nor done in order to avoid the application of the procedural safeguards entailed by the criminal law,[97] then this should form a major part of the necessary review of the preparatory and pre-emptive offences. Such a review would also consider forms of civil sanction, and would have to confront several problems (such as the appropriate standard of proof, the question of enforcement methods, and compliance with EU law) that relate to both practice and principle.

---

[91] For discussion, see RA Duff, 'Crimes, Regulatory Offences and Criminal Trials', in H Müller-Dietz, H Egon Müller, and KL Kunz (eds.), *Festschrift für Heike Jung* (Baden-Baden: Nomos, 2007), 87–98; 87.

[92] Law Commission, *Criminal Law in Regulatory Contexts Consultation Paper No. 195* (London: Law Commission, 2010).

[93] Law Commission, *Criminal Law in Regulatory Contexts Consultation Paper No. 195*, para. 3.5.

[94] Law Commission, *Criminal Law in Regulatory Contexts Consultation Paper No. 195*, para. 3.138.

[95] See A Ashworth, *Sentencing and Criminal Justice* (Cambridge: Cambridge University Press, 2010), 297–9.

[96] Duff, 'Perversions and Subversions of Criminal Law' (n 1), 102–5.

[97] See Section 4.3.

5.5 Conclusions

The prevention of harm, as an aspect of the duty to protect, is one of the state's core functions. The criminal law is primarily an institution for censuring people for committing public wrongs, but it also and inevitably has a preventive element. In Section 5.1 we considered the many ways in which the criminal law has been used for preventive ends, leading to certain tensions with standard criminal law doctrine that were drawn out in Section 5.2. One justification advanced for creating preparatory and pre-inchoate offences in anti-terrorist legislation was that these are necessary in order to 'defend further up the field' against terrorism. 'Defending further up the field' involves authorizing the law enforcement and security services to intervene at a much earlier stage in the process of planning an offence than would the traditional legal category of inchoate offences.[98] What 'defending further up the field' means in practice is earlier criminalization, earlier interventions by law enforcers, and earlier and more intrusive policing, much closer to everyday behaviour (since discussions with friends, acquiring timetables, buying weed-killer, etc. could all, if accompanied by a relevant intention, be sufficient to constitute offences in categories (4) or (5)).

To what extent it is necessary to 'defend further up the field' against terrorism is difficult to assess, and will be considered in context in Chapter 8. Looking more widely, the Law Commission and parliamentary draftsmen have embraced the inchoate mode of definition (category (3)) with increasing regularity, but without any analysis of the need thus to criminalize a wider range of conduct. While the Independent Reviewer of Terrorism Legislation comments on the form of anti-terrorist laws and on the ways in which they are used, there is no similar institution or procedure for what might be termed 'ordinary' criminal offences. This is an important lacuna, which should be addressed as soon as possible. Such a review body would examine both principle and practice. In this chapter we have focused on formulating principles—derived from standard criminal law doctrine—appropriate for reviewing and restraining the widespread use of preventive offences. It is not suggested that there are no arguments in favour of some offences in categories (3) to (9). It is more that the arguments in favour tend to have been pursued to the neglect of arguments of principle that should be no less important in a liberal legal order—arguments that respect individuals' rights just as much as the preventive rationales that drive these extensions of the criminal law.

---

[98] Anderson, 'Shielding the Compass: How to Fight Terrorism without Defeating the Law' (n 23).

6

Risk Assessment and the Preventive Role of the Criminal Court

The premise that it is possible to assess risk accurately stands behind much preventive endeavour, whether it is pursued through policing and law enforcement, civil preventive measures, or the prosecution of criminal offences. If the deprivations entailed by preventive measures are to be warranted, appropriate, and proportional, it is necessary to calculate both the gravity of the risked harm and the likelihood of it occurring. Where there is doubt about the validity of risk-assessment tools or the accuracy of their findings, much preventive endeavour becomes difficult to justify. It follows that the technological capacity for, and limitations of, risk assessment are an integral facet of preventive justice. It would be a mistake, however, to think that the issues here are solely technical ones of statistical validity or predictive accuracy. Risk calculation is not isolated from the social and political environment within which it occurs: perceptions of risk vary over time and by jurisdiction. While the scientific calculation of risk may be more or less robust, what is perceived and targeted as hazardous at any one time is partly a matter of social construction, susceptible to changes in public toleration and shifting perceptions of what threatens. Risk is also a political construct defined by the priorities of public policy, political climate, and changes in official views about the prevailing threats to public safety and national security. It follows that to technical questions about the reliability of risk-assessment tools must be added social and political questions about which risks are deemed most serious, which methods of assessment are preferred, and how these vary over time.

The political premium on public protection and the high level of interest in, and intense media coverage of, 'dangerous' offenders also generates risks to the organizations charged with managing them. The greater the anticipated threat, the greater the distortion caused when criminal justice professionals and agencies seek to avoid 'getting it wrong'. Decision-making is liable to be skewed by attempts by criminal justice professionals to avoid reputational risks that call into question their judgment and expertise. Generally, underestimating a threat poses a greater risk to reputation than overestimating it. Little blame attaches to the public servant who takes too cautious an approach if no threat arises; whereas failure to take preventive measures may result in reputational loss or worse if harm eventuates. Recognizing these contextual factors is an important corrective to purely technical analyses of the validity of risk-assessment tools.

Against pressures to assess risk accurately and to tread cautiously, criminal justice agencies and the courts face countervailing stresses. They operate in a world in which the 'precautionary principle' has been widely adopted as a framework for public decision-making in the face of the risk of serious harm. The precautionary principle was first developed in respect of risks to the environment and it states that 'where there are threats of serious or irreversible damage, lack of full scientific certainty shall not be used as a reason for postponing cost-effective measures'.[1] This precautionary approach arises from recognition that absence of hard evidence of a threat is not the same as absence of threat. As Ramsay points out, stronger articulations of the principle go further to make uncertainty 'a valid or compelling reason for taking preventive action'.[2] In the case of grave potential harm, the principle generates pressure on officials to take precautionary steps even in the absence of clear scientific evidence.[3] The benefit of this approach is that it licenses officials to take preventive measures, particularly in cases where the potential harm is life-threatening or gravely damaging to human safety or health. The problem is that the precautionary principle may license arbitrary and unfounded decision-making with serious adverse consequences for individual liberties. An important question is whether and to what extent the hazards inherent in the precautionary principle can be limited by insisting that it should stand alongside and be reconcilable with other key legal principles, such as proportionality and equality. This chapter considers not only the technical but also the political and organizational aspects of risk assessment: it focuses in particular on the role of risk decision-making in the criminal court.

Section 6.1 looks at the ways in which risk labels are deployed generally and Section 6.2 focuses on their use in the criminal justice process. Section 6.3 analyses whether we have a right to be presumed harmless, how we lose that right, and who, therefore, is liable to risk assessment. Section 6.4 examines how risk is defined, categorized, and calculated, and explores how risk labels are applied. Section 6.5 examines the task of assessing risk and the conflicted role played by expert witnesses

---

[1] Principle 15 of the UN Rio Declaration on Environment and Development. <http://www.un.org/documents/ga/conf151/aconf15126-1annex1.htm>. E Fisher, 'Precaution, Precaution Everywhere: Developing a "Common Understanding" of the Precautionary Principle in the European Community', *Maastricht Journal of European and Comparative Law* 9(1) (2002), 7–28; 9.

[2] P Ramsay, 'Imprisonment under the Precautionary Principle', in GR Sullivan and I Dennis (eds.), *Seeking Security: Pre-Empting the Commission of Criminal Harms* (Oxford: Hart Publishing, 2012), 194–218; 201–2.

[3] K Haggerty, 'From Risk to Precaution: The Rationalities of Personal Crime Prevention', in R Ericson and A Doyle (eds.), *Risk and Morality* (Toronto: University of Toronto Press, 2003), 193–214.

in the criminal court. It goes on to examine the timing of risk assessments, the bases upon which they are made and by whom, as well as questions of scientific validity. Finally, Section 6.6 considers the disjuncture between mass actuarial risk assessment and the calculation of the risk posed by any single individual, in particular where actuarial instruments are used as the basis for depriving individuals of their liberty.

6.1 Identifying Risk and Applying Risk Labels

Risk is an increasingly commonly applied term in criminal law and criminal justice but it is used to connote diverse types and levels of danger.[4] Sometimes risk refers simply to variables known to be associated with a higher likelihood of future offending. Particular background characteristics, patterns of behaviour, specific locales, or membership of certain demographic, ethnic, or socio-economic groups have all been identified as highly correlated with offending behaviour and used to justify preventive or risk-reductive interventions. Sometimes, risk is used to refer to conduct deemed inherently risky such as drinking, drug-taking, or speeding. Risk is also identified in present behaviour which becomes risky if done with the requisite mental state or intent to endanger, for example, buying a map of the underground with the intent to bomb it. Other risks pertain to behaviour that is not presently but only prospectively risky or, more remotely still, only prospectively risky as a result of third-party intervention—the shopkeeper who fails to secure his liquor section, for example. In short, risk is an umbrella term for widely differing hazards and degrees of liability. A more discriminating vocabulary would permit greater analytical clarity by distinguishing between present and prospective risks, between agent-dependent and agent-independent risks,[5] and by grading more finely different levels of culpability, gravity of risk, and degrees of likelihood in play.[6]

The importance of weighing the gravity of an offence has been well understood in respect of past crimes. Sentencing bodies have developed sophisticated ordinal scales that grade the seriousness of offences. The exact placement of particular crimes upon the scale and their relative ranking may be contested but that there should be such a scale is now accepted.[7] The ordinal ranking of offences forms the

---

[4] L Alexander and KK Ferzan, 'Danger: The Ethics of Preemptive Action', *Ohio State Journal of Criminal Law* 9(2) (2012), 637–67.

[5] RA Duff, 'Criminalising Endangerment', in RA Duff and SP Green (eds.), *Defining Crimes: Essays on the Special Part of the Criminal Law* (Oxford: Oxford University Press, 2005), 43–64.

[6] See A Ashworth, *Sentencing and Criminal Justice* (Cambridge: Cambridge University Press, 2010), 152; K Baker, 'More Harm Than Good? The Language of Public Protection', *Howard Journal of Criminal Justice* 49(1) (2010), 42–53.

[7] See, eg, the guidelines set out at <http://sentencingcouncil.judiciary.gov.uk/guide lines/guidelines-to-download.htm>.

basis for a proportional system of punishment that ties coercive consequences closely to the gravity of the offence.[8] The need for a similar scale to be used in respect of risk is no less pressing, though it would need to be set upon not one but two axes to address not only the gravity but also the likelihood of occurrence. A risk-assessment scale requires, first and most obviously, an assessment of the gravity of the harm in prospect. Second, it requires separate assessment of the degree of probability that it will actually occur.[9] Without these dual axes, risk assessments may appropriately gauge the gravity of a prospective risk but give insufficient attention to the probability of it occurring or vice versa. A third, and more challenging, calculus relates to the relationship between the gravity of the prospective harm and likelihood of its occurrence. As yet, little systematic consideration has been given to the question of whether the probability requirement should be varied according to the gravity of the harm in prospect. It might be argued that it would be appropriate to weight the scale so that a higher level of probability is required for less serious harms, a lower level of probability for more serious harms, and a lower level still for potentially catastrophic harms. This would not go so far as to underwrite liberty deprivation in the face of uncertainty—as some iterations of the precautionary principle allow—but it would place the probability requirement on a sliding scale tied to the gravity of the prospective harm.

Risk is a common focus of deliberation in the criminal court, but what exactly is being claimed, and upon what basis, is often less clear. Individual risk assessments may be based upon no more than past conduct or past convictions or may rely upon the expertise of criminal justice professionals or judicial wisdom. Clinical evaluations conducted by psychologists or forensic psychiatrists might appear to offer a more scientific basis, but opinions as to the reliability of clinical risk assessment vary widely. Lidz, Mulvey, and Gardner conclude that 'clinical judgment has been undervalued in previous research',[10] whereas Skeem and Monahan conclude that 'clinicians are relatively inaccurate predictors of violence'.[11] The dominance of purely clinical assessment has been challenged by the growing number of recognized actuarial instruments. These actuarial risk-assessment instruments (ARAIs) forecast the likelihood that those who share the characteristics of a particular

---

[8] A von Hirsch and A Ashworth, *Proportionate Sentencing: Exploring the Principles* (Oxford: Oxford University Press, 2005).

[9] F Schauer, 'The Ubiquity of Prevention', in A Ashworth, L Zedner, and P Tomlin (eds.), *Prevention and the Limits of the Criminal Law* (Oxford: Oxford University Press, 2013), 10–22; 12–16; N Walker, 'Harms, Probabilities and Precautions', *Oxford Journal of Legal Studies* 17(4) (1997), 611–20.

[10] C Lidz, E Mulvey, and W Gardner, 'The Accuracy of Predictions of Violence to Others', *Journal of the American Medical Association,* 269(8) (1993), 1007–11, 1010.

[11] J Skeem and J Monahan, 'Current Directions in Violence Risk Assessment.', *Current Directions in Psychological Science,* 21(1) (2011), 38–42, 39; R Ericson, 'Ten Uncertainties of Risk-Management Approaches to Security', *Canadian Journal of Criminology and Criminal Justice,* 48(3) (2006), 345–57.

population will go on to commit acts of wrongdoing or criminal harm (their validity will be discussed in further detail below). Although a sharp division between clinical and actuarial modes has long characterized the field, the clinical–actuarial (or unstructured versus structured) dichotomy has been partially eroded by the development of hybrid forms of partially structured forms of assessment that take account of both aggregate risk factors and those rarer individual factors that might otherwise be missed.[12] Despite considerable technological advances in statistical modelling, the development of structured clinical decision-making (or 'structured professional judgment'), and increasingly sophisticated techniques of enquiry and data analysis, nonetheless risk assessment remains a precarious business.[13]

Irrespective of the approach taken or robustness of the methodology applied, risk assessment often has the effect of applying enduring (even indelible) labels to an individual. Labelling is an acknowledged problem in respect of past offending because it adversely affects how individuals are perceived and treated, and how they come to perceive themselves.[14] Labelling individuals as 'high risk' also assigns them to a categorical status that is difficult to escape and, as a consequence, often self-fulfilling. Risk labels are arguably more problematic than those applied in respect of past offences because, being prognostic, they are apt to fix the future.[15] To apply the label 'high risk' makes the questionable assumption that the individual before the court is indistinguishable from their future (and perhaps not so risky) self. The further into the future this assumption is extended the more questionable it becomes since other variables (getting a job, marrying, securing a home) may reduce an individual's risk profile. The longer the interval, the more problematic is the prediction because it leaves open no possibility of change over time. Risk assessments based on past offending behaviour or other fixed criteria are particularly objectionable as they do not allow that the individual might develop in ways that would reasonably qualify them for recategorization as less, or not at all, risky. Static or backward-looking assessments cannot adequately take into account the inherently fluid quality of risk.[16]

---

[12] DJ Cooke and C Michie, 'Violence Risk Assessment: Challenging the Illusion of Certainty', in B McSherry and P Keyzer (eds.), *Dangerous People: Policy, Prediction, and Practice* (New York: Routledge, 2011), 147–61; 159–60.

[13] See especially L Johnstone, 'Assessing and Managing Violent Youth: Implications for Sentencing', in B McSherry and P Keyzer (eds.), *Dangerous Offenders: Policy, Prediction, and Practice* (New York: Routledge, 2011), 123–45; 126.

[14] D Downes and P Rock, *Understanding Deviance* 5th edn (Oxford: Oxford University Press, 2007), Ch. 7.

[15] L Zedner, 'Fixing the Future? The Pre-Emptive Turn in Criminal Justice', in S Bronitt, B McSherry, and A Norrie (eds.), *Regulating Deviance: The Redirection of Criminalisation and the Futures of Criminal Law* (Oxford: Hart Publishing, 2009), 35–58.

[16] M Brown, 'Calculations of Risk in Contemporary Penal Practice', in J Pratt and M Brown (eds.), *Dangerous Offenders* (London: Routledge, 2000), 93–108.

6.2 Risk Assessment in the Criminal Justice Process

Risk assessment in the criminal court is, of course, not simply a descriptive tool but an instrumental one from which serious consequences may follow, not least of which is preventive detention. Risk assessment plays a part in every decision to sentence an offender to indefinite detention. In some US states, for example Virginia, the use of actuarial assessment is even prescribed by the sentencing statute, which also specifies which actuarial tool is to be used and sets the score required to trigger commitment.[17] It is questionable whether the criminal court is structurally well suited to manage the dynamic nature of risk because its determinations are typically one-off affairs. In its conventional criminal trial role, this is not a major problem because the task is to determine liability for past wrongs. Saving new evidence or procedural impropriety, there is ordinarily no need to revisit that decision at a later date. The judgment is one-off and dichotomous: guilty/not guilty. By contrast, risk is prospective and, as such, requires continuing reassessment, at least regarding those factors that are not static (like past history), but fluid or dynamic and apt to change over time (age, substance abuse, or marital status). Continuing assessment sits ill within the structure and workings of the criminal court.[18] Yet, a one-off risk assessment poses a danger of doing injustice to those whose risk profile may change radically.[19] Where a risk assessment made by the court results in an indeterminate sentence there is, of course, provision for ongoing review while detained in prison.[20] However, the difficulty of subsequently satisfying the Parole Board that one

---

[17] For discussion of the use of actuarial assessment within the Virginia sentencing statute, see R Wandall, 'Actuarial Risk Assessment. The Loss of Recognition of the Individual Offender', *Law, Probability and Risk* 5 (2006), 175–200. The use of risk assessment as a basis for incapacitative civil detention in the US, for example in respect of the civil commitment of sexual offenders, has also been very controversial because, although it is technically non-punitive, the implications for those then held under indefinite detention are profound. N Demleitner, 'Abusing State Power or Controlling Risk?: Sex Offender Commitment and Sicherungsverwahrung', *Fordham Urban Law Journal* 30 (2003), 1621–69; E Janus, 'Civil Commitment as Social Control', in M Brown and J Pratt (eds.), *Dangerous Offenders: Punishment and Social Order* (London: Routledge, 2000), 71–90.

[18] M Shapiro, *Courts—a Comparative and Political Analysis* (Chicago: University of Chicago Press, 1981), Ch. 1.

[19] Brown, 'Calculations of Risk in Contemporary Penal Practice' (n 16); P Maurutto and K Hannah-Moffat, 'Assembling Risk and the Restructuring of Penal Control', *British Journal of Criminology* 46 (2006), 438–54; R McLeod, A Sweeting, and R Evans, *Improving the Structure and Content of Psychiatric Reports for Sentencing: Research to Develop Good Practice Guidance* (London: Ministry of Justice, 2010), 17.

[20] On the necessity of review, see the discussion in Section 7.3 of *Vinter and Others v the United Kingdom* (Grand Chamber: Application Nos. 66069/09, 130/10, and 3896/10).

is safe to release into the community evidences the difficulty of escaping the original judicial designation as a 'dangerous offender'.[21]

It is a characteristic of risk assessment that risk labels are applied not only to particular conduct or patterns of behaviour but also to people. Particular concerns arise where the question before the court is not 'under what conditions or subject to what difficulties, provocations or triggers is this person at risk of reoffending?' but 'does this person pose a risk?' or, more problematically still, 'is this a high risk individual?' Risk assessment of this sort may exclude relevant considerations in two important ways. First, the individual may become the sole object of assessment to the exclusion of external circumstances, hazards, and opportunities. Second, assessment tends to focus upon one aspect of the defendant's disposition—riskiness—to the exclusion of other considerations (such as character, attributes, and personal prospects). This narrowing of focus on risk reduces the person's external circumstances and their capacity for change to a single categorical label or ascription of probability. It also shifts attention from risky conduct to the identification of risky people, be they anti-social youths, sexual offenders, dangerous offenders, or terrorists. Yet, which groups are so designated can change radically over time and is often contested. As political priorities and popular concerns shift to identify new 'dangerous' populations the target groups change.

By way of example, consider how risk assessment was deployed under the Criminal Justice Act (CJA) 2003 in respect of Imprisonment for Public Protection (IPP).[22] Section 229(1) CJA 2003 stated that an offender was to be deemed dangerous if 'the court is of the opinion that there is a significant risk to members of the public of serious harm occasioned by the commission by him of further specified offences'. And yet the structured Offender Assessment System (OASys) risk-assessment tool,[23] upon which the court ordinarily made its determination, assesses likelihood of reconviction in terms of 'low', 'medium', or 'high' risk and assesses 'risk of serious harm' as 'low', 'medium', 'high', or 'very high'. Despite claims that there is 'a measure of compatibility' between these terms,[24] it remained unclear how the categories generated by the actuarial tools related to those specified in the legislation.[25] Unsurprisingly, the courts struggled to come up with a

---

[21] B McSherry and P Keyzer, '"Dangerous" People: An Overview', in B McSherry and P Keyzer (eds.), *Dangerous People: Policy, Prediction, and Practice* (New York: Routledge, 2011), 3–12.

[22] Imprisonment for Public Protection has been replaced by the provision for Extended Determinate Sentences under the Legal Aid, Sentencing and Punishment of Offenders Act 2012 (see further Ch. 7).

[23] See HM Prison Service Order Offender Assessment and Sentence Management OASys Order Number 2205:<https://www.google.co.uk/#q=oasys+risk+assessment+tool&revid=2110127836>.

[24] HM Chief Inspector of Prisons, *The Indeterminate Sentence for Public Protection* (2008), 14.

[25] Prison Reform Trust, *Unjust Deserts: Imprisonment for Public Protection* (London: PRT, 2010), 26.

satisfactory definition of 'significant risk' under the CJA 2003 in order to determine whether or not an IPP sentence was appropriate or not (see further Chapter 7).

In the leading case of *Lang*,[26] the Court of Appeal held that 'significant risk' means 'noteworthy, of considerable amount or importance', but it can hardly be said that this definition made the task of the court easier. Significantly, the judgment in *Lang* concludes:

It would be inappropriate to conclude these proceedings without expressing our sympathy with all those sentencers whose decisions have been the subject of appeal to this Court. The fact that, in many cases, the sentencers were unsuccessful in finding their way through the provisions of this Act, which we have already described as labyrinthine, is a criticism not of them but of those who produced these astonishingly complex provisions.[27]

In *Pedley, Martin and Hamadi*,[28] the Court confirmed the indication given in *Lang* that a 'significant risk' presented a higher threshold than a mere possibility of occurrence but, again, it did not consider that any further definition of the term would be helpful. In particular, the Court rejected the invitation of counsel for the appellants to redefine risk in terms of numerical probability or percentage of likelihood. So the disjuncture between the use of numerical risk-assessment tools and the legal definition of risk remained. More worryingly still, it appears that not all those sentenced to IPP orders were subject to formal risk assessment. A study by HM Inspector of Prisons found that of 48 offenders subject to IPP, three had had no pre-sentence report and a further five had no OASys assessment completed before sentencing. Of those upon whom reports had been completed, Her Majesty's Chief Inspector concluded that the risk had been falsely inflated in 16 cases and that, of 48 cases, the risks posed by 19 offenders could have been managed by a different, less restrictive sentence.[29]

The relationship between the present offence and assessment of future risk was addressed by the Court of Appeal in *Johnson*.[30] The Court held that it did not automatically follow from the absence of actual harm caused by an offender to date that the risk that he would cause serious harm in the future was negligible.[31] There may, of course, be legitimate reason to conclude that an individual who has not yet caused serious harm may, nonetheless, pose a significant risk of serious harm for the future. Yet, the figures for the use of IPP suggest that the courts were far too ready to reach this conclusion. If an offender had committed one of the listed 'relevant

[26] *R. v Lang* [2005] EWCA Crim 2864.   [27] *R. v Lang* [2005] EWCA Crim 2864.

[28] *Pedley, Martin and Hamadi* [2009] EWCA Crim 840. The Court also found that a sentence of IPP imposed when the judge is satisfied that the defendant poses a significant risk of serious harm to the public is wholly compatible with both Arts 3 and 5(1)(a) of the European Convention. See further <http://www.cps.gov.uk/legal/s_to_u/sentencing_and_dangerous_offenders/#a01>.

[29] Chief Inspector of Prisons, *The Indeterminate Sentence for Public Protection* (n 24), 19.

[30] *R. v Johnson* [2006] EWCA Crim 2486.

[31] *R. v Johnson* [2006] EWCA Crim 2486.

offences' under s. 224, the courts were, in any case, obliged to reach this conclusion by the requirement that 'the court must assume that there is a such a risk' unless it considered that 'it would be unreasonable to conclude that there was such a risk': s. 229(3) CJA 2003.[32] According to evidence from the Parole Board, until 2008 half of IPP prisoners received a tariff sentence of 20 months or less and 20 per cent received a tariff sentence of less than 18 months.[33] According to the Prison Reform Trust, in the first years of the IPP some individuals were given tariff sentences 'of no more than a few months or even weeks'.[34] The justification for imposing extended sentences on these relatively low-tariff offenders was the assessment of their future riskiness. However, it is a cause for concern when 'a significant risk to members of the public of serious harm' is so routinely found in respect of those whose present offences merited such short sentences. To prevent offenders with very low tariff sentences being indefinitely detained, the Criminal Justice and Immigration Act 2008 required that a tariff sentence be at least two years before an IPP order could be imposed.[35] Despite this change, by 2012 6,500 IPP prisoners were held in British prisons—a figure that makes clear the relative ease of entering the high-risk category resulting in indefinite incarceration and the relative difficulty of escaping that categorization to secure release once it has been made (see further Chapter 7). Recognizing that risk assessments are not merely classificatory measures but instruments with profound consequences for individual liberty invites closer attention to the ways in which they are used by the courts and to what ends. The next chapter explores in detail how the IPP sentence deployed risk assessment to justify incarceration beyond the tariff term of imprisonment.

In addition to the determinations made in respect of the indeterminate sentencing of dangerous offenders, risk assessment also plays an important role in many other aspects of criminal justice decision-making. Six may be mentioned here by way of illustration:

(1) Risk assessment underpins the decision whether an offender is placed on bail or remanded to custody awaiting trial. Under s.4 Bail Act 1976, remand is permitted if there are substantial grounds for believing that the defendant, if released on bail, would fail to surrender to custody, commit an offence while on bail, interfere with witnesses, or otherwise obstruct the course of justice. In the English case, these procedural grounds for remand may be met by

---

[32] This presumption of dangerousness was subsequently removed by an amendment under the Criminal Justice and Immigration Act 2008.

[33] House of Commons Justice Committee, *Towards Effective Sentencing* (HC 184–I, 2008), 21.

[34] Prison Reform Trust, *Unjust Deserts: Imprisonment for Public Protection* (n 25), 24.

[35] The Criminal Justice & Immigration Act 2008 provided that IPP could be imposed only where either of two conditions was met: either the immediate offence attracted a notional minimum term of at least two years; or the offender had on a previous occasion been convicted of one of the offences in the extensive list set out in the new Schedule 15A to the 2003 Act. See further Section 7.3.

reference to backward-looking criteria, such as the defendant's record in respect of previous grants of bail; their character, antecedents, and community ties; and prior criminal record. As Ashworth and Redmayne observe, the question of whether character and antecedents suffice as a basis for prediction of future risk 'has attracted surprisingly little legal analysis or empirical inquiry' and they criticize the making of such assumptions solely on the basis of prior record unless the previous conviction is 'recent, relevant and of a certain seriousness'.[36] By contrast, a 1996 amendment to the Irish Constitution requires that pre-trial detention may be imposed only where there is a risk of a 'serious offence'.[37]

(2) Risk assessment figures in *pre-sentence reports* used in the allocation of requirements attached to a community sentence (s. 147 CJA 2003), particularly in respect of those with preventive element such as curfews and electronic tagging. As with indefinite custodial sentences, tensions occur between judicial judgments and the use of actuarial tools.

(3) In respect of *probation decision-making* more generally, probation services use the OASys of risk assessment as well as a variety of specialist risk-assessment tools.[38] In practice, there are strains between assessments based upon the experience, values and 'craft-skills' of probation officers, and the use of these numerical risk inventories. A common cause for concern is that there is a deeper underlying tension between welfare and rehabilitation and the pressure to protect the public.[39]

(4) Risk assessment is also central to the requirement, under the CJA 2003, that local criminal justice agencies work in partnership to make arrangements, known as *Multi-Agency Public Protection Arrangements* (MAPPA), to identify, assess, and manage the risk posed by serious sexual and violent offenders in their area. MAPPA applies to registered sex offenders, offenders sentenced to 12 months or more for a sexual or violent offence, and to anyone else who poses a 'risk of serious harm to the public'. MAPPA is a mechanism that

---

[36] A Ashworth and M Redmayne, *The Criminal Process* 4th edn (Oxford: Oxford University Press, 2010), 237.

[37] U ni Raifeartaigh, 'Reconciling Bail Law with the Presumption of Innocence', *Oxford Journal of Legal Studies* 17(1) (1997), 1–21. See also Section 3.4.

[38] Specialist risk-assessment tools include the Risk Matrix 2000 for sexual offenders, the Spousal Assault Risk Assessment Guide for domestic violence, and ASSET in respect of young offenders. See C Logan, 'Managing High-Risk Personality Disordered Offenders', in B McSherry and P Keyzer (eds.), *Dangerous People: Policy, Prediciton, and Practice* (New York: Routledge, 2011), 233–47; 238. H Kemshall, *Understanding the Community Management of High Risk Offenders* (Maidenhead: Open University Press, 2008).

[39] H Kemshall, *Understanding Risk in Criminal Justice* (Maidenhead: Open University Press, 2003), 102. P Raynor, 'Community Penalties: Probation, and Offender Management', in M Maguire, R Morgan, and R Reiner (eds.), *The Oxford Handbook of Criminology* 5th edn (Oxford: Oxford University Press, 2012), 954–28; 946.

promotes information sharing among all relevant agencies, assesses risk, classifies offenders into one of three risk categories, and institutes management plans to ensure more effective supervision and better public protection.[40] Offenders regarded as high or very high risk, whose risks to others are judged to be potentially imminent, and whose cases are very complex or difficult are allocated to the highest level—Level 3.[41]

(5) Risk provides the dominant rationale for the growth of *civil and hybrid civil-criminal preventive orders* such as Anti-Social Behaviour Orders (ASBOs) (see Chapter 4), Control Orders and their replacement TPIMs (see Chapter 8), Serious Crime Prevention Orders, and Sexual Offences Prevention Orders (see Chapter 4).

(6) Risk assessment is also central to *release decision by the Parole Board*. Here too, tensions arise between clinical assessment and use of actuarial tools, many of which rely upon static risk factors. The Parole Board is generally considered to be cautious in its decisions about release, partly because s. 28(6)(b) of the Crime (Sentences) Act 1997 states that 'an indeterminate sentenced prisoner can be released if the Parole Board is satisfied that it is no longer necessary for the protection of the public that he be confined'. This statutory test sets a high bar because Parole Board members need to have a high level of confidence that a prisoner whom they release will not go on to commit a serious offence or otherwise pose a danger to the public or themselves.[42] The Board bases its decision in part upon a dossier that contains reports from prison and probation staff. The dossier also contains a variety of formal risk assessments based on offending history, behaviour in prison, courses completed, and, sometimes, psychological assessments. It also holds oral hearings that can include the legal representative of the prisoner, together with a public protection advocate representing the Secretary of State and the victim, as well as witnesses such as the prisoner's offender manager and prison psychologist.[43]

As this brief overview makes clear, risk assessment is central to court decisions to impose coercive measures, many of which invade individual liberty beyond the tariff term or result in the extension of indefinite sentences, as well as to a whole

---

[40] Ministry of Justice, *MAPPA Guidance 2012. Version 4* (2012). See also discussion in J Peay, 'Mentally Disordered Offenders, Mental Health and Crime', in M Maguire, R Morgan, and R Reiner (eds.), *The Oxford Handbook of Criminology* 5th edn (Oxford: Oxford University Press, 2012), 426–49; 428–9.

[41] Logan, 'Managing High-Risk Personality Disordered Offenders' (n 38), 239.

[42] N Padfield, R Morgan, and M Maguire, 'Out of Court, out of Sight? Criminal Sanctions and Non-Judicial Decision-Making', in M Maguire, R Morgan, and R Reiner (eds.), *The Oxford Handbook of Criminology* 5th edn (Oxford: Oxford University Press, 2012), 955–85; 977–8.

[43] The Parole Board for England and Wales, *Annual Report and Accounts 2012/13 HC 346* (London: The Stationery Office, 2013), 5.

range of other criminal justice disposals. Recognizing that risk assessment licenses state coercion beyond proportional punishment makes it all the more important that its foundations are methodologically sound and morally defensible.[44] Before turning to the methodological questions, first let us consider what moral claims are being made when risk is assessed for preventive purposes.

6.3 The Presumption of Harmlessness

It might be thought that any state that is serious about averting risk should subject the entire population to regular risk assessment. In practice, the law allows this only in places or at times of particularly high security: airport authorities, for example, screen all passengers before they are permitted to enter the 'airside' area of airports. The greater threats to security posed in respect of air travel are said to justify the erosion of civil liberties (not least the right to privacy) that is entailed by mass screening. Outside such high-risk milieux, universal risk assessment is generally not permitted, although risk assessment may be made a condition of certain activities (air travel in the example above) or for those working with children, for which Disclosure and Barring Service checks are required. One reason given against universal risk assessment is that those who have yet to offend are said to enjoy the right 'to be presumed free of harmful intentions'.[45] Famously, Floud and Young argued that those who: 'have not yet committed any violent act have the right to assume that the State will take no preventive action against them; they are to be presumed free of whatever harmful intentions they may have'.[46] This presumption does not extend to the convicted offender 'since he has already manifested harmful intentions in his present conviction'.[47] Walker argues even more strongly that, 'someone who has harmed, or tried to harm, another person, can hardly claim a right to the presumption of harmlessness: he has forfeited that right, and given society the right to interfere in his life'.[48] His claim is that the harm someone has

---

[44] H Kemshall, 'Crime and Risk: Contested Territory for Risk Theorising', *International Journal of Law, Crime and Justice* 39(4) (2011), 218–29.

[45] J Floud and W Young, *Dangerousness and Criminal Justice* (London: Heinemann, 1981), 44; J Floud, 'Dangerousness and Criminal Justice', *British Journal of Criminology* 22 (1982), 213–28.

[46] In this quote, Bottoms and Brownsword paraphrase the views of Floud and Young. AE Bottoms and R Brownsword, 'The Dangerousness Debate after the Floud Report', *British Journal of Criminology* 22 (1982), 229–54; 236.

[47] Bottoms and Brownsword, 'The Dangerousness Debate after the Floud Report' (n 46), 236.

[48] N Walker, 'Ethical and Other Problems', in N Walker (ed.), *Dangerous People* (London: Blackstone, 1996), 1–12; 7. Note that whereas Floud speaks of the 'right to be presumed free of harmful intentions' in order to limit the discussion to intentional harms, Walker uses the term 'right to the presumption of harmlessness'.

caused 'is part of the moral justification for subjecting that person to a precautionary measure'.[49]

The claim that such right as we have to be presumed free of harmful intentions is forfeit on conviction is problematic. To say that an offender has 'already manifested harmful intentions in his present conviction' plays fast and loose with the concept of intention, which is not an enduring state of mind but specific to the time and circumstances in which it is formed. A past harmful intention in respect of a single circumstance or victim cannot simply be extended into the future. The claim also overlooks the obvious fact that intention is not required for all serious offences, some of which may be committed recklessly or even negligently. We have therefore discarded the notion of a right to be presumed free from harmful intentions in favour of referring to the presumption of harmlessness. In our view, insufficient attention has been paid to questions about the circumstances, type of crime, and level of seriousness at which the presumption should be foregone, especially given the potential adverse consequences of risk assessment for the individual.[50] These are not merely theoretical objections: they also have implications for the basis upon which a court should assess risk and determine what intervention or restraint may be imposed to avert it.

The relationship between the presumption of harmlessness and the presumption of innocence also merits scrutiny. Although the two are not synonymous, loss of the presumption of harmlessness has serious implications for the presumption of innocence, which is rightly considered to be a fundamental principle of criminal justice.[51] It requires that the prosecution prove all the elements of the offence with which the individual has been charged and that any defence or exception is unfounded before the presumption can be rebutted and an individual be found guilty. The core presumption that, in the absence of proof, one is to be deemed innocent of past offences has been subject to erosions and statutory reversals of the burden of proof, particularly in respect of excuses and exceptions.[52] However, it has also been strengthened by Article 6(2) of the European Convention on Human Rights which provides that: '[e]veryone charged with a criminal offence shall be presumed innocent until proved guilty according to law.' The nub of this is that each time one appears in the dock, and no matter how many previous convictions, one has the right to be presumed innocent of the present charges until proven otherwise.

---

[49] Walker, 'Ethical and Other Problems' (n 48), 7.

[50] Some of these questions are addressed in the Floud Report but for cogent criticism see Bottoms and Brownsword, 'The Dangerousness Debate after the Floud Report' (n 46).

[51] A Ashworth and M Blake, 'The Presumption of Innocence in English Criminal Law ', *Criminal Law Review* (1996), 306–17; V Tadros, 'Rethinking the Presumption of Innocence', *Criminal Law and Philosophy* 1 (2007), 193–213.

[52] A Ashworth, 'Four Threats to the Presumption of Innocence', *South African Law Journal* 123 (2006), 62–96.

Insofar as individual risk assessment makes a predictive claim about the probability of future wrongful conduct, it does damage to the values underpinning the presumption of innocence. There is, of course, a temporal distinction in that that presumption relates to crime past, the assessment of risk to crimes future. However, it can be said that every positive risk assessment constitutes a denial of the presumption of harmlessness and that this denial cannot easily be squared with the maintenance of the right to be presumed innocent of future crimes. On this view, to designate someone as posing a risk ahead of time is to undermine their right to be presumed innocent into the future. Famously, the Swedish Council for Crime Prevention claimed that sentencing upon the basis of risk assessment is tantamount to an individual serving 'a sentence for a crime he did not commit' and that the practice 'can be compared to the sentencing of an innocent person'.[53]

In sum, to accept the right of the criminal court to assess convicted offenders for future risk is not to downplay the hazards that risk assessment may entail for fundamental legal principles. Moreover, risk assessment may dictate interventions that extend well beyond proportionate punishment and this departure from desert stands in need of special justification (see Chapter 7). Having examined who is the rightful object of enquiry and explored some of the implications of risk assessment for basic rights, we now turn to the process itself—to ask whether present methods of assessment furnish a sufficiently reliable basis upon which to impose preventive sentences.

6.4 The Calculation of Risk

As we noted at the outset of this chapter, much preventive endeavour is predicated upon the contention that it is possible to calculate risk accurately. That contention has long been contested. In the early 1990s, Feeley and Simon raised concerns about 'actuarial justice', questioned the validity of risk-assessment tools, and warned of the consequences of deploying them in the criminal court.[54] Their warnings were very influential in academic circles and spawned a rich literature dedicated to exploring the perils of risk assessment as a tool of crime control.[55] They did little, however, to

---

[53] National Swedish Council for Crime Prevention, *A New Penal System* (1978) cited in Walker, 'Ethical and Other Problems' (n 48), 2.

[54] M Feeley and J Simon, 'The New Penology: Notes on the Emerging Strategy of Corrections and Its Implications', *Criminology* 30(4) (1992), 449–74; M Feeley and J Simon, 'Actuarial Justice: The Emerging New Criminal Law', in D Nelken (ed.), *The Futures of Criminology* (London: Sage, 1994), 173–201.

[55] For example, B Harcourt, *Against Prediction: Profiling, Policing, and Punishing in an Actuarial Age* (Chicago: University of Chicago Press, 2007); P O'Malley (ed.), *Crime and the Risk Society* (Aldershot: Ashgate, 1998); P O'Malley, *Risk, Uncertainty and Government* (London: The Glasshouse Press, 2004).

halt the development of ARAIs or hinder their spread and rapid entrenchment in the daily workings of the criminal court. Simon later adopted a rather more sanguine view of the capacity of ARAIs to predict risk accurately.[56] As enormous sums and intellectual resources are invested in the development of ever more sophisticated tools, Simon sees room for optimism in the fact that as risk assessment becomes more 'scientific', it is subject to the restraints self-imposed by scientific method. One important example is the $8 million MacArthur Violence Risk Assessment Study,[57] a sophisticated research study which sought 'to do the best "science" on violence risk assessment possible'.[58] The MacArthur Study undertook clinical trials to integrate the predictions made by several different risk-assessment models and, ultimately, generated new 'violence risk assessment software' that more reliably predicts violence.

Part of the improvement in risk assessment comes down to improvements in technology, part to a fundamental change in the claims being made for the tools. Recognition that dichotomous dangerous/not dangerous evaluations are problematic has led to the increasing use of assessments that instead measure whether an individual falls above a designated threshold for risk or that make probabilistic forecasts of future violence.[59] Probabilistic forecasts avoid the problem of false positives because they do not claim to foretell whether a given offender will or will not offend, but only to estimate a given population's propensity for violence. However, the problem is that probabilistic assessments continue to form the basis for dichotomous decisions within the court room, not least whether to impose a fixed term or an indeterminate and therefore potentially grossly disproportionate sentence. The ability to state with any confidence that there is a 40 per cent risk of future violence in a given population group is clearly better than no knowledge, but it is questionable whether it suffices to underwrite the decision to deprive an individual of liberty indefinitely. Furthermore, probabilistic assessments are impossible to refute since non-offending does not disprove the assessment because the claim is not that a given offender *will* offend but merely that there is a 40 per cent risk of someone with the offender's characteristics doing so.

No less problematic is Feeley and Simon's claim that the rise of the 'new penology'[60] entailed a shift from individual to aggregate determinations of risk and to the management of risky populations. Although the rise of mass surveillance

---

[56] J Simon, 'Reversal of Fortune: The Resurgence of Individual Risk Assessment in Criminal Justice', *Annual Review of Law and Social Science* 1 (2005), 397–421, esp. 411 ff.

[57] J Monahan, *Rethinking Risk Assessment: The Macarthur Study of Mental Disorder and Violence* (New York: Oxford University Press, 2001).

[58] See <http://www.macarthur.virginia.edu/risk.html>. See also J Monahan et al., 'An Actuarial Model of Violence Risk Assessment for Persons with Mental Disorders', *Psychiatric Services* 56 (2005), 810–15.

[59] Skeem and Monahan, 'Current Directions in Violence Risk Assessment' (n 11).

[60] Feeley and Simon, 'Actuarial Justice: The Emerging New Criminal Law' (n 54), 178.

and other aggregate risk measures partially bear out this claim, it remains the case that, in the dock of the criminal court, a lone individual is the singular object of risk assessment. ARAIs are tools with which to assess the probability that those who belong to a particular class or population will re-offend or pose a threat of future violence. The assessment is an aggregate one, which maintains that of population X, Y per cent will reoffend. Even in respect of their capacity to make this aggregate claim difficult methodological issues arise concerning the size of sample, the selection of the population, and the margin of error.[61] There are also serious questions about the impartiality of ARAIs, particularly when applied to members of minority populations for whom these standardized tools may fail to provide a reliable assessment.[62] More problematic still is the application of aggregate prediction tools to the individual. As Hart and colleagues observe, 'moving the focus of analysis from groups to individuals changes the way in which risk is conceptualised'.[63] Group risk assessments are predictive statements about the proportion of people within a given population who will offend: here the margin of error is uncertainty regarding that proportion. When applied to the individual, the question shifts to become one of how likely that *particular individual* is to reoffend. Hart and colleagues argued that 'the margin of error or uncertainty for an individual prediction is not the same as—and indeed, logically, must be considerably greater than—that for groups'.[64]

It is questionable whether one can distinguish between aggregate and individual risk assessment in this way because, as their critics were quick to point out, 'if all one knows about an individual is his membership of a risk group what can "individual risk" mean?'[65] In response Hart and colleagues suggested that individual risk is 'unknown or incalculable' and they concluded that ARAIs are not capable of making assessments about individual risk. Hanson and Howard challenge this conclusion and defend the predictive utility of actuarial tools,[66] as do Skeem and

[61]   SD Hart, C Michie, and DJ Cooke, 'Precision of Actuarial Risk Assessment Instruments: Evaluating the "Margins of Error" of Group v. Individual Predictions of Violence', *Journal of Psychiatry* 190 (2007), 60–5.

[62]   EEH Griffith, 'Ethics in Forensic Psychiatry: A Cultural Response to Stone and Appelbaum', *Journal of the American Academy of Psychiatry and the Law* 26 (1997), 171–84. This is a particular problem in the US, where the Constitution prohibits the inclusion of race as a variable in risk assessment instruments.

[63]   Hart, Michie, and Cooke, 'Precision of Actuarial Risk Assessment Instruments: Evaluating the "Margins of Error" of Group V. Individual Predictions of Violence' (n 61), 61. See also Peay, 'Mentally Disordered Offenders, Mental Health and Crime' (n 40), 444.

[64]   Hart et al., 'Precision of Actuarial Risk Assessment Instruments' (n 61), 61.

[65]   D Mossman and T Sellke, 'Avoiding Errors About "Margins of Error"', *British Journal of Psychiatry* 191 (2007), 561–2, 561. See also GT Harris, ME Rice, and VL Quinsey, 'Shall Evidence-Based Risk Assessment Be Abandoned?', *The British Journal of Psychiatry* 192 (2008), 154.

[66]   RK Hanson and P Howard, 'Individual Confidence Intervals Do Not Inform Decision-Makers About the Accuracy of Risk Assessment Evaluations', *Law and Human Behaviour* 34(4) (2010), 275–81.

Monahan who point to the ubiquitous, effective use made of actuarial data to set individual premia by the insurance industry.[67] Yet, Cooke and Michie suggest that life insurance is 'a false analogue for violence risk assessment' on the grounds:

> The life insurance actuary achieves a profit by predicting the *proportion* of insured lives that will end within a particular time period. The actuary has no interest in predicting the deaths of particular individuals and recognizes the impossibility of doing so. By way of contrast, the decision-maker in court is only interested in the accused in front of him or her, not the properties of any statistical group from which the accused may be derived.[68]

These objections demonstrate the extremely contested character of current prediction tools, yet these disagreements do not seem to limit the reliance placed upon them in determining sentences in practice.

Another contentious issue is whether and to what extent risk assessment can or should be regarded as separable from risk management. If one goal of risk assessment is to calculate the likelihood of future violence, another is to assess risk with a view to treatment. In the latter case it makes sense to incorporate treatment-related variables, but, obviously, these add value only if they are followed by risk-reductive treatment.[69] So a further complication is the issue of resources: to the extent that the validity of the assessment is predicated upon subsequent treatment, that validity is radically undermined if treatment is not forthcoming (on which issue, see further Chapter 7). It should by now be clear that almost every aspect of risk assessment is contentious. Perhaps the key issue is whether, all things considered, ARAIs should be regarded as providing data that makes it possible to 'help us make better decisions that we otherwise could'[70] or whether the aggregate basis upon which ARAIs calculate risk render it indefensible to apply them to individuals. The key issue is surely that while a 'better decision' is desirable, it still may not suffice to justify the deprivation of liberty.

6.5 The Role of Expert Witnesses in Court

Although much of the risk literature presumes the dominance of ARAIs as technical tools of risk knowledge,[71] professional experts retain a key role in interpreting

---

[67] Skeem and Monahan, 'Current Directions in Violence Risk Assessment' (n 11); Ericson, 'Ten Uncertainties of Risk-Management Approaches to Security' (n 11).

[68] Cooke and Michie, 'Violence Risk Assessment: Challenging the Illusion of Certainty' (n 12), 154.

[69] K Heilbrun, 'Prediction Versus Management Models Relevant to Risk Assessment: The Importance of Legal Decision-Making Context', *Law and Human Behaviour* 21 (1997), 347–59.

[70] Mossman and Sellke, 'Avoiding Errors About "Margins of Error"' (n 65), 561.

[71] Harcourt, *Against Prediction: Profiling, Policing, and Punishing in an Actuarial Age* (n 55), 32; Skeem and Monahan, 'Current Directions in Violence Risk Assessment' (n 11).

actuarial data for the criminal court.[72] In respect of policing and community crime prevention, much risk assessment is carried out by multi-agency teams that combine a variety of criminal justice expertise and rely upon semi-structured prediction tools that frame, but do not dictate, decision-making.[73] Similarly, those making risk assessments to inform sentencing do not mechanically apply the data generated by the ARAIs; rather they interpret them using their professional judgement and experience.[74] In the criminal court, ARAIs are commonly interpreted by probation officers—whether or not they have the statistical expertise to interpret this complex data is subject to little scrutiny. Given the close correlation between mental illness and dangerousness, psychologists and forensic psychiatrists also play a key role as expert witnesses called upon by the court to offer authoritative determinations as to the threat posed by putatively dangerous offenders.[75] Recent academic debates in criminal law and criminology have focused almost entirely on the challenges of actuarial justice[76] and have paid little heed to the continuing importance of clinical experts in court.[77] Parallel debates in psychiatry about the dilemmas posed by the making of clinical determinations of risk in the criminal court[78] and the moral and jurisprudential issues they raise have largely escaped wider notice.

---

[72] B Hebenton and T Seddon, 'From Dangerousness to Precaution: Managing Sexual and Violent Offenders in an Insecure and Uncertain Age', *British Journal of Criminology* 49 (2009), 343–62; 351.

[73] Kemshall and Maguire found that use of these tools 'did not imply slavish acceptance of the outcomes'. H Kemshall and M Maguire, 'Public Protection, Partnership and Risk Penality: The Multi-Agency Risk Management of Sexual and Violent Offenders', *Punishment and Society* 3(2) (2001), 237–64; 248.

[74] So much so that Ansbro observes 'it is somewhat artificial to see actuarial and clinical information as mutually exclusive'. M Ansbro, 'The Nuts and Bolt of Risk Assessment: When the Clinical and Actuarial Conflict', *The Howard Journal of Criminal Justice* 49(3) (2010), 252–68; 254.

[75] McLeod, Sweeting, and Evans, *Improving the Structure and Content of Psychiatric Reports for Sentencing: Research to Develop Good Practice Guidance* (n 19), 23.

[76] M Feeley, 'Actuarial Justice and the Modern State', in G Bruinsma, H Elffers, and J De Keijser (eds.), *Punishment, Places, and Perpetrators: Developments in Criminology and Criminal Justice Research* (Devon, Cullompton: Willan Publishing, 2004), 62–77; B Harcourt, 'The Shaping of Chance: Actuarial Models and Criminal Profiling at the Turn of the Twenty-First Century', *The University of Chicago Law Review* 70 (2003), 105–28; Harcourt, *Against Prediction: Profiling, Policing, and Punishing in an Actuarial Age* (n 55); Wandall, 'Actuarial Risk Assessment. The Loss of Recognition of the Individual Offender' (n 17).

[77] This is so despite the fact that the Law Commission has publically voiced its concerns about the validity of expert evidence and about the ability of judges, advocates, and jurors to appreciate its limitations. The Law Commission, *The Admissibility of Expert Evidence in Criminal Proceedings in England and Wales* (London: The Law Commission, 2009). This Consultation Paper proposes a new statutory admissibility test for the reliability of expert evidence to be applied by the judiciary.

[78] For an overview, see N Eastman, 'The Psychiatrist, Courts and Sentencing: The Impact of Extended Sentencing on the Ethical Framework of Forensic Psychiatry', *The Psychiatrist* 29 (2005), 73–7; A Stone, 'The Ethical Boundaries of Forensic Psychiatry: A View from the Ivory Tower', *Journal of the American Academy of Psychiatry and the Law* 36(2) (2008), 167–74. (Reprint of a seminal article first published in 1984.)

Despite the fact that their validity is fiercely debated within the psychiatric profession, risk assessments are often presented to the court as unassailable scientific evidence. Psychiatrists are called as expert witnesses and their medical qualifications, experience, and skills are routinely recounted by barristers ahead of their cross-examination to affirm the scientific standing of their testimony. Like other witnesses, psychiatric experts are called upon to tell the truth but what constitutes truth here is of a different order than the recollections of a witness about a past event. Instead, it is a complex and often highly contested reading of actuarial and clinical data that makes claims about future conduct that is as yet unknowable. Although criminal liability for past offences is attributable only when the court is satisfied beyond reasonable doubt, the ability of ARAIs to predict future risk is, as we have seen, much less certain. Despite the growing sophistication of actuarial tools, there are continuing heated and often acrimonious debates within the psychiatric profession about what reliance can be placed upon them, especially where they are used to license extended or indeterminate detention.[79]

A recurring focus of psychiatric debate is whether prediction meets the criteria of scientific validity or whether it rather expresses professional value judgements about what ought to result.[80] Risk assessments in the criminal court are not merely abstract statements of probability but made in full knowledge of their consequences for individual liberty. Clinicians recognize that predictive risk assessments sit uneasily with the legal presumption of individual responsibility and that, to the extent that ARAIs deal in the aggregate probabilities of risky behaviour by cohorts of offenders, they do not treat each individual as morally autonomous.[81] Some claim that expert testimony is not predictive but merely descriptive; others deny that free will is a necessary condition of legal responsibility.[82] Despite these claims, the danger remains that risk assessment entails a degree of determinism injurious to individual moral autonomy and the right to be author of one's fate in a manner consistent with a liberal legal order.[83]

Psychiatrists also vigorously debate the ethical dilemmas that arise from the conflict between the duties owed to patients and to the court. The role of the

---

[79] Hart, Michie, and Cooke, 'Precision of Actuarial Risk Assessment Instruments: Evaluating the "Margins of Error" of Group V. Individual Predictions of Violence' (n 61), 154; A Buchanan, 'Risk of Violence by Psychiatric Patients: Beyond the "Actuarial Versus Clinical" Assessment Debate', *Psychiatric Services* 59(2) (2008), 184–90.

[80] N Eastman, 'Public Health Psychiatry or Crime Prevention', *British Medical Journal* 318 (1999), 549–51. Eastman, 'The Psychiatrist, Courts and Sentencing: The Impact of Extended Sentencing on the Ethical Framework of Forensic Psychiatry' (n 78).

[81] Wandall, 'Actuarial Risk Assessment. The Loss of Recognition of the Individual Offender' (n 17).

[82] S Morse, 'The Non-Problem of Free Will in Forensic Psychiatry and Psychology', *Behavioral Sciences & the Law* 25 (2007), 203–20.

[83] A Brudner, *Punishment and Freedom: A Liberal Theory of Penal Justice* (Oxford: Oxford University Press, 2009),140 ff.

psychiatrist as physician is ordinarily to act in the best interests of the patient by pursuing the optimal therapeutic outcome. However, where forensic psychiatrists are called upon as expert witnesses, they fulfil a dual role—as physician to their patients and as advisor to a court engaged in upholding the public interest in protection. An irresolvable tension thus arises between their medical and their court expert roles, generating dilemmas with serious implications for their testimony. On the one hand, psychiatrists recognize the danger that they may be tempted to conceal or twist data in a bid to serve the best interests of their patient, for example to ensure a welfare- or treatment-based disposal rather than a punitive or incapacitative one. On the other, they worry that their duty to the court and the interests of justice may incline them to offer assessments that do not fulfil the duty to promote the best interests of their patient. Putting truth or justice before patient welfare raises a conflict of interests between their obligations to law and to medicine. Broadly, one camp argues that testifying in court entails taking 'a grave moral risk';[84] the other that presenting evidence in court is a primary task of the forensic psychiatrist, governed by a different ethic based not on beneficence but on truth-telling.[85] At the risk of over-generalization, it seems that American psychiatrists are more at ease in their 'forensic' role, seeing themselves first and foremost as servants of the court to whom obligations are owed over and above individual patient welfare.[86] By contrast, British psychiatrists generally appear more conflicted about the tension between their professional training and self-identification as doctors devoted to patient welfare and the opposing demands placed on them as expert witnesses, particularly where long-term or indefinite incarceration is in view. Gunn puts it simply: 'I find it very difficult to understand how a doctor can stop being a doctor.'[87] For those who see themselves first and foremost as doctors, being called as an expert in court required to act in the interests of justice or public protection sits very uneasily with their clinical role and therapeutic obligations.

These conflicted loyalties stand behind and inform clinical interpretation of the ARAI results, the reports written by expert witnesses, and the answers they give under cross-examination. A clinician who is persuaded that his or her patient's best interests would not be served by long-term incarceration may feel a strong pressure to down play indicators of future dangerousness. Equally, clinicians whose primary loyalty is to the court may find themselves acting as double agents, gleaning information from patients only to use it against them in court. This uncomfortable

---

[84]   GH Miller, 'Alan Stone and the Ethics of Forensic Psychiatry: An Overview', *Journal of the American Academy of Psychiatry and the Law* 36(2) (2008), 191–4; 191.

[85]   PS Appelbaum, 'Psychiatric Ethics in the Courtroom', *Bulletin of the American Academy of Psychiatry and Law* 12(3) (1984), 225–31.

[86]   Eastman, 'The Psychiatrist, Courts and Sentencing: The Impact of Extended Sentencing on the Ethical Framework of Forensic Psychiatry' (n 78), 75.

[87]   J Gunn, 'Future Directions for Treatment in Forensic Psychiatry', *British Journal of Psychiatry* 176 (2000), 332–8; 337.

situation is only partially assuaged by making clear to patients the nature of the expert witnesses' obligations to the court.[88] Some psychiatrists even refuse to examine defendants in person ahead of appearing in court in order to avoid creating a doctor–patient relationship. They seek thereby to minimize possible conflicts of interest by generating no false expectations and engaging in no deception to *their* patient.[89] In resolving one problem this device only creates another: namely how much reliance can be placed upon a risk assessment made remotely. No less fraught is the conflict that arises between individual patient welfare and the larger public health interest in protection from violent attack or other harm. Even those psychiatrists who have no difficulty in privileging their medical over their forensic obligations find themselves torn by the divergent interests of individual versus public welfare.[90] The ethical duty of care to the individual is here challenged by the countervailing duty of care to the health and well-being of the public at large.

Precisely because psychiatrists are called as expert witnesses and their testimony is privileged as the telling of a scientific truth that is independent and impartial, they may be seen as a quasi-inquisitorial intrusion on the adversarial process. Although there is little reason to doubt that those called upon to testify as experts tell the truth such as they honestly believe it to be, the effect of being designated as experts risks placing their testimony beyond challenge. Much is made in court of their professional or medical credentials and the validity of the ARAIs upon which they draw, so it is little wonder that the impartial authority of their risk assessment comes to be accepted uncritically. An equally important, but again largely unasked, question is how well equipped lawyers and law courts are to assess and judge the validity of scientific evidence. Unless they are equally well versed in the intricacies of statistical inference and psychiatric diagnosis, lawyers may lack the expertise to challenge expert evidence, to test claims as to scientific validity or statistical significance, or to challenge a psychiatric diagnosis of pathology so as to provoke jurors to question its apparent unassailability. Instead, the criminal court seems to take the claims of science on trust, even as psychiatrists question the scientific status of their discipline and their diagnoses, as they dispute the reliability of ARAIs, and as they publicly debate their role and even their competence as expert witnesses. One possible improvement is the calling of expert witnesses for both sides in the hope that this may render their respective allegiances transparent and diminish the conflicts of interest in play. However, use of partisan expert witnesses introduces the further

---

[88] See the differences of opinion between: Stone, 'The Ethical Boundaries of Forensic Psychiatry: A View from the Ivory Tower' (n 78); PS Appelbaum, 'Ethics and Forensic Psychiatry: Translating Principles into Practice', *Journal of the American Academy of Psychiatry and the Law* 36 (2008), 195–200.

[89] Stone, 'The Ethical Boundaries of Forensic Psychiatry: A View from the Ivory Tower' (n 78), 172.

[90] Eastman, 'Public Health Psychiatry or Crime Prevention' (n 80).

difficulty that, in fulfilment of their partisan role, witnesses make one-sided assessments whose partiality is obscured by pretensions to scientific reliability and truth-telling.

Greater awareness among criminal lawyers of these dilemmas would alert the court to the contested status of ARAIs and difficulties of interpreting their data that are already so hotly debated within the psychiatric profession.[91] Inviting experts for each side to comment upon the validity of the other's testimony might help to expose the limits and uncertainties inherent in their respective assessments. And yet a lack of authoritative determination by the experts brings new dangers: creating a power vacuum that others may be quick to fill. Take, for example, the 'Dangerous and Severe Personality Disorder' (DSPD), a label that is contested in medical circles but that has been adopted as a basis for underwriting preventive detention policies.[92] As Gunn observes, '[p]sychiatry is confused and illogical in its approach to the concepts embodied under the broad umbrella of personality disorder' and he speculates whether the profession's 'philosophical muddle about terminology and the concepts behind the terminology handed politicians new devices for social control?'[93] Despite a woeful lack of clarity about what DSPD might mean, how it is to be identified, how it might be treated, or if it is treatable, this construction, bolstered by public concern about dangerous offenders, has been central to legislative developments like the introduction of Imprisonment for Public Protection. IPP permitted the imposition of thousands of indeterminate sentences and had a very significant impact on the overall size of the prison population (see further Chapter 7). Yet, as Peay observes of DSPD, 'there is no agreed definition, no clear diagnosis, no agreed treatment, no means of assessing when the predicted risk may have been reduced'.[94]

If psychiatrists are concerned about the ways in which their assessments of risk feed into determinations by the court, practising lawyers are also becoming uneasy about what use they should make of ARAIs and of expert analysis alike. In its damning report on IPP, the Prison Reform Trust cites legal respondents who describe actuarial determinations of risk as 'formulaic', 'mechanistic', and 'sausage-machine-ish', it decries the practice of 'trying to make statistical something that is actually a guess', and deplores the fact that the courts are not helped 'in their difficult task by tick-box assessments'.[95] The Prison Reform Trust has little more faith in the

---

[91] For example, research that suggests practitioners find it easier to override a low ARAI score than to override a high one. Ansbro, 'The Nuts and Bolt of Risk Assessment: When the Clinical and Actuarial Conflict' (n 74), 266.

[92] T Seddon, 'Dangerous Liaisons: Personality Disorder and the Politics of Risk', *Theoretical Criminology* 10 (2008), 301–17. See also Section 9.4.

[93] Gunn, 'Future Directions for Treatment in Forensic Psychiatry' (n 87), 336.

[94] Peay, 'Mentally Disordered Offenders, Mental Health and Crime' (n 40), 443.

[95] Prison Reform Trust, *Unjust Deserts: Imprisonment for Public Protection* (n 25), 25–7.

'quasi-scientific' claims made upon the basis of 'necessarily subjective judgment' by clinicians.[96] And yet, running seamlessly alongside this scepticism and anxiety, is the enormous and terrifying confidence evinced by judges about their own ability to assess risk.[97] By way of illustration, take just a few of the responses made by judges to the Prison Reform Trust:

> 'You kind of know instinctively if someone is dangerous or not ... Follow your instincts—they're probably right.'
>
> 'Usually it's overwhelming that an offender is dangerous. I only pass [an IPP] if I'm absolutely 100 per cent sure, and usually they stare out at you.'
>
> 'I don't think I've found any difficulties [in assessing risk]. ... You have to have that comforting belief in your abilities if you're going to be a judge, don't you!'
>
> '[Risk assessment] is an instinctive thing. ... It's a value judgment, isn't it, and the decision is as good as the person making the value judgment.'
>
> 'There are some people, particularly after a trial and you've watched them in the witness box, and you've seen the person and felt the presence—and you know.'[98]

Quite possibly the English case is singular. In Scotland, for example, the Risk Management Authority set up in 2005 is charged with ensuring robust and effective risk-assessment and risk-management practices.[99] These include the accreditation of risk assessors to carry out duties on behalf of the High Court and many measures that seek to improve the scientific validity of assessment. However, the above quotations surely call into question Simon's optimistic view that '[t]oday, risk assessment has established a new scientific paradigm that is in a position to reshape much of practice'.[100] No matter how scientific the tools and the data they produce—and this remains a contested issue—the role of human agency in using and applying them continues to call into question whether they provide a sufficiently robust basis for extending deprivations of liberty on grounds of prevention.

---

[96] Prison Reform Trust, *Unjust Deserts: Imprisonment for Public Protection* (n 25), 25–7.

[97] The extent of judicial licence to determine risk was made clear in the national guide for IPP, issued by the National Offender Management Service (NOMS) in June 2005, which stated: 'it will ultimately be a matter for the court how they form their opinion of risk'. Criminal Justice Joint Inspections *Indeterminate Sentences for Public Protection: A Joint Inspection by HMI Probation and HMI Prisons* (2010) <www.justice.gov.uk/downloads/publications/inspectorate-reports/hmiprobation/joint-thematic/IPP_report_final_2-rps.pdf>.

[98] Prison Reform Trust, *Unjust Deserts: Imprisonment for Public Protection* (n 25), 29. For a careful analysis of the proper extent of the judicial role concerning risk assessment, see M Wasik, 'The Test for Dangerousness', in GR Sullivan and I Dennis (eds.), *Seeking Security: Pre-Empting the Commission of Criminal Harms* (Oxford: Hart Publishing, 2012), 243–64.

[99] See <http://www.rmascotland.gov.uk/about-the-rma/>.

[100] Simon, 'Reversal of Fortune: The Resurgence of Individual Risk Assessment in Criminal Justice' (n 56), 417.

6.6 Conclusions

Individualization is a hallmark of the criminal justice system. It dictates that legal institutions show respect for the individual offender, which in turn requires that offenders are treated as morally autonomous beings whose independence and dignity calls for a distinct and appropriate response, and that they should not be treated as objects of an aggregate policy or collective decision-making. This chapter has explored whether the use of ARAIs is consistent with respect for individual autonomy. It has considered the idea of a presumption of harmlessness and has asked whether and under what conditions that presumption might be rebutted. To allow that the presumption is rebuttable in cases of significant risk only raises questions about what constitutes a significant risk, if it can safely be determined, and if so how, by whom, at what level of probability, and in respect of what gravity of harms? It has been suggested that more finely graded conceptions of risk would ensure that measures taken are proportionate to the likelihood, as well as to the gravity, of the prospective risk and that closer attention needs to be given to the appropriate relationship between gravity and likelihood to allow that the more serious the prospective harm the lower the probability requirement might be.

This chapter has also pointed out some difficulties entailed in determining who or what the subjects of risk assessment are. It has explored some hazards entailed in using actuarial data, focusing on questions of interpretation and the problems they throw up, particularly for clinicians. This in turn has raised difficult questions about the role of expert witnesses and the status of clinical judgement in the criminal court. At the heart of these lie heated debates in forensic psychiatry about what it is possible to learn about risk from ARAIs and, in particular, whether an assessment of individual risk can safely be derived from aggregate data relating to populations. Although there is much more to be said about questions of validity, confidence intervals, and margins of error, quite enough has been said here to make worryingly clear that risk tools, risk data, and their interpretation are so contested as to render judgments based upon them a source of concern. The government admitted as much when it observed: 'The limitations in our ability to predict future serious offending also calls into question the whole basis on which many offenders are sentenced to IPPs and, among those who are already serving these sentences, which of them are suitable for release.'[101] This recognition of our limited ability to predict risk signalled the death knell of the IPP. It also suggests a more general need for restraint in recourse to any coercive preventive measure that is predicated upon the questionable assumption that it possible to foresee accurately who poses a risk and who does not. At the close of Chapter 7 we suggest some limiting principles for

---

[101] Ministry of Justice, *Breaking the Cycle: Effective Punishment, Rehabilitation and Sentencing of Offenders* Cm 7972 (London: Ministry of Justice, 2010), 55.

application to risk assessment made in respect of preventive detention. The question remains, however, whether in respect of potentially catastrophic or irreversible harms, the rationale behind the precautionary principle, namely that uncertainty should not be a ground for inaction, should tilt decision-making in the opposite direction (a question about which we have more to say in Chapter 8).

7

Preventive Detention of the Dangerous

> Certainly the prisoner who after serving a three-year sentence is told that his punishment is over but that a seven-year period of preventive detention awaits him and that this is a 'measure' of social protection, not a punishment, might think he was being tormented by a barren piece of conceptualism—though he might not express himself in that way.[1]

Many states have powers to detain those deemed dangerous, that is, thought to pose a risk of serious harm to the public or themselves. Dangerousness is, of course, a social and cultural construct whose meaning varies over time and by jurisdiction.[2] Preventive detention is also an umbrella term: detention may occur ahead of proven wrongdoing; beyond the period of proportionate punishment; or in parallel systems of civil commitment.[3] Pre-trial detention; extended or indefinite sentences of imprisonment on grounds of public protection; and post-sentence detention provisions for those considered too dangerous to release all come within its remit. Preventive detention is also pursued in other domains such as national security, public health, and immigration, and these will be considered separately in Chapters 8, 9, and 10. Pre-trial detention has already been discussed in Chapter 3. The present chapter focuses on provisions for the detention of those reckoned to pose an immediate threat of criminal wrongdoing or risk of future harm to others so serious as to necessitate incarceration.

In Chapter 1 we examined what distinguishes prevention from punishment; whether particular measures are better conceived as preventive or punitive; and what may follow from these distinctions. These issues are not merely a matter of academic debate: they inform decisions about the preconditions, parameters, and purposes of preventive detention, as well as the legal protections owed to those

---

[1] HLA Hart, *Punishment and Responsibility* (Oxford: Oxford University Press, 1968), 166–7.
[2] M Brown and J Pratt (eds.), *Dangerous Offenders: Punishment and Social Order* (London: Routledge, 2000). See especially Part I 'Dangerousness: a sociological history'.
[3] Several types of preventive detention are explored in B McSherry and P Keyzer, *Sex Offenders and Preventive Detention: Politics, Policy and Practice* (Sydney: Federation Press, 2009).

detained.[4] Analysing the very different ways in which these issues are resolved in different domains, and also in different jurisdictions, reveals the varied and contingent nature of preventive detention and its legally contested character. Examination of the arrangements for and practices of preventive detention makes clear significant differences in structure and practice; for example, proceedings may be pursued in civil or criminal channels and, if criminal, can be imposed at the time of sentencing, as occurs in the UK, or post-sentence as in Australia. Whether preventive detention is indefinite or finite, and, if finite, whether it is renewable or not, are also important variants in its exercise. No less important are questions concerning the institutional conditions under which detention is imposed and the procedural protections attached. An issue of particular importance is the availability of risk-reduction programmes and these have been identified as a prerequisite of preventive detention regimes by the Strasbourg Court.[5]

Preventive detention constitutes one of the most coercive powers that the liberal state can exert over the individual so its exercise calls for close attention to its underlying justifications. Section 7.1 asks upon what grounds preventive detention is justly imposed, on whom, and in what circumstances. Section 7.2 examines the different practices and conditions of detention. Section 7.3 examines sentences of preventive detention, while Section 7.4 looks at post-sentence civil commitment— and both sections consider the limits that apply and protections that should be afforded to those detained. Section 7.5 examines the purported ends of preventive detention to determine if they could be pursued in other, less liberty-depriving ways and it suggests some principles that might guide and restrain its practice.

7.1 Justifying Preventive Detention

The right to liberty and security is assured by many national and supranational human rights instruments. Yet all these instruments specify exceptions. As we observed in Chapter 3, Article 5 ECHR declares the right to liberty of the person but permits detention post-conviction; following lawful arrest or non-compliance with the lawful order of a court; in order to bring an individual before a court; or when it is reasonably considered necessary to prevent an individual from committing an offence or fleeing after having done so.[6] The breadth of these exceptions raises questions about what justifies such substantial deprivations of

---

[4] See the sophisticated discussion in RL Lippke, 'No Easy Way Out: Dangerous Offenders and Preventive Detention', *Law and Philosophy* 27(4) (2008), 383–414.

[5] *James, Wells and Lee v United Kingdom* (2013) 56 EHRR 399. See also K Drenkhahn, C Morgenstern, and D van Zyl Smit, 'Preventive Detention in Germany in the Shadow of European Human Rights Law', *Criminal Law Review* (2012), 167–87; 177.

[6] In addition, special provisions under Article 5 permit detention 'for the prevention of the spreading of infectious diseases, of persons of unsound mind, alcoholics or drug addicts or

liberty and whether and to what extent the state is warranted in imposing detention preventively.

As noted in Chapter 1, punishment self-evidently requires justification because it entails the deliberate infliction by the state of hard treatment upon the individual. Although preventive detention imposes all the deprivations of confinement, often under the most restrictive conditions within high-security environments, it is often justified by no more than passing reference to a poorly articulated claim that the general public has a right to protection.[7] It was also established in Chapter 1 that the duty to protect falls principally upon the state. What the exercise of this duty entails in practice raises questions about when preventive confinement is required in the name of public protection, on what evidential bases, at what cost, and to whom it should be applied. These and other questions have been the subject of much academic discussion and of deliberation by the courts, where the extent of the state's duty to protect the public by resorting to preventive detention and the rights of those consequently detained have been contested.[8] Central to these deliberations is the question of what positive obligations the state has to protect life under Article 2 ECHR. In the important case of *van Colle*, the ECtHR reaffirmed the test set out in *Osman*,[9] namely that there will be a breach of the positive obligation if the authorities knew or ought to have known at the time of the existence of a real and immediate risk to the life of an identified individual or individuals from the criminal acts of a third party and if they failed to take measures within the scope of their powers which, judged reasonably, might have been expected to avoid that risk. However, in *van Colle*—a case in which a witness, Giles van Colle, was tragically murdered by the man against whom he was due to give evidence in a criminal trial—it was held that there was no point at which the police knew or ought to have known that a real and immediate risk to van Colle's life existed. Although the scope of the general duty set out in *Osman* is potentially wide, the Strasbourg jurisprudence has sought to ensure that positive duties to protect imposed upon the state are clearly identified and narrowly delimited.[10]

vagrants' and to prevent unauthorized entry into the country or in respect of deportation or extradition. For further discussion, see Chs 9 and 10.

[7] This, of course, begs the question of who are the public for the purposes of protection and whether the public extends to those behind the prison walls, what degree of protection is owed to other detainees and to prison employees, and at what cost.

[8] See the discussion in L Lazarus, 'Positive Obligations and Criminal Justice: Duties to Protect or Coerce?', in L Zedner and JV Roberts (eds.), *Principles and Values in Criminal Law and Criminal Justice: Essays in Honour of Andrew Ashworth* (Oxford: Oxford University Press, 2012), 135–55; A Ashworth, *Positive Obligations in the Criminal Law* (Oxford: Hart Publishing, 2013), Ch. 8.

[9] *Van Colle v United Kingdom* (2012) (Application No. 7678/09) citing *Osman v United Kingdom* (1998) 29 EHRR 245.

[10] Lazarus, 'Positive Obligations and Criminal Justice: Duties to Protect or Coerce?' (n 8), 139.

It is also the case that pursuit of protection through the engine of detention stands in direct tension with other goods, not least liberty of the person and freedom of movement and of choice. Its provision by the state is hugely expensive and competes directly for limited funding for education, health, welfare, and employment. In what follows we consider the circumstances in which preventive detention might be warranted, the grounds upon and conditions under which it is legitimately imposed, as well as the limits to state power to detain.

If preventive detention were a preventive measure *tout court*, logically all members of society would be legitimate subjects of detention if it could be proven that they posed a sufficient risk. But, as we observed in Chapter 6, we do not engage in universal screening for risk in this way. Even where there are good grounds to anticipate that an individual poses a danger, preventive detention is not generally available. Instead, scrutiny with a view to detention is restricted to specific groups such as serious offenders, the mentally disordered, those with dangerous contagious diseases, and unlawful migrant status (these groups will be discussed in subsequent chapters). Mass detention on grounds of security has been tolerated in liberal states only in times of exceptional danger and, even then, it has rightly attracted critical scrutiny.[11]

In Chapter 6 we discussed the presumption of harmlessness—that those who have not yet been convicted of any violent act have the right to assume that the state will take no preventive action against them. In practice, the presumption is readily dispensed with in high-risk locales or at times of heightened security. Mass screening of airline passengers, for example, places all travellers under scrutiny and subjects them to intrusive searches of property and person. The crossing of borders and entry to high-security locations commonly entails restrictions on conduct, communication, and the freedom to carry specified categories of goods. It is clear, therefore, that the presumption of harmlessness is conditional, and, in any case, apt to be curtailed on grounds of security. Indeed, the very existence of civil preventive orders, discussed in Chapter 4, relies upon a willingness to assess and label people as risky or anti-social or dangerous ahead of criminal wrongdoing that signifies a very significant attenuation of this presumption. As we saw in Chapter 2, this is hardly a new phenomenon.[12]

To the extent that individuals enjoy a presumption of harmlessness, this is contingent on not posing a threat sufficient to vitiate the presumption. Those who become defendants in the criminal process join a suspect population, in respect of whom further enquiries as to future risk are considered warranted. While the

---

[11] AWB Simpson, *In the Highest Degree Odious: Detention without Trial in Wartime Britain* (Oxford: Oxford University Press, 1992); D Rose, *Guantanamo: America's War on Human Rights* (London: Faber & Faber, 2004).

[12] See also E Janus, 'The Preventive State, Terrorists and Sexual Predators: Countering the Threat of a New Outsider Jurisprudence', *Criminal Law Bulletin* 40 (2004), 576–98.

criminal case against the defendant provides *prima facie* grounds for questioning their future intentions, such enquiry sits ill with the presumption of innocence. Moreover, it is unclear why the state should bear any greater liability for the actions of a criminal defendant than it does for other members of the population, unless it can be said that the fact of prosecution places the state on notice (on which see Section 3.4). Certainly, in practice, if an individual subject to criminal proceedings goes on to commit a serious offence, state officials may be regarded as negligent for failing to identify and avert the risk posed to the public. How negligent and what criticisms officials may face depends upon on the gravity of the criminal charge, the defendant's prior record, and his or her compliance with previous court orders. Together these may suggest a risk profile sufficient to warrant further enquiry, which in turn informs the decision to bail or remand.

As regards the convicted offender, we noted in the previous chapter that the Floud Report concluded that conviction for a serious violent crime proves the offender's moral capacity for criminal wrongdoing such that thereafter the state is justified in enquiring into the risk posed.[13] In that chapter we suggested that proof of a harmful intention in respect of a past offence cannot safely be said to evidence a continuing disposition to wrongdoing in the future. An alternative approach is suggested by Walen who contends that convicted offenders 'have, at least for a while, lost the moral basis for claiming the right to benefit from the respect that grounds the immunity to LTPD' (long-term preventive detention).[14] He argues that whereas the state ought normally to accord its citizens the presumption that they will be law-abiding 'as a matter of basic respect for their autonomous moral agency',[15] conviction for a very serious crime or string of serious crimes demonstrates 'that they do not deserve the presumption that they will be law-abiding'.[16] Yet, here too, it is unclear for what period this loss of status should persist or how it might be regained. Walen avers that his approach preserves the presumption of innocence in respect of future charges and thus avoids vulnerability to undeserved punishment, though his claim relies upon the ability and willingness of the courts to observe this fine distinction in practice. It relies also on acceptance of the claim that preventive detention is not punishment because it is not intended by the court as such and does not express censure for wrongs done (of which more below).[17]

---

[13] J Floud and W Young, *Dangerousness and Criminal Justice* (London: Heinemann, 1981), 44.

[14] A Walen, 'A Punitive Precondition for Preventive Detention: Lost Status as a Foundation for a Lost Immunity', *San Diego Law Review* 48 (2011), 1229–72; 1231.

[15] Walen, 'A Punitive Precondition for Preventive Detention' (n 14), 1230–1.

[16] Walen, 'A Punitive Precondition for Preventive Detention' (n 14), 1231.

[17] As it was held in respect of pre-trial detention in the leading case, *U.S. v Salerno and Cafaro* (1987) 481 U.S. 739 at 746–7, discussed in Section 3.4. Reference to legislative intent may be central to the distinction between punishment and regulation in the US but the Strasbourg Court has insisted that legislative labels alone are not determinative of whether a measure is in substance criminal or not, *Engel v Netherlands* (1979) 1 EHRR 647.

Even if we accept that conviction changes the status of the individual, this nonetheless leaves open the issue of whether conviction for any offence suffices to justify formal risk assessment with a view to preventive detention. While conviction for a serious sexual or violent offence provides *prima facie* grounds for risk assessment, it is debatable whether conviction for lesser offences should suffice. On one view an enquiry into dangerousness should be allowed only where the circumstances, type of crime, and level of seriousness are such as to justify it.[18] Conviction for a minor, non-violent offence should not ground further intervention. An alternate view is that even if the predicate offence is minor, should it or the circumstances surrounding it indicate a serious risk, then the conviction ought to be regarded as sufficient to ground a risk assessment. The fact of conviction, combined with an assessment that indicates a more serious risk, might be said to place the state on notice of a potential threat, such that it may no longer claim to be unaware of the danger posed. However, even if a significant risk of future danger can be established, conviction for a less serious crime poses justificatory difficulties since a period of preventive detention is likely to be disproportionate to the predicate offence. It follows that the post-tariff preventive part of the sentence calls for separate and stronger justification.

Another issue that has attracted considerable attention is the question of how to square the tacit denial of responsibility entailed in saying that an individual is incapable of restraining their dangerous violent or sexual impulses with the judgement that the same individual can justly be held responsible for past criminal conduct.[19] Concern about the deprivation of liberty occasioned by preventive detention is only partially mitigated in the case of those whose faculties are so limited that they are judged incapable of acting autonomously. The question of whether preventive detention on grounds of mental disorder, mental incapacity, or insanity is more readily justified because it entails a smaller loss of autonomy will be considered further in Chapter 9. The preventive detention of those of full capacity is arguably more problematic because it entails curtailing the freedom of choice of those who can meaningfully enjoy their freedom. Those with capacity can be held to account as responsible citizens, justifiably be subject to prosecution within the criminal justice process, and, if found guilty, punished in proportion to the gravity of their offence. To detain beyond the tariff inflicts disproportionate restrictions on liberty.

Moreover, preventive detention relies upon the prediction of future conduct that can be said to erode individual autonomy in two significant ways. First, the high

---

[18] See AE Bottoms and R Brownsword, 'The Dangerousness Debate after the Floud Report', *British Journal of Criminology* 22 (1982), 229–54.

[19] See, eg, SJ Morse, 'Fear of Danger, Flight from Culpability', *Psychology, Public Policy, And Law* 4 (1998), 250–67. L Alexander and KK Ferzan, 'Danger: The Ethics of Preemptive Action', *Ohio State Journal of Criminal Law* 9(2) (2012), 637–67; Walen, 'A Punitive Precondition for Preventive Detention' (n 14).

level of predictive accuracy claimed, whether by ARAIs or by clinical assessment, arguably constitutes an outright denial of autonomy. The judgement that an individual poses a significant risk of serious harm rests on the claim that he does not have the capacity to choose to do right, for if he did, logically, the prediction could not be accurate. At the very least, it relies upon accepting the ARAI's prediction that, even though the individual has capacity, he will not in fact exercise that capacity to restrain himself. Whereas conviction for a crime past rests upon the claim that the individual acted culpably at a particular point in time, the decision to detain preventively thus relies upon the assertion that the character traits of the detainee are enduring and predictable.[20] Second, during the period of preventive detention the individual is denied the moral opportunity to exercise choice to reflect, repent, and to resist temptations to engage in wrongdoing in the wider world.[21] This too constitutes a denial of autonomy insofar as autonomy has little meaning without a realm within which to exercise the freedom to choose to do right or wrong.

Yet, here too, counter considerations abound. First, the argument from autonomy cannot deny all forms of state interference or restriction. There are a great many examples of commonly accepted state limitations on individual freedom, such as taxation, compulsory education, immunisation, and, in some countries, military service. Second, respect for autonomy should apply no less to prospective victims, whose freedoms may be radically eroded (even unto disablement or death) were serious harm to eventuate. So, it is argued, the right of the individual not to be deprived of his liberty unnecessarily must be set against 'the claim of an innocent (unconvicted), unknown person (or persons), not to be deprived of the right to go about their business without risk of grave harm at the hands of an aggressor'.[22] Rawls's 'first principle', that 'each person is to have an equal right to the most extensive total system of equal basic liberties compatible with a similar system of liberty for all', suggests that limitations on the dangerous offender's freedom of action could be justified by the need to ensure respect for the potential victim's freedom of action.[23] However, this argument fails to weigh the certain and known deprivations imposed by preventive detention that fall immediately upon a known offender against the fact that the other side of the balance is peopled only by future and, as yet, typically unidentified potential victims.

Penal theory will only take us so far in justifying preventive detention. A strictly retributivist stance suggests detention is warranted only in respect of and in

---

[20] D Husak, 'Preventive Detention as Punishment? Some Possible Obstacles", in A Ashworth, L Zedner, and P Tomlin (eds.), *Prevention and the Limits of the Criminal Law* (Oxford: Oxford University Press, 2013), 178–93.

[21] S Smilansky, 'The Time to Punish', *Analysis* 54(1) (1994), 50–3; 52.

[22] J Floud, 'Dangerousness and Criminal Justice', *British Journal of Criminology* 22 (1982), 213–28; 219.

[23] J Rawls, *A Theory of Justice* (Oxford: Oxford University Press, 1973), 302.

proportion to a crime for which the individual stands convicted.[24] A more nuanced account of retributivism acknowledges that the preventive element is central to the justification of the penal sanction, because 'it supplies a prudential reason for desistance from offending... tied to the normative reason conveyed by censure'.[25] On this view, hard treatment fulfils an essential preventive role that censure alone might not achieve (see discussion in Chapter 1). On either account of retributivism, the sanction must be proportionate to the gravity of the offence for which the offender stands convicted. Detention beyond this term is *prima facie* disproportionate. It follows that serious difficulties arise in justifying pre-trial detention and most other forms of preventive detention too. In systems that set high maximum sentences, the gap between the tariff sentence and the period of detention deemed necessary for preventive purposes, and therefore the justificatory difficulties, may be less than in those systems that employ greater restraint at sentence. This is not to endorse high-tariff sentences, to the contrary, parsimony in sentencing guards against excessive punishment and it limits the social, financial, and psychological costs of incarceration. However, it also throws up the problem of the gap between the tariff term and need for longer protective sentences for the most dangerous offenders. This problem is not uncommonly resolved by resort to a twin-track system of proportionate sentences for the majority and limited provision for extended protective sentences for those who are judged to pose a serious risk of harm.[26] Extended sentences are justified here by reference to the exceptionally serious dangers that would otherwise result in 'extraordinary losses of utility' such that the infringement on the individual's liberty can be said to be justified.[27] Systems that operate recidivist offender 'enhancements' or that target persistent offenders are difficult to defend on retributive grounds but are often justified on the basis that prior convictions increase the risk of future offending. However, such schemes leave unresolved questions about how much 'enhancement' is justified and how far beyond normal proportionality constraints it is justifiable to go.

It is quite another matter to adopt a purely utilitarian approach. This would seem to license most forms of preventive detention, provided it could be shown, first, that the increase in general welfare outweighed the detriment to the individual and, second, that preventive detention outperformed all other alternatives.[28] Sentencing

---

[24] M Moore, *Placing Blame: A Theory of the Criminal Law* (Oxford: Oxford University Press, 2010).

[25] A von Hirsch and A Ashworth, *Proportionate Sentencing: Exploring the Principles* (Oxford: Oxford University Press, 2005), 22–3.

[26] These may be fixed term extended sentences, as introduced in England under the Criminal Justice Act 1991, or indefinite sentences, such as IPP sentences introduced by the Criminal Justice Act 2003, amended by the Criminal Justice and Immigration Act 2008, and abolished by the Legal Aid, Sentencing and Punishment of Offenders Act 2012.

[27] Von Hirsch and Ashworth, *Proportionate Sentencing: Exploring the Principles* (n 25), 53.

[28] C Slobogin, 'Prevention as the Primary Goal of Sentencing: The Modern Case for Indeterminate Dispositions in Criminal Cases', *San Diego Law Review* 48 (2011), 1127–71.

schemes not bound by the strictures of proportionality may permit extended sentencing on consequentialist grounds of prevention or rehabilitation to preventive ends (see Chapter 1).[29] Yet, research evidence does not appear to support the contention that longer incapacitative sentences result in significant crime preventive effects.[30] Given the danger that a purely consequentialist approach will sacrifice the individual to public utility and the lack of firm evidence that utility will in fact be increased, the larger task is to articulate justifications of preventive detention that serve preventive ends while observing retributive standards of respect for individual autonomy.

To think in terms of justifications *plural* acknowledges that there are many variant forms of preventive detention and that it is unlikely that a single unitary justification could satisfactorily cover all instances. Although several commentators purport to have developed a single coherent principle or overarching approach applicable to all categories,[31] the justifications for pre-trial detention surely differ from those that underlie detention post-conviction or under civil commitment regimes. The grounds for detaining the criminally insane or those with dangerous contagious diseases are unlikely to be the same as those that justify detention of individuals whose danger derives from their own volition. Distinguishing justifications applicable to particular instances of preventive detention is just as important, therefore, as seeking to identify those that are common to all.

Attempts to establish what grounds preventive detention, how it might be justified, and how subject to limits, tend to presume that it is possible to formulate one concrete conception applicable to all to forms. Yet preventive detention is arguably characterized more by divergence than uniformity of form or purpose. What follows attempts to delineate a rough taxonomy of preventive detention, in order to achieve greater clarity about what exactly is entailed when preventive regimes are proposed, defended, or subject to critique.

7.2 Practices of Preventive Detention

To identify what does and does not constitute an exercise of preventive detention is more difficult than may first appear. Aside from the core instances discussed below,

---

[29] Such schemes were common in the UK until the 1990s when the Criminal Justice Act 1991 set desert as the primary rational of sentencing, although its provisions were substantially undone by subsequent legislation.

[30] A Ashworth, *Sentencing and Criminal Justice* (Cambridge: Cambridge University Press, 2010), 207.

[31] A Walen, 'A Unified Theory of Detention', *Maryland Law Review* 70(4) (2011), 871–938; Alexander and Ferzan, 'Danger: The Ethics of Preemptive Action' (n 19); C Slobogin, 'A Jurisprudence of Dangerousness', *Northwestern University Law Review* 98(1) (2003), 1–62.

there are many practices not labelled as such but that are nonetheless used for preventive purposes. Of the United States, for example, Cole observes: 'Those who warn that we are dangerously unprepared to protect ourselves because of the absence of a preventive-detention statute overstate the case; many existing laws and authorities can be and have been invoked in an emergency to effectuate preventive detention.'[32] It follows that the task is not only to identify all those instances of detention that are labelled preventive but, no less importantly, all those that share the qualities of preventive detention irrespective of their name.

All this is to presume that preventive detention occurs post-conviction and within penal institutions. Too little attention has been paid to the deprivation of liberty entailed by remand or other forms of detention prior to a trial,[33] even though these generally proceed on an evidential basis far below that of conviction (see Section 3.4). As noted in Chapter 4, substantial restrictions on liberty short of detention on preventive grounds may also be imposed in the civil process, without the benefit of conviction at trial, on grounds of risk assessment alone.[34] For example, the TPIM[35] includes an 'overnight residence requirement' that may be imposed for one year on the basis of no more than 'reasonable belief' by the Home Secretary concerning the subject's involvement in terrorist-related activity and renewable for a further year.[36] Although overnight residence requirements replace the imposition of curfews that were possible under Control Orders, case law suggests that restrictions up to 16 hours will not normally be regarded as a deprivation of liberty.[37] The very expansive powers available relating to prevention of terrorism will be discussed in greater detail in Chapter 8. It suffices for the moment to observe that preventive restrictions on liberty, short of outright deprivation, are possible outside the criminal process, at a much reduced standard of proof. These

---

[32] D Cole, 'Out of the Shadows: Preventive Detention, Suspected Terrorists, and War', *California Law Review* 97 (2009), 693–750; 694.

[33] Though see, RA Duff, 'Pre-Trial Detention and the Presumption of Innocence', in A Ashworth, L Zedner, and P Tomlin (eds.), *Prevention and the Limits of the Criminal Law* (Oxford: Oxford University Press, 2013), 115–32.

[34] For example, Sexual Offences Prevention Orders may be imposed in civil proceedings on the application of the police when an individual, who has previously been convicted of a sexual offence, has 'acted in such a way as to give reasonable cause to believe that it is necessary for such an order to be made'. Sexual Offences Act 2003, s. 104(5)(b).

[35] Introduced by the Terrorism Prevention and Investigation Measures Act 2011, TPIMs replace Control Orders, though they have been labelled 'control orders-lite' by critics also.

[36] Parliament also proposes the introduction of Enhanced TPIMs that will permit the imposition of much more extensive restrictions broadly similar to those previously available under the old Control Order regime on an individual basis in 'exceptional circumstances'. Joint Committee on Human Rights, *Draft Enhanced Terrorism Prevention and Investigation Measures Bill* (London: HMSO, 2012).

[37] In *AP*, the Supreme Court held that 'for *a* control order with a 16-hour curfew (a fortiori one with a 14-hour curfew) to be struck down as involving a deprivation of liberty, the other conditions imposed would have to be unusually destructive of the life the controlee might otherwise have been living'. *R. (AP) v SSHD* [2010] UKSC 24.

lesser procedural and evidential requirements are said to be justified on grounds of security, but it should be noted that pursuit of the majority interest in public protection has the effect of substantially restricting individual liberty. To recognize individual security against state incursion as a legitimate, competing security interest would appear to be but a slender brake on coercive deprivations of liberty of this sort.

7.3 Preventive Detention at Sentence

Before examining sentences of preventive detention, it should be noted that several non-custodial sentences that restrict liberty for preventive purposes, but do not result in the deprivation of liberty entailed by detention, are available to the courts. The curfew order,[38] typically backed up by electronic monitoring, is one obvious example of a measure designed to restrain offenders at times when they are most likely to offend by requiring them to remain at home during specified hours. By keeping offenders away from sources of temptation and places of risk, it has the potential to reduce opportunistic crimes like assaults after pub-closing hours or night-time burglaries. Given that curfews can only be applied for limited periods, this protective effect applies only where offending is to some degree time-specific.

Seen positively, the curfew order is a sensible, parsimonious means of restraining non-dangerous offenders without resort to carceral detention.[39] Regarded negatively, however, the curfew order invades erodes civil liberties—not least privacy, particularly since it is often enforced by means of electronic tagging, which also impinges upon the body. Devoid of rehabilitative content, the curfew maintains control over offenders, in the name of risk reduction and protecting the public, but it does not address the problems that led to the offending behaviour and it may leave the offender as likely to offend at its conclusion as before. Where it is applied to those who would not otherwise have been sent to prison, the claim that it is less intrusive and less costly is undermined. This is all the more true since the maximum period in any day for which the court may impose a curfew requirement was increased from 12 to 16 hours and the maximum period for which a curfew requirement could be imposed was increased from six to 12 months.[40] The curfew

---

[38] Curfew orders were introduced in the UK under the 1991 Criminal Justice Act, s. 12, as amended by s. 204 of the Criminal Justice Act 2003.

[39] So-called Home Detention Curfews may also follow a period of incarceration. All prisoners serving sentences of three months or over but less than four years (and unless they fall into one of the excluded categories) are eligible for release on licence on a Home Detention Curfew (Criminal Justice Act 1991, s. 34A, as amended by the Crime & Disorder Act 1998, ss. 99–100).

[40] s. 71 of the Legal Aid, Sentencing and Punishment of Offenders Act (LASPO) 2012 amended s. 204 of the CJA 2003.

can be said to transform the offender's home into a place of detention and turn other members of the household into fellow inmates or quasi-warders of the person under curfew.

Other less controversial non-custodial measures which involve preventive restrictions on liberty include several of the possible requirements of the Community Sentence,[41] including the prohibited activity requirement, the exclusion requirement, the residence requirement, the mental health, drug rehabilitation, and alcohol treatment requirements, the supervision requirement and the attendance centre requirement.[42] In imposing these requirements, the courts must satisfy a threshold test as to seriousness. Courts are also restrained by guidance from the Sentencing Council that they should not impose a community sentence where the offender has a low risk of future offending.[43]

A more pressing issue is the rapid increase in numbers of those offenders deemed dangerous by the courts who are sentenced to serve extended, indefinite, or life sentences in prison on preventive grounds.[44] These sentences constitute core cases of preventive detention, though there is considerable variety in their form and substance. Life imprisonment without parole (LWOP, as it is known in the United States) or the 'whole life order' is typically imposed only following conviction for the most serious crimes and it is debatable whether it is better understood as primarily punitive or preventive.[45] Schedule 21 to the Criminal Justice Act 2003 empowers the court to set 'whole life' imprisonment as the maximum penalty in 'exceptionally serious cases, such as premeditated killings of two or more people, sexual or sadistic child murders, or political murders'.[46] The ECtHR, in the landmark judgment in *Vinter v United Kingdom*,[47] has held that where a legal system fails to provide for the possibility of review of a life sentence and, therefore, the possibility for release, it violates Article 3 of the Convention. Review is necessary 'to consider whether any changes in the life prisoner are so significant, and such progress towards rehabilitation has been made in the course of the sentence, as to mean that continued detention can no longer be justified on legitimate penological

---

[41] Criminal Justice Act 2003, s. 177.

[42] For further discussion of these various restrictions see Ashworth, *Sentencing and Criminal Justice* (n 30), 341–4.

[43] See Sentencing Council, *Assault: Definitive Guideline* (London: Sentencing Council, 2011), Annex: Fine Bands and Community Orders.

[44] In England and Wales there were 13,685 people serving indeterminate sentences in 2012 compared with fewer than 3,000 in 1992. Prison Reform Trust, *Bromley Briefings Prison Factfile* (November 2012), 20.

[45] See further our discussion in Ch. 1.

[46] Ashworth, *Sentencing and Criminal Justice* (n 30), 118.

[47] *Vinter and Others v the United Kingdom* (Grand Chamber: Application Nos. 66069/09, 130/10, and 3896/10).

grounds'.[48] Since English law has abolished its previous provision for review after 25 years, it is in violation of the Convention.[49]

There is continuing debate about the status of life imprisonment without parole, particularly in the United States where its use has increased very considerably in recent decades.[50] On the one hand, the absence of periodic review and impossibility of release suggests that the preventive element is subsidiary to the punitive.[51] Even if it could be shown decisively that the prisoner no longer posed a risk, release is not an option. On the other hand, the sentence has a preventive aspect in that it is reserved for those considered to pose the gravest of risks and the bar on parole is aimed at protecting the public from them.[52] Advocates of life without parole stress the primacy of this protective aspect, particularly in those jurisdictions where it functions as an alternative to the death penalty or where it was the basis for its abolition. However, the preventive status of life without parole has been placed in question, not least by research evidence that suggests reviewable life sentences are very effective and that conviction rates for lifers released on licence are lower than for any other sanction.[53] Moreover, controlling inmates who have no prospect of parole is problematic; so the sentence arguably buys protection for the general public partly at the expense of all those within prison.[54]

The Mandatory Life Sentence imposed in English law under the Criminal Justice Act 2003, ss. 269–277 on conviction for murder and the Discretionary Life Sentence (CJA 2003, s. 225)[55] have a more clearly preventive element in that, once the

---

[48] *Vinter and Others v the United* Kingdom (n 47), [119].

[49] See discussion in R English, 'Convicted murders win Article 3 case against whole life sentences in Strasbourg' at UK Human Rights Blog <http://ukhumanrightsblog.com/2013/07/09/convicted-murderers-win-article-3-case-against-whole-life-sentences-in-strasbourg/>.

[50] C Ogletree and A Sarat, *Life without Parole: America's New Death Penalty?* (New York: New York University Press, 2013); C Appleton and B Grover, 'The Pros and Cons of Life without Parole', *British Journal of Criminology* 47(4) (2007), 597–615; 600–1.

[51] In *Hindley* it was held that there was no reason in principle why life-long incarceration could not be regarded as pure punishment (*R. v Secretary of State for the Home Department, ex p Hindley* [2000] All ER 385 (HL)).

[52] Appleton and Grover, 'The Pros and Cons of Life without Parole' (n 50), 603.

[53] Home Office, *Life Licences: Reconviction and Recall by the End of 1995: England and Wales* (London: HMSO, 1997).

[54] Appleton and Grover, 'The Pros and Cons of Life without Parole' (n 50), 604. See also N Padfield, *Beyond the Tariff: Human Rights and the Release of Life Sentence Prisoners* (Cullompton: Willan Publishing, 2002).

[55] The Court of Appeal held that the discretionary sentence of life imprisonment should be 'reserved for cases of the utmost gravity' in which it would be 'unduly lenient to impose any other sentence'. *R. v Wilkinson; R. v Ali; R. v Olawaiye; R. v Bennett (Att-Gen's Reference No. 43 of 2009)* [2009] EWCA Crim 1925. In his commentary on these cases, Thomas argues that the sentence of life imprisonment under Criminal Justice Act 2003, s. 225 is not discretionary on the grounds: 'If the sentencing judge makes the judgment that there is a significant risk of serious harm occasioned by the commission by the offender of further specified offences and the seriousness of the offence or offences is such as to justify the

minimum term set by the court has been served, the prisoner is eligible to be considered by the Parole Board for release on licence. The Parole Board must make a risk assessment with the primary aim of preventing further offending and will only direct that a Life Sentence Prisoner should be released when it is satisfied that it is no longer necessary for the protection of the public that the prisoner should be confined.[56] Those sentenced to life imprisonment remain on licence for the rest of their lives. The licence may be revoked at any time and the lifer recalled to prison. Recall to prison while on licence is not dependent on conviction for a new offence: it may be justified by 'other risk factors' that give 'reasonable cause for considering the lifer to be a risk to the public'.[57] Accordingly, Appleton describes revocation of licence as principally 'a preventive measure' since 'recall may frequently involve sentencing someone to an indefinite term of detention for something they have not yet done but which they *might* do'.[58]

Here, yet again, problems of prediction arise. Research by Padfield and Maruna suggests that recall is based frequently upon proxies for risk, most obviously breach of licence conditions. They attribute a sharp increase in recalls to a parallel rise in the number and stringency of licence conditions, combined with a growing tendency 'to err on the side of over-caution than to risk the media attention that might surround a probationer who . . . commits a heinous crime while allegedly under state supervision'.[59] Identified as a presumptively high-risk group,[60] parolees are expected to adhere strictly to the terms of their licence: there is little toleration for any departures and the Parole Board is very risk averse in its judgments.[61] Moreover, the claim that recall and subsequent incarceration are implemented 'solely with a view to the prevention of risk and the protection of the public and not at all by way of punishment' has been contested in the courts on the grounds both that return to prison is in practice experienced as punishment and that detention until the end of

imposition of a sentence of imprisonment for life, the court must impose a sentence of imprisonment for life.' *R. v Wilkinson* [2010] Crim LR 69–75 at 75.

[56] Padfield observes: 'It seems curious that, while Parliament has attempted to structure judicial discretion in sentencing, the wide powers of the Parole Board—which decides the length of a sentence in practice—should be left wide open.' N Padfield, *Text and Materials on the Criminal Justice Process* (Oxford: Oxford University Press, 2008), 464.

[57] C Appleton, *Life after Life Imprisonment* (Oxford: Oxford University Press, 2010), 83.

[58] Appleton, *Life after Life Imprisonment* (n 57), 36.

[59] N Padfield and S Maruna, 'The Revolving Door at the Prison Gate: Exploring the Dramatic Increase in Recalls to Prison', *Criminology and Criminal Justice* 6(3) (2006), 329–52; 339.

[60] M Lynch, 'Waste Managers? The New Penology, Crime Fighting and Parole Agent Identity', *Law and Society Review* 32 (1998), 839–69.

[61] R Hood and S Shute, *The Parole System at Work: Home Office Research Study No. 202* (London: HMSO, 2000); R Hood and S Shute, *Reconviction Rates of Serious Sex Offenders and Assessments of Their Risk* Research Findings 164 (London: HMSO, 2002).

sentence, without the benefit of subsequent supervision on licence, may not be the best way of protecting the public.[62]

Further down tariff, instances of preventively motivated detention include indeterminate sentences, recidivist offender sentencing premiums, and provisions for extended detention on grounds of public protection. Many countries have regimes of extended or indefinite detention whether at or post-sentence.[63] In England and Wales, IPP sentences were designed to protect the public from potentially dangerous offenders, whose offence did not merit a life sentence, by imposing a tariff sentence of imprisonment followed by indefinite detention on preventive grounds. Offenders were held until the Parole Board determined that the risk was sufficiently reduced that they need no longer be detained for public protection. Introduced by the Criminal Justice Act 2003, the IPP came into force in 2005, resulting in an increase in the UK lifer population of 31 per cent in the following year.[64] IPP applied in cases where an offender had been convicted of a specified offence and where 'the court is of the opinion that there is a significant risk to members of the public of serious harm occasioned by the commission by him of further specified offences' (CJA 2003, s. 229(1)). Serious harm was defined as 'death or serious personal injury, whether physical or psychological'. If these conditions were fulfilled, the 2003 Act then imposed a duty to assume risk (CJA 2003, s. 229(3)) so denying the court the ability to exercise discretion in the interests of justice. The Criminal Justice and Immigration Act 2008 removed the mandatory presumption of risk and restored discretion to the court not to impose an IPP sentence. However, in exercising this discretion, the countervailing interest in public protection continued to weigh heavily.[65]

As we observed in Chapter 6, the threshold tests for IPP sentences were set relatively low.[66] In *Johnson*, it was held that IPP was concerned only with future risk and future protection of the public, and not with punishing the present offence. The worrying willingness of the courts routinely to find 'a significant risk to members of the public of serious harm' posed by those sentenced to relatively low-tariff terms resulted in an amendment by s. 225 of the Criminal Justice and

---

[62] Simon Brown LJ in R. *(Smith) v Parole Board*; R. *(West) v Parole Board* [2005]. In dissent, Hale LJ said 'to the person concerned it is experienced as punishment, whatever the authorities may say'. Quoted in N Padfield, 'Back Door Sentencing: Is Recall to Prison a Penal Process?', *Cambridge Law Journal* 64 (2005), 276–9; 277.

[63] It is notable that some countries, for example Sweden, do not.

[64] *James, Wells and Lee v United Kingdom* (2013) 56 EHRR 399.

[65] L Zedner, 'Erring on the Side of Safety: Risk Assessment, Expert Knowledge, and the Criminal Court', in GR Sullivan and I Dennis (eds.), *Seeking Security: Pre-Empting the Commission of Criminal Harms* (Oxford: Hart Publishing, 2012), 221–41.

[66] In *Lang* the Court of Appeal held that 'significant risk' means 'noteworthy, of considerable amount or importance': R. *v Lang* [2005] EWCA Crim 2864. In *Pedley, Martin and Hamadi*, the Court confirmed that a 'significant risk' presented a higher threshold than a mere possibility of occurrence: *Pedley, Martin and Hamadi* [2009] EWCA Crim 840.

Immigration Act 2008. This limited IPP to cases where the tariff sentence was more than two years or, as an exception to the seriousness threshold, when an offender had previously been convicted of a listed very serious offence. Nonetheless, the numbers of those detained continued to rise. By 2012, there were more than 6,500 IPP prisoners and yet less than 4 per cent of post-tariff detainees had been released, partly due to the difficulty they faced in persuading the Parole Board that their detention was 'no longer necessary for the protection of the public' (Crime (Sentences) Act 1997, s. 28(6)).[67] Although some Parole Board members thought the shock of an indeterminate sentence offered a 'wake-up call' and an opportunity to address offending behaviour,[68] the IPP order faced mounting criticism.

Continuing controversy over the attachment of IPP to low-tariff sentences; doubts about the reliability of the ARAIs upon which it was based (see Chapter 6);[69] and lack of clarity about the gravity of prospective harm required together undermined faith in IPP. The most serious failing was the lack of resources for rehabilitative programmes by which IPP prisoners might tackle the causes of their dangerousness. In *James, Wells and Lee v UK* (2012), the ECtHR found that the period of post-tariff detention served by the applicants was 'arbitrary and therefore unlawful within the meaning of Article 5 §1' ECHR.[70] It heard evidence that, despite the fact that IPP had been premised on rehabilitative treatment being made available to prisoners, there had been considerable delays in its provision, such that the applicants 'had no realistic chance of making objective progress' towards parole.[71] The Court accepted that 'any review of dangerousness which took place in the absence of the completion of relevant treatment courses was likely to be an empty exercise'.[72] It found that there had been a systemic failure by the Secretary of State to put in place the resources necessary to implement rehabilitation, despite the fact that rehabilitation was 'a necessary element of any part of the detention which is to be justified solely by reference to public protection'.[73] It found that the Secretary of State had breached his public law duty.[74] The judgment could, therefore, pave

---

[67] Ministry of Justice, *Breaking the Cycle: Effective Punishment, Rehabilitation and Sentencing of Offenders Cm 7972* (London: Ministry of Justice, 2010), 55; Prison Reform Trust, *Unjust Deserts: Imprisonment for Public Protection* (London: PRT, 2010).

[68] R Epstein and B Mitchell, 'Indeterminate Imprisonment for Public Protection and the Impact of the 2008 Reforms', *Criminal Law and Justice Weekly* (2009).

[69] Zedner, 'Erring on the Side of Safety' (n 65).

[70] *James, Wells and Lee v United Kingdom* (2013) 56 EHRR 399, [221].

[71] *James, Wells and Lee v United Kingdom* (n 70), [220].

[72] *James, Wells and Lee v United Kingdom* (n 70), [212].

[73] *James, Wells and Lee v United Kingdom* (n 70), [209]. In reaching this conclusion, the Court rejected the contention of Lord Phillips that the primary object of the IPP sentence was to protect the public from the risks posed by dangerous offenders and not to rehabilitate offenders.

[74] The decision of the Court was made final when a request to refer the case to the Grand Chamber was rejected in February 2013 (<www.humanrightseurope.org/2013/02/judges-reject-uk-demand-for-new-hearing-on-prisoners-human-rights-case/>).

the way for damages claims brought on behalf of all those held under IPP sentences post-tariff, as well as those IPP prisoners who have been released but who were themselves arbitrarily deprived of their liberty as a result of the failings noted by the Court. As of February 2012, 5,920 people were held on indeterminate IPP sentences, of which 3,528 had passed their tariff. As a consequence, the British government must decide what to do with the nearly 6,000 prisoners currently serving IPPs, particularly those who have completed their original tariff and who may now be in a position to seek release and/or damages. The judgment places the government under urgent pressure to ensure the provision of rehabilitation programmes for IPP prisoners, and to consider setting a lower threshold test for the release of those presently held post-tariff under IPP and whose detention could also be said to be arbitrary and unlawful.

The decision of the UK government to abolish the IPP sentence under the LASPO prevents new sentences being passed but does not address the continuing plight of those already held. An 'Extended Sentence of Imprisonment for Public Protection', which had permitted extended determinate sentences to be imposed in less serious cases, was also replaced under s. 124 of the LASPO by an Extended Determinate Sentence for dangerous offenders who are convicted of specified violent or sexual offences (listed in Schedule 15 of the Act) and who are 'adjudged to present a significant risk to the public of serious harm' (that is, at risk of committing further such serious offences). An Extended Determinate Sentence is a custodial sentence commensurate with the seriousness of the offence, after which and provided that the Parole Board 'is satisfied that it is no longer necessary for the protection of the public that P should be confined', the prisoner is released on licence. Prisoners are not eligible for release on licence until two-thirds of the sentence has been served, instead of the usual halfway point.[75] The period of licence (the 'extension period') is 'of such length as the court considers necessary for the purpose of protecting members of the public from serious harm occasioned by the commission by the offender of further specified offences' up to five years for a violent offence and eight years for a sexual offence. The Extended Determinate Sentence seeks preventive ends within a loosely proportionate framework, limited by the fact that the sum of the custodial term and the extension period on licence must not together exceed the maximum penalty for the offence. Section 122 of the LASPO also introduced Mandatory Life Sentences for the most serious adult offenders convicted of a second violent or sexual offence where the sentence imposed for both offences was ten years or more—a so-called 'two strikes' policy.[76]

---

[75] Release at the two-thirds point is automatic where the custodial term is less than 10 years but at the discretion of the Parole Board where the custodial term is 10 years or more or in cases where the prisoner has committed one of the most serious offences, listed in CJA 2003, Schedule 15B.

[76] <www.justice.gov.uk/downloads/legislation/bills-acts/legal-aid-sentencing/ipp-fac tsheet.pdf>.

The court must impose a life sentence unless it is of the opinion that it would be 'unjust to do so in all the circumstances' (LASPO, s. 122(1)).

The difficulty of proving that detainees no longer pose a risk such that they might be released may be no less a problem under the new legislation than the old.[77] Under s. 125 of the LASPO, release for determinate sentence prisoners is now subject to the test that the Parole Board must be 'satisfied that it is no longer necessary for the protection of the public that P should be confined'. The Parole Board decision had previously involved a balancing of benefits to public and offender of early release into the community under supervision, which might help rehabilitation and thus lessen the risk of reoffending in the future, against the benefits of safeguarding the public by continuing to detain the offender. This balancing approach was rejected in the case of an IPP prisoner in *Foley* (2012),[78] and it would appear that the focus of the s. 125 test on public protection rules out balancing the benefits of early release in favour of a so-called 'risk only' approach. A further difficulty is that the legislation fails to specify from which crimes the public are to be protected. Worryingly, the Parole Board's own guidance note asks 'Protect the public from what?' and notes that '[t]here is no direct case law to guide the Board'.[79] The guidance note speculates that 'it is likely that the courts will interpret the wording of the statute "protection of the public" as meaning violent and/or sexual offending' but that remains for the courts.[80] The fact that the Parole Board is left unclear as to what level of protection should apply and for which precise offences is unsatisfactory and in need of clarification by the courts.

The sentencing provisions of the LASPO pertaining to dangerous offenders, together with the IPP and Extended Sentences that preceded them, reflect a clear willingness to depart from the strictures of proportionality and determinate sentencing in the name of public protection. This results in protective sentences that may be effective during the term of incarceration only at the expense of the longer-term safety that might be secured by less onerous and exclusionary measures, such as release on licence under supervision.[81] The decision to adopt a 'risk only' approach to release decisions also signifies the abandonment of an earlier willingness to consider the extended preventive benefits of early release, especially when combined with rehabilitative and reintegrative programmes within the community.[82]

---

[77] P Ramsay, 'Imprisonment under the Precautionary Principle', in GR Sullivan and I Dennis (eds.), *Seeking Security: Pre-Empting the Commission of Criminal Harms* (Oxford: Hart Publishing, 2012), 194–218; 216.

[78] *R. (Foley) v Parole Board* [2012] EWHC 2184 (Admin).

[79] The Parole Board for England and Wales, *Guidance to Members on LAPSO* [sic] (2012), 4.

[80] The Parole Board for England and Wales, *Guidance to Members on LAPSO* [sic] (2012), 4.

[81] As the House of Lords acknowledged in respect of parole in *R. (Smith) v Parole Board*; *R. (West) v Parole Board* [2005] UKHL 1, [2005] 1 WLR 350. See Padfield, 'Back Door Sentencing: Is Recall to Prison a Penal Process?' (n 62), 278.

[82] Appleton, *Life after Life Imprisonment* (n 57).

With the exception of those sentenced to whole life terms without parole, the fact that those identified as dangerous will one day be released into the community would seem to call for a more constructive approach to their eventual reintegration than the present regime permits.

What principles might be invoked to guide and restrain the use of preventive detention at sentence? First, one might require a 'principle of proven serious wrongdoing': this would respect the presumption of harmlessness and only allow enquiry into risk post-conviction for a crime of sufficient gravity (denoted by a list of specified offences, or by reference to the maximum sentence for the offence, or both). Application of this principle would constitute a potentially significant curb on the preventive function, since it can be that commission of a lesser offence presages much graver future wrongdoing. However, the very ready resort to the IPP sentence discussed above suggests that to operate in the absence of such a requirement is to remove a much-needed brake upon judicial recourse to preventive detention. As Ashworth and von Hirsch have argued, 'the requirement of a serious conviction offence acts as a failsafe. It provides the assurance that, if someone were to transgress the criminal laws, he exposes himself to the risk of a lengthy extension of his criminal sentence only if he chooses to commit a grave act of violence.'[83] Further, a 'grievous risk principle' would require that the prospective harm is adjudged to be so serious as to justify the deprivation of liberty suffered by the individual detained. This should be combined with a 'high probability requirement', that the predicted occurrence is of such imminence and high likelihood as to justify detention. Given the limited predictive capacity of ARAIs and of clinical diagnosis, documented in Chapter 6, the grievous risk and high-probability principles should be regarded as conditional on the prior requirement of conviction for sufficiently serious wrongdoing.

Moreover, accepting that preventive detention constitutes a departure from a strict desert rationale should not entail abandoning all proportionality constraints. A valuable limiting prescription might be that which applies to the new Extended Determinate Sentences, namely that together the tariff term and the preventive period should not ordinarily exceed the maximum sentence for the offence. This would operate as a principle of qualified-desert—qualified, that is, by the exceptional provision that in rare cases of extreme severity the preventive term might be extended beyond this point in order to avert grave harm. To avoid extensions on preventive grounds becoming grossly unjust, sentences should be set for a fixed term, renewable only on grounds of proven need; subject to periodic review; and under conditions that abide by a principle of minimum restraint consistent with the demands of security. Following the judgment in *James, Wells and Lee*, adequately resourced provision of risk-reductive rehabilitative treatment for every detainee

---

[83] Von Hirsch and Ashworth, *Proportionate Sentencing: Exploring the Principles* (n 25), 56.

must be made available during the tariff period, and thereafter, such that they have a realistic prospect of reducing their risk to a level consistent with their eventual release.

7.4 Post-Sentence Civil Commitment

Implementing these principles, constraints, and requirements would do much to restrain unwarranted or disproportional resort to preventive detention. It is more difficult to ensure restraint when preventive detention is imposed not in the criminal system but as civil confinement, since the limiting principle of proportionality stemming from the desert rationale no longer applies. In Chapter 9 we examine systems of public health detention unconnected with criminal justice: these include forms of quarantine and civil commitment provisions for those who suffer from a contagious disease or mental disorder and who are deemed to pose a serious danger to themselves or others. Those who cannot be held responsible on grounds of unfitness to plead, acquittal, or a finding of not guilty by reason of insanity may be subject to long-term or indefinite detention within special hospitals in Britain and other forms of civil commitment elsewhere.[84] In the US, there is no constitutional limit on detention of persons so committed, so even a minor property crime may serve as a predicate offence for civil commitment on grounds of dangerous following an acquittal on grounds of insanity.[85] The finding that an individual is so incapacitated as to be incapable of being held culpable for criminal wrongdoing, and for whom punishment constrained by the limiting principle of proportionality is irrelevant, thus opens the door to civil commitment on grounds of pure prevention.

A more complex middle-ground is occupied by provisions for those who are sufficiently responsible to stand trial and who have been convicted of and sentenced for serious sexual or violent offences. In some jurisdictions, including many US states, where both an element of mental abnormality (not necessarily clinical disorder) and dangerousness are proven, an offender may be liable to post-sentence civil commitment. Forms of 'disease-based detention'[86] and the indefinite civil commitment of sexual predators post-sentence thus occupy a hybrid space between criminal and civil detention. Such detention typically applies to those who are not considered to be legally insane and who are, therefore, held criminally responsible for their conduct and ineligible for ordinary civil commitment. Whether post-sentence civil commitment is better understood as criminal or civil has been a matter of legal controversy. The constitutionality of the post-sentence civil commitment

---

[84] Morse, 'Fear of Danger, Flight from Culpability' (n 19).

[85] *Jones v United States* (1983) USSC. See discussion in SJ Morse, 'Neither Desert nor Disease', *Legal Theory* 5 (1999), 265–309; 278.

[86] Morse, 'Fear of Danger, Flight from Culpability' (n 19), 250.

of sexually violent offenders with a mental abnormality or personality disorder was upheld by the US Supreme Court in *Kansas v Hendricks*[87] on the grounds that the purpose was not punitive but primarily to protect the public and that this preventive function rendered the detention civil.

Provisions for post-sentence civil commitment have been subjected to searching analysis and critique, not least because, notwithstanding the designation of sexual offender commitment as civil, it shares many of the qualities of punishment. Both Morse[88] and Robinson[89] deprecate the confused manner in which contemporary laws contain a promiscuous combination of desert and danger, of preventive measures and punishment, and of civil and criminal procedures. Moreover, the imposition of civil commitment at the end of sentence is premised on holding that an offender is simultaneously both responsible and incapable of self-control. Accordingly, as Janus observes, 'civil commitment as a means to violence-control produces the contradictory holding that a criminal can be at the same time held responsible and yet be unable to control their behaviour'.[90] Similarly, Steiker observes the inconsistency between finding the offender criminally liable at point of sentence and yet suffering from a mental abnormality or personality disorder 'which predisposes the person to commit sexually violent offences in a degree constituting such person a menace to the health and safety of others'[91] so dangerous as to require indefinite commitment post-sentence.[92] Morse criticizes the decision in *Kansas v Hendricks* more strongly, arguing:

It is utterly paradoxical to claim that a sexually violent predator is sufficiently responsible to deserve the stigma and punishment of criminal incarceration, but that the predator is not sufficiently responsible to be permitted the usual freedom from involuntary civil commitment that even very predictably dangerous but responsible agents retain because our society wishes to maximise the liberty and dignity of all citizens. Even if the standards for responsibility in the two systems need not be symmetrical, it is difficult to imagine what adequate conception of justice would justify blaming and punishing an agent too irresponsible to be left at large. Our society must decide whether sexually violent predators are mad or bad and respond accordingly.[93]

---

[87] (1997) 117 S. Ct. 2072 in which a self-confessed molester of young children was sentenced for his offences, and then ordered to undergo indefinite civil commitment on release from his sentence. Note that in *Kansas v Crane* (2002) USSC 534 U.S. 407 it was held that purely preventive civil detention based upon dangerousness alone was not sufficient and proof of lack of control was needed.

[88] Morse, 'Fear of Danger, Flight from Culpability' (n 19).

[89] PH Robinson, 'Punishing Dangerousness: Cloaking Preventive Detention as Criminal Justice', *Harvard Law Review* 114(5) (2001), 1429–56.

[90] E Janus, 'Civil Commitment as Social Control', in M Brown and J Pratt (eds.), *Dangerous Offenders: Punishment and Social Order* (London: Routledge, 2000), 71–90; 82.

[91] Section 59–29a02(b). Kansas: Sexually Violent Predator Act.

[92] C Steiker, 'The Limits of the Preventive State', *Journal of Criminal Law and Criminology* 88 (1998), 771–808; Morse, 'Fear of Danger, Flight from Culpability' (n 19).

[93] Morse, 'Fear of Danger, Flight from Culpability' (n.19).

Whereas the decision in *Hendricks* merely required a mental condition creating a likelihood of such conduct in the future, it is arguable that the law should require a formal psychiatric diagnosis and followed up with a treatment programme.[94] Although Hendricks may well have been very dangerous, he was not psychotic and he was able to make rational decisions. As Morse points out, 'our society routinely and regretfully releases from prison inmates we know are highly likely to re-offend, because culpability limits the term of possible confinement'.[95] It follows that it is anomalous to commit someone to post-sentence civil commitment on grounds of risk alone.

Morse characterizes post-sentence civil commitment provisions as being reliant upon an unhappy hybrid of 'desert/disease'-based justifications,[96] since the offender is deemed responsible enough to be held liable for an offence, so mentally disordered as to be dangerous, yet not so reduced in capacity as to be held criminally insane. The judgment in *Hendricks* fails to clarify what degree of impairment is needed to licence indefinite incarceration and leaves ambiguous the level of treatment that should be provided in order that a regime be civil not punitive. Accordingly, Steiker concludes that the judges in *Hendricks* 'failed to use the case as an opportunity to clarify important issues regarding whether and what limits exist on the non-punitive use of civil confinement to deal with dangerous individuals'.[97] Significantly, the Californian sexually violent predator laws, unlike those in other US states, require an application for extension of the commitment every two years, at which point it must be decided beyond reasonable doubt that the offender is a sexually violent predator. On one view, this does not constitute a system of indefinite but rather of renewable fixed term detention on preventive grounds that must be proven if the detention is to be extended. On the other hand, Vess points out that it is a form of 'commitment that is renewable indefinitely', particularly since he judges the renewal requirement to be little more than a formality.[98]

In light of the US jurisprudence, it is instructive to note how the status of preventive detention has been judged in Europe. In the landmark decision of *M v Germany*, the Strasbourg Court was asked to rule on the claim that the German form of civil commitment, *Sicherungsverwahrung*, was not punitive by virtue of its preventive rationale.[99] The case arose in respect of a prisoner M who was sentenced,

---

[94] *Kansas v Hendricks*, 521 U.S. 346 (1997). In the subsequent case of *Kansas v Crane* (2002) 534 U.S. 407, it was held that proof of lack of control was also needed.

[95] Morse, 'Fear of Danger, Flight from Culpability' (n 19), 253.

[96] SJ Morse, 'Protecting Liberty and Autonomy: Desert/Disease Jurisprudence', *San Diego Law Review* 48(4) (2011), 1077–125.

[97] Steiker, 'The Limits of the Preventive State' (n 92), 791–2.

[98] J Vess, 'Preventive Detention versus Civil Commitment: Alternative Policies for Public Protection in New Zealand and California', *Psychiatry, Psychology and Law* 12(2) (2005), 357–66; 360–2.

[99] *M v Germany* [2009] ECHR No. 1939/04.

according to the law at the time, to the maximum of ten years' preventive detention in addition to a five-year tariff term for attempted murder and robbery. The law was then changed to allow courts to impose indefinite preventive detention, and this was imposed on M retrospectively. The German Constitutional Court considered the claim that post-sentence preventive detention was a 'penalty' within Article 7 of the ECHR and therefore the retrospective increase was not permissible. Against this claim, the German authorities argued that this element of M's detention was not a penalty, pointing to the distinction in German law between penalties (*Strafen*) and so-called measures of correction and prevention (*Massregeln der Besserung und Sicherung*). The German Constitutional Court held that preventive detention fell into the latter category, being 'of a purely preventive nature aimed at protecting the public from a dangerous offender' and, in so doing, it accepted that a new law permitting extension beyond ten years could be applied retrospectively to prolong M's preventive detention indefinitely.[100] However, the ECtHR rejected this decision. It ruled that the order for preventive detention was a penalty on the grounds that detention took place in ordinary prisons in conditions similar to those of ordinary prisoners; there were no or few special measures to enable those detained to reduce the danger they presented and thereby limit the period of detention; it operated, therefore, as additional punishment and contained a clear deterrent element; it was ordered by the criminal courts; and the detriment to the offender was greater than the punitive sentence itself. Moreover, as an indeterminate order, it was among the most severe orders that could be made under the German Criminal Code.

Subsequent judgments of the ECtHR have established that preventive detention provisions must 'satisfy the constitutional requirement of establishing a distance between preventive detention and prison sentences'; that preventive detention must be undertaken solely for preventive purposes; that the legislature must ensure than no burdens beyond the deprivation of liberty are imposed through the conditions of preventive detention; that detention must have 'a clear therapeutic orientation' designed to reduce the dangerousness of the offender and that therapy should be a legally enforceable right exercisable by the detainee; and that the detention must be subject to annual judicial review. Where preventive detention is imposed retrospectively it is a violation of both Articles 5 and 7.[101]

The determination of the Strasbourg Court to go beyond labels to discover the true character of detention sits in stark contrast to the judgment of the High Court

---

[100] It should be noted here that in Germany the concept of a 'dangerous offender' is not limited to those who are thought to present a risk of sexual or violent offending. Indeed, in *Grosskopf v Germany* (judgment of 21 October 2010) the ECtHR upheld an order of preventive detention imposed on a persistent burglar, who was not released because he refused to undergo therapy or to reappraise his criminal past. The imposition of indefinite detention in order to prevent burglary raises serious issues of proportionality.

[101] *Mautes v Germany* (no. 20008/07) (13 January 2011); *Kallweit v Germany* (no. 11792/07) (13 January 2011); *Schummer v Germany* (no. 27360/04 and 42225/07) (13 January 2011).

of Australia in *Fardon* that the Queensland scheme of post-sentence preventive detention[102] did not transgress the double jeopardy rule and that it was not punitive.[103] This decision, controversial in Australia, has since been criticized by the UN Human Rights Committee, which held that it was incompatible with the prohibition against arbitrary detention under art. 9(1) of the International Covenant on Civil and Political Rights and considered that it might also contravene the prohibition against double punishment under art. 14(7) and against retroactive punishment under art. 15(1).[104]

In principle, as argued in Section 1.6, the key question should be whether the detention is punitive in substance, irrespective of whether it is also preventive in purpose. This approximates to the position adopted by the ECtHR. It means that a measure which is punitive–preventive must abide by all the procedural require-ments and safeguards of a punishment or penalty, whereas a measure that is predominantly preventive (and not in substance punitive) is not subject to those particular safeguards and requirements. This means that our distinction is not quite that proposed by Robinson, who argues for a clear line to be drawn between punitive and preventive regimes. However, we agree with Robinson that 'if preventive detention is needed beyond the prison term of deserved punishment, it ought to be provided by a system that is open about its preventive purpose and is specifically designed to perform that function'.[105] This openness about the prevent-ive function would impose upon governments the obligations of periodic review, non-punitive conditions, use of least restrictive alternatives, and the right to treat-ment.[106] A civil commitment system that abided by such requirements would have greater moral credibility and might offer better protection.

7.5 Conclusions

This chapter has analysed various provisions that constitute parts of the family of preventive detention. This not to deny that there are significant differences in the grounds for the exercise of coercive state power in each case: rather, it is to suggest that there are significant parallels and similarities among them, such that they might

---

[102] Under the Dangerous Prisoners (Sexual Offenders) Act 2003 (Qld).

[103] *Fardon* (2004) 210 ALE 50.

[104] *Fardon v Australia*, UN Doc. CCPR/C/98/D/1629/2007 (12 April 2010).

[105] Robinson, 'Punishing Dangerousness: Cloaking Preventive Detention as Criminal Justice' (n 89), 1432. For an opposing view, see D Husak, 'Lifting the Cloak: Preventive Detention as Punishment', *San Diego Law Review* 48 (2011), 1173–204; Husak, 'Preventive Detention as Punishment? Some Possible Obstacles' (n 20), 178.

[106] Robinson, 'Punishing Dangerousness: Cloaking Preventive Detention as Criminal Justice' (n 89), 1447.

be regarded as being of the same class and subject to many of the same limiting principles.

One advantage of this approach is that, insofar as the courts have developed a jurisprudence of prevention and set out minimum requirements, procedural protections, and limiting principles in one sphere, these may be transferable to other preventive measures to cabin the power of the state and to protect those detained. Limiting principles are already well developed in respect of punishment by imprisonment—for example, the principle of restraint in the use of custody (using it only where it is the least restrictive appropriate alternative), the custody threshold (using imprisonment only for serious offences), and the proportionality principle (keeping sentences of imprisonment proportionate to the seriousness of the offence). These principles derive from well-founded fears about the dangers of unjustified, excessive, or inhumane treatment. Preventive detention is no less in need of justification. Where the curtailment of rights is less than deprivation of liberty, one might argue that the requirements may reasonably be attenuated accordingly. So, for example, in respect of TPIMs which are restrictive of liberty but do not entail its deprivation, the requirements set are less demanding. Where the measure entails full deprivation of liberty—as in the case of preventive detention—the requirements need to be correspondingly higher. A fully developed jurisprudence of preventive detention is all the more necessary because deprivation of liberty here often occurs ahead of the anticipated wrongdoing which it is its purpose to prevent, without the benefit of the usual evidential and other safeguards of the criminal process and trial, and may be imposed for indefinite periods, with little scope for effective challenge, escape, or redress.

The task ahead is to develop a body of restraining principles applicable to coercive preventive endeavour by the state.[107] During the discussions in this chapter and in Chapter 6, we have provided arguments in favour of the following principles relating to deprivation of liberty for predominantly preventive purposes:

(1) In principle, every citizen has a right to be presumed harmless, and this presumption of harmlessness can be rebutted only in exceptional circumstances (set out in (2)and (4)).

(2) The state's duty to protect people from serious harm may justify depriving a person of liberty if that person has lost the presumption of harmlessness by virtue of committing a serious violent offence and is classified as dangerous.

(3) Deprivation of liberty should not be considered unless it is the least restrictive appropriate alternative.[108]

---

[107] A task already begun by Christopher Slobogin, Stephen Morse, and Douglas Husak among others.

[108] Illustrated in the ECtHR case of *Enhorn v Sweden* 56529/00 (2005) discussed in Section 9.2.

(4) Any judgment of dangerousness in this context must be approached with strong caution. It should be a judgment of this person as an individual, not simply as a member of a group with certain characteristics and with an overall probability rating. The state should bear the burden of proving that the person presents a significant risk of serious harm to others and the required level of risk should vary according to the seriousness of the predicted harm. Decision-makers should bear in mind the contestability of judgments of dangerousness and the scope for interpretation that they leave and individuals should have rights of challenge and appeal.

(5) If it is decided to add time to the proportionate sentence in response to a judgment of dangerousness, in principle that additional time should be the shortest period necessary to respond to the anticipated danger, and the time should be served under different conditions (see (9) below).

(6) In exceptional circumstances, where a person is adjudged to present a very serious danger to others, and where that person has a previous conviction for a very serious offence, the court may consider an indeterminate sentence of detention. The court should determine that no lesser sentence would be effective in protecting the public from a significant risk of serious harm.

(7) If the preventive sentence is indeterminate, there should be provision for regular review of the continued need for detention; review proceedings should involve procedures and legal assistance to ensure that the offender's fair trial rights are respected.

(8) If the sentence is extended or indeterminate, adequately resourced risk-reductive rehabilitative treatment and training courses should be made available from the beginning of the tariff period of a criminal sentence (not just at its end), or throughout the entirety of a purely preventive term, to give the offender the opportunity to work towards release.

(9) Any preventive detention going beyond the proportionate sentence should be served in non-punitive conditions with restraints no greater than those required by the imperatives of security. Where possible, detention that is purely preventive and not punitive should take place in a separate facility, not part of the prison system.

An opportunity-to-challenge principle would require that no deprivation of a fundamental right be permitted without provision for the individual to challenge the decision upon which it is based. This principle would require that an individual who stands to lose their liberty should be provided with reasons for the deprivation of that right, as well as with procedural avenues for challenge, appropriate legal aid, and such legal assistance as is necessary to pursue their challenge. Questions remain as to what provisions and resources should be made available to those facing lesser restrictions and what quality of legal representation and of procedure should suffice.[109]

These are just some preliminary constraining principles. The question remains, however, whether it is possible to articulate principles that cover all cases of preventive detention in such a way as to mitigate possible abuses of power on grounds of public protection. Preventive detention is one of the most coercive exercises of state power over the individual. It imposes deprivation of liberty ahead of wrongdoing; it grants considerable discretion to criminal justice professionals and to the courts; it is based upon predictions of dubious reliability; and it risks creating arbitrariness in its varied forms and practices. The threshold for imposing preventive detention; the criteria according to which it is applied; the due process protections offered to the detainee; the character and conditions of the regime under which detainees are held; and the period of detention all require a more robust, principled approach if the liberty of the individual is not to be sacrificed in the name of prevention.

---

[109] For example, it is questionable whether the UK special advocate regime and resort to closed material procedures are an adequate substitute for proper disclosure. See, eg, <www. justice.org.uk/resources.php/33/secret-evidence>.

8

Counterterrorism Laws and Security Measures

The threat of terrorism constitutes one of the strongest reasons for the state to enact and deploy coercive measures to protect the public. If there are good reasons to create a realm of action and powers with which to prevent ordinary offences, how much stronger is the case for preventing the potentially catastrophic harms entailed by terrorist attacks.[1] Counterterrorism laws and measures may be defended on the grounds of national security and public protection but nonetheless have profound implications for the civil liberties of those against whom they are deployed.

Britain has a long history of tackling terrorism ranging from its experience as a colonial power, against which very many anti-imperial acts of political violence were carried out, to the long-running campaigns of violent political protest in Northern Ireland and the British mainland by Irish terrorists, notably the Irish Republican Army (IRA).[2] More recently, the events of 9/11 in the US and the subsequent bombings in London in July 2005 created a powerful imperative for the British government to introduce counterterrorist legislation and extensive counter-terrorism programmes to combat the threat from Al-Qaeda and other groups. The period since 9/11 has been one of 'hyper-legislation'[3] in which a welter of counterterrorism laws were passed as a response to these attacks, in reaction to international pressures and directives, to address credible security threats, as well as to meet the public's need for reassurance.[4]

Counterterrorism laws and measures seek to provide security against future attack but they also create a different security risk, namely the risk to individual security posed by the coercive power of the state. The grave risks of terrorism have led governments to introduce extensive police powers, specific terrorism offences that

---

[1] J Braithwaite, 'Pre-Empting Terrorism', *Current Issues in Criminal Justice* 17(1) (2006), 96–114.

[2] Between 1969 and the signing of the Belfast Agreement (the 'Good Friday Agreement') in April 1998, more than 3,500 people died in the UK in attacks by the Irish Republican and Loyalist terrorist groups.

[3] K Roach, *The 9/11 Effect: Comparative Counter-Terrorism* (Cambridge: Cambridge University Press, 2011).

[4] See B Ackerman, *Before the Next Attack: Preserving Civil Liberties in an Age of Terrorism* (New Haven: Yale University Press, 2006).

significantly expand the scope of the criminal law, as well as civil, administrative, and extra-legal measures that infringe individual liberties without the accompanying protections of the criminal process. Counterterrorism measures give rise to some of the most coercive instances of prevention and, as such, constitute some of the greatest justificatory challenges. Unsurprisingly, considerable academic and political attention has been paid to debating how to monitor and review state counterterrorism laws and measures; how to ensure accountability (especially in respect of secret operations by security services and police); how to ensure that effective prevention is consistent with the preservation of basic liberties; and how to ensure principled restraint.[5]

This chapter analyses the ways in which terrorism is defined and what follows from these definitional decisions. It examines the declaration of a 'War on Terror' and the military, intelligence, and security measures undertaken at national and international level. It explores domestic efforts to prevent terrorist activity through the exercise of police powers, pre-trial detention, and preventive detention of foreign national suspects. It examines the curtailments of civil liberties and side-stepping of procedural protections entailed by civil preventive orders. It also examines the UK's *Prevent* strategy, which seeks to target individuals at risk of recruitment into terrorist organizations, and it explores the tensions and blurring between *Prevent* and coercive methods deployed by policing and security services. Finally, the chapter examines possible constraints on preventive endeavour in the field of counterterrorism. These include pre- and post-legislative scrutiny, independent review, procedural protections, and sunset clauses in respect of special measures. It concludes by considering whether these suffice to limit some of the most invasive preventive powers exercised by the modern state.

8.1 The Definition of Terrorism

The legal definition of terrorism delineates the conduct targeted by counterterrorist legislation and terrorism offences and delimits the scope of preventive measures.[6] However, the definition is contested, differing among jurisdictions and between

---

[5] D Cole and J Dempsey, *Terrorism and the Constitution: Sacrificing Civil Liberties in the Name of National Security* (New York: W. W. Norton & Co, 2002); R Dworkin, 'Terror and the Attack on Civil Liberties', *The New York Review of Books* 50(17) (2003); M Ignatieff, *The Lesser Evil: Political Ethics in an Age of Terror* (Edinburgh: Edinburgh University Press, 2004); J Waldron, *Torture, Terror and Trade-Offs: Philosophy for the White House* (Oxford: Oxford University Press, 2010).

[6] K Hardy and G Williams, 'What Is "Terrorism"? Assessing Domestic Legal Definitions', *UCLA Journal of International Law and Foreign Affairs* 16(1) (2011), 77–162; J Hodgson and V Tadros, 'The Impossibility of Defining Terrorism', *New Criminal Law Review* 16(3) (2013), 494–526.

international and domestic law. The UN Security Council Resolution 1566 sets out a relatively focused definition that targets intentional killing or serious bodily injury to civilians. It defines terrorism as

criminal acts, including against civilians, committed with the intent to cause death or serious bodily injury, or taking of hostages, with the purpose to provoke a state of terror in the general public or in a group of persons or particular persons, intimidate a population or compel a government or an international organization to do or to abstain from doing any act, which constitute offences within the scope of and as defined in the international conventions and protocols relating to terrorism.[7]

UK law departs from this internationally agreed definition. Section 1 of the Terrorism Act 2000 (UK) adopts a broader conception of terrorism that encompasses serious damage to property and serious interference with and disruption of an electronic system.[8] Whereas the UN definition designates the purpose as being to 'compel a government or any international organization', UK law requires only that the threat be intended 'to influence the government or an international governmental organization'. While UK law provides that 'the use or threat is made for the purpose of advancing a political, religious, racial or ideological cause', no reference to purpose is made in UN Security Council Resolution 1566 or under the more restrained definition of terrorism set out in the US Patriot Act which, like Resolution 1566, focuses on violence and danger to human life.

The expansiveness of the UK definition extends the scope of the terrorism offences and the target range of counterterrorism measures; and, thereby, expands the realm of preventive endeavour. The breadth and vagueness of the definition creates ambiguity about what is legally delineated as terrorism and has the effect of incorporating acts that cannot properly be described as terrorist (resulting in the use of stop-and-search powers under former s. 44 of the Terrorism Act 2000 against peaceful political protestors: notoriously, to eject and detain a heckler, 82-year-old Walter Wolfgang, at the 2005 Labour Party Conference).[9] As Hardy and Williams observe, the inclusion of property damage, interference with electronic systems, and serious risks to health and safety within the UK definition potentially encompasses

---

[7] UN Security Council, *Security Council Resolution 1566 (2004) Concerning Threats to International Peace and Security Caused by Terrorism*, 8 October 2004, S/RES/1566 (2004), at <http://www.refworld.org/docid/42c39b6d4.html>.

[8] The UK's Terrorism Act 2000 defines terrorism as the use or threat of action designed to influence the government or to intimidate the public or a section of the public in order to advance a political, religious, or ideological cause. 'Action' involves serious violence against a person, serious damage to property, endangering the life of another, creating a serious risk to the health or safety of the public or a section of the public, or serious interference with or disruption of an electronic system.

[9] P Johnston, 'The police must end their abuse of anti-terror legislation', *The Telegraph* (3 October 2005). <http://www.telegraph.co.uk/comment/personal-view/3620110/The-police-must-end-their-abuse-of-anti-terror-legislation.html>. See also Section 3.2.

'a wide range of less serious and more uncertain harms'.[10] They conclude that this results from a 'tendency to err on the side of over-inclusion in order to account for all possible future manifestations of terrorist violence'.[11] While breadth creates greater scope for preventive action against possible threat, arguably it contravenes the principle of legality which requires criminal offences to be specified clearly and precisely (see discussion in Section 5.3, principle (3)). It permits counterterrorism measures to be used against those for whom the legislation was not intended (for example non-violent political protestors) and it endows officials with dangerously broad discretion. The widely varying and sometimes vaguely specified definitions of terrorism deployed in different jurisdictions and at international and domestic levels create confusion about what precisely constitutes the legitimate target of preventive laws. This makes it difficult for individuals to know in advance when they will be in breach of the law and to amend their conduct accordingly. The rule-of-law values incorporated in principle (6) in Section 5.3 should apply here no less strongly. In the aftermath of the 7/7 bombings, for example under Terrorism Act 2000, s. 44 powers, a group of trainspotters was detained and searched, as *The Telegraph* reported: '[b]y taking photographs of carriages and noting down serial numbers, the spotters were accused of behaving like a reconnaissance unit for a terrorist cell'.[12]

8.2 Is Preventing Terrorism a Matter of War or Crime?

The decision to classify terrorist atrocities as acts of war or as crimes has important implications for the pursuit of prevention. On one view, deciding in which realm to pursue counterterrorism depends upon answers to predetermined analytical and evaluative criteria. Feldman argues that where terrorism is deemed to challenge the very life of the nation, it may be designated a military threat to which the laws of war apply.[13] Where the threat is less pressing or the scale is smaller, terrorist acts violate the criminal law but arguably do not challenge state sovereignty in such a way as to enter the realm of war. Other determinative considerations include the identity of the actors involved—whether they are individual or state actors, whether they are domestic or foreign nationals; and their intentions—whether or not their

---

[10] Hardy and Williams, 'What Is "Terrorism"? Assessing Domestic Legal Definitions' (n 6), 160.

[11] Hardy and Williams, 'What Is "Terrorism"? Assessing Domestic Legal Definitions' (n 6), 160.

[12] P Johnston, 'The police must end their abuse of anti-terror legislation', *The Telegraph* (3 October 2005). <http://www.telegraph.co.uk/comment/personal-view/3620110/The-police-must-end-their-abuse-of-anti-terror-legislation.html>.

[13] N Feldman, 'Choices of Law, Choices of War', *Harvard Journal of Law and Public Policy* 25(2) (2002), 457–85.

aim is to challenge the very legitimacy of the state.[14] An alternative view, advanced by Lowe, is that these definitional criteria are slippery and none are decisive, so the choice whether to designate terrorism as an act of war carried out by enemy combatants or as a criminal act whose perpetrators should be prosecuted is less a legal than a policy decision made by states in response to their assessment of threats posed at any one time.[15] Whatever the basis of the decision, it is one from which important legal consequences follow.

In the immediate aftermath of the 9/11 attacks, the US declared a 'War on Terror', which has entailed both the real wars in Iraq and Afghanistan, and the designation of terrorist suspects as enemy combatants at home; the use of quasi-military measures such as extraordinary rendition; detention by military authorities (most notoriously at the camp within the Guantanamo Bay naval base); and trial by military commissions. The justification given for recourse to war rested on the scale of the attacks on 9/11; the belief that the security of the nation was under threat;[16] and the consequent priority given to security over due process protections. Indeed, these protections were widely regarded as unnecessary and even hazardous obstacles to the prevention of further attacks.[17] Resort to extra-legal measures, as well as administrative and military detention, rested on the claim that the US was engaged in an ongoing war against Al-Qaeda. The war model has attracted strong criticisms on the grounds that it dispenses with the ordinary requirements of due process and legality; that it is predicated upon the idea that the 'war' is winnable; and that it would be possible to determine when victory—in the form of assured national security and the absence of threat—might be achieved. Yet, as experience has shown, victory against terrorism is a chimera since any claim to security is continually challenged by threats as yet unknown.[18]

---

[14] Feldman, 'Choices of Law, Choices of War' (n 13), 459–60.

[15] V Lowe, '"Clear and Present Danger": Responses to Terrorism', *International and Comparative Law Quarterly* 54 (2005), 185–96; 187. Historically, the campaign against the IRA in Northern Ireland was met by military action and those held were granted the status of paramilitary prisoners. However, in 1976, the British government removed this special status and, with it, their rights as prisoners of war. Reclassified as ordinary criminals, they were confined in the Maze Prison near Belfast. More recently, debate about the proper categorization of terrorism has had a profound impact on the conduct of the 'War on Terror'. See, eg, C Savage, 'Debating the Legal Basis for the War on Terror', *The New York Times* (16 May 2013). <http://www.nytimes.com/2013/05/17/us/politics/pentagon-official-urges-congress-to-keep-statute-allowing-war-on-terror-intact.html?nl=todaysheadlines&emc=edit_th_20130517&_r=1&>.

[16] Hence, the setting up of the US Department for Homeland Security under the Homeland Security Act 2002.

[17] See, eg, V Dinh, 'Freedom and Security after September 11', *Harvard Journal of Law and Public Policy* 25 (2002), 399–406; B Ackerman, 'The Emergency Constitution', *Yale Law Journal* 113(5) (2004), 1029–91; 1034–7.

[18] L Zedner, *Security* (London: Routledge, 2009), 20.

The pursuit of a war model also licensed resort to extraordinary measures that might not otherwise have been contemplated. The then Attorney-General, John Ashcroft, declared the US administration willing to use any possible legal, and significant extra-legal, measures to combat terrorism, arguing, '[a]ggressive detention of lawbreakers and material witnesses is vital to preventing, disrupting, or delaying new attacks'.[19] One such measure—the US Bail Reform Act 1984—permits material witnesses to be held in detention to ensure that they give evidence in criminal proceedings. Since 9/11, this provision has been used not only to detain witnesses but also to hold terrorist suspects without charge for indefinite periods prior to, or in place of, trial. Faced with claims of national security, US courts have complied uncritically with applications to detain witnesses and they have rarely probed the grounds for suggesting that a witness would fail to appear at trial or abscond. Nor have the courts considered whether lesser restrictions might suffice to address risk of flight. Secrecy surrounding these proceedings makes it particularly difficult to ascertain how far formal protections are breached, against whom they are being used, and in what ways.[20] The Department of Justice has not released numbers of persons detained as material witnesses since 9/11, but in the period up to 2005 at least 70 people were detained.[21] Ostensibly held as witnesses, they have been incarcerated under very harsh conditions of high security or in solitary confinement, shackled, subjected to strip searches, repeatedly interrogated, and held under bright lights for 24 hours a day for weeks or months. Yet, in *Ashcroft v al-Kidd* (2011),[22] the Supreme Court held that there was no clearly established constitutional law which prohibited the use of material witness warrants to preventively detain terrorism suspects. The majority went further to hold that it did not matter whether or not the government actually intended to use a detainee as a witness in a prosecution; even if the warrant was a pretext to preventively detain a suspected terrorist without charge. The use of material witness detention has not passed without criticism. The US organization Human Rights Watch insists, 'Holding as "witnesses" people who are in fact suspects sets a disturbing precedent for future use of this extraordinary government power to deprive citizens and others of their liberty. The rule of law itself suffers when a law is

---

[19] 'Attorney-General Ashcroft Outlines Foreign Terrorist Tracking Task Force', 31 October 2001 <http://permanent.access.gpo.gov/websites/usdojgov/www.usdoj.gov/ag/speeches/2001/agcrisisremarks10_31.htm>.

[20] DQ Cochran, 'Material Witness Detention in a Post-9/11 World: Mission Creep or Fresh Start?', *George Mason Law Review* 18(1) (2010), 1–41.

[21] Human Rights Watch, *Witness to Abuse* (2005), 4. <http://www.hrw.org/reports/2005/us0605/us0605.pdf>.

[22] *Ashcroft v al-Kidd* 563 U.S. (2011). The Supreme Court further held that former Attorney-General Ashcroft was entitled to qualified immunity from suit because he was acting within the scope of his duties. <http://www.supremecourt.gov/opinions/10pdf/10-98.pdf>.

used as a pretext to sidestep longstanding checks on the arbitrary exercise of executive power.'[23] The abuse of material witness detention indicates the importance of ensuring that coercive measures are used solely for the purposes for which they were introduced and of instituting checks to ensure that they are not misapplied for other ends entirely (see Section 5.3(b) above).

The characterization of the terrorist atrocities of 9/11 as acts of war by the US administration thus made possible a host of strategies that test the very limits of the rule of law. Although the war on terror constituted a significant retreat from a criminal justice-based approach to combating terrorism,[24] prosecution of terrorist suspects continued. Under the Bush administration, from 2001 to 2009, 828 prosecutions were mounted against terrorist suspects, and the percentage of successful convictions rose from 38 per cent in 2006–2007 to 89 per cent in 2009.[25] On election in 2009, President Obama declared his intention to try more terrorist suspects in civilian rather than military courts and during the first two years of his administration the annual number of terrorist-related prosecutions doubled.[26] The move was controversial and has been repeatedly opposed since,[27] but it was welcomed by liberals like Waldron who applauded it as a 'welcome return to the criminal justice model'.[28] The 'return' has been at best partial. Obama's repeated pledges to close the detention facility at Guantanamo Bay have met with steep resistance, and indefinite detention at Guantanamo and the use of military commissions continue.[29]

---

[23] Human Rights Watch, *Witness to Abuse Human Rights* (n 21), 2.

[24] Waldron, *Torture, Terror and Trade-Offs: Philosophy for the White House* (n 5), Ch.1; L Zedner, 'Terrorizing Criminal Law', *Criminal Law and Philosophy* 8(1) (2014).

[25] Center on Law and Security, NYU *Terrorism Trial Report Card: September 11 2001– September 11, 2009* (New York: NYU) at ii. <http://www.lawandsecurity.org/Portals/0/ documents/02_TTRCFinalJan142.pdf>.

[26] Center on Law and Security, NYU *Terrorism Trial Report Card: September 11 2001* (New York: NYU), 2. Approximately 87 per cent of all resolved cases resulted in a conviction. *Terrorism Trial Report Card*, 7. <http://www.lawandsecurity.org/Portals/0/Documents/ TTRC%20Ten%20Year%20Issue.pdf>.

[27] See, eg, M Mukasey, 'Civilian Courts Are No Place to Try Terrorists', *The Wall Street Journal* (19 October 2009) <http://online.wsj.com/article/SB1000142405274870410720- 4574475300052267212.html>. B Wittes and J Goldsmith, 'Skip the trials for terrorists', *The Washington Post* (19 November 2010) <http://www.washingtonpost.com/wp-dyn/content/ article/2010/11/18/AR2010111806074.html>.

[28] Waldron, *Torture, Terror and Trade-Offs: Philosophy for the White House* (n 5), 17.

[29] See 'Barack Obama says Guantanamo Bay prison must close' (30 April 2013) *BBC News* <http://www.bbc.co.uk/news/world-us-canada-22358351>. Of 166 inmates held at Guantanamo Bay in April 2013, five were due to be tried by military tribunal, 36 were identified as triable in either military or civilian court, and 48 were classified as too dangerous to release but could not be taken to trial. Source: 'Q&A: Guantanamo detentions', *BBC News* (30 April 2013) <http://www.bbc.co.uk/news/world-us-canada-12966676>.

In Britain, debates since 9/11 about whether prevention of terrorism is better pursued under the military or crime model and the practices of prevention themselves have been more complex and less easily classified. Britain was a coalition partner in the wars in Iraq and Afghanistan. Outside these theatres of war, successive British governments have resisted pressure to treat terrorism as a military threat.[30] Yet, despite the official commitment to prosecute terrorism as a crime, the British government has readily and frequently adopted the language and practices of security. Compared with the United States, Britain has been less ready to resort to extra-legal and executive measures, and has shown a greater commitment to legalism. However, as Roach points out, this commitment is double-edged in that 'the overriding theme of the British response is a commitment to a legislative war on terrorism that is prepared to impose robust limits and derogations on rights normally enjoyed in the nonterrorist context'.[31] One example of this approach is resort to legislation that introduces administrative and civil measures, such as Control Orders and their successors, Terrorism Prevention and Investigation Measures (TPIMs), that substantially side-step the protections of the criminal process in pursuit of security (see further discussion below). In part, these departures from the ordinary legislative order derive from judgements made about the scale and likelihood of terrorist threats. In the period since 9/11, Britain is the only one of the Council of Europe's 47 Member States to have derogated from the ECHR under Article 15, which provides for derogation from the Convention 'in time of war or other emergency threatening the life of the nation': it did so in order to introduce indefinite preventive detention of foreign nationals suspected of involvement in terrorism (discussed below). The sense of emergency in Britain was greater still in the aftermath of the bombings that killed 52 civilians and injured more than 700 in London in July 2005, as a result of which the official terrorist threat assessment was raised to the highest level. Since 2005, the official terrorist threat assessment in Britain has rarely dropped below its present level—'substantial', which denotes that an attack is a strong possibility.[32] Moreover, the police and MI5 are reported to foil plots on a similar scale to the 7/7 bomb attacks every year.[33] The continuing threat of further attack frames debates about pre-empting terrorism, the special legal powers needed to do so, and consequent limits to procedural protections owed to suspects.

---

[30] D Cole, 'English Lessons: A Comparative Analysis of UK and US Responses to Terrorism', *Current Legal Problems* 62(1) (2009), 136–67.

[31] Roach, *The 9/11 Effect: Comparative Counter-Terrorism* (n 3), 238.

[32] <https://www.gov.uk/terrorism-national-emergency/terrorism-threat-levels>.

[33] <http://www.telegraph.co.uk/news/uknews/terrorism-in-the-uk/9946806/Major-terror-attack-on-scale-of-77-foiled-every-year-in-UK-police-reveal.html>.

8.3 Preventing Terrorism through the Criminal Law

The definition of acts of terrorism as crimes is problematic. On the one hand, ordinary criminal law could cover almost all forms of terrorist act; and the malign intent of the perpetrators and the grave harms risked by terrorist activity justify criminalization. Successful terrorist attacks typically result in serious harm to persons and property and, as such, fall within the core of serious criminal offences such as murder, arson, and criminal damage endangering life. On the other hand, it is questionable whether the criminal law can capture the distinctive and exceptional features of successful terrorist attacks. The sheer scale and catastrophic harm to life and property, together with the intent to terrorize the population, to challenge the sovereignty of the state and, in some cases, to secure specific political ends place terrorist atrocities beyond the scope of even the most serious offences. As Waldron observes: 'a special sort of moral outrage should be reserved for terrorist crimes, as distinguished from other homicides or acts of destruction . . . we put definitional pressure on our ability to articulate this sense that special outrage is appropriate for these offences'.[34] It is not easy to capture this outrage or the terror that takes terrorism out of the realm of ordinary crime. Specifying this terror within the definition of a criminal offence is enormously difficult. Yet, no defensible creation of criminal offences can proceed unless it is possible to articulate precisely the phenomenon that is to be criminalized.

Furthermore, the principles of maximum certainty and of fair labelling require that the definition of criminal conduct is clear, unambiguous, and precise enough for the rules to provide fair warning, so that individuals can determine what is unlawful and make their decisions accordingly. Fair labelling also ensures that the censure that attaches to conviction and the punitive response that follows is proportionate to the wrong done.[35] This said, the principles of maximum certainty and fair labelling are predicated on the assumption that offenders are autonomous rational agents who may be deterred by the threat of censure and punishment. The determination of many would-be terrorists to pursue their goals irrespective of the risks and their willingness to die in this pursuit calls into question this assumption. Suicide bombing is a common characteristic of contemporary terrorism that radically undermines the criminal law's potential deterrent effect, since perpetrators are unlikely to be inhibited by the threat of punishment. Moreover, although the creation of terrorist offences is commonly justified partly by deterrence, there is little evidence that more expansive criminal laws or harsher punishments in fact

---

[34] Waldron, *Torture, Terror and Trade-Offs: Philosophy for the White House* (n 5), 49.
[35] A Ashworth and J Horder, *The Principles of Criminal Law* 7th edn (Oxford: Oxford University Press, 2013), 62–5; 77–9.

deter.[36] The labelling of these offences as heinous wrongs may be more important for its declaratory effect and for reassuring the general public than for their power to deter would-be offenders.

The more catastrophic the potential consummate offence, the greater the imperative to prevent, and the more it can justly be said that prosecution and punishment of the completed offence comes too late, which is why a significant feature of terrorism offences is that they criminalize pre-inchoate, preparatory, facilitative, and associative offences (for details, see Section 5.1).[37] The urgent need to prevent terrorist attacks and the relative infrequency of successfully completed terrorist atrocities mean that, in practice, the prosecution of completed terrorist offences is rare. Even if would-be terrorists are willing to die in the execution of their plans, they nonetheless wish to complete the attack successfully. So, while terrorists may not be easily deterred, they may be halted by the criminalization of remote or early conduct since this permits the police to interrupt them in the initial planning stages. Terrorism offences create a sphere of operation in which police and security officials may monitor, stop and search, interrogate, and detain would-be terrorists with the aim of forestalling the consummate harm.

The drive to prevent terrorism by expanding the operational realm and investigatory powers of the police and security services has significantly widened the ambit of the criminal law.[38] As we observed in Section 5.3(b), it has led to the creation of offences defined in broad and imprecise terms that target conduct temporarily and causally remote from the substantive harm. A prominent example given in Section 5.3(b) was the offence, under the Terrorism Act 2006, of encouraging or glorifying terrorism, which is more widely defined than its purported justification allows. Thus, as shown in Chapter 5, criminalization as a means of preventing terrorism carries the risk of rendering unlawful forms of conduct that do not satisfy the usual requirements of mens rea and actus reus, and that only weakly satisfy the harm principle. The conduct may not itself be harmful and it may be only tenuously causally related to the consummate harm, and the perpetrators may have little normative involvement in the subsequent acts of the principal agents.[39]

For all the criticisms that may legitimately be made of the broad framing and questionable bases of many terrorism offences,[40] the criminalization of terrorist

---

[36] MC Melia, 'Terrorism and Criminal Law: The Dream of Prevention, the Nightmare of the Rule of Law', *New Criminal Law Review* 14(1) (2011), 108–22; 114.

[37] A Goldsmith, 'Preparation for Terrorism: Catastrophic Risk and Precautionary Criminal Law', in A Lynch, E Macdonald, and G Williams (eds.), *Law and Liberty in the War on Terror* (Annandale, NSW: The Federation Press, 2007), 59–74; C Murphy, *EU Counter-Terrorism Law: Pre-Emption and the Rule of Law* (Oxford: Hart Publishing, 2012).

[38] See Ch. 5.

[39] A Simester and A von Hirsch, *Crimes, Harms and Wrongs: On the Principles of Criminalization* (Oxford: Hart Publishing, 2011), Ch. 4.

[40] V Tadros, 'Justice and Terrorism', *New Criminal Law Review* 10(4) (2007), 658–89; V Tadros and J Hodgson, 'How to Make a Terrorist out of Nothing', *Modern Law Review* 72(6) (2009), 984–98.

activity at least requires that actions against terrorist suspects are pursued in criminal proceedings. This promises a more constrained exercise of state power and greater procedural protections than military action, security measures, or civil preventive measures. It also offers a stronger prospect of openness, transparency, and accountability than the covert operations of intelligence and securities services.[41] Most obviously, those suspected of the most serious offences can be brought before the criminal courts and, if found guilty, they can be sentenced to commensurately long periods of imprisonment.[42] The average sentence in the UK for individuals convicted of a terrorist offence in 2011 was 17 years.[43] The continuing counterarguments against prosecution include the fact that intelligence may not be admissible as evidence and that the imperatives of security may not be consistent with trial in open court. Indeed, the Independent Reviewer has observed what he terms 'an unpalatable truth: that while it [ie prosecution] should always be the first and preferable option for dealing with suspected terrorists, the criminal justice system—whose open nature may prevent some relevant national security evidence from being used—is not always enough to keep the public safe'.[44]

8.4 Preventing Terrorism outside the Criminal Process

It is perhaps not surprising therefore that, notwithstanding its formal commitment to prosecuting terrorist suspects, the UK government has introduced many laws and measures outside the criminal process. These rely upon administrative or civil proceedings and entail fewer protections for those whom they target. This strategy of prevention through civil and administrative channels is by no means confined to terrorism. As we observed in Chapter 4, recourse to civil and hybrid civil-criminal preventive measures has been an important feature of lawmaking since the 1990s, as evidenced by the introduction of the ASBO, the Serious Crime Prevention Order, and the many other civil preventive orders. However, it is in respect of the potentially catastrophic risks posed by terrorism that the most intrusive and far-reaching measures, with the greatest impact upon individual liberty, have been

---

[41] Goldsmith, 'Preparation for Terrorism: Catastrophic Risk and Precautionary Criminal Law' (n 37), 63.

[42] See further Zedner, 'Terrorizing Criminal Law' (n 24).

[43] Europol TESAT 2012: EU Terrorism Situation and Trend Report. European Police Office 14 at <https://www.europol.europa.eu/sites/default/files/publications/europoltsat.pdf>.

[44] D Anderson, *Terrorism Prevention and Investigation in 2012: First Report of the Independent Review on the Operation of the Terrorism Prevention and Investigation Act 2011* (London: TSO, 2013), 62.

introduced.[45] Various forms of preventive detention on grounds of national security including extended investigative detention by the police, indefinite administrative detention (until it was ruled unlawful in 2004), and immigration detention have all been deployed to detain those suspected of preparing terrorist attacks but against whom no criminal charge has been brought.[46] As we shall see below, lesser but nonetheless onerous and enduring restrictions have been imposed under Control Orders and to a more limited degree by their successors, TPIMs.

How has this resort to preventive measures outside the criminal process come about? Britain is no stranger to the threat of terrorism and recourse to non-criminal measures was an enduring feature of the British government's tactics in seeking to prevent terrorist attacks by the IRA during the 1970s and 1980s.[47] Resort to administrative detention resulted in the internment of almost 2,500 people suspected of involvement in terrorism in Northern Ireland in 1971–1972, and these regulations themselves derived from earlier British laws in former colonies such as Singapore, Malaysia, and Palestine. The use of administrative detention in Northern Ireland was widely criticized for imposing detention without the due process protections of a criminal trial, for creating conditions conducive to radicalization within detention facilities, and for generating a strong sense of injustice and grievance in the population outside. Yet, recourse to civil measures and administrative detention continue to be important features of counterterrorism (on the use of immigration detention for counterterrorism, see further Chapter 10). Part of the explanation is that in the UK, as in the US, the catastrophic scale of the 9/11 attacks was deemed to change the legal landscape. In the immediate aftermath of 9/11, then British Prime Minister Tony Blair announced that 'the rules of the game have changed'.[48] The legal protections of the criminal process were regarded by many, even those usually committed to civil liberties, as too favourable to suspects and as obstacles to the pursuit of security.[49] Those who championed them were seen as stubborn 'liberty partisans', incapable of seeing that the world had changed.[50] To avoid the protections of the criminal trial, and the human rights protections that attached to it under Article 6, it was again proposed that preventive measures be pursued in administrative and civil domains.[51] This move perhaps reflects

[45] A Lynch, E Macdonald, and G Williams (eds.), *Law and Liberty in the War on Terror* (Sydney: The Federation Press, 2007).

[46] For a masterly analysis of these provisions, see Roach, *The 9/11 Effect: Comparative Counter-Terrorism* (n 3).

[47] See the discussion in Roach, *The 9/11 Effect* (n 3), 244–62.

[48] P Wintour, 'Blair vows to root out extremism' *The Guardian* (6 August 2005). <http://www.guardian.co.uk/politics/2005/aug/06/terrorism.july7>.

[49] See discussion in Waldron, *Torture, Terror and Trade-Offs: Philosophy for the White House* (n 5), 7.

[50] Zedner, 'Terrorizing Criminal Law' (n 24).

[51] L Zedner, 'Seeking Security by Eroding Rights: The Side-Stepping of Due Process', in B Goold and L Lazarus (eds.), *Security and Human Rights* (Oxford: Hart Publishing, 2007), 257–76.

Dershowitz's claim that: '[t]he need for preventive intervention becomes more obvious in a society that has circumscribed the formal process of criminal justice with safeguards that make conviction more difficult.'[52] The problem, as we observed in Chapter 4, is that although the safeguards and thresholds may be lower in respect of purely preventive measures, the burdens imposed are not necessarily less punitive.

Just two months after the 9/11 attacks, the Anti-Terrorism, Crime and Security Act 2001 was passed: under Part IV this provided that the Home Secretary could detain indefinitely any non-British citizens he suspected of terrorist activity, either pending deportation or in cases where deportation was not possible for fear of torture.[53] Between 2001 and 2004, 17 foreign nationals suspected of terrorism were thus detained at Belmarsh Prison in London,[54] until such detention was ruled unlawful by the House of Lords on the grounds that the provision was disproportionate and that it discriminated unfairly against foreign nationals.[55] Lord Hoffman agreed that the appeals should be allowed but dissented from the majority decision on the grounds that the entire scheme was incompatible with the UK constitution and its commitment to human rights. In respect of the indefinite detention of terrorist suspects, he concluded that 'such a power in any form is not compatible with our constitution. The real threat to the life of the nation, in the sense of a people living in accordance with its traditional laws and political values, comes not from terrorism but from laws such as these.'[56]

The matter went to the ECtHR in *A v UK* (2009),[57] in respect of 11 terrorist suspects who had been preventively detained indefinitely. The Court held unanimously that there had been a violation of the right to liberty and security, of the right to have lawfulness of detention decided by a court, and of the right to be compensated for such violations. It held that the detention of terrorist suspects based 'solely or to a decisive degree on closed material' always amounts to a breach of procedural fairness as guaranteed by the ECHR. And it further held that Article 5(4) ECHR requires that suspects be given sufficient detail of the allegations against them

---

[52] A Dershowitz, *Preemption: A Knife That Cuts Both Ways* (New York: W.W. Norton, 2006), 40.

[53] H Fenwick, 'The Anti-Terrorism, Crime and Security Act 2001: A Proportionate Response to 11 September?', *Modern Law Review* 65(5) (2002), 724–62; PA Thomas, 'Emergency and Anti-Terrorist Powers 9/11: USA and UK', *Fordham International Law Journal* 26(4) (2003), 1193–233.

[54] The regime at Belmarsh was condemned, perhaps implausibly, as 'Britain's Guantanamo Bay'. See, eg, 'Belmarsh—Britain's Guantanamo Bay?' *BBC News* (6 October 2004) <http://news.bbc.co.uk/1/hi/magazine/3714864.stm>.

[55] Following the 'Belmarsh case'. *A and others v Secretary of State for the Home Department* [2004] UKHL 56.

[56] *A and others v Secretary of State for the Home Department* [2004] UKHL 56. For a penetrating analysis of the role of the courts in this and subsequent cases, see A Tomkins, 'National Security and the Role of the Court: A Changed Landscape?', *Law Quarterly Review* 126 (2010), 543–67.

[57] *A v UK* (2009) 49 EHRR 29.

in order for them to give effective instructions to their special advocate. Although the UK government took the view that no further general measures were necessary to implement this judgment, because the legal regime found to have violated the ECHR (namely indefinite detention under ATCSA Part IV) had been repealed, it is arguable that the case has important implications for the use of special advocates and closed material proceedings more generally.

Denied resort to indefinite detention, the government introduced hybrid civil-criminal measures—Control Orders—under the Prevention of Terrorism Act (PTA) 2005 which were immediately imposed on all those who had been held at Belmarsh. Control Orders applied to both citizens and non-citizens and could be used against those for whom prosecution or deportation was not possible.[58] Control Orders came in two forms: derogating orders, which were in practice never used, and non-derogating orders which enabled the Home Secretary to impose stringent restrictions on those whom he thought to pose a threat. Under PTA, s. 2(1)(a), a Control Order could be imposed where the Home Secretary had '... reasonable grounds for suspecting the individual is or has been involved in a terrorist related activity' and that 'it is necessary, for purposes connected with protecting members of the public from a risk of terrorism', but in respect of whom prosecution was not deemed possible.[59] Control Orders were an alternative to prosecution; conviction for a criminal offence was not required. The 'reasonable grounds' threshold set the standard of proof far below that which is applicable in criminal cases. Control Orders permitted the Home Secretary to impose multiple onerous restrictions:[60] these included lengthy curfews of up to 16 hours per day,[61] significant restrictions on place of residence and on movement, on communication, use of the internet, and association with others, restrictions on work or other occupation, the breach of which resulted in criminal conviction and sanction by up to five years' imprisonment. Controlees were liable to surrender of passport, electronic monitoring and other surveillance, regular home searches, and they were required to comply with demands for information or surrender of possessions. A sunset clause required the scheme to be reviewed annually, but in practice it was repeatedly renewed each year

---

[58] For an extended, critical analysis of the resort to Control Orders, see V Tadros, 'Controlling Risk', in A Ashworth, L Zedner, and P Tomlin (eds.), *Prevention and the Limits of the Criminal Law* (Oxford: Oxford University Press, 2013), 133–55.

[59] Or for whom deportation was not available because the suspect was a British national or could not be deported for risk of torture or inhumane treatment.

[60] For a full list, see Liberty, *From War to Law: Liberty's Response to the Coalitions Government's Review of Counter-Terrorism and Security Powers 2010* (London: Liberty), 16 fn 12. <http://www.liberty-human-rights.org.uk/pdfs/policy10/from-war-to-law-final-pdf-with-bookmarks.pdf>.

[61] An 18-hour curfew was held to be a deprivation of liberty in breach of the controlee's rights and was quashed in *SSHD v JJ & Others* [2008] 1 AC 385. In this case it was held that the lengthy curfew combined with the exclusion of visitors amounted in effect to 'solitary confinement'. Liberty, *From War to Law* (n 60), 24.

almost without debate. Individual Control Orders could be renewed indefinitely and several individuals were subject to a Control Order for years. A particularly grievous aspect of the regime was provision for forced relocation by which controlees were moved hundreds of miles from their community, family, and friends, and obliged to live under curfew in considerable isolation or 'internal exile'.[62]

Unsurprisingly, the Control Order was subject to sustained criticism and several challenges in the courts on questions of their compatibility with the ECHR.[63] In the leading case of *AF*, Lord Hope described the most onerous Control Orders as imposing conditions 'not far short of house arrest'.[64] Other judgments addressed their failure to respect the rights of freedom of movement, privacy, family life, and the right to a fair trial of those subject to them.[65] Judicial concern about Control Orders revolved broadly around two main issues. First, the orders provided a potent means of protecting citizens from terrorism but at the cost of very substantial restrictions on the liberty of those subject to them, some of which were deemed to amount to a deprivation of liberty.[66] Because the orders were imposed at a very early stage in, or in the absence of, criminal proceedings, they breached basic common law principles: the presumption of innocence, the right to a fair trial, and duty of the state to prove its case against individuals before subjecting them to severe curtailment of their liberty. The second central issue addressed by the courts was the right of controlees to know the case against them (as required under Article 6 ECHR). In *AF*, the House of Lords held that an individual subject to a Control Order must be informed of the case against him and that 'non-disclosure cannot go so far as to deny a party knowledge of the essence of the case against him'.

In *AN v SSHD* (2010),[67] the Court of Appeal held that it was a breach of the right to a fair trial under Article 6 to hold someone under a Control Order without sufficient information about the case against him even where the case was based

---

[62] Liberty, *From War to Law* (n 60), 12.

[63] See, eg, the analysis in D Feldman, 'Deprivation of Liberty in Anti-Terrorism Law', *Cambridge Law Journal* 67(1) (2008), 4–8.

[64] Lord Hope in *Secretary of State for the Home Department v AF & Others (No. 3)* [2009] UKHL 28, 77. See discussion in A Kavanagh, 'Special Advocates, Control Orders and the Right to a Fair Trial', *Modern Law Review* 63(5) (2010), 836–57; 836.

[65] See discussion of these cases in A Hunt, 'From Control Orders to TPIMs: Variations on a Number of Themes in British Legal Responses to Terrorism', *Crime, Law and Social Change* (forthcoming); S Macdonald, 'ASBOs and Control Orders: Two Recurring Themes, Two Apparent Contradictions', *Parliamentary Affairs* 60(4) (2007), 601–24; L Zedner, 'Preventive Justice or Pre-Punishment? The Case of Control Orders', *Current Legal Problems* 59 (2007), 174–203; C Walker, 'Keeping Control of Terrorists without Losing Control of Constitutionalism', *Stanford Law Review* 59(5) (2007), 1395–464.

[66] For example, it was held that a Control Order that imposed 18 hours of house arrest violated the right to liberty (though it was subsequently decided that 16 hours constituted a mere 'restriction' on liberty and did not). On the distinction between deprivation and restriction of liberty, see *SSHD v JJ & Others* [2008] 1 AC 385; *Secretary of State v MB* [2007] UKHL 46.

[67] *AN v SSHD* [2010] EWCA Civ 869.

upon 'closed materials', disclosure of which would compromise national security. The Court not only required that the orders be revoked but that those held be compensated so as to remedy the breach. Following the decision, the Secretary of State decided to revoke the individual Control Orders in question rather than reveal the security sensitive information that formed the basis of the case against the controlees. This decision resulted in part from the countervailing claim, made by the security services and the police in respect of closed material proceedings, that to disclose security-sensitive secret evidence in open court would be to risk the lives of operatives, informants, and others; the workings of the security services; and in some cases the security interests of other nations.

In 2010, the Joint Committee on Human Rights (JCHR) concluded that the Control Order regime was no longer sustainable on the grounds that the orders had a 'devastating impact' on controlees, their families, and their communities, and that the cost of the system was 'out of all proportion to the supposed public benefit'.[68] The JCHR called for the government to abolish Control Orders in favour of more vigorous pursuit of prosecution of terrorist suspects in general and intensive surveillance of those few who could not be prosecuted. On coming to power, the coalition government announced an urgent review as part of the Counter Terror and Security Powers Review 2010, the purpose of which was 'to determine whether it might be possible to roll back some of the measures imposed by counter-terrorism and other legislation over the last decades, consistent with public safety'.[69] Responses to the Review were overwhelmingly critical, arguing that Control Orders should be abolished,[70] and the Review itself recognized that 'the present control order regime acts as an impediment to prosecution'.[71] In 2011, Control Orders were abolished and replaced with TPIMs under the Terrorism Prevention and Investigation Measures Act 2011.

Swiftly branded 'Control Orders-lite',[72] TPIMs continue to impose significant restrictions upon individuals who have not been charged with any criminal offence. The threshold for imposition has been raised from 'reasonable grounds for suspecting' to 'reasonable belief'; overnight residence requirements substituted for lengthy curfews; a warrant is required before their property is searched; and relocation requirements have been abolished, but the TPIM regime is otherwise only slightly

---

[68] JCHR, *Counter-Terrorism Policy and Human Rights (Sixteenth Report): Annual Renewal of Control Orders Legislation* (HL Paper 64, HC 395, 2010).

[69] K Macdonald, *Review of Counter-Terrorism and Security Powers Cm 8003* (London: HMSO, 2011), 2.

[70] HM Government, *Review of Counter-Terrorism and Security Powers: Summary of Responses to the Consultation CM 8005* (London: HMSO, 2011), 14.

[71] Macdonald, *Review of Counter-Terrorism and Security Powers Cm 8003* (n 69), 9.

[72] <https://www.liberty-human-rights.org.uk/human-rights/terrorism/control-orders/index.php>.

less onerous than its predecessor.[73] It is also questionable whether and to what extent the TPIM regime is more compatible with the government's avowed commitment to give priority to prosecution. Notwithstanding the name change, the restrictions imposed by TPIMs are based principally upon averting the threat that the individual is thought to pose rather than for the purposes of investigation or punishment. Insofar as TPIMs label terrorist suspects as known to the authorities, limit their movement, communication, and associations, this will clearly have the effect of inhibiting the collection of evidence and so militate against successful prosecution. Although they are also civil measures, TPIMs, like Control Orders before them, include a power to imprison for up to five years for breach of the conditions of the order.

TPIMs also provide a level of security palpably inferior to that supplied by imprisonment. If the surveillance, oversight, and restrictions on movement, association, and communication imposed by Control Orders had no more than a limited power to prevent terrorism,[74] and since TPIMs impose less restrictive conditions, it seems unlikely that they will be more effective. It is unclear upon what basis the Independent Reviewer concludes that 'TPIMs are likely to have been effective in preventing terrorism-related activity during 2012', particularly since he goes on to concede that there has as yet been no full-scale analysis of the extent to which would-be terrorists have been prevented by TPIMs.[75] A particular concern is that the two-year limit imposed upon TPIMs provides no means of preventing further terrorist activity after the expiry of the term and may encourage some would-be terrorists to wait out the period in order then to resume activity.[76] At least a third of those subject to Control Orders were deemed sufficiently dangerous to be subject to those orders for more than two years and some for more than four years. It would, therefore, appear that the two-year limit on TPIMs (in the absence of evidence of new terrorist-related activity) removes necessary restrictions on those who may well continue to be a danger to the public. As Hunt points out, it would

---

[73] Liberty have produced a table comparing Control Orders and TPIMs, see <http://www.liberty-human-rights.org.uk/pdfs/policy11/tpim-and-control-order-comparison-table-october-2011-.pdf>. See also C Walker and A Horne, 'The Terrorism Prevention and Investigations Measures Act 2011: One Thing but Not Much the Other?', *Criminal Law Review* (2012), 421–38; 421–3; Hunt, 'From Control Orders to TPIMs: Variations on a Number of Themes in British Legal Responses to Terrorism' (n 65).

[74] As evidenced, not least, by the fact that seven of those subject to Control Orders absconded. Equality and Human Rights Commission Human Rights Review 2012, 183 <http://www.equalityhumanrights.com/human-rights/human-rights-review/>.

[75] Anderson, *Terrorism Prevention and Investigation in 2012: First Report of the Independent Review on the Operation of the Terrorism Prevention and Investigation Act 2011* (n 44), 6; 87.

[76] The Independent Reviewer observes that on expiry: 'Some subjects who have been judged by the Home Secretary and by the courts to be potentially dangerous will then, absent prosecution or new evidence of terrorism-related activity, be free and unconstrained.' Anderson, *Terrorism Prevention and Investigation in 2012* (n 44), 7.

appear inconsistent to require that the government deems it necessary to impose and maintain TPIMs to protect national security and public safety, but to provide for mandatory release without regard for necessity after two years.[77]

A particularly controversial aspect of Control Orders—representation by special advocates and use of closed materials proceedings—is perpetuated under the TPIM regime. Special advocates are lawyers who have been security cleared and appointed by the Attorney General to act in closed material proceedings where these are necessitated by the sensitivity of the intelligence material at issue. Special advocates act as representatives in these cases but they are not permitted to communicate with suspects once they have seen the evidence against them.[78] The continuing use of special advocates and of closed material proceedings is problematic because it substantially undermines the ability of those subject to proceedings to know the case against them.[79] Although the courts have held that Article 6 requires 'a "core irreducible minimum" of procedural fairness such that "[t]he controlled person must be given sufficient information about the allegations against him to give effective instructions to the Special Advocate"', it is questionable whether the present arrangements suffice to create equality of arms.[80] Moreover, it can be argued that the stipulations applied by the courts to the use of secret materials and special advocates in order to render them compatible with human rights protections have succeeded only in legitimizing their use. This legitimizing effect is evidenced most powerfully by the fact that closed proceedings have been extended to other civil proceedings that involve sensitive intelligence relating to national security under the Justice and Security Act 2013.

TPIMs are above all preventive measures, whose purpose is to impede the planning and execution of terrorist plots by those subject to them. Although TPIMs also have an investigative remit, the individual's awareness that they are under scrutiny, together with the limits imposed upon the individual's freedom of movement, communication, and association, make it much less likely that admissible evidence can be collected about them.[81] The consequence of this 'chilling'

---

[77] See discussion in Hunt, 'From Control Orders to TPIMs: Variations on a Number of Themes in British Legal Responses to Terrorism' (n 65), 20–1.

[78] A Tomkins, 'National Security and the Due Process of Law', *Current Legal Problems* 64(1) (2011), 215–53; 216–23.

[79] Justice, *Secret Evidence* (London: Justice, 2009). See also 'Justice and Security Green Paper: Response to Consultation from Special Advocates' at <http://consultation. cabinetoffice.gov.uk/justiceandsecurity/wp-content/uploads/2012/09_Special%20Advo cates.pdf>.

[80] Kavanagh, 'Special Advocates, Control Orders and the Right to a Fair Trial' (n 64), 838, quoting the decision in *SSHD v AF* (2009).

[81] Anderson, *Terrorism Prevention and Investigation in 2012: First Report of the Independent Review on the Operation of the Terrorism Prevention and Investigation Act 2011* (n 44), 6.

effect is to make prosecution less plausible than it would otherwise be, even though the justice of allowing allegedly dangerous offenders to escape prosecution is dubious. The argument that TPIMs should be permitted to persist only so long as investigation is ongoing was not accepted.[82] Instead, a watered-down provision, that tacitly acknowledged the difficulty of tying the TPIM to a live prosecution, requires only that the Secretary of State must keep under review the 'ongoing necessity' of the measure during the period that the TPIM is in force.[83] The continuing use of civil preventive measures against terrorist suspects side-steps the criminal process, denies those subject to them the right to a fair and timely trial in an open court; the right to confront witnesses, to know and to dispute the evidence against them; and the right to legal advice, legal aid, their choice of legal representation, and confidentiality in communication with their lawyers.[84] No other civil preventive measures of comparable severity have so far been imposed upon individuals who have not been convicted of a crime.[85] It is also troubling that four of those presently subject to TPIMs have previously been acquitted of charges that form at least part of the case against them.[86] Although this practice has been justified by the lower standard of proof required and the fact that intelligence may not be capable of being used as evidence in a criminal trial, it is, nonetheless, disquieting that those who have been acquitted by a criminal court are then subject to such intrusive measures. As a matter of principle, an individual who has been acquitted by a criminal court should not then be subject to coercive measures.

Even where prosecution is in view, the ordinary protections of the criminal process do not apply. Changes to provisions for pre-charge detention allow the detention of terrorist suspects for extended periods prior to charge. In Britain, the normal maximum period of pre-charge detention is 96 hours (four days) but under s. 23 of the Terrorism Act 2006 those suspected of terrorist activity could be held for up to 28 days, though this has since reverted to 14 days.[87] Even this constitutes a very significant departure from the normal maximum, and again it is rationalized on the grounds that investigations in such cases face special difficulties, as well as on grounds of the gravity of the prospective harm.

---

[82] As made by the former DPP, Ken Macdonald, in his capacity as head of a government review of counterterrorism and security powers, Macdonald, *Review of Counter-Terrorism and Security Powers* Cm 8003 (n 69), 9–10.

[83] Terrorism Prevention and Investigation Measures Act 2011, s. 11.

[84] A Ashworth, 'Security, Terrorism and the Value of Human Rights', in B Goold and L Lazarus (eds.), *Security and Human Rights* (Oxford: Hart Publishing, 2007), 203–26.

[85] Anderson, *Terrorism Prevention and Investigation in 2012: First Report of the Independent Review on the Operation of the Terrorism Prevention and Investigation Act 2011* (n 44), 10.

[86] Anderson, *Terrorism Prevention and Investigation in 2012* (n 44), 46.

[87] The statutory period of 28-day detention lapsed in January 2012 and the maximum term reverted to 14 days. The Protection of Freedoms Act 2012, part 4 permanently reduces the maximum term to 14 days.

Substantial restrictions may also be imposed upon terrorist suspects by way of bail conditions. For example, in the case of the radical Muslim cleric and terrorist suspect Abu Qatada, stringent bail conditions included a 22-hour curfew during which Qatada could not even enter his garden, imposition of a very restricted area of movement for the remaining two hours, surrender of passport, electronic tagging, a ban on use of phones, computers, and data storage devices, a ban on communicating with anyone (bar his wife and children) without prior approval, and a ban on making any statement without prior approval of the Home Secretary.[88] Abu Qatada was subsequently held to have breached his bail conditions and returned to prison pending his deportation to Jordan in July 2013 where he now faces charges. The use of bail rather than pre-trial detention is compatible with the principle of the least restrictive alternative, but that principle also requires each restriction incorporated in the bail conditions to be justified.

Elsewhere, detention without trial or judicial review persists despite strenuous campaigns by lawyers and civil liberties advocates to end it. As we have observed, numerous promises to close the US facility at Guantanamo Bay have come to nothing and the detention of terrorist suspects continues. Against the argument that criminal prosecution is the best means to provide adequate procedural protections and to ensure adherence with the rule of law, the claims of national security license preventive detention of those deemed too dangerous to release but against whom investigation is pending or in respect of whom prosecution is not possible. Cochran defends this, arguing that, 'in the context of long-term detention, national security may require non-criminal detention of terrorists who cannot be tried but are too dangerous to release'.[89] This view has been contested by powerful critics, such as Waldron, who argues that, while there may be instances in which detention without trial is justified, 'it is hard to think of methods of ensuring that this power is not abused, that it does not get out of hand, and that detention does not turn into "disappearance"'.[90] Quite apart from the issue of injustice, coercive measures like detention without trial exacerbate problems of alienation and exclusion that conduce to radicalization. Counterterrorism laws and measures that are overly harsh or unwarranted create grievances among those who are targeted. Practices such as the profiling and targeting of terrorist suspects on grounds of ethnicity or religious faith, oppressive surveillance techniques, aggressive police operations, and dawn raids also generate hostility and disaffection that feeds religious radicalization, political extremism, and recruitment by terrorist groups.

---

[88] See 'Abu Qatada released under strict bail conditions', *The Telegraph* (13 February 2012) <http://www.telegraph.co.uk/news/uknews/law-and-order/9080137/Abu-Qatada-released-under-strict-bail-conditions.html>.

[89] Cochran, 'Material Witness Detention in a Post-9/11 World: Mission Creep or Fresh Start?' (n 20), 33.

[90] Waldron, *Torture, Terror and Trade-Offs: Philosophy for the White House* (n 5).

8.5 The *Prevent* Strategy

Recognition that overly coercive counterterrorism policies are likely to be counterproductive has led to the development of 'soft' security endeavours. These stand some distance from the 'hard' preventive measures with which this book is primarily concerned, but they are important to the UK security strategy in seeking a means of prevention that does not rely wholly on coercion to fulfil its aims. Since 2007 a central plank in the UK's counterterrorism policy has been the *Prevent* strategy.[91] This has had among its main aims to 'prevent people from being drawn into terrorism and ensure that they are given appropriate advice and support' and to 'work with sectors and institutions where there are risks of radicalisation'.[92] However, the use of 'soft' power under *Prevent* merges into more intrusive and liberty-eroding security strategies, such as surveillance, monitoring, intelligence gathering, and use of informants. While the role of the police under *Prevent*, as initially conceived, was to build good community relations, they also sought to persuade members of those same communities to act as informants to provide intelligence about suspicious or problematic behaviour.[93] *Prevent* requires neighbourhood police officers to gather information about the circulation of extremist ideologies, particularly where those ideologies endorse violence.[94] Tensions between surveillance and the attempt to build trust have caused problems. Individuals with whom one branch of the police is seeking to build trust in order to prevent their radicalization may simultaneously be the subject of covert surveillance or investigation by another.[95]

---

[91] *Prevent* is one of the four streams of the overall UK strategy for countering terrorism, *CONTEST*. It was begun in 2007, and relaunched in 2011 following a major review.

[92] HM Government, *Prevent Strategy* Cm 8092 (2011). The current *Prevent* strategy builds upon earlier endeavours that sought to increase understanding and encourage interaction between communities with the aim of reducing hostility and disaffection. Multi-agency partnerships, or Regional Resilience Forums, assess risks in their areas, prepare, and test plans to tackle them. In addition, the *Channel Project* is a community-based multi-agency initiative to support vulnerable individuals using existing partnerships between the police, local authorities, and communities. The project takes referrals of individuals considered susceptible to recruitment by violent extremist groups and it institutes programmes of intervention designed to avert this risk. HM Government, *Channel: Protecting Vulnerable People from Being Drawn into Terrorism. A Guide for Local Partnerships* (2012).

[93] M Innes et al., *Hearts and Minds and Eyes and Ears: Reducing Radicalisation Risks through Reassurance Oriented Policing* (Cardiff: Cardiff University, 2007), 13.

[94] B Spalek and L Zahra McDonald, *Preventing Religio-Political Extremism Amongst Muslim Youth: A Study Exploring Police-Community Partnership* (Birmingham: University of Birmingham, 2011), 15. Innes et al., *Hearts and Minds and Eyes and Ears: Reducing Radicalisation Risks through Reassurance Oriented Policing* (n 93), 13.

[95] Spalek and Zahra McDonald, *Preventing Religio-Political Extremism Amongst Muslim Youth: A Study Exploring Police-Community Partnership* (n 94), 20. The government denies that *Prevent* itself has been used to spy on communities, averring: 'We can find no evidence to support these claims.' Yet the same report continues: '*Prevent* must not be used as a means for covert spying on people or communities. Trust in *Prevent* must be improved.' HM Government, *Prevent Strategy* (n 92), 6.

Where trust is exploited in order to gain intelligence, police–community relations suffer. Early endeavours also attracted accusations that counterterrorist funding was being diverted into community integration projects and that 'that the Government was supporting cohesion projects only for security reasons and in effect "securitising integration"'.[96]

The attempt to identify and target those vulnerable to radicalization has been criticized for its reliance on dubious criteria, its use of beliefs and practices (most obviously Islamic) as proxies for risk, and its overestimation of vulnerability.[97] The expansive scope of liability for terrorism-related offences (see further Chapter 5) creates a fine line between identifying vulnerable individuals and identifying suspects chargeable with preparatory or associative offences. In addition, the *Pursue* branch of CONTEST is aimed at 'detecting and investigating threats at the earliest stage, disrupting terrorist activity before it can endanger the public and, wherever possible, prosecuting those responsible'.[98] Openness and honesty are important attributes fostered by de-radicalization programmes but they render individuals liable to formal investigation for terrorist-related offences. Many of those targeted under the *Prevent* strategy were liable to prosecution, with the result that the division between *Prevent* and the *Pursue* strategy became blurred. Radicalization in prisons and in the immigration detention system, especially among young detainees who may be alienated, isolated, and susceptible to recruitment by extremists, is also a significant problem but not one that admits of easy resolution.[99]

The *Prevent* strategy now focuses on three narrower targets: to 'respond to ideological challenge', to 'prevent people from being drawn into terrorism', and to 'work with sectors and institutions where there are risks of radicalisation'.[100] The first of these goals is arguably the most problematic in that it specifies that 'preventing terrorism will mean challenging extremist (and non-violent) ideas that are also part of a terrorist ideology'.[101] The determination to challenge the non-violent espousal of 'terrorist ideology' places a very wide range of views and beliefs under scrutiny and permits much earlier intervention than conventional preventive policing. In short, despite the designation of *Prevent* as a form of 'soft' power, it is clear that it has coercive aspects and may render individuals more liable to coercive or, at least, intrusive measures.

---

[96] Respondents to consultation reported in HM Government, *Prevent Strategy* (n 92), 30.

[97] Spalek and Zahra McDonald, *Preventing Religio-Political Extremism Amongst Muslim Youth: A Study Exploring Police-Community Partnership* (n 94), 24.

[98] <https://www.gov.uk/government/policies/protecting-the-uk-against-terrorism/supporting-pages/pursue>.

[99] P Neumann, *Prisons and Terrorism: Radicalisation and De-Radicalisation in 15 Countries* (London: ICSR, 2010).

[100] HM Government, *Prevent Strategy* (n 92), 7.

[101] HM Government, *Prevent Strategy* (n 92), 6.

8.6 Review and Accountability Mechanisms

The question of how best to ensure that counterterrorism mechanisms are necessary, appropriate, and accord with human rights protections, due process, and with domestic and international law is fiercely contested. In large part the issue is a political one in that it depends upon political judgements about what preventive measures are necessary and defensible. These judgements vary according to perceptions of external threat and the security measures needed to avert it, assessments of the public demand for protection, and relative political commitments to individual liberties. On taking office, the UK coalition government made, as an urgent priority, a commitment to review counterterrorism and security powers to assess their impact on civil liberties and 'where possible, to provide a correction in favour of liberty'.[102] It undertook a Counter-Terrorism Review, in which the Home Secretary further elaborated the government's intention to 'correct the imbalance that has developed between the State's security powers and civil liberties, restoring those liberties wherever possible and focussing those powers where necessary'.[103] Whether and to what extent the subsequent changes brought about by the Protection of Freedoms Act 2012 suffice to meet this aim is questionable.[104]

Domestic accountability mechanisms play an important role in ensuring that there is adequate pre- and post-legislative scrutiny to ensure that bills are consistent with domestic law, human rights requirements, and principles of criminal and public law. The JCHR scrutinizes bills with significant human rights implications for compatibility and plays an important role where UK courts and the ECtHR find breaches and remedial orders are required to bring legislation in line with the ECHR. However, calls by the JCHR to overhaul or to repeal existing provisions have frequently been rejected by the government.[105] The role of the Independent Reviewer of Terrorism Legislation also has the potential to subject counterterrorism laws to dispassionate, critical scrutiny. However, the fact that the Reviewer is appointed by the Home Secretary and the post is not advertised raises the risk that the appointee will be sympathetic to the government and insufficiently detached and critical.[106] It is notable that the present incumbent, David Anderson, has called

---

[102] Theresa May, the Home Secretary, quoted in E Cape, 'The Counter-Terrorism Provisions of the Protection of Freedoms Act 2012: Preventing Misuse or a Case of Smoke and Mirrors?', *Criminal Law Review* (2013), 385–99; 385.

[103] HM Government, *Review of Counter-Terrorism and Security Powers*, Cm 8004 (2011), 3.

[104] See discussion in Cape, 'The Counter-Terrorism Provisions of the Protection of Freedoms Act 2012: Preventing Misuse or a Case of Smoke and Mirrors?' (n 102).

[105] J Blackbourn, *Independent Reviewers of Anti-Terrorism Laws as Effective Oversight Mechanism: Australia and the UK Compared* (unpublished paper).

[106] Blackbourn, *Independent Reviewers of Anti-Terrorism Laws as Effective Oversight Mechanism*, 'Evaluating the Independent Reviewer of Terrorism Legislation', *Parliamentary Affairs* (2012), 1–14.

for his post to be advertised. Certainly, if the Reviewer is regarded as being too close to the government or insufficiently critical of the preventive measures brought in to tackle terrorist threats, then his independence, objectivity, and their effectiveness as a source of external review become open to question. That said, the reports of the Reviewer provide the opportunity publicly to review legislation; to question its necessity and its effectiveness; to identify misuses of the law; and to inform public and parliamentary debate.[107]

Rightly, there has been resistance to introducing extraordinary executive powers to prevent terrorism on a permanent basis.[108] The use of sunset clauses and the requirement of periodic renewal of counterterrorism powers is one means of seeking to ensure that preventive measures are not perpetuated longer than is absolutely necessary.[109] The original conception that renewal debates would permit a critical review of the continuing necessity of the measures was belied by the failure of MPs to attend: according to the former Independent Reviewer of Terrorism Legislation, Lord Carlile, renewal debates became 'a bit of a fiction'.[110] Thus, renewal requirements may merely serve to underscore a general presumption against the use of exceptional preventive powers by the executive.[111] Under s. 21 of the Terrorism Prevention and Investigation Measures Act 2011, review will occur only every five years and it remains to be seen whether, without the requirement of annual renewal, parliamentary committees like the JCHR will produce reports on the operation of TPIMs with as much regularity as was the case for Control Orders. It is, likewise, an open question whether the reports of the Independent Reviewer of Terrorism Legislation will attract the same level of political attention to TPIMs and have the same degree of salience now that there is no requirement of annual debate. Much depends upon the role of lobby organizations (such as Liberty, Justice, and Amnesty International), of lawyers, and of the press in keeping issues requiring scrutiny in the public eye. As is evident from the analysis throughout this chapter, perhaps the single most important scrutiny is that provided by the courts and, not least, by the judgments of the ECtHR.[112]

---

[107] See, eg, R Brant, 'New terror laws could be less effective, warns watchdog' *BBC News UK* (26 March 2012) at <http://www.bbc.co.uk/news/uk-17511459>. Blackbourn, *Independent Reviewers of Anti-Terrorism Laws as Effective Oversight Mechanism: Australia and the UK Compared* (n 105).

[108] Witness the fact that the Enhanced TPIM Bill has yet to be enacted.

[109] J Ip, 'Sunset Clauses and Counterterrorism Legislation', *Public Law* (2013), 74.

[110] Quoted Walker and Horne, 'The Terrorism Prevention and Investigations Measures Act 2011: One Thing but Not Much the Other?' (n 73), 436.

[111] Quoted Walker and Horne, 'The Terrorism Prevention and Investigations Measures Act 2011: One Thing but Not Much the Other?'(n 73), 436.

[112] C Gearty, 'Human Rights in an Age of Counter-Terrorism: Injurious, Irrelevant or Indispensable?', *Current Legal Problems* 58 (2005), 25–46; Ashworth, 'Security, Terrorism and the Value of Human Rights' (n 84); Tomkins, 'National Security and the Role of the Court: A Changed Landscape?' (n 56).

8.7 Conclusions

One way to curtail abuse of preventive counterterrorism provisions might be to insist on adherence to *a principle of proper usage* to prevent legal powers intended for one purpose being used for another, as has been the case in the use of immigration detention for counterterrorism (see Chapter 11). This would prevent powers being used for other ends and avoid circumvention of criminal process protections. Many of the principles that apply to the deprivation of liberty within the criminal process apply equally to preventive measures that entail a substantial deprivation of liberty. The starting point is therefore to reassert the right to personal liberty and the presumption of innocence. The restraining principles may be restated here as follows:

(1) The necessity principle, that any restriction of, or deprivation of, liberty must be necessary for the prevention of terrorist activity, and should continue for no longer than is absolutely necessary for that purpose.

(2) The principle of the least restrictive appropriate means, that any restrictions on liberty must be a last resort and the least intrusive that are consistent with the preventive purpose.

(3) The principle of sufficient substantiating evidence, requiring a high standard of proof (beyond reasonable doubt) and avoiding the use of fallible secret intelligence.

(4) The right to a fair trial, including the principles of openness, transparency, and accountability, in terms of the right to know upon what grounds the measure is needed, open access to evidence, rights of challenge and appeal, legal assistance to do so, and a presumption in favour of open hearings. Use of secret evidence in closed material proceedings and other limitations on disclosure should be permitted only where they constitute the least restrictive means to further a compelling government interest, and special advocates should be used only where the grounds of national security are overwhelming.

It may seem practical to mention efficacy as a further ground for restraint, but there is a danger here. Efficacy alone cannot suffice to justify substantially liberty-eroding measures, not least when it blurs into efficiency and economy—as occurs in the conclusion by the Independent Reviewer that 'because a TPIM subject is considerably easier and cheaper to monitor than a person who is entirely free of constraint, TPIM notices were undoubtedly effective in releasing resources for use in relation to other pressing national security targets'.[113] Just as preventive counterterrorism measures should not be permitted to operate as a means of bypassing the strictures of the criminal process, neither should these most coercive of preventive measures be defended on grounds of economy.

---

[113] Anderson, *Terrorism Prevention and Investigation in 2012: First Report of the Independent Review on the Operation of the Terrorism Prevention and Investigation Act 2011* (n 44), 87.

9

Public Health Law, Prevention, and Liberty

There is no accepted definition of public health law, but Gostin refers to the government's 'authority and responsibility to persuade, create incentives or even compel individuals and businesses to conform to health and safety standards for the public good'.[1] On this view the state's responsibility includes the identification, prevention, and amelioration of risks to public health, and the promotion of good health (and reduction of harm) by measures that respect 'autonomy, privacy, liberty, proprietary or other legally protected interests'.[2] Among other things, public health law provides for the taking of liberty-restricting coercive measures against individuals in various contexts, including compulsory treatment and deprivation of liberty. In this chapter, our primary interest lies in restrictions and deprivations of liberty in two broad types of situation—where a person has a contagious disease which is thought to render them a danger to others, and where a person has a mental disorder which is thought to create a risk to themselves or others. In both instances the law provides for a range of voluntary and compulsory measures, the latter including community orders that may restrict subjects' movement and require them to fulfil certain requirements, and orders for detention. The problems of this interface between the state's duty to protect from harm and the rights of individuals have already been discussed in Chapter 7 in the context of preventive detention. In respect of public health law many of the same theoretical and practical problems arise, and, as we will see, many of the crucial judgements are made by health-care professionals operating within a relatively loose legal framework.

In this chapter, we begin (Section 9.1) by sketching the justifications for coercive measures based on public health rationales. We then move on to assess the legal provisions for imposing detention on three groups of people, those with contagious diseases (Section 9.2), those with mental disorder under civil powers (Section 9.3), and those with mental disorder under criminal powers (Section 9.4). In that analysis we examine the procedural safeguards for those subjected to these processes, and the institutional conditions in which any detention takes place. Close scrutiny of the powers available in English law (which are not markedly different, in most respects,

---

[1] LO Gostin, *Public Health Law* (University of California Press, 2000), 2.
[2] Gostin, *Public Health Law* (n 1).

from those of many other countries) suggests that, in matters of deprivation of liberty, there is a form of discrimination against the mentally disordered. The relevant threshold tests for detention are examined in Section 9.5, and some conclusions are drawn in Section 9.6.

9.1 Towards a Justification for Coercive Measures taken on Health Grounds

We have argued in Section1.4 that the state has a duty to prevent harm or, framed as a duty to protect, an obligation to take reasonable measures to protect people from harm. It was argued that prevention of harm is one of various obligations of the state, another being the duty to ensure that the relevant rights of individuals are safeguarded. One of the undisputed justifications for public health law is the prevention of harm. In most cases this means the prevention of harm to others, particularly when compulsory restrictions or even compulsory detention are being considered, but in relation to mentally disordered persons it also extends to the prevention of harm to self, a paternalistic extension that needs separate justification.

One source of actual and potential harm that has presented a challenge to states' duty to protect in recent years is that deriving from infectious diseases, whether naturally occurring or deliberately spread. Two examples of strategies of deliberate spreading of disease, known as bioterrorism, were the Sarin gas attacks on the Tokyo subway in 1995, and the deliberate dissemination of anthrax in the US in 2001. Responses to such incidents are usually based on anti-terrorist strategies (see Chapter 8). In relation to naturally occurring diseases, and leaving aside the challenge of HIV,[3] two examples were the outbreak of avian influenza H5N1 in 1997, and the widespread concern about SARS in 2003.[4] On the international stage, the World Health Organization convened a meeting in the wake of the SARS pandemic, and then published its *International Health Regulations*[5] which set out 'core capacity requirements' which countries are expected to meet in order to provide adequate surveillance and response to public health emergencies. In the United States this sphere of public health law is in the hands of the states, and a model

---

[3] The response to this is different in English law, which criminalizes the intentional or reckless transmission of HIV to others: for a critical appraisal, see M Weait, *Intimacy and Responsibility: The Criminalization of HIV Transmission* (London and New York: Routledge-Cavendish, 2007).

[4] S Gainotti et al., 'Ethical Models Underpinning Responses to Threats to Public Health: A Comparison of Approaches to Communicable Disease Control in Europe', *Bioethics* 22 (2008), 466.

[5] World Health Assembly, *International Health Regulations* 2nd edn (Geneva: World Health Organization, 2005).

statute drafted in 2002 has been adopted by most of the states.[6] That model statute includes provisions on planning for and the detection of infectious diseases, and special measures for the protection of individuals. In view of the fact that the United States experienced the intentional dispersal of anthrax through the mail in 2001, the model statute covers public health emergencies arising either naturally or through deliberate human agency. The need for compulsory preventive powers (eg testing, vaccination, treatment, isolation, and quarantine) is manifest if an acceptable degree of public protection is to be provided, but the model statute recognizes that there must be principled limitations on any such compulsory powers, and that due process safeguards should be available to those individuals adversely affected by restrictive measures.[7] More will be said about the principled limitations in Section 9.3, but it is important to signal at the outset that these are necessary restraints upon the design and use of special powers.

Turning to mentally disordered persons, legal systems tend to provide a range of compulsory powers. In most countries there is a compulsory power to detain mentally disordered persons who meet certain criteria; the English legislation will be examined in Sections 9.3 and 9.4. However, insofar as British public health law provides for the compulsory detention of individuals in certain circumstances, the justifications have to be in conformity with human rights documents, such as the ECHR. Article 5.1 proclaims 'the right to liberty and security of person', but then Article 5.1(e) goes so far as to accept that the right to liberty of the person is subject to an exception for:

the lawful detention of persons for the prevention of the spreading of infectious diseases, of persons of unsound mind, alcoholics or drug addicts or vagrants.

This is a staggeringly wide provision, and its justifications seem highly dubious. There is a straightforward public protection rationale for deprivation of liberty 'for the prevention of the spreading of infectious diseases', so long as this is retained as a last resort. But the public protection rationale cannot be stretched to any of the other conditions, which are listed in such broad and unqualified terms. As Gable and Gostin argue:

The categories present a series of characteristics based on a person's health or socio-economic status. The fact that an individual is in poor health from mental illness or dependence on alcohol or drugs or that she has no visible means of support does not, in itself, warrant detention. Additional findings of dangerousness and/or that the person will benefit from treatment are necessary to justify detaining people who belong to these groups.[8]

---

[6] LO Gostin et al., 'The Model State Emergency Powers Act: Planning for and Response to Bioterrorism and Naturally Occurring Infectious Diseases', *Journal of the American Medical Association* 288 (2002), 622.

[7] Gostin et al., 'The Model State Emergency Powers Act' (n 6).

[8] L Gable and LO Gostin, 'Human Rights of Persons with Mental Disabilities: The European Convention on Human Rights', in LO Gostin et al. (eds.), *Principles of Mental Health Law and Policy* (Oxford: Oxford University Press, 2010), 103–66; 129–30. The International Covenant

The focus of the discussion in this chapter will be upon the first two categories (preventing the spread of infectious diseases, and persons of unsound mind), but we should note the dubiousness of the exception to the right to personal liberty in relation to alcoholics, drug addicts, and vagrants—who ought to have a claim to support, rather than being treated as having no claim to liberty. In effect, the ECHR has been left behind by developments in equality and human rights. Thus, the UN Convention on the Rights of Persons with a Disability 2006 declares that states should ensure that persons with a disability (physical or mental) have equal liberty to others; and Article 14(1) states specifically that 'the existence of a disability shall in no case justify a deprivation of liberty', which may be taken as an authoritative rejection of the wording of Article 5.1(e) of the ECHR.

Being a 'person of unsound mind' is an insufficient justification for depriving such a person of liberty. The question of defining 'unsound mind' will be discussed below, but the category is obviously over-extensive as a justification for detention, since it is not confined to those who are 'dangerous'. It is shameful that a leading international human rights document subscribes to such an obviously flawed category, which implies that the liberty of a person is less worthy of protection if he or she is diagnosed as mentally disordered. The ECtHR has attempted through its jurisprudence to narrow the effects of this flawed provision, adopting the test of necessity and the principle of the least restrictive appropriate alternative when dealing with the detention of drug addicts and alcoholics.[9] In relation to 'persons of unsound mind', the Court has insisted on a necessity test for detention.[10] This and other judicial refinements, discussed in Section 9.3, have helped to rein in the overbreadth of Article 5.1(e) itself. Moreover, once a mentally disordered person is lawfully detained, the right to periodic review of the lawfulness of continued detention (required by Article 5.4 of the Convention) has been and is a means of promoting fair procedures and avoiding arbitrariness.

Before we consider the legal frameworks and their implications, three contrasts between those with contagious diseases and those with mental disorder should be noted. One contrast is that the numbers of those subjected to restrictive measures on grounds of (potential) contagion rarely exceed single figures (nine in 2010–2011; six in 2011–2012),[11] whereas the number of those subject to compulsory detention in

---

on Civil and Political Rights (1966) contains no specific provision relating to the deprivations of liberty to control infectious diseases or for the dangerous mentally disordered.

[9] D Harris et al., *Harris, O'Boyle & Warbrick: Law of the European Convention on Human Rights* 2nd edn (Oxford: Oxford University Press, 2009), 156–7.

[10] The leading case is *Winterwerp v Netherlands* (1979) 2 EHRR 387; for subsequent jurisprudence, see Harris et al., *Harris, O'Boyle & Warbrick* (n 9), 156–9.

[11] The English figures are for orders under the Health Protection (Part 2A Orders) Regulations 2010, accessible at <http://www.hpa.org.uk>.

hospital on grounds of mental disorder is much larger at 49,365 in 2010–2011;[12] another contrast is that contagious diseases tend to pose a high risk of harm, whereas those with mental disorder do not usually present a medium or high risk of harm, save for a relatively small sub-group; and a third contrast is that persons with contagious diseases cannot be treated against their will (unless they have lost mental capacity), whereas those with mental disorder can be subjected to compulsory treatment regardless of whether they have lost capacity to consent to treatment.

9.2 Deprivations of Liberty for Persons with Contagious Conditions

English law empowers a justice of the peace to make a compulsory order in respect of a person who is suffering from a contagious disease that is notifiable. There is a list of legally notifiable diseases, which includes cholera, leprosy, malaria, meningitis, tuberculosis, and typhoid fever.[13] The justice must be satisfied that the person (1) may be infected or contaminated to a degree that (2) could present a risk of significant harm to human health by (3) infecting or contaminating others. The justice may then make an order that involves submission to a medical examination, restrictions on movement, a requirement to wear protective clothing, detention in a hospital, or removal to isolation or quarantine.[14] In this context 'isolation' involves the confinement to a particular place (eg hospital, home) of a person who is diagnosed as having an infectious disease; 'quarantine' refers to the confinement of a person or person(s) suspected of having been exposed to an infectious disease and who might therefore develop it and/or infect others. These are far-reaching powers,[15] and the subject is entitled to be represented at the hearing before the justice, and to challenge the grounds put forward and the nature of the order to be made. Many cases can be dealt with consensually, without the need for a court

---

[12] English statistics on 'In-Patients Formally Detained in Hospitals under the Mental Health Act 1983—and Patients subject to Supervised Community Treatment' are published annually at <http://www.ic.nhs.uk>.

[13] Notification is now to the Health Protection Agency (part of Public Health England), which publishes statistics on Notifications of Infectious Diseases (NOIDs) at <http://www.hpa.org.uk>.

[14] Public Health (Control of Disease) Act 1984, s. 45G as substituted by s. 129 of the Health and Social Care Act 2008. Similar powers exist in other countries, such as the United States: see Gostin, *Public Health Law* (n 1), Ch. 8.

[15] It should be noted, however, that English law provides that there shall be no compulsory treatment (s. 45E of the Public Health (Control of Disease) Act 1984), unlike the laws of several other European countries: see Gainotti et al., 'Ethical Models Underpinning Responses to Threats to Public Health: A Comparison of Approaches to Communicable Disease Control in Europe' (n 4), 473.

order, but there are some cases where a court order is thought appropriate.[16] The legislation empowers the justice to make such order as is necessary to 'remove or reduce that risk': it is, therefore, this test of necessity that is crucial to the justification, particularly in the rare cases where detention is ordered. The test impliedly includes the principle of the least restrictive appropriate alternative—in the sense that a magistrate should not make an order for detention if some lesser intervention would suffice, since the more intrusive order would then not be 'necessary'.[17]

This interpretation is supported by the relevant jurisprudence of the ECtHR, dealing with the exception to Article 5(1) relating to 'the lawful detention of persons for the prevention of the spreading of contagious diseases'. In *Enhorn v Sweden*[18] the applicant had the HIV virus and had transmitted it to another man. The Swedish medical authorities placed him under conditions as to his behaviour, and, when he failed to observe those conditions, they sought and obtained an order that he be kept in compulsory isolation in a hospital. This order was renewed over a period of five years, although the applicant absconded several times and was in fact detained for about 18 months. He argued that his Article 5 right to liberty had been unjustifiably infringed. The Court held that the essential criteria for exception (e) to Article 5(1) are:

whether the spreading of the infectious disease is dangerous for public health or safety, and whether detention of the person infected is the last resort in order to prevent the spreading of the disease, because less severe measures have been considered and found to be insufficient to safeguard the public interest. When these criteria are no longer fulfilled, the basis for the deprivation of liberty ceases to exist.[19]

The Court went on to hold that Article 5 had been violated, because 'the compulsory isolation of the applicant was not a last resort' and, since his liberty was at stake, greater attention should have been paid to less restrictive means of protection.

The technique of this judgment and others is to approach the difficult task of devising appropriate limits to preventive deprivations of liberty by a procedural route, requiring consideration to be given to certain criteria. Three familiar Strasbourg principles are invoked—the principle of necessity, that it must be clear that the restrictions are necessary to prevent the harm; the principle of subsidiary, that less intrusive measures must have been considered and adjudged to be insufficient; and the principle of proportionality, that the measures taken must not be out of

---

[16]   For further discussion, see JW Nickel, 'Restraining Orders, Liberty and Due Process', in A Ashworth, L Zedner, and P Tomlin (eds.), *Prevention and the Limits of the Criminal Law* (Oxford: Oxford University Press, 2013), 156–77; 158–9.

[17]   Other legal systems explicitly require that detention be used only as a last resort: see the various Australian state laws listed by B McSherry, 'Sex, Drugs and "Evil" Souls: The Growing Reliance on Preventive Detention Regimes', *Monash University Law Review* 32 (2009), 238; 248–9. See also Public Health Act 2010 (NSW), s. 62(6) for a more recent example.

[18]   (2005) 41 EHRR 643.   [19]   (2005) 41 EHRR 643, [44].

proportion to the danger apprehended. It is easy to be sceptical of this kind of approach: it is merely procedural, and does not attempt to grapple with questions of substance (what kind of harm? what degree of risk?); and it relies on broad and malleable concepts that leave room for variable interpretations. On the other hand, this approach led to findings of a violation in both the leading European cases,[20] which demonstrates that the prevailing approach places considerable emphasis on the right to liberty. This suggests that deprivation of liberty for purely preventive purposes may be justifiable only *in extremis* and as a last resort, when nothing less will provide adequate public protection, and for as short a period as possible. Thus detaining an alcoholic for six hours was held to violate Article 5 because the Polish authorities had not tried less intrusive methods of controlling the applicant.[21]

In this discussion of infectious diseases it has been assumed thus far that there is no great problem of diagnosis. However, in the case of new viruses or new strains there may not be sufficient scientific research to enable confident predictions of risk, particularly in the early stages of awareness of a new strain. Whether the test be based on the principles of necessity, subsidiarity, and proportionality (as above), or on a significant risk of serious harm, the greater uncertainty of risk assessments might lead some to advocate a precautionary approach.[22] In that eventuality, there would be a choice between (1) insisting that ordinary human rights protections should be maintained until the evidential basis for risk assessments improves, and (2) allowing some reduction of normal human rights protections in view of the evidential uncertainty. It was argued in Chapter 6 that the precautionary principle is not well suited to the justification of measures taken against individuals, and therefore (1) is to be preferred.

It is important to keep fully in view the fact that we are discussing deprivation of the liberty of a person who should be respected as an autonomous individual and as a full member of society, and who is assumed not to have committed a criminal offence.[23] The deprivation of liberty means that the person is taken away from his or her family and employment, sometimes causing economic difficulties as well as emotional hardship and the various pains of incarceration. The rationale for requiring one person to give up freedom of movement is that this will prevent the infection of (and hence serious harm to) others: compulsory powers are justifiable for those who decline to

---

[20] The cases of *Enhorn* (n 18) and *Witold Litwa v Poland* (2001) 33 EHRR 1267.

[21] *Witold Litwa v Poland* (2001) 33 EHRR 1267.

[22] eg R Martin, 'The Exercise of Public Health Powers in Cases of Infectious Disease: Human Rights Implications', *Medical Law Review* 14 (2006), 132; 142; EP Richards, 'The Jurisprudence of Prevention: the Right of Societal Self-Defense against Dangerous Individuals', *Hastings Constitutional Law Quarterly* (1989) 16, 329, discussing US Supreme Court decisions.

[23] In English law there are criminal offences of transmitting diseases (on which see Weait, *Intimacy and Responsibility: The Criminalization of HIV Transmission* (n 3)); here, we are assuming a purely civil detention, as in Sweden (see the *Enhorn* case (n 18)).

enter voluntary isolation or quarantine, since they are 'by those very actions exposing others to an unjustified risk of harm' and this makes it 'legitimate to use coercion to prevent them from carrying through such wrongfully dangerous conduct'.[24] Where deprivation of liberty follows conviction of a crime, full procedural safeguards for the individual must be in place. Since there is no conviction in public health cases, it is all the more important that a step as momentous as deprivation of liberty should only be taken if procedural safeguards are in place. Moreover, the state has an obligation to ensure that the places of detention are adequately provided with facilities which are as normalized as possible,[25] and that the person detained is compensated for loss of income and amenity.[26] Respect for the detainee as an autonomous moral agent should not be lost through the decision to impose isolation or quarantine in order to prevent harm to others.

In his writings on the topic, John Stuart Mill argued that the analysis of 'necessity' in this context should take account of the wider social consequences of using detention, not merely the consequences for the individual. Although Mill did not believe in individual rights such as the right to liberty of the person, his utilitarian balancing of probable consequences led him to advocate the assessment of the wider costs (social costs, opportunity costs) of a policy of quarantine, rather than focusing on the costs for the particular individual.[27] However, it is doubtful whether this kind of social balancing exercise can properly be expected of courts in individual cases: it is suitable when legislatures are deciding on the shape of their public health laws, but courts should focus on the consequences for the individual. We will return, in Section 9.4, to the question of appropriate limiting principles and procedural safeguards.

9.3 Deprivation of Liberty and the Mentally Disordered (Civil Powers)

We have already noted that, while the exception in Article 5.1(e) relating to infectious diseases refers to its rationale ('the prevention of the spreading of infectious diseases'),

---

[24] RA Duff, 'Pre-Trial Detention and the Presumption of Innocence', in A Ashworth, L Zedner, and P Tomlin (eds.), *Prevention and the Limits of the Criminal Law* (Oxford: Oxford University Press, 2013), 115–32; 129.

[25] Gostin et al., 'The Model State Emergency Powers Act: Planning for and Response to Bioterrorism and Naturally Occurring Infectious Diseases' (n 6), 626–7.

[26] For a summary of provisions for compensation in European countries (including the UK), see Gainotti et al., 'Ethical Models Underpinning Responses to Threats to Public Health: A Comparison of Approaches to Communicable Disease Control in Europe' (n 4), 472.

[27] For discussion, see J Waldron, 'Mill on Liberty and the Contagious Diseases Act', in N Urbinati and A Zakaras (eds.), *J.S. Mill's Political Thought: A Bicentennial Reassessment* (Cambridge: Cambridge University Press, 2007), 11–42; and WE Parmet, 'J.S. Mill and the American Law of Quarantine', *Public Health Ethics* 1(3) (2008), 210–22. See further Section 2.4.

the wording of the 'mental disorder' exception in Article 5.1(e) refers merely to 'persons of unsound mind' without indicating a rationale for ever depriving them of liberty. Looking at the non-criminal statutory powers in England and Wales, the Mental Health Act 1983 (as amended) provides a considerable number of gateways to compulsory hospitalization. The starting point is section 131 of the Act, which provides that nothing in the legislation should be construed so as to prevent a person who requires treatment for mental disorder from being admitted to hospital for that purpose, without the use of compulsory powers. Informal voluntary admission under this section is widely used, but there are doubts about the degree to which it is truly voluntary in some cases—eg where members of the family say that they can no longer cope with the patient living with them, or where a doctor suggests that if the patient does not opt for voluntary admission then one of the compulsory orders will be sought.[28] It is arguable that the detention of a patient under section 131, in circumstances where the patient's admission is not truly voluntary (because he or she has been given the choice to consent or to be subjected to compulsory admission), may amount to a 'deprivation of liberty' requiring justification under Article 5 of the ECHR; that argument will be taken up below. Moreover, it is possible that some supposedly voluntary patients do not have sufficient moral agency to be fairly regarded as consenting to their admission to hospital.

Sections 2 and 3 of the Mental Health Act provide the principal gateways to civil confinement.[29] The criteria for admission under the two sections are broadly parallel, but section 2 concerns admission for assessment and section 3 relates to admission for treatment. Under section 2, a person may be detained for assessment if (1) that person is suffering from a mental disorder warranting detention in hospital for assessment, and (2) the person ought to be detained for his or her own safety or 'with a view to the protection of other persons'. The order may last for up to 28 days. Under section 3, a person may be detained for treatment if (1) that person is suffering from a mental disorder that makes it appropriate that he or she should receive medical treatment in hospital, (2) such treatment is necessary for the patient's health or safety or 'for the protection of others', and (3) appropriate treatment is available. The order lasts for six months and may then be renewed for a further six months and thereafter for 12 months at a time.

The operation of sections 2 and 3 depends to a considerable degree on clinical judgement. The terms of the legislation are largely permissive. The classification of a person's mental condition can have far-reaching effects, and yet the definition of mental disorder remains a contested issue. While mental disorder cannot be

---

[28] Cf. also the holding powers under s. 5 of the Mental Health Act 1983 (emergency power to detain in-patient for up to 72 hours).

[29] There are other provisions for emergency admission (ss. 4 and 5), for admission by the police on public order grounds (s. 136), and for admission by a magistrate (s. 135).

constituted by dependency on alcohol or drugs,[30] there has been a long-running controversy over the extent to which personality disorders fall within the statutory definition. The Mental Health Act 2007 removed the requirement of 'abnormally aggressive or seriously irresponsible conduct' that used to limit the category of 'psychopathic disorder', which means that the reach of 'personality disorder' is much greater but still susceptible to different interpretations by different psychiatrists.[31] Since mental disorder includes 'any disorder or disability of the mind', it 'acts like a concertina, expanding and contracting depending on the context in which it is applied'[32] to different client groups and by different psychiatrists.

Once a person is classified as having a mental disorder, it must be determined that the disorder 'warrants' detention in hospital or that this is 'appropriate'—both rather vague criteria which fall below any requirement of necessity. It is not obvious why different terms were employed in the two sections.[33] While those elements relate to the nature or extent of the mental disorder, there is a further requirement that detention in hospital is necessary (section 3) or ought to be arranged (section 2) either for the patient's own safety or for the protection of other persons. This is the explicitly preventive element, and although it is tied to a judgement of necessity, at least in relation to section 3, it rests on a prediction of risk of harm to self or to others. While most civil committals are based on clinical assessments, some authorities use prediction tools developed for the purpose, although it seems that the best of these risk-assessment tools underpredict and overpredict by some 25–30 per cent.[34] Moreover, the tools are not sufficiently well grounded to deal with some groups, notably persons with learning disabilities and also (surprisingly) women. Thus, because the statute itself resorts to vague terms and the value of the available assessment tools is debatable, 'the result is a detention system run largely on medical discretion'.[35]

---

[30] Mental Health Act 1983, s. 1(3).

[31] P Fennell, 'The Statutory Definition of Mental Disorder and the Availability of Appropriate Treatment', in LO Gostin et al. (eds.), *Principles of Mental Health Law and Policy* (Oxford: Oxford University Press, 2010), 71–102; J Peay, 'Mentally Disordered Offenders, Mental Health and Crime', in M Maguire, R Morgan, and R Reiner (eds.), *Oxford Handbook of Criminology* 5th edn (Oxford: Oxford University Press, 2012), 426–49; 442–3; L Zedner, 'Erring on the Side of Safety: Risk Assessment, Expert Knowledge, and the Criminal Court', in GR Sullivan and I Dennis (eds.), *Seeking Security: Pre-Empting the Commission of Criminal Harms* (Oxford: Hart Publishing, 2012), 221–41; 239.

[32] Peay, 'Mentally Disordered Offenders, Mental Health and Crime' (n 31), 432; see also the analysis in Chs 3 and 18 of J Peay, *Mental Health and Crime* (Abingdon: Routledge, 2011).

[33] G Richardson and O Thorold, 'Law as a Rights Protector: Assessing the Mental Health Act 1983', in N Eastman and J Peay (eds.), *Law without Enforcement* (Oxford: Hart Publishing, 1999), 109–32; 112.

[34] P Bartlett, 'Civil Confinement', in LO Gostin et al. (eds.), *Principles of Mental Health Law and Policy* (Oxford: Oxford University Press, 2010), 413–72; 420–1; see also Peay, *Mental Health and Crime* (n 32), Ch. 13.

[35] Bartlett, 'Civil Confinement' (n 34), 421.

What, then, are the safeguards for the individual in relation to these compulsory preventive measures? We have already noted that Article 5 of the Convention establishes a right to personal liberty but that Article 5.1(e) creates an exception in the case of detention of a person 'of unsound mind'. In the leading case of *Winterwerp v Netherlands*[36] the ECtHR held that the person to be detained must be reliably shown by objective medical expertise to be of unsound mind; that the mental disorder 'must be of a kind or degree warranting compulsory confinement'; and that detention must not continue if the mental disorder and the concomitant need for detention have subsided. The articulation of these criteria was a significant step in the Court's narrowing of Article 5.1(e): while they are stated in broad terms, the first principle points towards international medical opinion on forms of mental disorder; the second, in its use of the word 'warranting', indicates a threshold test of necessity (which might have been more tightly circumscribed if the term 'requiring' had been used);[37] and the third insists that the test of necessity should also apply throughout any detention, so as to ensure timely release. The *Winterwerp* judgment is rightly regarded as a landmark case, not least in view of the inadequacies of Article 5.1(e) itself.

Winterwerp was applied in the judgment in *HL v United Kingdom*,[38] which involved an applicant suffering from autism who was unable to consent or object to medical treatment. Following an incident of over-agitation, he was examined by a psychiatrist and admitted to hospital as an informal patient for three months, after which he was detained compulsorily. He brought an action for false imprisonment relating to the three months in which he was an 'informal patient'. Ultimately, the House of Lords concluded, by a majority, that he had been lawfully detained and, unanimously, that such detention was justified under the common law doctrine of necessity. However, the ECtHR held that he had been arbitrarily deprived of his liberty. Although the Court agreed that he was suffering from a mental disorder that warranted his compulsory confinement, it held that the common law doctrine of necessity had not developed any safeguards against arbitrary detention, such as procedural rules determining the admission to hospital of compliant incapacitated persons, the process of admission, or the duration of detention:

As a result of the lack of procedural regulation and limits, the Court observes that the hospital's health care professionals assumed full control of the liberty and treatment of a vulnerable incapacitated individual solely on the basis of their own clinical assessments completed as and when they considered fit: as Lord Steyn remarked, this left 'effective and unqualified control' in their hands. While the Court does not question the good faith of those professionals or that they acted in what they considered to be the applicant's best interests, the

---

[36] (1979) 2 EHRR 387.
[37] See further *Stanev v Bulgaria* (2012) 55 EHRR 696, at [155]–[160].
[38] (2005) 40 EHRR 761.

very purpose of procedural safeguards is to protect individuals against any 'misjudgment and professional lapses'.[39]

This judgment reasserts the indispensability of procedural safeguards against arbitrariness. Given the uncertainty about the accuracy of risk-assessment tools and of clinical assessments by health-care professionals (see Chapter 6), there must be proper procedures in place and it must be possible to challenge decisions relating to the deprivation of liberty. Such procedures may usually be found in legislation,[40] such as the provisions for access to a Mental Health Tribunal.

The key issue in many instances is whether there is a deprivation of liberty or mere restriction on liberty. On this point the jurisprudence of the ECtHR remains opaque. In the leading judgment of *Guzzardi v Italy*[41] the Court held that 'account must be taken of a whole range of criteria such as the type, duration, effects and manner of implementation of the measure in question'. The Court thus accepted that 'the difference between deprivation of and restriction upon liberty is nonetheless merely one of degree or intensity, and not one of nature or substance'.[42] In a mental health context the judgment in *HL* directs attention to the practical day-to-day control exerted by mental health professionals as an indicator of deprivation of liberty, but it must be said that the Court's general jurisprudence on Article 5(1) is unsatisfactory in the sense that it is often difficult to be sure whether or not there is a deprivation of liberty.[43]

Once a mentally disordered person who lacks capacity has been deprived of liberty, by being placed in a hospital or care home, English law now imposes various procedural safeguards. These were introduced following the judgment in *HL v United Kingdom*, and the details are to be found in a Schedule to the Mental Capacity Act 2005 added by the Mental Health Act 2007. The procedure is referred to as the deprivation of liberty safeguards (DOLS): essentially, the procedure is aimed at determining whether such a person's detention in the hospital or care home is in their best interests. The relevant health authority must appoint appraisers to determine whether the qualifying requirements for the detention are met, resulting in the issue of an authorization, and must also appoint a representative to maintain contact with the patient and to support her or him in matters relevant to deprivation

---

[39] (2005) 40 EHRR 761 at [122], repeated by the Grand Chamber in *Stanev v Bulgaria* (2012) 55 EHRR 696, at [140]–[141]. In this context, the Court in *HL* held, it did not matter whether the ward was locked or not, or whether the applicant had voluntarily agreed to enter hospital, not least because he was known to lack capacity.

[40] As in the Mental Health Act 1983 (England and Wales), and, eg, in Australian state legislation: see McSherry, 'Sex, Drugs and "Evil" Souls: The Growing Reliance on Preventive Detention Regimes' (n 17), 249.

[41] (1980) 3 EHRR 333.   [42] (1981) 3 EHRR 333, at [92]–[93].

[43] See the criticisms of the judgment in *Austin v United Kingdom* in Section 3.2.

of liberty.[44] This procedure is an important step forward in ensuring that compulsory preventive measures are only used where necessary and appropriate,[45] particularly if due attention is paid to the principle of the least restrictive appropriate alternative.[46]

Assuming that a patient is now in hospital under one of the civil powers, can a degree of compulsion be retained after release? When release into the community is being considered, there are two sets of compulsory powers, either of which may be imposed if the statutory conditions are fulfilled.[47] First, the Mental Health Act 2007 introduced a new form of Community Treatment Order (CTO), inserted as section 17A of the Mental Health Act 1983. This was put forward as a significant step towards deinstitutionalization of mental patients, but research shows that it has not led to any reduction in overall hospital admissions.[48] This creates doubt about whether its coercive framework of conditions is justifiable in many cases. A second possibility is a grant of leave, now under section 17 of the Mental Health Act 1983 as amended by the Mental Health Act 2007. Leave may be granted so long as the patient is still 'liable to be detained in hospital'; conditions are usually imposed, and treatment may be required, with recall to hospital a possible response to breach of conditions. If leave of more than seven days is contemplated, consideration should be given to supervised community treatment under a CTO instead. Both a CTO and leave have the same maximum duration as a hospital order (six months, six months, and then 12-month renewals), subject to challenge before a Tribunal.

In some cases, particularly where the criteria for leave or CTO are not met, discharge from hospital may be considered. The power to discharge may be exercised by the responsible clinician, by the hospital managers, or by the nearest relative, as well as by a Mental Health Tribunal. In particular, the responsible clinician and the hospital managers have a duty to keep under review whether the patient still fulfils the *Winterwerp* criteria for detention, and to discharge the

---

[44] For further discussion, see Bartlett, 'Informal Admissions and Deprivation of Liberty under the Mental Capacity Act 2005' in LO Gostin et al. (eds.), *Principles of Mental Health Law and Policy* (Oxford: Oxford University Press, 2010), 385–412.

[45] The Care Quality Commission reported in 2012 that the procedures had been implemented widely, but that in some institutions little staff training had taken place: <http://www.cqc.org.uk/public/news/second-annual-report-deprivation-liberty-safeguards-published-today>.

[46] As set out in s. 1(6) of the Mental Capacity Act 2005; see also s. 1(4) of the Mental Health (Care and Treatment)(Scotland) Act 2003, discussed by L Thomson, 'The Role of Forensic Mental Health Services in Managing High-Risk Offenders: Functioning or Failing?', in B McSherry and P Keyzer (eds.), *Dangerous People: Policy, Prediction and Practice* (Abingdon: Routledge, 2011), 165–82; 176–7.

[47] For detailed analysis, see J Dawson, 'Community Treatment Orders', in LO Gostin et al. (eds.), *Principles of Mental Health Law and Policy* (Oxford: Oxford University Press, 2010), 513–54.

[48] T Burns et al., 'Community Treatment Orders for Patients with Psychosis (Octet): A Randomised Controlled Trial', *The Lancet* 381 (2013), 1627.

patient if not. If discharge is being contemplated, Primary Care Trusts and social services authorities have a duty to provide after-care for discharged patients. The role of Mental Health Tribunals (MHTs) is to assess the lawfulness of continued detention, as required by Article 5(4) of the Convention. Although it remains possible to challenge certain decisions on admission to hospital and on treatment by means of judicial review, it is the MHTs that deal with the bulk of challenges. Once again, the test to be applied is that laid down by the *Winterwerp* judgment, ie whether the patient is still suffering from a mental disorder that warrants admission to hospital for treatment. Of the cases actually heard by an MHT (around half of all applications are withdrawn before hearing, often because the patient is released), some 15–17 per cent of applicants are discharged.[49]

In relation to persons with contagious diseases it was argued that, because they are detained for the benefit of other citizens rather than because of a conviction, they should be detained only in surroundings as normalized as possible and compensated for this deprivation of liberty. Similar reasoning should apply to the bulk of people in mental hospitals who are detained for the protection of others, but there is no sign of such an ethos. Indeed, the Care Quality Commission's recent review of the Mental Health Act revealed 'controlling practices that only seem to serve the hospital's needs', and in 1:5 visits by the CQC patients who were in hospital voluntarily 'were detained in all but name'.[50]

9.4 Deprivation of Liberty and the Mentally Disordered (Criminal Powers)

We now turn to the compulsory powers available to the criminal courts when dealing with a mentally disordered person. Compulsory powers may be exercised even though the mentally disordered person is not convicted. In some cases a person may be found unfit to plead (mental disability in relation to the trial), through inability to participate properly in the trial, to understand the indictment, to instruct lawyers, and so forth.[51] In other cases, a person may be found not guilty by reason of insanity, ie insane at the time of the offence. It is not necessary here to discuss the details of unfitness to plead or the insanity defence as doctrines of the criminal law.[52]

---

[49] For detailed analysis of the role of MHTs, see P Fennell, 'Review of the Lawfulness of Detention in the Courts and Mental Health Tribunals' in LO Gostin et al. (eds.), *Principles of Mental Health Law and Policy* (Oxford: Oxford University Press, 2010), 557–642.

[50] Care Quality Commission, *Monitoring the Mental Health Act 2011–2012* (2012), 33.

[51] See the discussion in Peay, *Mental Health and Crime* (n 32), Ch. 17.

[52] For detailed analysis of the law and practice, see RD Mackay, 'Mental Disability at the Time of the Offence', in LO Gostin et al. (eds.), *Principles of Mental Health Law and Policy* (Oxford: Oxford University Press, 2010), 721–56; RD Mackay, 'Mental Disability at the Time of the Trial', in LO Gostin et al. (eds.), *Principles of Mental Health Law and Policy* (Oxford:

Our interest is in the consequences of such findings by the courts. Under the Criminal Procedure (Insanity and Unfitness to Plead) Act 1991, as amended, the Crown Court now has a choice of three possible orders. First, where the defendant fulfils the *Winterwerp* criteria,[53] the court may make a hospital order (with or without restrictions); the details of these orders are discussed in the next paragraph. Second, if appropriate, the court may make a supervision order, which may require the defendant to submit to treatment during the period of the order, and to comply with any other conditions under the supervision of a probation officer or social worker. Third, where there is no need for treatment or supervision in the community, the defendant may be given an absolute discharge.

Many mentally disordered persons are convicted of a criminal offence, not having raised issues of fitness to plead or insanity either because their disorder does not involve a sufficient degree of cognitive distortion to meet the legal test of insanity or because their disorder goes unrecognized (or the defendant refuses to have it put to the court). On conviction, the court has all the measures normally available to it—such as discharges, fines, community sentences and imprisonment—plus some measures specifically designed for mentally disordered offenders. The least intrusive of those measures is the community order with a requirement of mental health treatment, based on the evidence of a registered medical practitioner.[54] Some 600–700 such orders are made each year, and the court has various powers on breach of the order, including imprisonment in cases of wilful or persistent failure to comply.

The principal order under the Mental Health Acts for offenders is the hospital order. Section 37 of the 1983 Act provides for the order to be made if the court has evidence from two qualified medical practitioners to the effect that the offender is suffering from a mental disorder of a nature or degree that makes detention for medical treatment appropriate; if the disorder is susceptible to treatment; and if a hospital has signified its willingness to admit the offender. However, section 37 also provides that the court must be satisfied that a hospital order is the most suitable method of dealing with the offender, a provision that underlines its permissive nature and leaves much to the judgment of the court. There is no provision similar to that in New South Wales, for example, requiring that the least restrictive appropriate alternative be chosen.[55]

The court also has the power, under section 41, to add a restriction order to the hospital order. It must first hear oral evidence from at least one of the registered medical practitioners, and must be satisfied that a restriction order is 'necessary for

---

Oxford University Press, 2010), 757–76. See also Law Commission, 'Criminal Liability: Insanity and Automatism, a Discussion Paper' (2013).

[53] See n 36 and accompanying text.   [54] Criminal Justice Act 2003, ss. 207–8.

[55] Mental Health Act 2007 (NSW), s. 12(1)(b): 'no care of a less restrictive kind is appropriate and reasonably available to the person'.

the protection of the public from serious harm'.[56] It has been held that where the potential harm from further offences is serious, a relatively low risk of repetition may be sufficient, whereas a high risk of relatively non-serious offences is not a sufficient justification.[57] For a restriction order to be added to a hospital order, all the requirements for making a hospital order must be fulfilled, most particularly the requirement that a hospital place be available. Many restricted patients go to a high-security hospital, admission to which is controlled by the Secretary of State.[58] If a high-security hospital place cannot be found for an offender who needs and is susceptible to treatment and who is also believed to represent a risk of serious harm, the court may conclude that it has little alternative but to impose a prison sentence.[59]

A restriction order is indefinite, and its effect is to confine the decision to release to either an MHT or the Minister of Justice, who acts on advice from the Mental Health Unit. In practice, it seems that some four-fifths of decisions to discharge patients are made by the Tribunal, with the Minister of Justice responsible for the remainder.[60] A Tribunal is bound to release a restricted patient if it concludes that the patient is no longer suffering from a mental disorder of a nature or degree that warrants detention—a criterion that says nothing about the risk of serious harm. However, the Mental Health Unit monitors all restricted patients from the time of their admission to hospital, receiving reports from their treatment teams and submitting a report to the Tribunal when it considers a particular case. The Tribunal does sometimes discharge offenders against the recommendation of the Ministry, and it appears that many officials believe 'that the Tribunal placed the system and the public at greater than necessary risk'.[61] However, that may simply be because the Unit proclaims its role as protecting the public and ensuring public confidence,[62] whereas the statutory obligations of the Tribunal in relation to discharge are different, being derived from the requirements of Article 5 of the Convention.[63]

According to Boyd-Caine, some 3,300 restricted patients were in hospital in the mid-2000s, about 1,000 of these not having been admitted on a hospital order with restrictions, but having been transferred to hospital under restrictions from a prison

---

[56] This wording may be compared with that applicable to the automatic sentence of imprisonment for life under the Legal Aid, Sentencing and Punishment of Offenders Act 2012, discussed in Ch. 7.

[57] See generally the judgment of Mustill LJ in *Birch* (1989) 11 Cr App R (S) 202.

[58] National Health Service Act 2006, s. 4.

[59] For discussion, see A Ashworth, *Sentencing and Criminal Justice* 5th edn (Cambridge: Cambridge University Press, 2010), 405–9.

[60] T Boyd-Caine, *Protecting the Public? Detention and Release of Mentally Disordered Offenders* (Abingdon: Routledge, 2012), 55.

[61] Boyd-Caine, *Protecting the Public?* (n 60), 56.

[62] Boyd-Caine, *Protecting the Public?* (n 60), 45.

[63] Note the comparison with civil confinement in the United States, discussed in relation to *Hendricks v Kansas* in Section 7.4.

(or, occasionally, from an immigration detention centre) for medical treatment. A further 1,300 restricted patients were on conditional release in the community.[64] These patients are subject to recall, a power that resides in the Minister of Justice and is conferred by section 42 of the Act without any reference to the grounds for recall. The recalled patient's case must be referred to the Tribunal within a month, and the Tribunal will then review the legitimacy of the recall. It is established that the *Winterwerp* test must be satisfied at this stage, as must the requirement that detention is necessary for the patient's health or safety or for the protection of other persons. If either test is not fulfilled, recall cannot be justified. However, in *R. (MM) v Secretary of State for the Home Department*,[65] the Court of Appeal held that recall could be justified by reasonable grounds for believing that the patient might commit an offence if not returned to hospital for treatment. The problem in this case was that the patient had a drug habit, and taking drugs tended to aggravate his paranoid schizophrenia. The Court accepted that the mere fact that he was in breach of his conditions of discharge by taking drugs was not a sufficient reason for recall. But the Court also accepted that recall could be justified if 'his condition is likely to deteriorate imminently and significantly if he takes illicit drugs'. The Court of Appeal held that it 'would not make sense' if recall had to be delayed until the drugs had been taken and the mental disorder triggered, because that might be too late.[66] This, therefore, extends the grounds for recall and legitimates it as an anticipatory mechanism, using the preventive rationale as a justification for extending what are admittedly unspecific statutory provisions.

The above reference to a mental condition brought on by the use of drugs brings the discussion to the use of imprisonment for mentally disordered offenders. Studies have long suggested that around a third of prisoners have a form of mental disorder, and that 2–7 per cent have a major psychotic disorder.[67] It is often said that prison is no place for a person suffering from mental disorder,[68] and indeed that for some prisoners the mental disorder is (partly) a result of their incarceration. Moreover, as

---

[64]   Boyd-Caine, *Protecting the Public?* (n 60), 45–6. Sections 36–8 of the Domestic Violence, Crime and Victims Act 2004 (as amended) entitle the victims of violent or sexual offences to make representations before a restricted patient is discharged from hospital: see Mackay, 'Mental Disability and the Sentencing Decision' in LO Gostin et al. (eds.), *Principles of Mental Health Law and Policy* (Oxford: Oxford University Press, 2010), 777–802; 800–1.

[65]   [2007] EWCA Civ 687.

[66]   [2007] EWCA Civ 687 per Toulson LJ at [47].

[67]   See Peay, *Mental Health and Crime* (n 32), 118–19, for references and discussion. See also S Fazel and J Danesh, 'Serious Mental Disorder in 23,000 Prisoners', *The Lancet* 359 (2002), 545–50, a meta-study of 62 research findings across 12 countries, which found that some 4 per cent of men and women prisoners had a psychotic illness; 10 per cent of men and 12 per cent of women had major depression; and 65 per cent of men and 42 per cent of women had a personality disorder.

[68]   See, eg, the reports examined by the Court of Appeal in *IA* [2006] 1 Cr App R (S) 521.

the Bradley report confirmed,[69] a significant proportion of mentally disordered persons who are sent to prison have problems of substance abuse (bearing in mind that dependence on alcohol or drugs is not of itself able to support a diagnosis of mental disorder). Sentencing law requires a court to obtain and consider a medical report before passing any custodial sentence on a person who appears to be mentally disordered,[70] and expressly preserves the court's power to mitigate sentence in the case of a mentally disordered offender.[71] However, it is well known that many offenders who are mentally disordered are sentenced to imprisonment.[72] There are two main reasons for this. First, as noted above, a hospital order cannot be made unless a hospital agrees to receive the offender-patient for treatment. If no hospital place is available, the court may have to choose between a community order with a mental health requirement[73] and prison. Second, there are cases where a hospital place is available but the court decides that a hospital order, with or without restrictions, would be unable to ensure the degree of public protection required. Often, this is because it is feared that an MHT may find the criteria for discharge satisfied while the offender is still thought to represent a danger. However, the Court of Appeal now scrutinizes such decisions keenly, and in some cases has quashed a sentence of life imprisonment in favour of a hospital order with restriction order so as to ensure that the offender receives treatment in an appropriate setting,[74] rather than relying on a transfer from prison to hospital under the Mental Health Act powers.[75] All those who receive an indeterminate prison sentence—such as life imprisonment or, formerly, imprisonment for public protection (IPP)—will only be released on licence and will be subject to conditions and liable to recall for the remainder of their life (unless discharged absolutely at a subsequent point). Studies of the operation of the Parole Board confirm that it adopts a distinctly cautious

---

[69] Lord Bradley, *The Bradley Report: Lord Bradley's Review of People with Mental Health Problems or Learning Disabilities in the Criminal Justice System* (London: COI for the Department of Health, 2009), Ch. 4; cf. Peay, *Mental Health and Crime* (n 32), 32.

[70] Criminal Justice Act 2003, s. 157.

[71] Criminal Justice Act 2003, s. 166(5).

[72] For detailed discussion, see K Gledhill, *Defending Mentally Disordered Persons* (London: LAG Education and Service Trust, 2012), Ch. 17.

[73] See n 47 and text thereat.

[74] eg *IA* [2006] 1 Cr App R (S) 521 and *Simpson* [2007] EWCA Crim 2666; cf. *Attorney-General's Reference (No. 54 of 2011)* [2012] 1 Cr App R (S) 637 for a case where the Court of Appeal quashed a hospital order with restrictions in favour of custody for life. For discussion of the different regimes, see the House of Lords in *Drew* [2003] UKHL 25.

[75] The powers under ss. 47 and 48 of the 1983 Act are discussed by Mackay, 'Transfer to Hospital' in LO Gostin et al. (eds.), *Principles of Mental Health Law and Policy* (Oxford: Oxford University Press, 2010), 803–20. Sometimes, such a transfer is made towards the end of a prison sentence, evidently for public protection reasons rather than treatment, which is not a proper use of the power: P Fennell, *Mental Health: Law and Practice* 2nd edn (Bristol: Jordan Publishing, 2011), 258–60.

release policy,[76] and indeed very few prisoners serving IPP sentences have been released at all.[77]

Finally, reference should be made to the Dangerous and Serious Personality Disorder(DSPD) initiative. For many years the definition of mental disorder did not extend to some forms of personality disorder, many of which were regarded as untreatable.[78] In 2000, the then government argued that a programme was needed to tackle offenders with DSPDs, and four units were established, two in special hospitals and two in high-security prisons. In terms of the success of treatment the evaluations have not been positive, and in any event the number of persons treated has been low. It remains unclear whether such persons should be regarded as mental health cases or not.[79]

9.5 Thresholds of Public Protection

Following that critical examination of the legal requirements for deprivation of liberty under English public health law, we now turn to some broader, normative questions. What should be the legal threshold for depriving a person of liberty on grounds of mental disorder or contagious disease? Is the inclusion of these groups within Article 5.1(e) of the ECHR discriminatory? In particular, to take up the argument in Section 9.1, is Article 5.1(e) discriminatory in terms of the UN Convention on the Rights of Persons with Disability 2006 (UNCRPD), in the sense that it fails to assure the equality of treatment that states undertake to provide in Articles 5 and 14 of that Convention?[80]

As explained in Section 9.3, civil confinement under section 3 of the Mental Health Act 1983 can be authorized if two conditions—the 'appropriateness' condition and the 'necessity' condition—are fulfilled. First, the person must be suffering from a mental disorder of a 'nature or degree' that makes it appropriate that he or she should receive medical treatment in hospital.[81] The key word in the section 3

---

[76] eg R Hood and S Shute, *Parole Decision-Making: Weighing the Risk to the Public* (London: Home Office, 2000); N Padfield and A Liebling, *An Exploration of Decision-Making at Discretionary Lifer Panels* (London: Home Office, 2000).

[77] The statistics are discussed in Section 7.3; see also the judgment in *James, Wells and Lee v United Kingdom* (2013) 56 EHRR 399.

[78] See n 31 and accompanying text.

[79] For discussion of the research and debate about the DSPD category, see Peay, *Mental Health and Crime* (n 32), Ch. 18; C Logan, 'Managing High-Risk Personality Disordered Offenders', in B McSherry and P Keyzer (eds.), *Dangerous People: Policy, Prediction and Practice* (London: Routledge, 2011), 233–47; 233; K Harrison, *Dangerousness, Risk and the Governance of Serious Sexual and Violent Offenders* (Abingdon: Routledge, 2011), 197–203.

[80] For a UNCRPD-based challenge to English mental health law, see G Richardson, 'Mental Disabilities and the Law: From Substitute to Supported Decision-Making', *Current Legal Problems* 65 (2012), 333; 343 ff.

[81] For controversy about the words 'nature or degree', see B Hale, *Mental Health Law* 5th edn (London: Sweet and Maxwell, 2010), 55–7.

formulation is 'appropriate'; the key absence from this formulation is any reference to the right to liberty of the person, and the grounds for deprivation of that liberty, despite the fact that the focus of the Mental Health Acts remains on hospital treatment. Section 37, on the making of a hospital order on a convicted offender, is no tighter in this respect. Section 37(2)(b) merely requires the court to be of opinion, having regard to the offender's characteristics and 'to the other available methods of dealing with him, that the most suitable method of disposing of the case is by means of an order under this section'. So, we must enquire: from what point of view is appropriateness or suitability to be considered? Is it that hospital would be the most convenient place, in case the patient wandered off and failed to attend the whole course of treatment, or that treatment in the controlled surroundings of a hospital would be more effective? Or should the finding of appropriateness be linked to the second condition, and to protecting the patient's own safety or protecting others? If so, is it not relevant that the authorization of section 3 detention (and section 37 too) automatically confers the power under section 63 to order compulsory treatment in the first three months, ie without consent? Whatever the answers to these questions, the statutory formulae in sections 3 and 37 provide no structure for the judgments they require, and, above all, fail to direct attention to the fact that what is being authorized is a deprivation of liberty. We noted above that Article 5.1(e) of the ECHR is no better in this respect, failing to advert to any justification for the detention of what it terms 'persons of unsound mind' and thus suggesting that such a condition itself gives adequate grounds for deprivation of liberty. We have seen that in its *Winterwerp* judgment[82] the ECtHR has imposed safeguards against arbitrary detention under Article 5.1(e), and has insisted that the mental disorder be of a kind or degree warranting compulsory confinement, thereby bringing the jurisprudence of 'deprivation of liberty' firmly into play. That is a step forward, but even the notion that certain disorders warrant compulsory confinement lacks the crucial details necessary to supply a convincing justification, and almost certainly violates the UNCRPD.

Turning to the second condition, the treatment must be necessary for the patient's own health or safety (a paternalistic intervention to prevent self-harming or suicide) or for the protection of others, a preventive rationale aimed at public protection. The same formula applies to the making of a CTO, and to the justification for a recall to hospital. But the second condition has no qualifying words, such as 'from serious harm', so the statutory requirement can be satisfied if there is any degree of risk of any harm to the person, which includes physical or psychological harm of an unspecified degree, and it seems indeed to extend beyond that to other unspecified forms of harm.[83] Given that degree of vagueness, the word

[82] See n 27 and accompanying text.
[83] Department of Health, *Mental Health Act Code of Practice* (2008), para. 4.8.

'necessary' in the second condition seems to have little effect.[84] The concepts of 'danger to other persons' and 'serious harm' may be found in other sections of the Mental Health Act,[85] which suggests that the drafting of section 3 deliberately set the threshold for detention at a low (or at least an uncertain) level.

The law relating to contagious diseases contains more restrictive requirements. First, a justice may only make an order if there is a 'risk of significant harm to human health': here we find an adjective, 'significant', which qualifies harm and indicates that clinicians must give evidence about the degree of harm to human health, on the basis of which the court must decide whether it achieves the threshold of significance. If that were transposed into mental health law, it would introduce into the second condition (in section 3) a phrase such as 'the protection of others from significant harm'. However, the law on contagious diseases refers only to 'a risk', without specifying the degree or imminence of the risk. That may just be acceptable in view of the second element, imported from the European Court's case law: the principle of the least restrictive appropriate alternative. This indicates that the decision-maker should give active consideration to all other measures before authorizing deprivation of liberty. This is a procedural requirement only, but the phrase 'a risk of significant harm' might be interpreted so as to vary the degree of probability according to the seriousness of the anticipated harm. However, given that the law on contagious diseases itself may be used to justify deprivation of liberty in some cases—even if this is being done for the benevolent purpose of facilitating contact with clinical services[86]—its parameters should surely be stated more firmly. The detainee is innocent of wrongdoing, and is being detained purely for the protection of others—a step that is regrettable and, if it is to be justified on grounds of public protection, really must be a last resort, must be confined to serious diseases, for as short a time as possible, and in as normalized a setting as feasible.

If we accept those prescriptions, should we not take the same approach to mentally disordered persons detained under civil powers? They are innocent of wrongdoing, and detaining them for the protection of others is a regrettable use of state power against an innocent person. Again, it ought to be a last resort and must be confined to situations in which serious harm is in prospect. Any detention should be for as short a time as possible, and in conditions as normal as feasible. All of this is persuasive because the deprivation of liberty is chiefly for the benefit of others.[87] Indeed, Stanton-Ife argues that detention in a mental hospital necessarily inflicts

---

[84] J Stanton-Ife, 'Preventive Detention at the Margins of Autonomy', in GR Sullivan and I Dennis (eds.), *Seeking Security* (Oxford: Hart Publishing, 2012), 143–68; 149–50.

[85] In ss. 25 and 41 respectively.

[86] But recalling that there can be no compulsory treatment for contagious diseases, unlike the compulsory treatment for the first three months of any Mental Health Act order for hospitalization.

[87] This would not apply where detention is chiefly for the health and safety of the individual concerned.

some 'hard treatment', inasmuch as it involves six forms of material deprivation characteristic of imprisonment (restrictions on movement, isolation from family, significant loss of autonomy, loss of privacy, exposure to risk of humiliation and/or harm, effect on friends and family members).[88] It also inflicts stigma—not the normative stigma or censure intentionally imposed by a criminal conviction, but a form of social and psychological stigma that seems to go inevitably with detention in a mental hospital, even when under civil powers.[89] This, then, supports the claim that the civil powers for detention of the mentally disordered are discriminatory. Similar powers are not available in respect of persons who are not mentally disordered, even if they may be thought to present a significant risk of serious physical harm to others.

In order to ensure that public protection arguments show proper respect for the liberty of individual citizens, the powers of civil confinement under section 3 (and the requirements for a hospital order on conviction) ought to be based on the protection of the patient or of others from personal harm that is serious. Given the six forms of material deprivation involved in detention in a psychiatric hospital, and building on the legislation on contagious diseases, the law should impose higher standards: the relevant harm should be confined to physical or psychological harm,[90] and the requirement should be raised to 'significant risk of serious physical or psychological harm'.[91] This formulation, used in the former sentence of IPP, has attracted a fair amount of criticism on the grounds of vagueness and consequent over-use,[92] and similar criticisms could be advanced against the requirement that restriction orders for mentally disordered offenders be 'necessary for the protection of the public from serious harm'. The challenge is to refine such formulae so as to give a clearer indication to courts and to 'experts' of where the threshold should be placed.

One approach that might be adapted for use in relation to hospital orders with restriction orders would be to require the court to specify a minimum term, as it does for life imprisonment (and as it formerly did for IPP), and then for the law to indicate a sentence-level below which the section 41 power should not apply. Thus, the power to make a restriction order (which must be indefinite) could be confined

---

[88] Stanton-Ife, 'Preventive Detention at the Margins of Autonomy' (n 84), 150–1, drawing on RL Lippke, *Rethinking Imprisonment* (Oxford: Oxford University Press, 2007).

[89] Stanton-Ife, 'Preventive Detention at the Margins of Autonomy' (n 84), 153.

[90] Cf. the similar proposal of the Richardson Committee, *Review of the Mental Health Act 1983: Report of the Expert Committee* (1999), para. 5.95.

[91] Department of Health, *Mental Health Act Code of Practice* (n 83) states that in deciding on the need for detention regard should be had to 'the severity of the potential harm' (para. 4.7); however, given the consequence of loss of liberty, the requirement should be tighter and in primary legislation.

[92] Cf. Zedner, 'Erring on the Side of Safety: Risk Assessment, Expert Knowledge, and the Criminal Court' (n 31), 227–30; M Wasik, 'The Test for Dangerousness', in GR Sullivan and I Dennis (eds.), *Seeking Security* (Oxford: Hart Publishing, 2012), 243–64; 248–50.

to cases in which the offence(s) would otherwise have justified a sentence of a specified level. There would need to be debate about the appropriate level: even the revised lower limit of four years for IPP sentences was probably too low,[93] so we would argue in favour of at least seven years' imprisonment. This would have the advantage of tying the exercise of this power to the sentencing guidelines. Some would argue that there is a large difference between the function of the sentencing guidelines, which is to indicate sentence levels proportionate to the seriousness of the crime committed, and the function of restriction orders under the Mental Health Act, which is to protect the public against the possibility of serious crimes being committed in the future. However, given the unreliability of predictions,[94] one could argue that no-one should be eligible for deprivation of liberty (especially an indefinite deprivation) unless they have committed an offence of a certain level of seriousness.

This discussion of the thresholds of public protection provides the foundation for the following general principles:

(1) The state is justified in taking compulsory powers in public health law to deal with dangers of serious harm to members of the public, whether arising from persons with contagious diseases or from persons who are mentally disordered.

(2) Any compulsory powers should, out of respect for the human rights of individuals, be the least restrictive appropriate alternative to deal with the anticipated danger.

(3) Compulsory powers should only be available to protect the public from a significant risk of serious harm, and should always be kept in proportion to the gravity of the prospective harm and the probability of it occurring.

(4) Where the compulsory powers involve the deprivation of liberty for the protection of others (and not primarily for the protection of the individual), and that deprivation of liberty is not in consequence of a criminal conviction, the state should additionally bear the burden of proving that deprivation of liberty is absolutely necessary, ie that it is the last resort and that lesser forms of intervention have proved or would be ineffective. The individual must have the right to challenge such a decision.

(5) If an individual is deprived of liberty under (4), the state should provide conditions of detention which are as close to normal as feasible; the individual should have the right to regular view of the necessity of detention, and the right to release as soon as the necessity subsides; and the individual should have the right to compensation for loss of income and amenity during the period of detention.

---

[93] The IPP sentence was abolished in 2012: see the discussion in Section 7.3; cf. also Peay, *Mental Health and Crime* (n 32), 112–13.
[94] On which see Ch. 6.

(6) Where the compulsory powers involve the deprivation of liberty following conviction of a criminal offence, such an order should not be made unless the court finds that treatment in a hospital is necessary, and (where the order involves indefinite detention) that no lesser order would be effective in protecting the public from a significant risk of serious harm and that the appropriate sentence for the offence (absent the mental disorder) would be at least seven years' imprisonment.

(7) Whether detention is in a hospital or a prison, the state should ensure that appropriate risk-reductive treatment is made available to detained persons.

(8) Where an individual is deprived of liberty under (6), there should be a right to regular review of the necessity for continued detention. After release on licence, any recall must be based on the need for further detention and not simply on a breach of licence conditions; if further detention is thought necessary, this must be subject to an early assessment, reviewable by the tribunal, of the need for continued detention in order to protect the public from a significant risk of serious harm.

9.6 Conclusions

In other chapters we have noted the frequent reference to the state's duty of prevention as a justification for a range of liberty-depriving measures—against suspected terrorists, against those behaving in a way that is labelled 'anti-social', and so forth. Similar observations will be made in Chapter 10 in relation to migrants. Thus, those who, Rose argues, are classed as 'monstrous individuals' attract this kind of approach:

a whole variety of paralegal forms of confinement are being devised, including pre-emptive or preventive detention prior to a crime being committed or after a determinate sentence has been served, not so much in the name of law and order, but in the name of the community that they threaten, the name of the actual or potential victims they violate. It appears that the conventions of 'the rule of law' must be waived for the protection of the community against a growing number of 'predators'.[95]

This may be taken as a salutary warning against the seductive rhetoric of public safety, public protection, prevention, and security. Yet, popular assumptions about the 'dangerousness' of mentally disordered people seem to persist, despite the constant finding that reconviction rates for disordered offenders are no higher than those for other offenders.[96] As we saw in Section 9.1, even Article 5 of the

---

[95] N Rose, 'Government and Control', *British Journal of Criminology Special Issue: Criminology and Social Theory* 40 (2000), 334.

[96] Peay, 'Mentally Disordered Offenders, Mental Health and Crime' n 31, 429; cf. S Fazel and M Grann, 'The Population Impact of Severe Mental Illness on Violent Crime', *American Journal of Psychiatry* 163 (2006), 1397.

ECHR appears to proceed on the basis that mentally disordered people are inherently dangerous and thus may properly be subject to detention in the name of public protection. Eastman and Peay point to a resurgence of protectionism in the 1990s, referring to various legislative provisions which emphasize the growing public-protective function of psychiatrists in the criminal justice system.[97] As we saw in Section 9.2, discretion abounds because of the broad language of the English legislation, and thus mental health-care professionals play a key role in deprivation of liberty (ie the admission of mentally disordered persons to hospital). They play a role in release procedures too, although these may also involve MHTs and (where the patient has been detained in hospital under what might be termed the 'criminal' provisions) the civil servants in the Mental Health Unit who advise the responsible Minister. Studies of Tribunals have consistently found that some psychiatrists continue to pursue a paternalistic/protective approach rather than recognizing patient rights, and that medical members of Tribunals seem reluctant to comply with the requirements of fair process.[98] Not only has the protective approach been very much alive among psychiatrists, but, in her research in the Mental Health Unit, Boyd-Caine found that the civil servants in the Unit adopted a strongly protective stance and were able subtly to shape the timing and deliberations of MHTs to a considerable degree, in order to maintain 'public confidence'.[99]

The dominance of the preventive/protectionist approach is evident from the first of the 'guiding principles' for making decisions under the Mental Health Act, as set out in the Code of Practice:

Decisions under the Act must be taken with a view to minimising the undesirable effects of mental disorder, by maximising the safety and wellbeing (mental and physical) of patients, promoting their recovery and protecting other people from harm.[100]

This 'purpose principle' proclaims a preventive approach as both its first and its last justifications, and says absolutely nothing about the loss of liberty. The enormous scale of the loss of individual rights flowing from decisions to detain people who are contagious[101] or mentally disordered should be identified as a prominent source of

---

[97] N Eastman and J Peay (eds.), *Law without Enforcement: Integrating Mental Health and Justice* (Oxford: Hart Publishing, 1999), 7.

[98] See eg J Peay, *Tribunals on Trial* (Oxford: Clarendon Press, 1989); G Richardson and D Machin, 'Judicial Review and Tribunal Decision-Making: A Study of Mental Health Review Tribunals', *Public Law* (2000), 494; and E Perkins, *Decision-Making in Mental Health Review Tribunals* (London: Policy Studies Institute, 2003).

[99] Boyd-Caine, *Protecting the Public? Detention and Release of Mentally Disordered Offenders* (n 60).

[100] Department of Health, *Mental Health Act Code of Practice* (n 83), para. 1.2.

[101] Compulsory powers relating to infectious diseases are rarely invoked in practice: see n 11.

concern. If we focus on those with contagious diseases and on civil powers relating to the mentally disordered,[102] it is insufficient simply to state, as does the Code of Practice:

People taking action without a patient's consent must attempt to keep to a minimum the restrictions they impose on the patient's liberty, having regard to the purpose for which the restrictions are imposed.[103]

Combined with the words of the Act, this fails to give sufficient weight to the fundamental nature of the right to personal liberty. It may be said to gesture towards a system of justice that is flexible rather than rights-respecting, and which proceeds on a crude model of balancing that can easily be made to give public protection priority over individual rights. This is facilitated by the wide statutory wording on admission to hospital, or recall to hospital, and at several other stages. As has been apparent through this chapter, there are four major issues that need to be addressed by standards and procedures set out in primary legislation. These issues are: (1) the definition of contagious disease or mental disorder; (2) the type of harm which is to be prevented; (3) the magnitude and likelihood of the risk against which there should be protection; and (4) the accuracy of the predictions on which preventive measures may be based.

The argument relating to these four issues may be summarized as follows. In relation to (1), the list of contagious diseases for which powers (including the power of isolation or quarantine) can be taken is open to extension, for example, to more common viruses. It is essential to be sure that the list contains only those conditions that can do serious harm to the well-being of others so long as they are untreated. As for the definition of mental disorder, this is notoriously contestable, particularly in relation to personality disorders.[104] The use of a broad concept such as 'mental abnormality or personality disorder' in certain US sexual predator laws, as a justification for civil commitment after the end of a sentence, raises strong concerns about the malleability of these concepts in the context of (sometimes indefinite) deprivation of liberty.[105]

Turning to (2), we noted in Section 9.5 the failure of legislatures always to insist on a suitably targeted form of harm. References to 'the prevention of harm' or, equally opaquely, 'protecting other people from harm'[106] suffer from a lack of specificity about the type and degree of harm required. The proposal here is that, whenever loss of liberty is a possible outcome, the legislation should specify 'serious

---

[102] The detention of mentally disordered people who offend raises issues of public protection similar to those discussed in Ch. 7.

[103] Department of Health, *Mental Health Act Code of Practice* (n 83), para. 1.3.

[104] See n 31 for references.

[105] SJ Morse, 'Protecting Liberty and Autonomy: Desert/Disease Jurisprudence', *San Diego Law Review* 484 (2011), 1077–125; 1077.

[106] As in the Department of Health, *Mental Health Act Code of Practice* (n 83), para. 1.2.

physical or psychological harm'. That safeguard should then be expanded in line with (3), so as to specify the degree of risk required by constructing a legislative formula such as 'a significant risk of serious physical or psychological harm'.[107] In this way, the statutory formula could give appropriate weight to the need for prevention and protection, and also show recognition of the fundamental nature of the right to personal liberty.

However, in the practical implementation of such a formula there remains a problem. Even if a sufficiently clear and rights-respecting statutory formula could be devised, there remains concern about the fragility of the predictions and risk-assessments that form the basis of decisions by clinicians. Our full discussion of these issues in Chapter 6 concluded that predictive accuracy is not high, and yet that courts tend to place greater weight on expert evidence than the experts themselves would claim. So, even if one could find a formula that identifies the level of risk (of serious harm) required before deprivation of liberty can be justified, there are bound to remain ineradicable uncertainties about the evidential foundations on which such judgments can be made.[108]

Having indicated the problems of framing a law that is suitably restrictive, we should conclude by reasserting the basic justifications and limiting principles that should be applicable in public health law. One of the animating purposes of public health law is to create a framework for treatment or control that is designed, among other things, to prevent (serious) harm to people.[109] There is a range of contexts in which that treatment and prevention can be delivered, and the principle of the least restrictive appropriate alternative should be insisted on. In the rare cases where detention is being considered, the principles ought to be that the fundamental right to personal liberty must be respected, and that deprivation of liberty may be justified only as a last resort in cases where there is a strong reason to believe that there is a significant or substantial risk of serious physical or psychological harm. Where the preconditions for detention are met, those deprived of their liberty for preventive reasons should be offered risk-reductive treatment.[110] Detention should be monitored so as to ensure that it is for the shortest period possible, and that the criteria for

---

[107] Some would argue for 'substantial' instead of 'significant'; but it has been held in the US that 'substantial' means a risk so great that it was almost certain to materialize if nothing was done: *Miller v Fisher* (2010), US Court of Appeals (7th Circuit), 23 June 2010.

[108] See further Peay, *Mental Health and Crime* (n 32), Ch. 6.

[109] The reference to 'and control' here recognizes that not all forms of mental disorder are treatable, and that there may be people who are agreed to be mentally disordered and to present a danger of serious physical or psychological harm to others. The rationale for detaining such people raises deep problems, since the purpose of treatment cannot be used as a justification, and so it is purely the presence of mental disorder that distinguishes them from other potentially dangerous citizens—for whom there is no general system of detention, unless they are made subject to a civil preventive order and then imprisoned for breach (see Ch. 4).

[110] As held in *M v Germany* (2010) 51 EHRR 976, discussed in Section 7.4.

detention are applied not merely on admission but also on a continuing basis, in relation to decisions about release and recall. Moreover, insofar as people with contagious diseases or mentally disordered people are deprived of their liberty in order to prevent harm to others, there is a principled argument that the conditions of their detention should be as normalized as possible, given the invasion of their fundamental rights.

10

Prevention and Immigration Laws

Much of the preventive endeavour with which this book has engaged concerns measures taken by states in respect of their own citizens. This chapter turns its attention to preventive laws and measures taken against those who are not citizens. Mass mobility is a core feature of contemporary globalization that makes possible the creation of global markets, meets demands for labour in developed nations, and helps to sustain developing economies. The rate and scale of migration has accelerated in recent decades with the lifting of prohibitions on emigration from Eastern bloc countries after the fall of the Berlin Wall; the relaxation of internal borders in the EU; and the increased number of Member States. Europe's relative prosperity and stability has made it a magnet for economic migrants and political refugees alike. However, these developments have also challenged the capacity of states to secure their borders, to enforce immigration controls, and to prevent the supposed hazards associated with unrestricted immigration (see Section 10.1).[1]

Border control is regarded as essential to the preservation of national security and the right to exclude non-citizens as 'the ultimate prerogative of sovereignty'.[2] As the present British government asserts in respect of national security, 'The first duty of any government is to keep this country safe.'[3] Yet, mass mobility, visa-exemption arrangements, and the obligations owed to refugees and asylum seekers under international law combine to limit the state's power to control immigration. A particular source of cross-party concern in the UK has been the relative permeability of borders and the need for stronger security measures to reassert control at the border. As Bosworth observes, the

---

[1] C Rudolph, 'Globalization and Security: Migration and Evolving Conceptions of Security in Statecraft and Scholarship', *Security Studies* 13(1) (2003), 1–32; A Dobrowolsky, '(In)Security and Citizenship: Security, Im/Migration and Shrinking Citizenship Regimes', *Theoretical Inquiries in Law* 8(2) (2007), 628–62; C Dauvergne, *Making People Illegal: What Globalization Means for Migration and Law* (Cambridge: Cambridge University Press, 2008).

[2] A Macklem, 'Borderline Security', in RJ Daniels, P Macklem, and K Roach (eds.), *The Security of Freedom* (Toronto: University of Toronto Press, 2001), 383–404; 389.

[3] HM Government, *The Coalition Together in the National Interest* (London: HMSO, 2013), 42.

desire to reduce, monitor and police who comes into the country, though underpinned in large part by economic factors, is increasingly being presented as a matter of 'security'; from concrete walls and barbed wire fences to so called 'e-borders', countries seek to close off entry points.[4]

The UK's coalition government has declared itself committed to admitting 'the brightest and best workers', ie the highly qualified and employable.[5] It is those considered to pose a threat to economic life, social order, or national security that states seek to limit, exclude, and remove. Although it may be an overstatement to claim that 'the only question asked about immigration policy at present is whether and how effectively it enhances the security of citizens',[6] security concerns have certainly become central to immigration law and policy.

Section 10.1 examines the hazards considered to attend mass migration and the threats against which immigration controls are intended to protect. Section 10.2 explores the preventive rationale of immigration law. Section 10.3 examines how violations of immigration regulations are increasingly made the subject of criminal law, a development that is consistent with the wider 'securitization' of immigration; though it also notes the continuing importance of administrative measures. In Section 10.4, we examine uses of detention of foreign nationals for preventive purposes: these include detention of foreign national prisoners in prisons beyond their tariff term for preventive purposes, and detention in immigration detention and deportation centres prior to expulsion. Finally, Section 10.5 examines the ways in which immigration laws and measures have been used as tools of security and counterterrorism. As this chapter will demonstrate, the preventive dimensions of immigration control take many forms. This chapter is concerned less with systems of surveillance, monitoring, and regulation—oppressive though they may be: rather it focuses on those laws and measures that are directly coercive in that they entail significant curtailment of civil liberties.

10.1 The Hazards of Mass Migration

Mass migration is a fact of modern life that brings incalculable benefits. It allows people freedom of movement to pursue the educational and employment oppor- tunities that accompany globalization and it generates a mobile, flexible workforce capable of fulfilling the needs of modern economies. It enables those from transi- tional or failing economies to seek education and work elsewhere, and to send home remittances to support their families. Yet, at the same time, immigration is

---

[4] M Bosworth, 'Border Control and the Limits of the Sovereign State', *Social and Legal Studies* 17(2) (2008), 199–215; 200.
[5] HM Government, *The Coalition Together in the National Interest* (n 3), 35.
[6] Macklem, 'Borderline Security' (n 2), 384.

said to imperil the job security of domestic workers, to burden the education and welfare system, and to threaten social cohesion, particularly if immigrant communities are relatively closed or do not integrate socially.

Foreigners, refugees, and would-be immigrants are often regarded as presumptively untrustworthy. While trust can be established relatively easily by those in receipt of the requisite papers, bank balance, and bona fide travel plans, those who are undocumented or 'irregular' aliens are quickly categorized as objects of distrust. As Hudson observes, 'The other figure at the borders of community is the *alien* . . . The alien is not-yet-classified, the *undecided* who has yet to persuade that she is friend not foe.'[7] Ramsay has identified, as an important characteristic of contemporary penal politics, the emphasis placed upon the vulnerability of citizens, the consequent popular demand for reassurance, and the intolerance of those who, by virtue of their conduct or characteristics, are deemed to pose a threat.[8] Immigrants, it would seem, fall squarely into the category of those who, in Ramsay's terminology, 'fail to reassure' (see discussion in Section 4.3).[9]

A range of social problems—from minor issues of social order and anti-social behaviour to racial and religious hatred, gangs, and interracial violence—have been attributed to immigrants. In political debate and popular discourse, immigrants are commonly associated with criminality. Notwithstanding evidence that levels of offending within migrant communities are 'in line with the rate of offending in the general population'[10] it is often assumed that they are more crime prone than the rest of the population.[11] Immigrants come from diverse ethnic groups and yet little account is taken of evidence that ethnic minority suspects and defendants are

---

[7] B Hudson, 'Punishing Monsters, Judging Aliens: Justice at the Borders of Community', *Australian & New Zealand Journal of Criminology* 39(2) (2006), 232–47; 239. See also RA Duff, 'Dangerousness and Citizenship', in A Ashworth and M Wasik (eds.), *Fundamentals of Sentencing Theory* (Oxford: Clarendon, 1998), 141–64.

[8] P Ramsay, *The Insecurity State: Vulnerable Autonomy and the Right to Security in the Criminal Law* (Oxford: Oxford University Press, 2012), Ch.1.

[9] P Ramsay, 'The Theory of Vulnerable Autonomy and the Legitimacy of Civil Preventative Orders', in B McSherry, A Norrie, and S Bronitt (eds.), *Regulating Deviance: The Redirection of Criminalisation and the Futures of Criminal Law* (Oxford: Hart Publishing, 2009), 109–39; Ramsay, *The Insecurity State: Vulnerable Autonomy and the Right to Security in the Criminal Law* (n 8), Ch. 1. See also D Ohana, 'Trust, Distrust and Reassurance: Diversion and Preventive Orders through the Prism of *Feindstrafrecht*', *Modern Law Review* 73(5) (2010), 721–51; 724; S Krasmann, 'The Enemy on the Border: Critique of a Programme in Favour of a Preventive State', *Punishment and Society* 9(3) (2007), 301–18.

[10] *The Guardian*, 'Migrant Crime Wave a Myth: Police Study' (16 April 2008) <http://www.guardian.co.uk/politics/2008/apr/16/immigrationpolicy.immigration>.

[11] See L Solivetti, 'Who Is Afraid of Migration and Crime?', *The Howard Journal of Criminal Justice* 44(3) (2005), 322–5. For a counterview see SA Baker et al., 'More Sinned against Than Sinning? Perceptions About European Migrants and Crime', *Criminology and Criminal Justice* 13(3) (2013), 262–78; 263.

subject to unequal treatment in the criminal justice system, more likely to be arrested, prosecuted (as opposed to cautioned), subject to pre-trial detention, and given a custodial sentence.[12]

Mass migration also raises concerns about so-called 'crimes of mobility': transnational organized crime; the trafficking of people, drugs, and other goods; and the illegal arms trade. The threat of terrorism, in particular that inspired or incited by al-Qaeda, is commonly perceived as a primarily foreign threat.[13] Accordingly, foreign national terrorist suspects have been particular targets of counterterrorism laws and measures (see Section 10.6). The neo-liberal assumption that the market should be permitted to determine the global movement of peoples thus stands in direct tension with the aspiration of the sovereign state to provide for national security and to protect its citizens and territory from those deemed to pose a threat or, in the case of terrorists, to challenge its very existence. Widespread political, media, and popular concern identifies would-be migrants as a menace to public safety and recasts immigration as a security issue.[14] As Macklem observes, 'systematic explanations cannot compete with the simplicity and emotive power of invoking the spectre of the foreigner as an intrinsic menace to national security'.[15] Even where foreign nationals are recognized as the victims of transnational crime, for example in human trafficking, the prosecution of traffickers is accompanied by immigration enforcement as a means of preventing illegal movement of peoples.[16]

Mobility permits refugees to flee from armed conflict, religious or political oppression, ethnic strife, detention, and torture in order to seek shelter in safer and more stable jurisdictions. And yet, even the most vulnerable migrants, such as refugees and asylum seekers, are not immune from being considered a threat.[17] Concern about 'bogus' asylum seekers is a staple of media coverage and political debate. Anti-immigrant pressure groups and lobby organizations allege that many asylum seekers do not have genuine grounds for claiming refugee status but use the cover of asylum to gain entry for economic reasons.[18] Overtly xenophobic political organizations, such as the English Defence League and the British National Party,

---

[12] Statistics published under s. 95 of the Criminal Justice Act 1991. Ministry of Justice, *Statistics on Race and the Criminal Justice System 2010* (2012).

[13] J Goodey, 'Whose Insecurity? Organised Crime, Its Victims and the EU', in A Crawford (ed.), *Crime and Insecurity: The Governance of Safety in Europe* (Cullompton: Willan Publishing, 2002), 135–58.

[14] J Huysmans, *The Politics of Insecurity: Fear, Migration and Asylum in the EU* (London: Routledge, 2006), especially Ch. 4. RC Mawby and W Gisby, 'Crime Fears in an Expanding European Union: Just Another Moral Panic?', *The Howard Journal of Criminal Justice* 48(1) (2009), 37–51.

[15] Macklem, 'Borderline Security' (n 2), 384.

[16] JM Chacón, 'Tensions and Trade-Offs: Protecting Trafficking Victims in the Era of Immigration Enforcement', *University of Pennsylvania Law Review* 158 (2010), 1609–53.

[17] J Banks, 'The Criminalisation of Asylum Seekers and Asylum Policy', *Prison Service Journal* 175 (2008), 43–9.

[18] <http://www.migrationwatchuk.co.uk/>.

view most asylum seekers and immigrants as, at best, undeserving scroungers, at worst, as dangerous criminals, and they campaign for the removal of all non-white immigrants. In consequence, immigration control is an intensely politicized arena in which dispassionate assessment of the risks associated with uncontrolled immigration is all but impossible.

The perception that immigrants pose a threat is not confined to far right or xenophobic groups. In the UK, the rise of immigration up to 2010[19] led to claims by the government that the 'traditional tolerance' of British society was

under threat. It is under threat from those who come and live here illegally by breaking our rules and abusing our hospitality . . . The challenge for the Government is to maintain public confidence in the system by agreeing immigration where it is in the country's interests and preventing it where it is not.[20]

Such claims increased markedly in the aftermath of the July 2005 London bombings—notwithstanding the fact these atrocities were the work of 'home-grown' terrorists and that the vast majority of immigrants posed no threat to security.[21] As Bosworth observes, 'issues that have traditionally been conceptualized as problems of "assimilation", these days are articulated as questions of risk to the security of the host population due to the challenges they pose to "social cohesion". Integration . . . is thus presented as a safeguard of all sorts of aspects of community well-being and security.'[22] The subsequent government announcement of plans to introduce a 'robust machinery' to 'manage migration and protect British values' relied on the unsubstantiated claim that, post-7/7, immigration posed a particular threat to security and public order, social stability, and economic welfare. Such views sustain a political environment in which the ill-founded identification of immigrants as threats licenses exclusionary and often highly coercive measures.

---

[19] According to the organization Migration Watch, net migration rose 'from 50,000 in 1997 to 250,000 in 2010. Over 3 million immigrants have arrived since 1997. Net migration fell to 163,000 in the year to June 2012 as government policies took effect.' <http://www.migrationwatchuk.co.uk/>. However, the UKBA reported in 2013 that '[n]et migration is now at its lowest level for a decade, falling from 242,000 in the year to September 2011 to 153,000 in the year to September 2012'. UKBA, 'New statistics show net migration has decreased', <http://www.ukba.homeoffice.gov.uk/sitecontent/newsarticles/2013/may/72-migration-statistics>.

[20] Former British Prime Minister Tony Blair in his 'Forward' to the 2005 White Paper on immigration: Home Office, *Controlling Our Borders: Making Migration Work for Britain. Five-Year Strategy for Asylum and Immigration* (London: Home Office, 2005), 5–6.

[21] Former British Prime Minister, Tony Blair, 'The Duty to Integrate: Shared British Values', speech on multiculturalism and integration, delivered at 10 Downing Street, London, for the 'Our Nation's Future' Lecture (8 December 2006), quoted in Dobrowolsky, '(In)Security and Citizenship: Security, Im/Migration and Shrinking Citizenship Regimes' (n 1), 660.

[22] Bosworth, 'Border Control and the Limits of the Sovereign State' (n 4), 203.

10.2 The Preventive Rationale of Immigration Laws

Preventive justifications underpin much policy-making and legislative endeavour with respect to immigration control. To take just one example, the 2005 UK White Paper on immigration control speaks of 'a new drive to prevent illegal entry'; 'effective control to prevent those who do not meet our criteria from getting here'; improvements to the justice system to 'prevent it being used to delay or circumvent our control'; 'accepting genuine refugees but preventing abuse of the asylum system'; 'work with carriers overseas . . . preventing undocumented passengers reaching the UK'; and '[p]reventing applicants concealing their identity to frustrate removal'.[23]

The preventive rationale also operates at the international level in attempts to pre-empt travel by those without requisite documentation and visas; in the strengthening of external borders by both physical structures and the enforcement of border checks and controls; and in the extensive systems of controls and registration requirements of those who have already crossed the border. The drive to pre-empt illegal immigration stands behind the formation of transnational surveillance systems such as *Eurosur* (European Border Surveillance System); data-collection requirements—for example, requirements to collect and exchange Passenger Name Records (PNR) and to collect and share data on asylum seekers (eg using *Eurodac*, a database of the fingerprints of asylum seekers); and the setting up of the European border policing agency *Frontex*.[24] Co-operative international policing arrangements, for example that under the Schengen Agreement (1995), sought to relax border controls by simultaneously increasing profiling, surveillance, and checks on those deemed to pose a risk.[25] Together, these various international agreements, policies, and measures seek to pre-empt illegal immigration well before the border is attained. Supra-national security arrangements thus decouple national security from the territory of the nation state and involve a partial ceding of the state's sovereign right to control its own border. In practice, states now also export controls to the borders of the EU and, further afield still, to airline companies and local border control authorities that seek to prevent illegal migrants at the point of departure. The Immigration, Asylum and Nationality Act 2006 introduced further provisions to obtain passenger, crew, and service data from carriers in advance of all movements into and out of the UK, and imposed a duty on border agencies to share that data. In 2013, the United Kingdom Border Agency (UKBA) asserted that 'controls overseas ensure that we can

---

[23] Home Office, *Controlling Our Borders: Making Migration Work for Britain. Five-Year Strategy for Asylum and Immigration* (London: HMSO, 2005) at 6, 7, 8, 9, and 10 respectively.

[24] KF Aas, ' "Crimmigrant" Bodies and Bona Fide Travelers: Surveillance, Citizenship and Global Governance', *Theoretical Criminology* 15(3) (2011), 331–46; 333.

[25] Aas, ' "Crimmigrant" Bodies and Bona Fide Travelers' (n 24), 337–8.

prevent abuse of our immigration laws at the earliest possible point, which reduces risks and costs'.[26]

Notwithstanding this partial export of border security,[27] domestic immigration laws, border controls, and security remain important means of preventing illegal immigration at the point of entry; to curb trade in illicit goods and arms; and to prevent trafficking of people and of drugs. The Border Policing Command (BPC), a specialist unit within the National Crime Agency (NCA), co-ordinates intelligence relating to organized crime and illegal immigration. Border controls also play an important role in preventing the importation of material that might be used for criminal purposes, or in pursuit of a terrorist attack, in particular, explosives and radioactive materials.

'Inland enforcement', as it is called, has its focus on the regulation of those non-citizens who—though physically resident—may have broken immigration rules or overstayed their visa. The role of domestic law enforcement in the policing of immigration has a long history, dating back at least to the Immigration Act of 1971 which gave immigration officers and the police considerable powers to detain and question those whom they suspected of being in breach of immigration law.[28] Internal enforcement of immigration laws carried out by the police relies on profiling suspected illegal immigrants and targeted spot checks[29] as a means of checking immigration status.[30] Powers of administrative detention under immigration law allow police to make checks on suspect individuals and, according to Weber and Bowling: 'even more controversially, Immigration Act detention powers are sometimes used pre-emptively as crime prevention measures'.[31] Joint enforcement operations between police and immigration officials, large-scale raids, and routine use of the police to monitor suspect individuals and asylum applicants further involve the police in immigration control.

---

[26] Home Office, *UKBA Business Plan 2011–2015* (London: HMSO, 2011a), 9.

[27] KF Aas, '(In)Security-at-a-Distance: Rescaling Justice, Risk and Warfare in a Transnational Age', *Global Crime* 13(4) (2012), 235–53.

[28] B Bowling and C Phillips, 'Policing Ethnic Minority Communities', in T Newburn (ed.), *Handbook of Policing* 2nd edn (London: Routledge, 2012), 611–14; 612.

[29] See, eg, D Doffey, 'Government adviser's warning over spot check for illegal immigrants', *The Guardian* (3 August 2013). <http://www.theguardian.com/uk-news/2013/aug/03/government-adviser-spot-checks-illegal-migrants>. M Townsend, 'Even if illegal immigration is an issue, targeting skin colour is unacceptable', *The Guardian* (3 August 2013). <http://www.theguardian.com/uk-news/2013/aug/03/illegal-immigration-issue-unacceptable-walthamstow>.

[30] L Weber, '"It Sounds Like They Shouldn't Be Here": Immigration Checks on the Streets of Sydney', *Policing and Society* 21(4) (2011), 456–67; L Weber and B Bowling, 'Policing Migration: A Framework for Investigating the Regulation of Global Mobility', *Policing & Society* 14 (2004), 195–212; 200.

[31] Weber and Bowling, 'Policing Migration: A Framework for Investigating the Regulation of Global Mobility' (n 30), 201.

The progressive tightening of immigration controls can be demonstrated by outlining some of the most important recent UK legislation. The Nationality, Immigration and Asylum Act 2002 provisions included extended powers to detain asylum seekers at any point during their application; in 2005 the government announced a five-year strategy entitled 'Controlling our borders'; and the Immigration, Asylum and Nationality Act 2006 introduced restrictions on visa appeals processes. The Borders Act 2007 equips immigration officers with police-like powers, including entry, search-and-seizure powers, as well as powers of detention at airports.[32] The secondment of police officers to immigration services and the use of police officers to train immigration officials further blur the distinction between immigration control and policing. In addition to primary legislation, extensive secondary immigration rules and regulations seek to prevent and curtail illegal immigration. The scale of operations is vast: the e-Borders programme, for example, vetted around 125 million people in 2010 resulting in more than 2,800 arrests.[33]

The toughening of immigration control measures by the Labour government up to 2010 included new electronic checks on those seeking to enter and leave the UK; a 'clamp down on illegal immigration'; and fingerprinting of visa applicants abroad. The Borders, Citizenship and Immigration Act 2009 introduced complex new regulations designed to raise the requirements for acquisition of citizenship and to limit access by new immigrants to social security benefits and to housing. It also weakens their legal status by introducing a provisional trial status of 'probationary citizenship', during which the commission of even minor crimes is a bar to progress.[34] Those with conditional immigration status are particularly vulnerable to abuse, open to exploitation, subject to poor working conditions, and at risk of homelessness.[35] The coalition government has further strengthened controls to prevent illegal entry by would-be immigrants. In 2012, the Border Force, which is responsible for entry control and customs functions, was split off from UKBA.[36] High-profile removal operations have been carried out against foreign nationals living in the UK without valid immigration status or who have overstayed their visa.

---

[32] Under the 2007 Act, immigration officers are empowered to arrest and detain suspects for up to three hours at the border in the absence of a police officer if it is thought that the individual may be liable to arrest or is subject to a warrant for arrest.

[33] Home Office, *UKBA Business Plan 2011–2015* (n 26) at 13. By the end of 2014, it is hoped to cover 95 per cent of those entering the UK.

[34] L Zedner, 'Security, the State and the Citizen: The Changing Architecture of Crime Control', *New Criminal Law Review* 13(2) (2010), 379–403; A Bostanci, *British Citizenship: A Debate of Paradoxes* (London: Friedrich Ebert Stiftung, 2008).

[35] Equality and Diversity Forum, *Response to 'The Path to Citizenship: The Next Steps in Reforming the Immigration System'* (London, 2008). Liberty, *Liberty's Evidence to the Joint Committee on Human Rights Call for Evidence on the Draft Legislative Programme 2008–09* (London, 2008).

[36] UKBA remains responsible for asylum and immigration cases, enforcement activity within the UK, and immigration operations overseas.

The government has also launched a National Allegations Management System to track allegations by members of the public of immigration law breaches. More controversial still has been the Home Office practice of driving vans through London boroughs with high immigrant populations that display advertising hoardings which invite those in the UK illegally to 'Go home or face arrest'.[37]

Special provisions apply in respect of those foreign nationals suspected or convicted of committed criminal offences. Following 'Operation Nexus', UKBA posted immigration officers in police custody suites in order to identify foreign national offenders liable for removal from the UK. This operation was endorsed by Immigration Minister Mark Harper, who declared:

we will take all possible action against individuals who pose a risk to the public and remove them from the country at the earliest opportunity. Through our combined work with the police we are using the full force of immigration powers on those who seek to commit crime and damage our communities. The success of this operation proves that foreign nationals who continue to offend in this country will be arrested and removed from the UK.[38]

In addition, the Crime and Courts Act 2013 provided for the establishment of a dedicated Border Police Command, as part of the new National Crime Agency, which the government believes will improve co-ordination of border control and security operations.[39]

In 2013, the government announced plans to abolish the long-criticized UKBA[40] and on 1 April 2013 UKBA was split into two separate operational units which are now situated within the Home Office. The units are: UK Visas and Immigration—responsible for handling applications for visas and to extend stay, applications for asylum, and appeals, and Immigration Enforcement—responsible for 'investigating immigration offences, detaining and removing individuals with no right to be in the UK, preventing abuse of the immigration system'.[41] The Immigration Enforcement unit is described by the Home Office as 'an organization

---

[37] See, eg, 'Campaign to persuade illegal immigrants to leave UK', BBC News (22 July 2013): <http://www.bbc.co.uk/news/uk-england-london-23406479> and 'Council "horrified" over scheme for immigrants to go': <http://www.bbc.co.uk/news/uk-england-london-23419848>.

[38] <http://www.ukba.homeoffice.gov.uk/sitecontent/newsarticles/2013/january/02-nexus>.

[39] House of Commons Library (2013), *Immigration and Asylum Policy: Government Plans and Progress Made Standard Note SN/HA/5829*, 12. <http://www.parliament.uk/briefing-papers/SN05829>.

[40] On the grounds that it was a 'troubled' organization with a 'closed, secretive and defensive culture', and that it has been prone to 'poor enforcement of its own policies'. A Travis, 'UK Border Agency to be abolished, Theresa May announces', *The Guardian* (26 March 2013).<http://www.guardian.co.uk/uk/2013/mar/26/uk-border-agency-broken-up>.

[41] <http://www.ukba.homeoffice.gov.uk/aboutus/organisation/>.

that has law enforcement at its heart and gets tough on those who break our immigration laws'.[42] Despite this institutional endeavour to separate immigration regulation and crime control, in its mid-term review the government continued to blur the distinction between illegal immigration and criminal activity: 'We will strengthen our borders with a new Border Policing Command, to ensure that illegal goods are seized, illegal immigrants are dealt with and networks of organised criminals are targeted and disrupted—both overseas and at ports up and down the UK.'[43] Stronger measures to control illegal immigration are expected in the Immigration Bill 2013/14 to require private landlords to check on tenants' immigration status, to double fines for those who employ illegal workers, and to ensure that, other than in exceptional circumstances, foreign nationals who commit serious crimes are deported.[44]

10.3 The Criminalization of Immigration Violations

A prominent feature of contemporary immigration law is the criminalization of what were formerly administrative violations of immigration regulations—or 'crimmigration' as it is called.[45] Aliverti points out that criminal sanctions for breach of immigration regulations have existed for more than 200 years, but notes that whereas just 70 immigration offences were enacted in Britain between 1905 and 1996, 84 new immigration offences were created in the 13 years 1997–2010 in six Acts passed by the then Labour government.[46] The Immigration and Asylum Act 1999 alone introduced 35 new immigration-related offences, including deception

---

[42] <http://www.ukba.homeoffice.gov.uk/sitecontent/newsarticles/2013/may/11-transi tion>. The creation of this more robust agency was, in part, a response to perceived failures by the existing regime. See, eg, 'Only one in every 100 reports of illegal immigration results in deportation' *The Telegraph* (4 August 2013). <http://www.telegraph.co.uk/news/ uknews/immigration/10183826/Only-one-in-every-100-reports-of-illegal-immigration- results-in-deportation.html>.

[43] HM Government, *The Coalition Together in the National Interest* (n 3), 42.

[44] <http://www.gov.uk/government/uploads/system/uploads/attachment_data/file/ 197434/Queens-Speech-2013.pdf >, 64–6.

[45] J Stumpf, 'The Crimmigration Crisis: Immigrants, Crime and Sovereign Power', *Lewis & Clark Law School Legal Research Paper Series* Paper No. 2007-2 (2007), 1–44. For the US, McLeod has documented that between 1990 and 2010 'immigration offenses became the most common federally prosecuted crimes in the United States'. AM McLeod, 'The US Criminal-Immigration Convergence and Its Possible Undoing', *American Criminal Law Review* 49 (2012), 105–78; J Stumpf, 'Doing Time: Crimmigration Law and the Perils of Haste', *UCLA Law Review* 58 (2011), 1705–48.

[46] See discussion in A Aliverti, *Making Home Safe? The Role of Criminal Law and Punishment in British Immigration Controls*. Oxford DPhil Thesis (2012), 85; 102; 103.

intended to circumvent immigration enforcement actions; false or dishonest representation by asylum claimants; failure by a sponsor to maintain claimants; and offences relating to the enforcement of discipline inside Immigration Removal Centres (IRCs). The Nationality, Immigration and Asylum Act 2002 added more offences, including assisting unlawful immigration to a Member State by a non-EU citizen; helping an asylum seeker to enter the UK 'knowingly and for gain'; and assisting entry to the UK in breach of a deportation or exclusion order. Further offences were added by the Asylum and Immigration Act 2004, which made failure to produce a passport, and failure to co-operate with deportation or removal procedures, without a reasonable excuse, crimes; as well as by the UK Border Agency Act 2007 and the Borders, Citizenship and Immigration Act 2009.[47] Breaches of immigration regulations generally have a criminal sanction attached.[48] Prosecution and conviction rates for immigration crimes rose between 2000 and 2005 and continued to rise in the Crown Court but have decreased in the magistrates' courts since 2005.[49]

The extension of criminal liability to what were once regulatory and administrative matters under immigration law has not passed without criticism.[50] While recognizing that states have a legitimate interest in controlling their borders, the former European Commissioner for Human Rights, Thomas Hammarberg, nonetheless insists: 'Criminalization is a disproportionate measure which exceeds a state's legitimate interest in controlling its borders.... Immigration offences should remain

---

[47] Aliverti, *Making Home Safe?* (n 46); A Aliverti, 'Making People Criminal. The Role of the Criminal Law in Immigration Enforcement', *Theoretical Criminology* 16(4) (2012), 417–34.

[48] Home Office, *Protecting Our Border, Protecting the Public. The UK Border Agency's Five Year Strategy for Enforcing Our Immigration Rules and Addressing Immigration and Cross Border Crime* (London: Home Office, 2010), 26.

[49] Prosecutions in the magistrates' courts declined from 1,083 in 2005 to 552 in 2011, and convictions in the magistrates' courts declined from 686 to 156 over the same period. Aliverti attributes the decline to guidance from UKBA, which said that prosecution of immigration offences should be reserved for the most serious offences. Prosecution in the Crown Court rose from 364 in 2005 to 505 in 2011 and convictions also rose over the same period from 293 to 403. A Aliverti, *Immigration Offences: Trends in Legislation and Criminal and Civil Enforcement: Migration Observatory Briefing* (Oxford: COMPAS, University of Oxford, 2013). <http://www.migrationobservatory.ox.ac.uk/sites/files/migobs/Briefing%20-20Immigration%20Offences_0.pdf>.

[50] T Miller, 'Citizenship & Severity. Recent Immigration Reforms and the New Penology', *Georgetown Immigration Law Journal* 17 (2003), 611–66; T Miller, 'Blurring the Boundaries between Immigration and Crime Control after September 11th', *Boston College Third World Law Journal* 25 (2005), 81–124; Stumpf, 'The Crimmigration Crisis: Immigrants, Crime and Sovereign Power' (n 45); JM Chacón, 'Managing Migration through Crime', *Columbia Law Review* 109 (2009), 135–48; JM Chacón, 'Overcriminalizing Immigration', *Journal of Criminal Law & Criminology* 102(3) (2012), 613–52; McLeod, 'The US Criminal-Immigration Convergence and Its Possible Undoing' (n 45); DA Sklansky, 'Crime, Immigration, and Ad Hoc Instrumentalism', *New Criminal Law Review* 15(2) (2012), 157–223.

administrative in nature.'[51] Hammarberg's case against criminalization rests chiefly on the deleterious consequences of stigmatization and marginalization; the over-burdening of courts; and the resultant overcrowding of prisons and detention centres.[52] Less attention has been paid to the fact that many immigration offences fail to satisfy basic principles of criminal law and are predicated upon questionable assumptions about the hazards that illegal immigration is feared to pose to the domestic polity. Many immigration offences do not satisfy the requirement that some non-trivial harm is risked or caused; they include, for example, failure to produce documents before an immigration judge or failure to supply information requested by the authorities by employers or financial institutions.[53] Comprehen-sive review of existing offences and careful prelegislative scrutiny of proposed offences might curb the over-readiness to criminalize breaches of immigration law. This might inhibit the use of immigration law for crime prevention purposes, particularly where the creation of offences is justified by reference to dubious claims that offences will serve as effective deterrents. It would check the exercise of the police power over non-citizens by limiting immigration offences to those that are fairly labelled, clearly wrongful, and entail harms of a sufficient gravity to merit criminalization.

Those who are prosecuted are entitled to all the protections that attach to the criminal process irrespective of their status as citizens or non-citizens. However, s. 32 of the Border Act 2007 provides that an individual who is not a British citizen, who is convicted in the UK of an offence and is either sentenced to a period of at least 12 months' imprisonment or imprisoned for an offence specified as a *'serious criminal offence'* (under s. 72(4)(a) of the Nationality, Immigration and Asylum Act 2002), must be subject to a deportation order. Part 10 (ss. 130–137) of the Criminal Justice and Immigration Act 2008 gives the Secretary of State power to subject those designated foreign criminals to electronic monitoring, to impose conditions as to their residence, employment, and movement, as well as reporting requirements. Breach of these conditions is an imprisonable offence.

Despite the rightful concern about resort to criminalization of immigration violations, it is arguably less pressing an issue in the UK than in the US. As Aliverti points out, the number of immigration offence convictions in the UK remains very small compared with administrative actions. Administrative actions in the form of

---

[51] T Hammarberg, 'It is wrong to criminalize migration' (2008) <http://www.coe.int/t/commissioner/Viewpoints/080929_en.asp>.

[52] Hammarberg, 'It is wrong to criminalize migration' (n 51). For Hammarberg's views on the human rights implications, see also T Hammarberg, 'Criminalisation of Migration in Europe: Human Rights Implications'. <https://wcd.coe.int/ViewDoc.jsp?id=1579605>.

[53] Aliverti, 'Making People Criminal. The Role of the Criminal Law in Immigration Enforcement' (n 46), 6; A Simester and A von Hirsch, *Crimes, Harms and Wrongs: On the Principles of Criminalization* (Oxford: Hart Publishing, 2011), Ch. 3.

enforced removals and refusals of entry at port stood at 30,763 in 2011, whereas only 559 people were convicted of immigration offences that year in the UK.[54] In practice it would seem that, in the UK at least, the criminalization of immigration remains but a very small element in the larger scheme of administrative measures.

10.4 Detention, Deportation, and Removal

Deportation and removal are core tools of immigration control. Deportation is reserved for those who are considered to be 'an individual social threat', because they have a criminal record or for other reasons, for example as a risk to national security. Others, such as those who have overstayed their visa and failed asylum seekers, are subjected not to deportation but to 'administrative removal'.[55] Successful deportation or removal requires that the person has been located and is available for travel. In practice, the considerable time taken to resolve legal questions means that many foreign nationals are detained until they can be removed.

Powers to detain immigrants, while determining whether or not to admit them or pending removal, have a long history. The first UK immigration detention centre was built in 1969, prior to which immigration detainees were held in ordinary prisons. Detention is primarily a matter of administrative convenience to facilitate identity checks, information-gathering, and to test the basis of claims. It may be imposed at any point during the asylum process. Individuals can also be detained where there is a risk of absconding and where there is a risk of harm to the individual themselves or to the public. Detention may be deployed as part of fast-track asylum procedures or in support of the removal of failed asylum seekers. It is typically imposed upon those who are thought to have entered illegally, overstayed, or otherwise breached the terms of their residence and who are awaiting deportation. There is no limit on the length of time a person can be detained. Despite guidance that detention should occur only when removal is 'imminent', about 60 per cent of detainees are held for up to two months but some are held for many months and some (less than 10 per cent) are held for more than a year.[56] Detention

---

[54] Aliverti, *Immigration Offences: Trends in Legislation and Criminal and Civil Enforcement: Migration Observatory Briefing* (n 49), 6. There is also an extensive regime of civil penalties which are applied against employers for failure to check workers' documentation at 7. <http://www.migrationobservatory.ox.ac.uk/briefings/immigration-offences-trends-legislation-and-criminal-and-civil-enforcement>.

[55] M Bosworth, 'Deportation, Detention and Foreign-National Prisoners in England and Wales', *Citizenship Studies* 15(5) (2011), 583–95; 584.

[56] SJ Silverman and R Hajela, *Briefing: Immigration in the UK* (Oxford: Migration Observatory), 3. <http://www.migrationobservatory.ox.ac.uk/sites/files/migobs/Immigration%20Detention%20Briefing.pdf>.

has clearly become an important adjunct to deportation, ensuring that those whose case for asylum or immigration fails can speedily be removed.

The UK has a large immigration detention estate with a capacity of approximately 3,500 places. In 2011, around 27,000 people entered immigration detention in the UK,[57] and on average between 2,000 and 3,000 people are detained at any given time.[58] Individuals may be detained in one of ten IRCs,[59] in prisons, or for shorter periods in Short-Term Holding Facilities (STHFs) at airports and ports, in a special predeparture facility for families at Gatwick Airport, or in police cells. About half of those held in IRCs are 'time-served' foreign national prisoners who are deemed not to pose such serious security risk as to require continued detention in prison. The remainder of inmates are asylum seekers or visa 'over-stayers'.[60] Three IRCs are run by HM Prison Service; the rest are run by private companies. There is considerable variation in the physical estate and the restrictions imposed on detainees: some IRCs are built to restrictive Category B prison security standards, while others permit greater freedoms.[61] Several IRCs are situated in former or current penal institutions, or are run by former prison governors. IRCs thus sit on the margins of the penal estate and have many similarities with it, not least by being governed by concerns about security.

Foreign national prisoners (FNPs) may be detained in prison at the end of their sentence pending deportation. In 2006, a crisis arose when it was revealed that more than 1,000 FNPs had been released from prison, having served their sentence, before they could be considered for deportation.[62] The Borders Act 2007 ended discretionary deportation. All non-European Economic Area (EEA) offenders sentenced to 12 months' custody or more and EEA offenders sentenced to 24 months' custody or more now face automatic deportation. There is no possibility for appeal unless deportation would breach human rights and/or international

---

[57] Not including those detained in police cells. Silverman and Hajela, *Briefing* (n 56), 2. <http://www.migrationobservatory.ox.ac.uk/sites/files/migobs/Immigration%20Detention%20Briefing.pdf>.

[58] The Migration Observatory 'Immigration in the UK' at <http://migrationobservatory.ox.ac.uk/briefings/immigration-detention-uk>.

[59] Under the Nationality, Immigration and Asylum Act 2002 Immigration Detention Centres were relabelled Immigration Removal Centres.

[60] Following an earlier decision to end the detention of children, it was announced in 2013 that no children were any longer held in IRCs, though they could be held for up to one week at a special family facility prior to departure. House of Commons Library 2013. *Ending Child Immigration Detention—Commons Library Standard Note* at <http://www.parliament.uk/briefing-papers/SN05591>.

[61] M Bosworth, 'Immigration Detention: Policy Challenges', *The Migration Observatory* at <http://migrationobservatory.ox.ac.uk/policy-primers/immigration-detention-policy-challenges>.

[62] The crisis led to strong criticism of Home Office officials and prompted the dismissal of Charles Clarke as Home Secretary. E Kaufman, 'Hubs and Spokes: The Transformation of the British Prison', in KF Aas and M Bosworth (eds.), *The Borders of Punishment: Migration, Citizenship, and Social Exclusion* (Oxford: Oxford University Press, 2013), 166–82; 166.

obligations. On an average, more than 5,000 FNPs have been deported annually since the introduction of automatic deportation. FNPs should only continue to be held in prison as immigration detainees if they are considered to pose a threat to national security; have been involved in serious drugs, sexual, or violence offences; are deemed to pose a threat to security because, for example, they have previously escaped from custody or planned or assisted others to do so; or are deemed to pose serious problems of control.[63] On completion of their sentence, individuals should be treated as 'unconvicted prisoners'.[64]

IRCs have a preventive role in averting the supposed risks posed by those who have entered or remain in a country illegally and in facilitating deportation or removal. It is, however, questionable whether many of those detained pose a sufficient threat or are dangerous enough to justify incarceration.[65] Article 5 of the ECHR declares the right to liberty of the person. As already noted in Chapters 3 and 9, there are six exceptions to the right, which have been subject to interpretation by the European Court. Article 5.1(f) creates an exception for 'the lawful arrest or detention of a person to prevent his effecting an unauthorised entry into the country or of a person against whom action is being taken with a view to deportation or extradition'. On the face of it, this exception does not require the detention to be necessary or proportionate. Arguments in favour of implying such requirements—as the Court did in respect of the exception for mentally disordered persons[66]—were dismissed by the Grand Chamber in the leading decision in *Saadi v United Kingdom*.[67] The Grand Chamber held that the duration of any such detention should be no longer than reasonable for the stated purpose. It also insisted that the conditions of detention must reflect the fact that the detainees were not held for a criminal offence. But the failure to require that deprivation of liberty be necessary, in the sense that no less restrictive alternative would be appropriate, is an unfortunate subjugation of this right to an overblown notion of the state's territorial sovereignty.[68]

Although extensive use is made of immigration detention, it is questionable whether, given the loss of liberty and severe deprivations entailed, it is a just and

---

[63] Bosworth, 'Deportation, Detention and Foreign-National Prisoners in England and Wales' (n 55), 588.

[64] Prisoners may be asked to waive this right if the prison in which they are held cannot meet the requirements of increased time out of cell and greater access to visits, and prisoners may themselves waive this right, for example in order to retain access to work or drug treatment (which are not available to unconvicted inmates). M Bosworth, 'Immigration Detention: Policy Challenges', *The Migration Observatory*, 4 at <http://migrationobservatory.ox.ac.uk/policy-primers/immigration-detention-policy-challenges>.

[65] Bosworth, 'Immigration Detention' (n 61), 7.

[66] See the discussion in Section 9.3.

[67] (2008) 47 EHRR 427.

[68] G Cornelisse, 'A New Articulation of Human Rights, or Why the European Court of Human Rights Should Think Beyond Westphalian Sovereignty', in M Dembour and T Kelly (eds.), *Are Human Rights for Migrants? Critical Reflections on the Status of Irregular Migrants in Europe and the United States* (Abingdon: Routledge, 2011), 99–119; 102.

defensible means of border control.[69] Nor is it self-evident that it is proportionate to the risk to others that the individuals concerned supposedly pose. In order to address the question of harm risked, the UKBA developed a 'harm matrix' which identifies three categories 'High', 'Medium', and 'Low'. Prosecution is prioritized in respect of Category A, whereas low-level harms are supposed to be dealt with by caution and removal. While Category A includes serious criminal offences, such as terrorist activity, murder, rape, people trafficking, violent crime, and child abuse, the lowest Category C includes 'minor immigration offences, a drain on public funds and anti-social behaviour'.[70] Given the low-level risk of harm posed by those in the lowest category, detention and/or removal would seem to be a disproportionate response. As Bosworth observes, those who are not detained 'are required to report to various agencies including the police, while their cases are under consideration. They are also expected to provide the state with details about their residence and financial situation.'[71] As we argued in Chapter 9, liberty is a fundamental right and should not be taken away unless it is necessary to do so. Moreover, the principle of the least restrictive alternative requires that it is justifiable to deprive individuals of their liberty in the cause of border control only if less liberty-eroding measures would not suffice to minimize the risks entailed.

IRCs have been subject to criticism, not least because the conditions under which detainees are held are not dissimilar to imprisonment, notwithstanding the fact that those held need not have been convicted of a crime but are being held supposedly for the public good. Detainees do not enjoy the protection of judicial oversight, nor do they have access to the same amount or quality of legal representation as do those in prison.[72] Other than in the three IRCs run by HM Prison Service, the NHS does not provide routine health care to detainees. Moreover, there are few opportunities for work, fewer leisure activities, little by way of counselling, and no drug-treatment programmes.[73] Most importantly, those in detention, unlike most prisoners, may be held indefinitely.

In 2011, 14,225 persons were removed or departed voluntarily from the UK, of which 5,585 were enforced removals and notified voluntary departures.[74] The means by which removal is carried out are also controversial. In July 2013, a public inquest found that Jimmy Mubenga, an Angolan asylum seeker whose application

---

[69] M Bosworth, 'Human Rights and Immigration Detention in the UK', in M Dembour and T Kelly (eds.), *Are Human Rights for Migrants? Critical Reflections on the Status of Irregular Migrants in Europe and the United States* (Abingdon: Routledge, 2011), 165–83.

[70] Home Office, *Control of Immigration Quarterly Statistical Summary First Quarter 2011* (London: HMSO, 2011), 24.

[71] Bosworth, 'Border Control and the Limits of the Sovereign State' (n 4), 207.

[72] M Bosworth, 'Subjectivity and Identity in Detention: Punishment and Society in a Global Age', *Theoretical Criminology* 16(2) (2012), 123–40.

[73] Bosworth, 'Human Rights and Immigration Detention in the UK' (n 69), 173–4.

[74] Home Office, *Control of Immigration Quarterly Statistical Summary First Quarter 2011* (n 70), 22.

had been rejected, was unlawfully killed by private escorts during deportation proceedings.[75] The fact that deportation has been contracted out to private security firms has been much criticized because it has led to improper, and in this case fatal, use of restraints and because privatization hinders accountability about the manner in which removal is accomplished.

10.5 Immigration Appeals Procedure

A well-documented feature of immigration law is that it offers inadequate procedural protections for those who are subject to it, even where the consequences of its application extend to indefinite detention and to deportation. As Macklem argues, 'The truth is that laws that arouse deep concern about civil liberties when applied to citizens are standard fare in the immigration context.'[76] Yet (as we will argue further below), the procedural safeguards that should attach in cases where deprivation of the fundamental right to liberty is at issue apply no less to non-citizens than citizens.[77]

In 1969, the Immigration Appeals Act instituted a system of appeals against deportation decisions. Historically, foreign nationals who faced deportation on grounds of national security had limited rights of appeal. A statutory system for appeals against deportation was introduced in 1973 but it specifically excluded deportation on grounds of national security from its scope. If granted leave by the Home Secretary, those subject to deportation for reasons of national security could appeal to a special advisory panel within the Home Office: appellants could call witnesses and make representations on their own behalf but had no right to legal representation. Evidence that might compromise security or the safety of sources was not revealed to the appellant who, therefore, had no opportunity to test or rebut it. The Home Secretary, not the panel, decided how much information the appellant received, the appellant was not told of the panel's advice, and the Home Secretary was, in any case, not bound by it; judicial review was available but the court could not see the secret evidence, contained in closed materials, upon which the decision was based.[78]

---

[75] <http://www.guardian.co.uk/uk-news/2013/jul/09/jimmy-mubenga-unlawfully-killed-inquest-jury>.

[76] Macklem, 'Borderline Security' (n 2), 391.

[77] D Cole, *Enemy Aliens: Double Standards and Constitutional Freedoms in the War on Terrorism* (New York: The New Press, 2003), 11; D Cole, 'Against Citizenship as a Predicate for Basic Rights', *Fordham Law* 75 (2007), 2541–8.

[78] Justice, *Secret Evidence* (London: Justice, 2009), 38–9.

The use of secret evidence was a key issue in the landmark judgment, *Chahal v United Kingdom*.[79] Mr Chahal appealed on the grounds that if he was sent back to India he would face torture at the hands of the Indian authorities. He also argued that the procedures governing his deportation on national security grounds were unfair, in particular because he had no opportunity to view or challenge the evidence against him. The Grand Chamber in Strasbourg prohibited the UK from deporting Mr Chahal to India under Article 3 on the grounds that he faced a real risk of torture or inhuman or degrading treatment by the Indian authorities. The Court also held that the lack of procedures allowing Mr Chahal to challenge the evidence breached his right to liberty under Article 5(4) ECHR (because he had been detained pending his deportation) and his right to an effective remedy under Article 13 ECHR.

The decision in *Chahal* led to the establishment in 1997 of the Special Immigration Appeals Commission (SIAC) to hear appeals against decisions to deport or exclude individuals from the UK on grounds of national security or public interest. The SIAC Act 1997 also introduced closed material proceedings (CMPs) to permit security sensitive evidence to be heard in camera,[80] and special advocates—officially appointed, security-cleared barristers who are allowed to see secret intelligence and cross-examine secret witnesses, but not permitted to speak with appellants or to their lawyers without permission thereafter. SIAC rules authorize the appointment of special advocates where disclosure of evidence is deemed hazardous to security organizations or national security. Although intended to improve procedural fairness, SIAC is the sole means of appeal against decisions by the Home Secretary to deport on grounds of national security or international relations. While special advocates represent the interests of appellants, their chief rationale is to meet national security concerns—under s. 6(4) a special advocate 'shall not be responsible to the person whose interests he is appointed to represent'.[81] CMPs thus sacrifice due process and respect for the rule of law for security.[82]

In *Home Secretary v Rehman*,[83] it was held that the appointment of special advocates was only permissible 'in the most extreme circumstances. However considerations of national security can create situations where this is necessary. If this happens, the court should use its inherent power to reduce the risk of prejudice to the absent party so far as possible.'[84] The obvious problem is that the right of those subject to

---

[79] (1997) 23 EHRR 413.

[80] Justice, *Secret Evidence* (n 78), 38. The introduction of special advocates was modelled on the Canadian system.

[81] See discussion in T Endicott, *Administrative Law* 2nd edn (Oxford: Oxford University Press, 2011), 137–41.

[82] Endicott, *Administrative Law* (n 81), 141.

[83] *Home Secretary v Rehman* [2003] 1 AC 153 at 31–2.

[84] Lord Woolf in *Home Secretary v Rehman* [2003] 1 AC 153 at 31–2.

the CMPs to know the case against them is unsatisfactorily served by the practice of 'gisting'.[85]

10.6 Use of Immigration Law as a Tool of Counterterrorism

Recourse to immigration law as a tool of counterterrorism has a long history in the UK. During the period of the Troubles in Northern Ireland, the Prevention of Terrorism (Temporary Provisions) Act 1974, s. 3, incorporated immigration law to permit detention of individuals for up to 12 hours at ports between England and Northern Ireland, where this was expedient for the prevention of terrorism relating to Northern Ireland. On the same grounds, under s. 6 of the Act, Exclusion Orders could be imposed by the Secretary of State on non-citizens to prohibit them from being in, or entering, the UK or Northern Ireland. It was an offence to breach an order or to aid another in effecting entry and the maximum sentence for breach was five years' imprisonment or a fine or both. Like deportation, exclusion relies upon the fallacious assumption that a would-be terrorist is not dangerous if not on domestic territory. The 1974 Act was passed in response to sustained terrorist attacks by the IRA on the UK mainland (including the Birmingham bombings that killed 21 and injured 184). As its name implies, it was intended to be a temporary measure. Yet, it was re-enacted in 1976, 1984, and again in 1989: on each occasion as an emergency 'temporary' power subject to annual renewal.

The role of immigration control in anti-terrorism strategy grew significantly after the terrorist attacks of 9/11, and again after the London bombings of July 2007. This growth is attributable, first, to the wider securitization of immigration and the linking of immigration control with counterterrorism in public and political debate.[86] In the UK, within weeks of the 9/11 attacks, Prime Minister Tony Blair announced plans to 'increase our ability to exclude and remove those whom we suspect of terrorism and who are seeking to abuse our asylum procedures'. The leader of the opposition went further to denounce the constraints of human rights: 'The Home Secretary ought to be able to prevent individuals entering Britain and to deport them on the grounds of national security without the threat of his decisions being overturned as a result of the Human Rights Act 1998.'[87] Second,

---

[85] Gisting is the means by which sufficient material is disclosed to the appellant to enable them to give effective instruction to the special advocate who represents their interests in CMPs. See further Justice, *Secret Evidence* (n 78).

[86] J Huysmans and A Buonfino, 'Politics of Exception and Unease: Immigration, Asylum and Terrorism in Parliamentary Debates in the UK', *Political Studies* 56(4) (2008), 766–88.

[87] Cited in Huysmans and Buonfino, 'Politics of Exception and Unease' (n 86) at 768 and 769.

the importance of immigration control to counterterrorism was suggested by evidence that security lapses at the border played a part in the 9/11 attacks.[88] In the US, 9/11 resulted in large-scale recourse to immigration controls, administrative detention, and deportation as essential tools in the war on terror. As Chacón observed, 'the border has become the front line in the fight against terrorism'.[89] Third, the UN Security Council Resolution 1373,[90] paragraph 2(g), required states to 'prevent the movement of terrorists or their groups by effective border controls' and went on to require states to:

3(f) Take appropriate measures in conformity with the relevant provisions of national and international law, including international standards of human rights, before granting refugee status, for the purpose of ensuring that the asylum seeker has not planned, facilitated or participated in the commission of terrorist acts;

3(g) Ensure, in conformity with international law, that refugee status is not abused by the perpetrators, organizers or facilitators of terrorist acts, and that claims of political motivation are not recognized as grounds for refusing requests for the extradition of alleged terrorists.

Since none of the 9/11 bombers had entered the United States illegally or claimed refugee status, it is unclear why the UN Security Council singled these groups out as possible security threats.[91] In Resolution 1373, the UN called on states not to grant refugee status to suspected terrorists, even if they otherwise satisfied the definition of refugees facing political persecution. In so doing, it effectively condoned the breach of human rights. Roach observes that UN Security Council Resolution 1373 was read by many democracies as a cue to use immigration law as a tool of counterterrorism. He suggests: 'Immigration law was attractive for governments because it had broader liability rules, lower burdens of proof, and increased periods of investigative detention than even criminal laws that were amended in the wake of 9/11.'[92]

The availability of indefinite administrative detention under immigration law became an important tool of counterterrorism.[93] As discussed in Chapter 8, following 9/11 the UK government introduced indefinite detention without trial of

[88] Macklem observes: 'there seems little doubt that the utter inadequacy of security checks in airports across North America contributed to the outcome of 11 September'. Macklem, 'Borderline Security' (n 2), 383.

[89] N Demleitner, 'Misguided Prevention: The War on Terrorism as a War on Immigrant Offenders and Immigration Violators', *Criminal Law Bulletin* 40 (2004), 550–75; 563. Others have also questioned whether immigration control in the US really serves national security: JM Chacón, 'Unsecured Borders: Immigration Restrictions, Crime Control and National Security', *Connecticut Law Review* 39 (2007), 1827–91.

[90] Issued, after hurried consultation, by the UN on 28 September 2001.

[91] K Roach, *The 9/11 Effect: Comparative Counter-Terrorism* (Cambridge: Cambridge University Press, 2011), 40.

[92] Roach, *The 9/11 Effect* (n 91), 41.

[93] DQ Cochran, 'Material Witness Detention in a Post-9/11 World: Mission Creep or Fresh Start?', *George Mason Law Review* 18(1) (2010), 1–41; 9–10.

foreign national terrorist suspects who could not be prosecuted or deported.[94] Because Article 5(1)(f) ECHR permits detention of an individual only 'to prevent his effecting an unauthorised entry into the country or of a person against whom action is being taken with a view to deportation or extradition', the UK government could introduce indefinite detention only by seeking to derogate from the ECHR under Article 15.[95] Here again, it is questionable whether use of indefinite detention would have been politically acceptable had it been imposed on British citizens. As we noted in Chapter 8, in *A and others v Home Secretary* (the 'Belmarsh' case),[96] the House of Lords held that the law discriminated on the ground of nationality or immigration status by providing for detention without trial for foreign suspects but not for British citizens and it found that the law was irrational because the threat of terrorism is not confined to non-citizens. Although the Belmarsh case rendered the indefinite detention of foreign national terrorist suspects unlawful and although the civil preventive measures (Control Orders and later TPIMs) that replaced it apply to citizens and non-citizens alike, the evidence is that Control Orders were chiefly applied to non-citizens.[97]

Immigration law has been widely used as a means of expelling individuals deemed to pose a security threat. The Immigration, Asylum and Nationality Act 2006 strengthened powers of removal and deportation. Section 54 of the Act permits the government to deny refugee status to those found to have engaged in '(a) acts of committing, preparing or instigating terrorism (whether or not the acts amount to an actual or inchoate offence), and (b) acts of encouraging or inducing others to commit, prepare or instigate terrorism (whether or not the acts amount to an actual or inchoate offence)'. The 2006 Act further provides under s. 56 that the Home Secretary may 'deprive a person of citizenship status if the Secretary of State is satisfied that deprivation is conducive to the public good'. The provision was used to deprive Australian-born David Hicks, who had been detained at Guantanamo Bay, of his British citizenship just hours after he had been granted it on grounds of maternal heritage.[98]

Although the 2011 *Review of Counter-Terrorism and Security Powers* found that 'in some areas our counter-terrorism and security powers *are neither proportionate nor*

---

[94] C Walker, 'Prisoners of "War All the Time"', *European Human Rights Law Review* 1 (2005), 50–74.

[95] Article 15 of the European Convention permits derogation only in case of 'war or other public emergency threatening the life of the nation' and measures taken must be 'strictly required by the exigencies of the situation'.

[96] *A and others v Secretary of State for the Home Department* [2004] UKHL 56.

[97] Before they were abolished and replaced by TPIMs in 2011, 28 of the 48 Control Orders were imposed on foreign nationals. HM Government, *Review of Counter-Terrorism and Security Powers Review Findings and Recommendations Cm 8004* (London: HMSO, 2001), 36.

[98] V Dodd, 'Reid revoked citizenship of Guantanamo detainee', *The Guardian* (11 January 2007). <http://www.guardian.co.uk/uk/2007/jan/11/world.politics>.

necessary', it committed the government to make '[a] stronger effort to deport foreign nationals involved in terrorist activities in this country fully respecting our human rights obligations'.[99] The government seeks assurances from receiving states to ensure that deportation is consistent with its human rights obligations. However, deportation has been criticized by human rights groups and lawyers who argue that assurances from countries with poor human rights records are not to be trusted. It is questionable whether the assurances given are credible and reliable enough and the monitoring provisions adequate to satisfy the absolute prohibition on torture under the ECHR, particularly in respect of countries with poor human rights records and unstable regimes such as Algeria, Libya, and Jordan. A difficulty is that the courts may lack the expertise to determine the nature and extent of human rights abuses in those countries to which deportees are to be sent and they are therefore prone to defer to the executive.[100] Following *Chahal* (see above), the UK government sought to establish a Memorandum of Understanding (MoU) with each receiving country, in order to ensure that the deportee was not subjected to violations of Article 3. In the highly publicized case of Abu Qatada (the Jordanian preacher Omar Othman), the Strasbourg Court was eventually satisfied that the MoU with Jordan would avoid any violation of Article 3.[101] However, the Court found that the applicant's right to a fair trial in the receiving country was not assured, since evidence obtained by torture was admissible. It was only when the MoU was extended so as to exclude this possibility that Abu Qatada was finally deported in July 2013.

Protecting the civil liberties of deportees once they have been sent abroad requires independent monitoring and legal oversight in the country in question and adequate follow-up of deportees. Accordingly, the 2011 *Review of Counter-Terrorism and Security Powers* recommended that the government 'consider commissioning an annual independent report on deportations under this policy; and explore options for improving monitoring of individuals after their return'.[102] In so far as removal to questionable regimes may only render those deported liable to recruitment by terrorist organizations overseas, it is possible that deportation displaces, and in the longer term may even exacerbate, the risk of terrorism. It is somewhat ironic that the commitment to deporting terror suspects persists, despite the fact the associated risks of so doing were recognized as early as 2003 by the Newton Committee, which concluded: 'Seeking to deport terrorist suspects

---

[99] HM Government, *Review of Counter-Terrorism and Security Powers Review Findings and Recommendations Cm 8004* (n 97), 5–6.

[100] See, eg, *RB (Algeria) v Secretary of State* UKHL 20 (2009).

[101] The case was known as *Othman v United Kingdom* (2012) 55 EHRR 1; for a different and unsuccessful attempt at a satisfactory MoU, the UK government intervening, see *Saadi v Italy* (2008) 49 EHRR 730.

[102] HM Government, *Review of Counter-Terrorism and Security Powers Review: Findings and Recommendations Cm 8004* (n 97), 35.

does not seem to us to be a satisfactory response, given the risk of exporting terrorism ... it would not necessarily reduce the threat to British interests abroad, or make the world a safer place more generally.'[103]

In other respects, use of immigration law also sets lower standards of adjudicative fairness for non-citizens than the criminal prosecution of citizens allows. The use of secret evidence by SIAC has already been discussed above. In respect of counter-terrorism, secret evidence has taken on a particular importance as a means of keeping sensitive information out of the public domain and of protecting intelligence agencies and their operatives. Information-sharing between states is an important strategy in respect of international terrorist organizations like al-Qaeda. It is often accompanied by strict stipulations as to secrecy and typically imposes an obligation not to disclose any intelligence that might compromise the security of friendly states. International co-operation and bi-lateral agreements, in particular the so-called 'special relationship' between Britain and the US, thus increase the likelihood of non-disclosure of intelligence and resort to CMPs, with the accompanying hazards entailed by the use of secret evidence and special advocates.[104] In sum, the use of immigration proceedings as a tool of counterterrorism derives partly from the questionable assumption that foreign nationals pose a greater terrorist threat; partly because immigration law permits the pursuit of suspected terrorists outside the procedural protections of the ordinary criminal process in less demanding procedural channels; and partly because it is possible to introduce measures against non-citizens, including indefinite administrative detention, which would be politically unacceptable if applied to UK nationals.

In short, resort to immigration proceedings derives in no small part from the common view that we do not owe non-citizens the same legal protections that citizens enjoy. Contesting this view, Cole has developed four powerful arguments against the differential treatment of non-citizens and, in particular, against allowing the treatment of non-citizens suspected of involvement in terrorism to be traded for the security of citizens. First, to permit governments to treat foreign national suspects less favourably than citizens 'creates a template for how it will treat citizens tomorrow' not least because 'alienage discrimination is often closely tied to (and a cover for) racial animus, and is therefore particularly susceptible to being extended to citizens along racial lines'.[105] However, it could be argued that violations of non-citizens' rights are principally objectionable because they are wrong in their own

---

[103] Privy Council Review Committee, *Anti-terrorism, Crime and Security Act Review 2001: Report* quoted in C Walker, 'The Treatment of Foreign Terror Suspects', *Modern Law Review* 70(3) (2007), 427–57; 433.

[104] *A v SSHD* [2004] UKHL 56. A Kavanagh, 'Special Advocates, Control Orders and the Right to a Fair Trial', *Modern Law Review* 63(5) (2010), 836–57.

[105] Cole, *Enemy Aliens: Double Standards and Constitutional Freedoms in the War on Terrorism* (n 77), 7. See also Cole, 'Against Citizenship as a Predicate for Basic Rights' (n 77).

right, not because of the future impact they might have on citizens. Second, Cole suggests that to apply a double standard with respect to the basic rights accorded to citizens and non-citizens is 'likely to prove counterproductive as a security matter' because it undermines the legitimacy of government both domestically and over-seas.[106] Third, he argues that to insist on equitable treatment of citizens and non-citizens 'may help counteract our historic tendency to overreact in times of fear' and act as a 'prophylactic against such excesses'.[107] This argument is not limited to times of crisis. Permitting government to apply legislation only to non-citizens enables it to evade the 'natural political resistance' that might otherwise arise if controversial measures were applied to all.[108] Fourth, and most importantly, Cole insists that we should resist the temptation to trade the rights of non-citizens for citizens' security because 'it is morally and constitutionally wrong to do so'.[109]

Under the US Constitution, with the exception of the right to vote and the right to run for office, core political, religious, due process, and equal protection rights are not limited to citizens but apply to all 'persons' subject to US laws. In Britain, just as in the US, due process protections apply to all persons including aliens, whether their presence is lawful, unlawful, temporary, or permanent. The prescription that basic rights apply to all and are not the privilege of citizenship accords strongly with the presumption to be found in many constitutions and human rights instruments (including the ECHR) that fundamental rights extend to all persons regardless of nationality or citizenship status.[110] Cole's argument, while particularly powerful in respect of the treatment by the US government of 'enemy combatants' in the war on terror, is hardly less germane to the treatment of non-citizens in national security cases in the UK. Although Roach argues that the British government has shown a greater commitment to legalism and respect for human rights than countries such as the US,[111] it has been adjudged by the courts to have taken discriminatory measures against non-citizens in the name of preventing terrorism and it has deported suspects to regimes with dubious human rights records. An important feature of human rights law is that it provides safeguards for persons by virtue of their status as humans and out of respect for humanity, regardless of whether or not they are citizens. Article 6, for example, guarantees right to a fair trial that should apply no less to the foreigner and to the stateless person.[112]

---

[106] Cole, *Enemy Aliens* (n 77), 9.

[107] Cole, *Enemy Aliens* (n 77), 10–11.

[108] C Sunstein, *Laws of Fear: Beyond the Precautionary Principle* (Cambridge: Cambridge University Press, 2005).

[109] Cole, *Enemy Aliens* (n 77),

[110] See also the reasoning in the landmark decision *A v SSHD* [2004] UKHL 56; [2005] 2 WLR 87.

[111] Roach, *The 9/11 Effect: Comparative Counter-Terrorism* (n 91), 290.

[112] Walker, 'The Treatment of Foreign Terror Suspects' (n 103), 443 ff.

10.7 Conclusions

Immigration laws and measures target the most vulnerable, powerless, and marginalized people. Accepting that states have the right to control inward migration and that totally unrestricted migration would likely pose a threat to social order and to the ability of the state to ensure the welfare of all does not license the weakening of the rule of law or the diminution of ordinary due process protections.[113] The following principles might be applied to all use of immigration law for preventive purposes:

(1) The state is justified in taking compulsory powers in immigration law to ensure that its borders are secure and that migrants who have committed serious offences are deported.

(2) A sufficiently close connection should exist between the purpose of the relevant immigration law (eg preventing unauthorized entry) and the purpose of the coercive measure (eg facilitating a speedy and efficient decision).

(3) The application of any coercive power should, out of respect for the human rights of individuals, be the least restrictive appropriate measure to ensure one of the purposes in (1) above.

(4) In particular, special justifications should be given for making non-compliance with immigration laws into a criminal offence. Criminal offences should only be used in immigration law where the relevant conduct is seriously wrong and a regulatory law is adjudged to be an inadequate response. If criminal offences are deemed necessary and proportionate, their elements should be compliant with rule-of-law principles, particularly in requiring proof of mens rea for conviction.

(5) Detention of persons in order to assure one of the purposes in (1) above should also require special justification. Neither deprivation of liberty nor deportation/removal should be considered unless it is the least restrictive appropriate alternative. Before a migrant is deprived of liberty, even for a short period, there should be a judicial determination that this is absolutely necessary and that no less intrusive measure would be adequate.

(6) The application of coercive powers under immigration law should be accompanied by procedural protections, including access to legal advice, right to challenge decisions before a court, and fair and open hearings with reasons given for decisions. The case for such procedural protections becomes overwhelming when deprivation of a person's liberty is proposed. In principle, all hearings should be open unless compelling reasons for closed material proceedings are given in the particular case.

---

[113] It should be noted that not everyone accepts the case for immigration controls. See, eg, T Hayter, *Open Borders: The Case against Immigration Controls* (London: Pluto Press, 2004), or the campaign against immigration control by the organization No One is Illegal. <http://www.noii.org.uk/controls-must-go/>.

(7) The principles of equality and non-discrimination should be maintained in all cases involving migrants and would-be migrants: 'targeting' practices and the use of profiling by immigration officers and police are often based on dubious religious and racial grounds, and should be regarded as unacceptable.

(8) Where it is proposed to deport a person, the state must show that this is an appropriate and proportional measure. It must show that the deportation has a pressing and legitimate objective; that it is the least restrictive measure to achieve this objective; that it is necessary; and that the infringement of the deportee's rights is proportionate to the importance of the objective.

(9) Where it is proposed to deport a person, not only must the detention of the person pending deportation be justified (on the principle of no less restrictive appropriate alternative), but the state must prove that the potential deportee will not be subjected to torture or inhuman or degrading treatment in the receiving country, and will have a fair trial there.

(10) Any detention must be for the least possible duration necessary for accomplishing the objective, and must be in conditions that reflect the fact that the person is not being detained for punitive purposes.

If immigrants and asylum seekers are not to be subjected to measures that are unfair or disproportionate to the risk posed, then recourse to immigration detention, removal, and deportation needs to be subject to sustained review for adherence to the principles we have outlined and constrained by proportionality requirements.[114] The preventive measures analysed in this chapter are, by definition, applied to those who are not citizens and who generally have the most limited means to challenge decisions taken against them. Given the profound impact on individual autonomy of immigration detention and the life-changing effects of removal or deportation, the need for principled restraint is particularly acute.

---

[114] M Wishnie, 'Immigration Law and the Proportionality Requirement', *UC Irvine Law Review* 2 (2012), 415–52.

11

Conclusions: The Preventive State and Its Limits

This book began by articulating two senses of the term preventive justice (see Section 1.3). The first is broadly empirical: the study of preventive justice seeks to investigate and catalogue the extent and nature of preventive endeavour within the criminal law and beyond the criminal justice system. The second sense is theoretical and normative: preventive justice seeks critically to evaluate the preventive endeavour and to propose limits on it. These two facets of preventive justice are inextricable: the normative project of determining what powers the state may justly exercise in the name of prevention cannot be divorced from the task of identifying, categorizing, and analysing the preventive endeavour in all its considerable variety. So our critical examination of preventive measures has been followed swiftly by a concerted effort to articulate appropriate guiding values and limiting principles.

Our focus has been on those measures that are coercive for the simple reason that the exercise of coercion by the state for preventive purposes infringes individual autonomy and, as such, is in greatest need of justification and restraint. The manifestations of the preventive state with which this book has been concerned, therefore, are those that are aimed at the prevention of serious physical harm (including sexual harm), and to which deprivation of liberty is a response prescribed by law. Thus, the focus is not on coercive preventive measures in general, but on preventive measures that may involve the use or threat of deprivation of liberty. This is the focus, not an absolute dividing line, and hence we discuss some measures that lie on or close to the boundary between restrictions on and deprivations of liberty—eg stop-and-search and police containment (Chapter 3), civil preventive orders (Chapter 4), and TPIMs (Chapter 8)—and which, therefore, raise closely analogous questions. The measures falling most obviously within the remit of preventive justice are policing (Chapter 3) and the criminal law itself (Chapter 5), where the preventive rationale is certainly not a new phenomenon, as we demonstrate in Chapter 2. Also clearly within the ambit of the preventive state are the kinds of potentially liberty-depriving measures examined in Chapter 4 (civil preventive orders), Chapter 7 (preventive sentencing, especially indeterminate sentences), Chapter 8 (measures against terrorists, including some criminal offences), Chapter 9 (compulsory powers over people for public health reasons), and Chapter 10 (measures aimed at border security, including some criminal offences).

In this concluding chapter, we draw together some of the most important principles for which we have argued in the previous chapters, summarizing their rationales. Thus, in Section 11.1 we revisit the state's duty to prevent harm and indicate some of the problems to which recognition of that duty gives rise. In Section 11.2 we return to the idea of the preventive state, and consider what infringements of individual liberty it permits. Section 11.3 outlines a principled approach to deprivations of liberty on preventive grounds. Section 11.4 sketches a rationale for requiring heightened procedural protections before depriving a person of liberty for preventive purposes. In Section 11.5, we consider what the material conditions of detention should be when prevention is the rationale. Section 11.6 brings the discussion back to limiting principles that apply to the preventive aspects of the criminal law and criminal process, and Section 11.7 concludes with suggestions of how the principles may be put into practice.

11.1 The Irresistibility of Prevention

As we saw in Section 1.4, the state's duty to prevent harm is foundational and not, in principle, controversial.[1] Whether expressed as the duty to protect, to ensure security, to provide public protection, or to ensure public safety, it is widely accepted to be a core duty of the state.[2] The key question is how this duty to protect can be squared with the state's duty of justice (that is to treat persons as responsible moral agents, to respect their human rights), and the state's duty to provide a system of criminal justice (including police, prosecutors, courts, and a punishment system) to deal with those who transgress the criminal law.[3] Of course,

---

[1] Although, as we have already observed, scholars vary in their estimation of the priority of prevention over punishment and vice versa. For example, Slobogin goes so far as to argue that preventive sentencing 'cabined only very loosely by desert' is to be preferred over determinate, proportional sentencing. C Slobogin, 'Prevention as the Primary Goal of Sentencing: The Modern Case for Indeterminate Dispositions in Criminal Cases', *San Diego Law Review* 48 (2011), 1127–71; 2–4.

[2] The duty of the state to protect its citizens against crime is a core tenet of classical liberal theory. Although even this minimal conception of the 'night-watchman state' is called into question by libertarians like Nozick, who advocates a still more limited 'ultraminimal state'. R Nozick, *Anarchy, State and Utopia* (Oxford: Blackwell, 1974), 26. Some contemporary political thinkers embrace a much more expansive notion: Giddens, for example, argues that 'freedom from the fear of crime is a major citizenship right'. A Giddens, *Where Now for New Labour?* (Cambridge: Polity, 2002), 17. See also, I Loader and N Walker, 'Necessary Virtues: The Legitimate Place of the State in the Production of Security', in B Dupont and J Wood (eds.), *Democracy, Society and the Governance of Security* (Cambridge: Cambridge University Press, 2005), 165–95; I Loader and N Walker, *Civilizing Security* (Cambridge: Cambridge University Press, 2011); M Thorburn, 'The Constitution of Criminal Law: Justifications, Policing and the State's Fiduciary Duties', *Criminal Law and Philosophy* 5 (2011), 259–76.

[3] See also M Matravers, 'On Preventive Justice', in A Ashworth, L Zedner, and P Tomlin (eds.), *Prevention and the Limits of the Criminal Law* (Oxford: Oxford University Press, 2013), 235–51.

the norms guiding the fulfilment of these duties are contested, but core among them are the liberal values of respect for the autonomy of the individual, fairness, equality, tolerance of difference, and resort to coercion only where justified and as a last resort. More amorphous values such as trust also play an important role in liberal society and find their legal articulation in requirements of reasonable suspicion, proof beyond all reasonable doubt, and the presumption of innocence. Yet, the duty to prevent wrongful harms conflicts with these requirements since it may require intervention before reasonable suspicion can be established, on the basis of less conclusive evidence, or even in respect of innocent persons.[4] The imperative to prevent, or at least to diminish the prospect of, wrongful harms thus stands in acute tension with any idealized account of a principled and parsimonious liberal criminal law. In practice, as we have shown, that tension is almost always likely to be resolved in favour of prevention.

Preventing harm, particularly grave or more especially catastrophic or irreversible harms, is a political obligation that weighs heavily on politicians, mindful that they are answerable to an anxious public and that they will be called to account should calamity eventuate. The strong intuition that prevention is better than cure informs policymaking, the legislative process, and judicial decision-making. In Section 2.1 we referred to Blackstone's claim that 'preventive justice is, upon every principle of reason, of humanity, and of sound policy, preferable in all respects to punishing justice'.[5] Is this an exaggerated claim? At a general level it seems incontrovertible that it is better that a wrong is not perpetrated than that it is (harm is avoided, which must be good), and therefore that it is better to prevent a wrong than to wait until it has taken place and only then to take action. It is widely accepted that wrongs should be prevented where possible, and that this is a task of the state, the government and its officials.

However, there are two reservations that must be borne in mind when admiring Blackstone's enthusiastic articulation of what appears to be common sense. First, Blackstone conceived of preventive justice as relating to 'the means of *preventing* the commission of crimes and misdemeanours' and 'intended merely for prevention, without any crime actually committed by the party, but arising only from a probable suspicion that some crime is intended or likely to happen'.[6] In short, Blackstone's conception of preventive justice pertained only to crime, though it did not require that a crime had been committed before intervention was justified. In terms of the

---

[4] GR Sullivan, 'The Hard Treatment of Innocent Persons in State Responses to the Threat of Large Scale, and Imminent Terrorist Violence: Examining the Legal Constraints', in GR Sullivan and I Dennis (eds.), *Seeking Security: Pre-Empting the Commission of Criminal Harms* (Oxford: Hart Publishing, 2012), 293–322.

[5] W Blackstone, *Commentaries on the Laws of England in Four Books* (London: Routledge, 2001, 1753). Book IV, Chapter XVIII 'On the Means of Preventing Offences', 251. The homely adage 'prevention is better than cure' is attributed to Erasmus.

[6] Blackstone, *Commentaries* (n 5), 251, 252.

structure of this book, therefore, his remarks relate to Chapter 5 (on criminal law) and perhaps to Chapter 3 (on policing) and extend also to the preventive aspects of punishment, notably Chapter 7 (on preventive detention). Indeed, he goes so far as to claim that 'if we consider all human punishments in a large and extended view, we shall find them all rather calculated to prevent future crimes than to expiate the past'.[7] This view of punishment sits some way from the retributive paradigm that dominates current liberal penal theory, which finds the justification of punishment in deontological ethics and requires that punishment be proportionate to the gravity of the offence.[8] However, Blackstone's conception of preventive justice has nothing to say about the justifications for the many other types of preventive endeavour discussed in the other chapters of the book, for example, those relating to counter-terrorism, public health, or immigration.

To accept Blackstone's claim is, therefore, to say nothing about many spheres of preventive justice, spheres in which coercive measures (including deprivation of liberty) may be taken. In Section 2.4 we quoted Mill's concerns about resort to prevention as a general justification for the use of coercive powers by the state. Mill regarded the preventive function of the state as 'undisputed,' but went on to warn that it is:

far more liable to be abused, to the prejudice of liberty, than the punitory function; for there is hardly any part of the legitimate freedom of action of a human being that would not admit of being represented, and fairly too, as increasing the facilities for some form or other of delinquency.[9]

This important point should not be lost in the haste to embrace preventive measures. It is, in principle, right to put efforts into preventing harm from occurring rather than waiting until it happens; but 'the prevention of harm' can be and is used to justify a wide range of state powers, some of them involving considerable curtailments of liberty. Recognizing the coercive aspect of preventive justice makes it all the more necessary to enquire into the proper limits of the preventive state. That has been a central theme of this book, and more will be said about it in Sections 11.3–11.6. For the present, we set out the most prominent rights and principles relevant on the issue of coercive preventive measures and deprivation of

---

[7] Blackstone, *Commentaries* (n 5), 251–2.

[8] A von Hirsch and A Ashworth, *Proportionate Sentencing: Exploring the Principles* (Oxford: Oxford University Press, 2005). Steiker considers the possible ways that proportionality might be adapted for use in respect of preventive measures, particularly in respect of the duration and conditions of confinement for preventive purposes and she suggests limits to its likely efficacy as a robust constraint. C. Steiker, 'Proportionality as a Limit on Preventive Justice: Promises and Pitfalls', in A Ashworth, L Zedner, and P Tomlin (eds.), *Prevention and the Limits of the Criminal Law* (Oxford: Oxford University Press, 2013), 194–213.

[9] JS Mill, *On Liberty* (Harmondsworth, Middlesex: Penguin, 1979), 165.

liberty. These rights and principles, already articulated and discussed in previous chapters, are:

A. The right to liberty of the person.
B. The presumption of innocence.
C. The presumption of harmlessness.
D. The principle of the least restrictive appropriate alternative, and its close cousins the principle that deprivation of liberty should be a last resort, and the *ultima ratio* principle.
E. The principle of parsimony, that any interference with an individual's rights should be kept to a minimum consistent with security.
F. The necessity principle, that any deprivation of liberty should last no longer than is necessary to fulfil the stated purpose.

We now turn to the second reservation about Blackstone's claim. Even in the sphere to which it applies directly—preventing crime—it fails to deal with the vital question of how far ahead of the causing of harm it is proper for the state to intervene and what, therefore, are the proper limits of the criminal law. In other words, it leaves open the two contested issues of how remote from the harm-to-be-prevented it is justifiable for the criminal law to intervene, and how severe (given the distance from the ultimate harm) the penalty ought to be. As we observed in Section 5.3, there has been a lively academic debate about the criminalization of remote harms; the justifications for enacting so-called 'prophylactic crimes'; and the possible justifications for adopting an 'anticipatory perspective' on criminalization.[10] A strictly minimalist requirement that an individual should not be held liable until an irrevocable risk has been unleashed[11] leaves very little space for preventive intervention. Against this minimalist view, it has been argued that 'we have good reason to count intending criminals as criminally culpable and liable before they irrevocably unleash a risk of harm to others' protected interests'.[12] To these debates about the proper scope and limits of the criminal law must be added questions of political theory (what does the duty of the state to protect entail, what civic responsibilities do citizens have to one another to guard against their own future

---

[10] A Simester and A von Hirsch, *Crimes, Harms and Wrongs: On the Principles of Criminalization* (Oxford: Hart Publishing, 2011); AP Simester, 'Prophylactic Crimes', in GR Sullivan and I Dennis (eds.), *Seeking Security: Pre-Empting the Commission of Criminal Harms* (Oxford: Hart Publishing, 2012), 59–78; J Horder, 'Harmless Wrongdoing and the Anticipatory Perspective on Criminalisation', in GR Sullivan and I Dennis (eds.), *Seeking Security: Pre-Empting the Commission of Criminal Harms* (Oxford: Hart Publishing, 2012), 79–102.

[11] Of the sort advanced by Alexander and Ferzan, see L Alexander and KK Ferzan, 'Danger: The Ethics of Preemptive Action', *Ohio State Journal of Criminal Law* 9(2) (2012), 637–67.

[12] RA Duff, 'Risks, Culpability and Criminal Liability', in GR Sullivan and I Dennis (eds.), *Seeking Security: Pre-Empting the Commission of Criminal Harms* (Oxford: Hart Publishing, 2012), 121–42; 142.

wrongdoing) and policy questions about the exigencies of prevention (what time, what realm of operation, and what powers are necessary to permit effective intervention). In short, the issue of how far ahead the state may intervene is not only a moral but also a political and a practical question.

In discussing these issues in the context of anti-terrorist laws David Anderson, the UK's Independent Reviewer of Terrorism Legislation, uses the phrase 'defending further up the field' (discussed in Sections 5.2 and 5.5). He puts the argument that it is not the seriousness or uniqueness of terrorist acts that justifies extending the law beyond its normal limits, but rather the related operational demands of policing and prosecuting terrorism. There is, he argues:

a perceived need, in a footballing phrase also beloved of spies, to *defend further up the field*. That is a consequence of the highly destructive potential of single, concentrated terrorist attacks; the dangers of allowing such a plot to run; and so the resulting need to intervene at an earlier stage.[13]

Anderson recognizes that 'defending further up the field' also includes the use of non-coercive measures: he instances the *Prevent* strategy (discussed in Section 8.6), and we would add that the principle of the least restrictive appropriate alternative should also be applied, so as to give priority to strategies that do not involve deprivation of liberty—see Section 11.3. Anderson believes that in terrorist cases there is 'a need to intervene earlier than would normally be the case so as to pre-empt the possibility of a catastrophic incident'.[14] However, the catastrophic risks potentially entailed by terrorist attacks should not be allowed to license expansion of the criminal law or of police powers without careful consideration of the grounds for extending liability or awarding extra powers. The focus on the worst-case scenario should not obscure the fact that terrorism is ill-defined and the law is so broadly cast that less or even non-harmful activity may come under its remit.[15] As Anderson recognizes, the relevant laws 'call for the exercise of some very broad discretions by decision-makers', although he maintains the sceptical stance that 'the dangers of excessive reliance on the wise exercise of discretions are self-evident'.[16] More will be said about discretion in Section 11.7. For the present, we can conclude that the question of how far ahead of the harm-to-be-prevented it is right for the state to intervene can only be answered satisfactorily if there is cogent evidence of convincing operational imperatives, combined with the principled restrictions on the criminalization of remote acts examined in Section 5.3. Those principles, let us recall, take the following form:

---

[13] D Anderson, 'Shielding the Compass: How to Fight Terrorism without Defeating the Law', *European Human Rights Law Review* (2013), 233; 237.

[14] Anderson, 'Shielding the Compass' (n 13), 239.

[15] V Tadros and J Hodgson, 'How to Make a Terrorist out of Nothing', *Modern Law Review* 72(6) (2009), 984–98; J Hodgson and V Tadros, 'The Impossibility of Defining Terrorism', *New Criminal Law Review* 16(3) (2013), 494–526.

[16] Anderson, 'Shielding the Compass' (n 13), 245.

G. The more remote the conduct criminalized is from the harm-to-be-prevented, and the less grave that harm, the weaker the case for criminalization.

H. If criminalization is thought to be justified because of the gravity of the harm-to-be-prevented, there is a compelling case for higher-level fault requirements such as intention and knowledge.

I. In principle, a person may be held liable for the future acts of others only if that person has a sufficient normative involvement in those acts (for example, he or she has encouraged, assisted or facilitated), or where the acts of the other were foreseeable, with respect to which the person has an obligation to prevent a harm that might be caused by the other.

J. All offences, including those enacted on a preventive rationale, ought to comply with rule-of-law values, such as maximum certainty of definition, fair warning, and fair labelling, so as clearly to identify the wrong that they penalize, for the purpose of guiding conduct and publicly evaluating the wrong done.

K. All offences, including those enacted on a preventive rationale, should be so drafted as to require the court to adjudicate on the particular wrong targeted, and not on some broader conduct.

11.2 The Contours of the Preventive State

In Section 1.6 we referred to 'the contrast between the extensive research and writing on "theories of punishment" and the more limited normative debate about preventive measures', and we went on to set out a theoretical framework for such a debate in Sections 1.6 and 1.7. In Section 11.1, we noted that Blackstone's conception of preventive justice was largely confined to preventing crime. On reflection, this reference to crime constitutes less of a restriction than might at first appear since we have seen in Chapters 3 (policing), 5 (criminal law), 8 (terrorism), and 10 (immigration) how the ambit of the criminal law has been extended in order to criminalize a range of behaviour that the state wishes to prevent. In another sense, however, the subject matter of this study is wider than the prevention of crime, since it is concerned with the prevention of serious physical and sexual harms that are not necessarily criminal. The clearest example of this is the state's coercive powers in response to serious infectious diseases (as discussed in Chapter 9), but other examples are to be found in civil preventive orders (Chapter 4) and in respect of some mentally disordered persons (Chapter 9).

We recognize the necessity in some cases for deprivations of liberty of people who have not committed criminal offences on grounds of public protection. As stated in Section 11.1, we accept that the state has a duty to protect, or to provide security. Whether that is capable of justifying a particular coercive power of the state depends on at least two lines of argument. One is the practical argument about necessity, about why such powers are necessary, whether lesser or different powers would be no less effective or even more effective, and so on. These are fundamentally questions of evidence, and they have been explored in Chapter 6 (on risk assessment) and Chapter 8 (terrorism), among others. Laws and coercive measures that grant extra liberty-depriving powers 'further up the field' require strong justifications based on substantial evidential foundations. If the 'irresistibility of prevention' is to be withstood, claims of operational necessity ought not to be accepted too readily or without concrete evidence that they are necessary and the least restrictive measures available.

If the first line of argument is practical and evidential, the second line of argument is principled and rights-respecting. The starting-point (see Section 1.4) is that the state has not only a duty to protect but also a duty of justice, that is, a duty to respect the rights of individuals. This leads to the paradox of liberty: that a major justification for taking preventive powers is to secure or enhance the liberty of individuals, but that one possible effect of such powers is to deprive some individuals of their liberty. The paradox cannot be resolved by saying that it is all a question of balance, and that the loss of liberty for some has to be balanced against the overall gain in liberty generally. That is an unsatisfactory argument because it fails to respect liberty as a fundamental right, and also fails to recognize that the loss of liberty may fall disproportionately upon certain minorities or groups.[17] If liberty is to be duly respected, the state's powers—justified as the minimum necessary powers to achieve an acceptable degree of prevention—should be so adjusted as to ensure that the liberty of all persons involved is preserved so far as possible. According to one formula in human rights law, the encroachment on a right must be kept to a minimum, and must be sufficiently counterbalanced by other measures:[18] this kind of adjustment differs from balancing, but it does not rule out the possibility that in certain circumstances there may be sufficient justification for depriving an individual of the right to liberty entirely. The question has been raised in several of the foregoing chapters: under what conditions may an individual properly be deprived of liberty for preventive purposes? Those 'conditions' are in part substantive (what level of harm, and what degree of probability, should be required?), in part procedural (what rights should persons about to be subjected to such deprivations be accorded?), and in part consequential (if a person is properly detained, for how long and under what material conditions should such detention take place?).

[17] J Waldron, 'Security and Liberty: The Image of Balance', *Journal of Political Philosophy* 11(2) (2003), 191–210; see also L Zedner, 'Securing Liberty in the Face of Terror: Reflections from Criminal Justice', *Journal of Law and Society* 32(4) (2005), 507–33; and David Luban's reference to 'OPR theory'—that other people's rights count for less—in D Luban, 'Eight Fallacies About Liberty and Security', in RA Wilson (ed.), *Human Rights in the War on Terror* (Cambridge: Cambridge University Press, 2005), 242–57; 243–4.

[18] See, eg, *Doorson v Netherlands* (1996) 22 EHRR 330.

11.3 Prevention and Deprivation of Liberty

We have already referred to the right to liberty. Another right centrally involved here is the presumption of innocence or, since many of the instances of prevention do not involve an accusation of crime, the right to be presumed harmless. Thus, when the state is contemplating the exercise of coercive powers against an individual, that individual has a right to be treated as presumptively harmless, unless he or she has been proven to have perpetrated a serious harm in the recent past. This qualification of the right to liberty is strongly contested, as discussed in Section 6.2. It goes right to the issue of when the state may justifiably curtail a person's liberty on grounds of supposed 'dangerousness'. If it is proven that an individual has committed a prior serious wrongful harm, does that not make it prudent, even necessary, for the state to pursue its duty to provide security by taking measures to prevent a repetition? This leaves open the question of what the nature of the prior act should be: need it be a crime or would conduct that poses an imminent risk of serious harm suffice?[19]

Two points may be made in answer to this question. The first is that in a rights-respecting jurisdiction the state ought to apply the principle of the least restrictive appropriate alternative. The reason for this is obvious: since we are dealing here with the right to liberty and with a form of the presumption of innocence (the presumption of harmlessness), any exercise of state coercion should respect those fundamental rights so far as possible. The formulation of the principle adopted here uses the word 'appropriate', since the least restrictive measure is always to do nothing or a little, whereas the application of the principle can only be assessed properly in relation to the particular individual concerned and the risk he or she is considered to present. The emphasis should, therefore, be on the least restrictive measure, given the situation and the characteristics of the person concerned and the risk assessments made. One obvious question is whether in place of the deprivation of liberty entailed by detention, other measures such as registration, reporting requirements, limits on movement, or curfews backed up by electronic monitoring might serve preventive ends just as effectively. For some brief deprivations of liberty, such as stop-and-search and arrest, 'reasonable grounds for suspicion' combined with the principle of minimum intervention may be the most appropriate approach.

The second point concerns the degree of probability of the harm occurring, the degree of seriousness of the likely harm, the procedural protections, and the standard of proof that should apply. In Section 9.3 it was argued that the test of

---

[19] Slobogin distinguishes between the 'triggering act', which he labels the 'predictive conduct' and the 'act or acts sought to be prevented', which he labels the 'object conduct'. He further argues that if the predictive conduct/triggering act is not a crime then it must be proven to be imminently risky. Slobogin, 'Prevention as the Primary Goal of Sentencing: The Modern Case for Indeterminate Dispositions in Criminal Cases' (n 1).

'a significant risk of a serious harm' was the minimum that might be acceptable as a justification for loss of liberty. In this formulation, 'significant' suggests less than a 50 per cent probability, and some might argue that this is too low a threshold, particularly in view of the fallibility of predictions discussed in Chapter 6. A more demanding test, formulated in Section 7.3, is the 'grievous risk' principle, applicable only to individuals who have been proven to have committed grievous harm on at least one previous occasion. This would justify preventive detention only if there was a high probability of a prospective harm so serious as to justify that loss of liberty. This test not only sets the bar high, but also raises that bar where indefinite detention is proposed, rightly requiring the prospect of a very serious harm in such cases. Some would argue that, where the prospective harm is extremely serious or (in the case of anticipated terrorist attacks) 'catastrophic', a reduced degree of probability would be appropriate. It should be recalled that under the precautionary principle, in the case of catastrophic or irreversible harms, lack of full scientific certainty is not a ground for inaction. However, we would reject a stronger formulation of the precautionary principle which suggests that, in respect of the most serious harms, precautionary measures should be taken even if there is uncertainty about the probability of the risk eventuating or about the efficacy of the proposed measures.[20] The argument for action in the face of uncertainty may be persuasive where the costs of so doing fall upon those well able to bear these burdens (for example, governments, pharmaceutical companies, or the nuclear industry) but they cannot apply where individual liberties are at stake. The greater the prospective loss of individual liberty, the higher the degree of certainty that should be required. Rather than lowering the bar, active consideration should be given to ways of ensuring that more robust and effective risk-assessment and risk-management practices are in place (as discussed in Section 6.5).

In Chapters 7, 9, and 10 we articulated principled restrictions on deprivations of liberty for public protection. They may be restated here as follows:

L. In principle, every citizen has a right to be presumed harmless, and this presumption of harmlessness can be rebutted only in exceptional circumstances.

M. The state's duty to protect people from serious harm may justify depriving a person of liberty if that person has lost the presumption of harmlessness (by virtue of committing a serious violent offence) and is classified as dangerous.

N. Deprivation of liberty should not be considered unless it is the least restrictive appropriate alternative.

---

[20] P Ramsay, 'Imprisonment under the Precautionary Principle', in GR Sullivan and I Dennis (eds.), *Seeking Security: Pre-Empting the Commission of Criminal Harms* (Oxford: Hart Publishing, 2012), 194–218; 201.

O. Any judgment of dangerousness in this context must be approached with strong caution. It should be a judgement of this person as an individual, not simply as a member of a group with certain characteristics and with an overall probability rating. The state should bear the burden of proving that the person presents a significant risk of serious harm to others: the required level of risk should vary according to the seriousness of the predicted harm, and the assessment of risk should be based upon current best available research evidence and professional expertise.[21]

P. If it is considered justifiable to add time to the proportionate sentence in response to a judgment of dangerousness, extended sentences should not exceed the maximum sentence for the offence. If it is deemed necessary to exceed that maximum, in principle that additional time should be the shortest period necessary to respond to the anticipated danger, and the time should be served under different conditions (see principle X below).

Q. In exceptional circumstances, where a person is adjudged to present a very serious danger to others, and where that person has a previous conviction for a very serious offence, the court may consider an indeterminate sentence of detention. The court should determine that no lesser sentence would be effective in protecting the public from a significant risk of serious harm.

11.4 Prevention and Procedural Safeguards

Human rights instruments such as the International Covenant on Civil and Political Rights and the ECHR attach special procedural rights to criminal cases, and this can be justified on the basis of the censure and punishment that criminal proceedings involve, and hence the importance of imposing them only on someone who has had an opportunity for full and informed defence. Clearly, that rationale cannot apply to preventive measures outside the criminal law. So the question is whether there is a justification for any special procedural rights here, or whether predominantly preventive measures constitute a jurisprudential black hole[22]—with no impediment to imposing them retrospectively, without a requirement to give

---

[21] This draws upon the guiding principles set out by the Scottish Risk Management, *Framework for Risk Assessment, Management and Evaluation: Frame* (Paisley: Scottish Risk Management, 2011), Ch. 4 <http://www.rmascotland.gov.uk/files/8613/2887/2321/FRAME_CHAPTER_4_GUIDING_PRINCIPLES.pdf>.

[22] This question has attracted academic attention, but, as yet, no fully developed response. C Slobogin, 'A Jurisprudence of Dangerousness', *Northwestern University Law Review* 98(1) (2003), 1–62; L Farmer, 'The Jurisprudence of Security: The Police Power and the Criminal Law', in MD Dubber and M Valverde (eds.), *The New Police Science: The Police Power in Domestic and International Perspective* (Stanford CA: Stanford University Press, 2006), 145–67; EP Richards, 'The Jurisprudence of Prevention: The Right of Societal Self-Defense against Dangerous Individuals', *Hastings Constitutional Law Quarterly* 16 (1989), 329–92.

reasons, and without provision for legal assistance, etc. Recalling that we are dealing with coercive measures that may involve deprivation of liberty, and that therefore at least one fundamental right is engaged, the question is whether this deprivation of rights should trigger the granting of any procedural rights. There is certainly a long-standing principle in the English law of evidence and procedure that the standard of proof required in court should increase with the severity of the possible consequences. This principle is well established in the civil law.[23] It was applied to civil preventive orders by the House of Lords, arguing that, because the possible consequence of breaching an ASBO was imprisonment of up to five years, the standard of proof should be equivalent to that in criminal proceedings (that is, beyond reasonable doubt).[24]

Since deprivation of liberty is a serious consequence in any rights-respecting country, and deprivation for a long or indeterminate period is very serious, this supports a high standard of proof in such cases. Does it then strengthen the case for other safeguards? There is certainly a strong case for requiring law enforcement officers to give reasons for stop-and-search and for arrest. This may also help to promote the principle of equality and non-discrimination. Where a person stands to lose his or her liberty, there is a strong case for legal assistance to be provided on the same basis as in criminal cases, that is 'to be given it free when the interests of justice so require'.[25] To prevent arbitrariness the state's powers should be clearly described and the individual concerned should be given the right to challenge any decision or proposal that might compromise a basic right such as liberty. Any challenge should be based on the principle of equality of arms, the principle of full disclosure, and the principle of open justice—principles which were seen to be stretched and compromised in some of the anti-terrorist measures, such as closed material proceedings, discussed in Chapter 8.

The general conclusion is that there should be no deprivation of liberty without the provision of appropriate procedural safeguards. The particular rights and principles relevant to the provision of safeguards in relation to the preventive deprivation of liberty, already articulated in previous chapters, are:

R. The principle of sufficient proof, that the standard of proof of factors leading to any deprivation of liberty should be as high as the criminal standard, in view of the severity of the potential consequences.

S. The principle of free legal assistance where the interests of justice so require, deprivation of liberty being a strong indicator that this is appropriate.

T. The right to challenge, before a court or other impartial tribunal, any decision to deprive a person of liberty.

---

[23] eg *Bater v Bater* [1951] P 55, and *Hornal v Neuberger Products* [1957] 1 QB 247.

[24] *Clingham v Royal Borough of Kensington and Chelsea; R. (McCann) v Crown Court at Manchester* [2002] UKHL 39, per Lord Steyn at [37] and Lord Hope at [83].

[25] ECHR, Art. 6.3(c).

U. The principle of open justice, that proceedings involving a challenge to detention should be held in public and that enough of the material upon which the case is based be made available to applicants' lawyers to permit individuals to contest the case against them.

V. The principle of equality of arms, that each side should have equal access to all case papers, including the principle of maximum disclosure (the right of access to evidence held by the state for or against the individual sufficient to mount a proper defence).

11.5 Prevention and the Material Conditions of Detention

If it is determined that an individual should be deprived of their liberty on preventive grounds, the question arises under what material conditions they should be held. In the US, the Supreme Court has interpreted the Due Process Clause of the 14th Amendment to mean that there must be a 'reasonable relation' between the nature and duration of the measure and the purpose for which the individual is committed.[26] When an offender is sentenced to imprisonment, following conviction for one of the preventive crimes discussed in Chapter 5, that sentence will be served in prison. In principle, the human rights of all prisoners should be respected, and the principle of human dignity underlies the discrete rights in the ECHR, the work of the European Committee for the Prevention of Torture, and other constitutional and international standards.

The conditions of detention should also be rights-respecting in relation to offenders imprisoned indefinitely on grounds of dangerousness, as discussed in Chapter 7. However, it is recognized that offenders serving sentences of life imprisonment—especially those with lengthy minimum terms, to be served before they can be considered for release—ought to be provided with opportunities for rehabilitation, so as to reduce their risk and the right to regular review to open up the possibility of release and reintegration in the event that it is considered safe to do so. As discussed in Chapter 7, the Grand Chamber of the ECtHR has developed this application of the principle of human dignity in order to ensure that rehabilitative courses are provided for long-term prisoners.[27]

A different approach is appropriate for persons who are remanded in custody pending trial. The presumption of innocence is taken to indicate that they should be treated differently than convicted prisoners: this should include the right to be held in non-punitive conditions and to enjoy as much freedom within detention as is

---

[26] *Jackson v Indiana*, 406 U.S. 715, 738 (1972).

[27] The most recent judgment is that in *Vinter v United Kingdom*, 9 July 2013.

consistent with the needs of security, together with certain privileges (such as more frequent visits) that are not available to convicted prisoners. However, the reality does not match the principle: many remand prisoners are housed in overcrowded conditions in local prisons, with a toilet in the cell and limited opportunities for exercise.[28] The gulf between principle and practice is immense, but is allowed to persist partly in order to avoid perverse incentives (ie if conditions for remand prisoners really were consistent with the presumption of innocence, too many defendants would be tempted to seek ways of postponing their trial). As argued in Section 3.4, the justifications for pre-trial detention require urgent scrutiny, and in principle those detained before trial for public protection should be held in non-punitive conditions.

Similar reasoning should apply to those detained for immigration purposes. Unless they are serving a sentence for an offence (in which case ordinary principles apply), it was argued in Chapter 10 that persons detained for the purposes of border security and immigration should be detained for the least possible duration, and in conditions that reflect the fact that the person is not being detained for punitive purposes. Where the preventive purposes of immigration control could be served by less restrictive measures (such as surveillance, reporting requirements or handing in the passport), these should be preferred over detention.

When it comes to depriving individuals of their liberty for public health reasons—ie isolation or quarantine of those having or suspected of having a serious infectious disease—the principle of the least restrictive appropriate alternative, the principle of last resort, and the principle of necessity should all be applied. If deprivation of liberty is thought to be justified, then it is accepted that it should not only be for the minimum period necessary, but also that it should be in conditions that are as normalized as possible, and that the individual should be compensated for the period of detention, as discussed in Section 9.2(1). The rationale for this is that a person who has done no wrong is being deprived of liberty in order to safeguard public health and therefore the public good. If this reasoning is sound, might it not also apply to other groups deprived of their liberty for the common good—mentally disordered persons (not including those detained for their own self-protection), immigration detainees, and even those prisoners serving indeterminate sentences who are detained beyond their minimum term? In respect of the last group, in principle its members have all been convicted of a serious offence, and that may be the distinguishing mark. But it remains to be decided why the other groups should not be treated in the same way as persons placed in isolation or quarantine.

---

[28] See HMIP, *Remand Prisoners: A Thematic Review* (London: HMIP, 2012); M Cavadino, J Dignan, and G Mair, *The Penal System: An Introduction* 5th edn (London: SAGE, 2013), 204–6.

The particular rights and principles relevant to the conditions of detention for preventive purposes, already articulated in previous chapters, are:

W. An individual who is deprived of liberty indefinitely should have the right to receive rehabilitative treatment designed to reduce their level of risk and the right to regular review of the continuing necessity for detention.

X. Where an individual is deprived of liberty for the public good, and not as a consequence of a criminal offence, the conditions of detention should be as close to normal as feasible; the individual should have the right to release as soon as the necessity subsides; and the individual should have the right to compensation for the period of detention.

Y. Where a person is remanded in custody pending trial, this decision should only be taken if it is the least restrictive appropriate alternative (last resort), and the conditions of detention should be as consistent as possible with the presumption of innocence.

11.6 Preventive Justice and the Rule of Law

Throughout this book we have tried to suggest substantive norms with which preventive justice ought therefore to comply and to articulate limiting principles. It is often said that the centrepiece of a liberal legal order is the requirement of the rule of law.[29] What the rule of law requires is, of course, contested, but there is general agreement that, at a minimum, laws should be enacted in compliance with established procedure, legal formality, and proper scrutiny; that they should be prospective and adequately publicized; that laws should be sufficiently clear and certain as to provide due warning; that they should have general, stable, consistent, fair, and equal application; and that they should be applied in appropriate legal channels with sufficient due process protections. These prerequisites have several important implications for preventive justice.[30] It is not consistent with the rule of law for the state to exercise coercive powers without prior democratic mandate, parliamentary scrutiny, and legislative authority. Nor may it designate measures as preventive retrospectively or without adequate warning. Neither is it consistent with the rule of law to enact preventive laws or measures that are overly broad or vague and which rely on the exercise of discretion by officials to ensure that they are not misapplied. It is a flouting of the rule of law if preventive laws and measures are

---

[29] PA Albrecht, *Securitized Societies. The Rule of Law: History of a Free Fall* (Cambridge: Intersentia, 2011).

[30] Or, to put it another way, preventive justice has profound implications for the rule of law. D Dyzenhaus, 'Preventive Justice and the Rule-of-Law Project', in A Ashworth, L Zedner, and P Tomlin (eds.), *Prevention and the Limits of the Criminal Law* (Oxford: Oxford University Press, 2013), 91–114.

applied erratically, inconsistently, or arbitrarily; if they are unfairly discriminatory, or target sections of the population without good reason. And it is a clear breach of the rule of law for state officials to take coercive preventive action outside the appropriate legal channels or in disregard of due process protections. Gardner vividly describes the government of 'Securitania' as one which engages in all these violations in the name of security and he asks:

Do any of these developments make the people of Securitania more secure? Probably not. But in one way they clearly make the people of Securitania a lot less secure. The people of Securitania are progressively being deprived of the rudimentary security of living under the rule of law.[31]

For Gardner, it is not sufficient that officials act within the law, 'the law itself must also live up to certain standards'.[32] These go beyond the rule-of-law requirements of certainty, clarity, and consistency (see principles J and K in Section 11.1) to entail potentially conflicting values like the right of all members of law's community to debate the proper limits of law and to question its authority—a right that inevitability raises the spectres of uncertainty, ambiguity, and unpredictability. If the rule of law is to serve as an effective protection against arbitrary intervention, the right to challenge is particularly important in cases where the stakes for individual liberty are high. As MacCormick argues, 'the Rule of Law . . . insists on the right of the defence to challenge and rebut the case made against it. There is no security against arbitrary government unless such challenges are freely permitted.'[33] But, here too, challenge opens the way to argument and contestation, and these necessarily undermine predictability. Indeterminacy is, of course, an enduring strain on the application of criminal law where the demands of maximum certainty are continually tested by the inherently disputatious workings of the adversarial system and the unpredictability of outcome of the criminal trial.

The potential for uncertainty in respect of preventive justice is even greater since its object—the harm to be prevented—is inherently unknowable and, as we observed in Chapter 6, the scientific basis upon which its probability is determined is itself debatable. It follows that if they are to abide by the rule of law, measures of preventive justice must adhere to the prescriptions of legality and aspire to the highest standards of certainty and fair warning, while tempering their commitment to certainty in recognition of the fact that prevention addresses a necessarily uncertain object, namely the future; that risk-calculation is an uncertain science; and that the efficacy of liberty-depriving measures for preventive purposes is contested. Moreover, it can be argued the right to challenge all aspects of the case for coercive intervention

---

[31] J Gardner, 'What Security Is There against Arbitrary Government?', *The London Review of Books* 28(5) (2006), 1–9; 1–2.

[32] Gardner, 'What Security Is There against Arbitrary Government?' (n 31), 3.

[33] N MacCormick, *Rhetoric and the Rule of Law: A Theory of Legal Reasoning* (Oxford: Oxford University Press, 2005), 27.

is no less—and in the case of indeterminate preventive detention, arguably even more—critical in respect of the coercive preventive laws with which this book has been concerned. In sum, insofar as preventive justice underwrites a warrant for the enactment and deployment of coercive laws and measures by the state, adherence to the rule of law requires that citizens have the inalienable right to challenge those laws. The right to challenge—notwithstanding the uncertainty that flows from it—is the chief protection against arbitrary or unwarranted coercion by the state.

11.7 Conclusions

The duty to protect the public is always liable to be laid down as a trump card. Preventive justice does not contest this duty,[34] but it does contest its claim to outplay all other values and insists that preventive measures should be subject to restraining principles. In this chapter we have not sought to draw together all the principles for which we have argued in the earlier chapters. Our purpose has rather been to show how the principles are interlinked, and how they bear on the main topic of the study—restraining principles for deprivations of liberty which are said to be based on preventive rationales. In the various chapters we have adopted a critical stance towards the justifications advanced for preventive laws and measures, and have used those criticisms as a basis for developing the various restraining principles. We hope that we have given sufficiently strong arguments for these principles to be used as a reference point by practitioners in the field—policymakers in government and elsewhere, legislators, legislative scrutineers, and of course the many persons (mostly officials) involved in implementing the various policies. Those persons include the police, prosecutors, courts, and the Parole Board, as well as immigration officers, psychiatrists, Mental Health Tribunals, and others.

We also hope that the principles that we have enunciated in this chapter and throughout the book will be read by academics, researchers, and students in the spirit that they are offered; namely as a provocation to further debate about the extent of the state's duty to protect and the proper limits on the powers it employs in fulfilment of this duty. The principles we articulate are not the last word on the subject but they are surely a start, even if they merit further deliberation and refinement. Thorny questions about the weight to be given to the different principles and the resolution of tensions and conflicts between them will require constant working out.

---

[34] For further discussion of this debate, see K Günther, 'Responsibility to Protect and Preventive Justice', in A Ashworth, L Zedner, and P Tomlin (eds.), *Prevention and the Limits of the Criminal Law* (Oxford: Oxford University Press, 2013), 69–90.

How such principles might be brought into play and what incentives might be created within the policymaking and legislative processes, as well as within the everyday working practices of criminal justice and other officials, to accord with these principles also demand further academic attention. Enhancing the role of prelegislative cross-party scrutiny and of independent review of the implementation of preventive laws and measures, and institutionalizing recourse to expert assessment and management of risk (for example, by establishing an independent risk-management authority) are just some of the potent means to translate principles into good practice. Yet, even if our proposed principles were warmly received by all those involved, they are not straightforward in their application, and we should conclude by drawing attention to two factors in their implementation. First, most of the principles include an open-textured concept that requires both interpretation and sensitive application to the factual situation. Examples of this would be terms such as 'reasonable suspicion', least restrictive 'appropriate' alternative, conditions of detention 'as close as possible' to normal life, 'maximum' certainty of definition, and so on. One way of maximizing the effect of the principles is to develop a code of practice or a set of working principles applicable to the particular spheres of operation.[35] Second, and relatedly, there is a considerable amount of judgement required of those who have the task of implementing the various coercive powers. Discretion pervades not only the criminal justice system but also the working of the preventive state. Thus, if the spirit of the principles is to be carried through into practice, there must be proper training and robust accountability systems,[36] to ensure that the exercise of discretion is based on recognition not only of the state's duty to protect but also of the rights of the individuals against whom the coercive powers are to be exercised. If there is to be security against arbitrary government, particularly when government purports to be acting in the very interests of security, then the task of articulating the principles, parameters, and aspirations of preventive justice cannot afford to stop here.

---

[35] An example of a sustained attempt to set out general standards and guidelines may be found in Scottish Risk Management, *Framework for Risk Assessment, Management and Evaluation: Frame*. See especially Ch. 4 'Guiding Principles' at <http://www.rmascotland.gov.uk/files/8613/2887/2321/FRAME_CHAPTER_4_GUIDING_PRINCIPLES.pdf>.

[36] For emphasis on practical training and supervision, as well as the articulation of principles, see Her Majesty's Inspectorate of Constabulary, *Stop and Search Powers: Are the Police Using Them Effectively and Fairly?* (London: HMSO, 2013), discussed in Section 3.2.

Bibliography

Aas, KF (2011), 'Crimmigrant' bodies and bona fide travelers: Surveillance, citizenship and global governance', *Theoretical Criminology* 15(3), 331–46.

——(2012), '(In)security-at-a-distance: rescaling justice, risk and warfare in a transnational age', *Global Crime* 13(4), 235–53.

——, Oppen Gundhus, H, and Mork Lomell, H (eds.) (2008), *Technologies of (In)security: The Surveillance of Everyday Life* (London: Routledge).

Ackerman, B (2004), 'The Emergency Constitution', *Yale Law Journal* 113(5), 1029–91.

——(2006), *Before the Next Attack: Preserving Civil Liberties in an Age of Terrorism* (New Haven: Yale University Press).

Albrecht, PA (2011), *Securitized Societies. The Rule of Law: History of a Free Fall* (Cambridge: Intersentia).

Alexander, L and Ferzan, KK (2009), *Crime and Culpability: A Theory of Criminal Law* (Cambridge: Cambridge University Press).

——and——(2012), 'Danger: The Ethics of Preemptive Action', *Ohio State Journal of Criminal Law* 9(2), 637–67.

——and——(2012), 'Risk and Inchoate Crimes: Retribution or Prevention?', in GR Sullivan and I Dennis (eds.), *Seeking Security* (Oxford: Hart Publishing), 103–20.

Aliverti, A (2012), 'Making home safe? The role of criminal law and punishment in British immigration controls'. Oxford DPhil Thesis.

——(2012), 'Making people criminal. The role of the criminal law in immigration', *Theoretical Criminology* 16(4), 417–34.

——(2013), *Immigration Offences: Trends in Legislation and Criminal and Civil Enforcement: Migration Observatory briefing* (Oxford: COMPAS, University of Oxford).

American Law Institute (1962), *Model Penal Code*.

Anderson, D (2013), 'Shielding the Compass: How to Fight Terrorism without Defeating the Law', *European Human Rights Law Review* 233–43.

——(2013), *Terrorism Prevention and Investigation in 2012: First Report of the Independent Review on the Operation of the Terrorism Prevention and Investigation Act 2011* (London: TSO).

Ansbro, M (2010), 'The Nuts and Bolt of Risk Assessment: When the Clinical and Actuarial Conflict', *The Howard Journal of Criminal Justice* 49(3), 252–68.

Appelbaum, PS (1984), 'Psychiatric ethics in the courtroom', *Bulletin of the American Academy of Psychiatry and Law* 12(3), 225–31.

——(2008), 'Ethics and Forensic Psychiatry: Translating Principles Into Practice', *Journal of the American Academy of Psychiatry and the Law* 36, 195–200.

Appleton, C (2010), *Life after Life Imprisonment* (Oxford: Oxford University Press).

——and Grover, B (2007), 'The Pros and Cons of Life without Parole', *British Journal of Criminology* 47(4), 597–615.

Ashworth, A (2004), 'Social Control and Anti-Social Behaviour Order: the Subversion of Human Rights?', *Law Quarterly Review* 120, 263–91.

——(2006), 'Four Threats to the Presumption of Innocence', *South African Law Journal* 123, 62–96.

——(2007), 'Security, Terrorism and the Value of Human Rights', in B Goold and L Lazarus (eds.), *Security and Human Rights* (Oxford: Hart Publishing), 203–26.

——(2010), *Sentencing and Criminal Justice* 5th edn (Cambridge: Cambridge University Press).

——(2011), 'Attempts', in J Deigh and D Dolinko (eds.), *Oxford Handbook of Philosophy of Criminal Law* (Oxford: Oxford University Press), 125–46.

——(2011), 'The Unfairness of Risk-Based Possession Offences', *Criminal Law and Philosophy* 5(3), 237–57.

——(2013), *Positive Obligations in the Criminal Law* (Oxford: Hart Publishing).

——(2013), 'Preventive Orders and the Rule of Law', in D Baker and J Horder (eds.), *The Sanctity of Life and the Criminal Law* (Cambridge: Cambridge University Press), 45–68.

——and Blake, M (1996), 'The Presumption of Innocence in English Criminal Law', *Criminal Law Review*, 306–17.

——and Horder, J (2013), *The Principles of Criminal Law* 7th edn (Oxford: Oxford University Press).

——and Redmayne, M (2010), *The Criminal Process* 4th edn (Oxford: Oxford University Press).

——and Zedner, L (2010), 'Preventive Orders: a problem of under-criminalization?', in RA Duff, et al. (eds.), *The Boundaries of the Criminal Law* (Oxford: Oxford University Press), 59–87.

——and——(2011), 'Just Prevention and the Limits of the Criminal Law', in RA Duff and SP Green (eds.), *Philosophical Foundations of the Criminal Law* (Oxford: Oxford University Press), 279–303.

——and——(2012), 'Prevention and Criminalization: Justifications and Limits', *New Criminal Law Review* 15(4), 542–71.

Asp, P (2013), 'Preventionism and the Criminalization of Noncomsummate Offences', in A Ashworth, L Zedner, and P Tomlin (eds.), *Prevention and the Limits of the Criminal Law* (Oxford: Oxford University Press), 23–64.

Association of Chief Police Officers (2010), *Manual of Guidance on Keeping the Peace.*

Association of Chief Police Officers (2012), *The National Decision Model.*

Bailey, V (1987), *Delinquency and Citizenship: Reclaiming the Young Offender 1914–1948* (Oxford: Oxford University Press).

Baker, K (2010), 'More Harm than Good? The Language of Public Protection', *The Howard Journal of Criminal Justice* 49(1), 42–53.

Baker, SA, et al. (2013), 'More sinned against than sinning? Perceptions about European migrants and crime', *Criminology and Criminal Justice* 13(3), 262–78.

Banks, J (2008), 'The criminalisation of asylum seekers and asylum policy', *Prison Service Journal* 175, 43–9.

Bartlett, P (2010), 'Civil Confinement', in LO Gostin, et al. (eds.), *Principles of Mental Health Law and Policy* (Oxford: Oxford University Press), 413–72.

——(2010), 'Informal Admissions and Deprivation of Liberty under the Mental Capacity Act 2005', in LO Gostin, et al. (eds.), *Principles of Mental Health Law and Policy* (Oxford: Oxford University Press), 385–412.

Beattie, JA (1986), *Crime and the Courts in England 1660–1800* (Oxford: Oxford University Press).

Beattie, JM (2007), 'Sir John Fielding and Public Justice: The Bow Street Magistrates' Court, 1754–1780', *Law and History Review* 25(1), 61–100.

Beck, U (1992), *The Risk Society: Towards a New Modernity* (London: Sage Publications).

Becker, G (1968), 'Crime and Punishment: An Economic Approach', *The Journal of Political Economy* 76(2), 169–217.

Bentham, J (1830), *Constitutional Code* (London: Robert Heward).

——(1838–43), *The Works of Jeremy Bentham*, ed. J Bowring (Edinburgh: William Tait).

——(1967, 1789), *An Introduction to Principles of Morals and Legislation* (Oxford: Blackwell).

Blackbourn, J (2012), 'Evaluating the Independent Reviewer of Terrorism Legislation', *Parliamentary Affairs*, 1–14.

——(2013), 'Independent Reviewers of Anti-Terrorism Laws as Effective Oversight Mechanism: Australia and the UK Compared' (unpublished paper).

Blackstone, W (1753), *Commentaries on the Laws of England in Four Books.*

Bostanci, A (2008), *British Citizenship: A Debate of Paradoxes* (London: Friedrich Ebert Stiftung).

Bosworth, M (2008), 'Border Control and the Limits of the Sovereign State', *Social and Legal Studies* 17(2), 199–215.

——(2011), 'Deportation, detention and foreign-national prisoners in England and Wales', *Citizenship Studies* 15(5), 583–95.

——(2011), 'Human Rights and Immigration Detention in the UK', in M Dembour and T Kelly (eds.), *Are Human Rights for Migrants? Critical Reflections on the Status of Irregular Migrants in Europe and the United States* (Abingdon: Routledge), 165–83.

——(2012), 'Subjectivity and identity in detention: Punishment and society in a global age', *Theoretical Criminology* 16(2), 123–40.

Bottoms, AE (1995), 'The Philosophy and Politics of Punishment and Sentencing', in C Clarkson and R Morgan (eds.), *The Politics of Sentencing Reform* (Oxford: Clarendon Press), 17–49.

——and Brownsword, R (1982), 'The Dangerousness Debate after the Floud Report', *British Journal of Criminology* 22, 229–54.

——and —— (1983), '"Dangerousness and Rights', in JW Hinton (ed.), *Dangerousness: Problems of Assessment and Prediction* (London: George Allen and Unwin), 233–7.

Bowling, B and Phillips, C (2012), 'Policing ethnic minority communities', in T Newburn (ed.), *Handbook of Policing* 2nd edn (London: Routledge), 611–41.

Boyd-Caine, T (2012), *Protecting the Public? Detention and Release of Mentally Disordered Offenders* (Abingdon: Routledge).

Bradley, Lord (2009), *The Bradley Report: Lord Bradley's review of people with mental health problems or learning disabilities in the criminal justice system* (London: COI for the Department of Health).

Braithwaite, J (2006), 'Pre-empting Terrorism', *Current Issues in Criminal Justice* 17(1), 96–114.

——and Pettit, P (1990), *Not Just Deserts: A Republican Theory of Justice* (Oxford: Oxford University Press).

Bright, S and Bakalis, C (2003), 'Anti-social behaviour: local authority responsibility and the voice of the victim', *Cambridge Law Journal* 62, 305–34.

Brown, M (2000), 'Calculations of Risk in Contemporary Penal Practice', in J Pratt and M Brown (eds.), *Dangerous Offenders* (London: Routledge), 93–108.

——and Pratt, J (eds.) (2000), *Dangerous Offenders: Punishment and Social Order* (London: Routledge).

Brudner, A (2009), *Punishment and Freedom: A Liberal Theory of Penal Justice* (Oxford: Oxford University Press).

Buchanan, A (2008), 'Risk of Violence by Psychiatric Patients: Beyond the "Actuarial Versus Clinical" Assessment Debate', *Psychiatric Services* 59(2), 184–90.

Burney, E (2005), *Making People Behave: Anti-Social Behaviour, Politics and Policy* (Cullompton, Devon: Willan Publishing).

——(2006), '"No Spitting": Regulation of Offensive Behaviour in England and Wales', in A von Hirsch and A Simester (eds.), *Incivilities* (Oxford: Hart Publishing), 195–218.

Burns T, et al. (2013), 'Community Treatment Orders for Patients with Psychosis (OCTET): a Randomised Controlled Trial', *The Lancet* 381, 1627–33.

Cape, E (2013), 'The counter-terrorism provisions of the Protection of Freedoms Act 2012: Preventing misuse or a case of smoke and mirrors?', *Criminal Law Review*, 5, 385–99.

Care Quality Commission (2012), *Monitoring the Mental Health Act 2011–2012*.

Carlile, Lord (2009), *Report on the Operation in 2008 of the Terrorism Act 2000*.

Cavadino, M, Dignan, J, and Mair, G (2013), *The Penal System: an Introduction* 5th edn (London: Sage).

Chacón, JM (2007), 'Unsecured Borders: Immigration Restrictions, Crime Control and National Security', *Connecticut Law Review* 39, 1827–91.

——(2009), 'Managing Migration through Crime', *Columbia Law Review* 109; 135–48.

——(2010), 'Tensions and Trade-Offs: Protecting Trafficking Victims in the Era of Immigration Enforcement,' *University of Pennsylvania Law Review* 158, 1609–53.

——(2012), 'Overcriminalizing Immigration', *Journal of Criminal Law & Criminology* 102(3), 613–52.

Chadwick, E (1829), 'Preventive Police', *London Review* 1, 252–308.

Chief Inspector of Prisons, HM (2008), *The Indeterminate Sentence for Public Protection*.

Chin, GJ (2012), 'The New Civil Death: Rethinking Punishment in the Era of Mass Conviction', *University of Pennsylvania Law Review* 160, 1789–833.

Clarke, RV (1995), 'Situational Crime Prevention', in M Tonry and N Morris (eds.), *Crime and Justice: An Annual Review of Research* 19 (Chicago: University of Chicago Press), 91–150.

Clarkson, C (2009), 'Attempt: the Conduct Element', *Oxford Journal of Legal Studies,* 29, 25–41.

Coady, CAJ (2012), 'Terrorism and the Criminal Law', in RA Duff, et al. (eds.), *The Constitution of the Criminal Law* (Oxford: Oxford University Press), 185–208.

Cochran, DQ (2010), 'Material Witness Detention in a Post-9/11 World: Mission Creep or Fresh Start?', *George Mason Law Review* 18(1), 1–41.

Cole, D (2003), *Enemy Aliens: Double Standards and Constitutional Freedoms in the War on Terrorism* (New York: The New Press).

——(2004), 'The Priority of Morality: The Emergency Constitution's Blind Spot', *Yale Law Journal* 113(8), 1753–800.

——(2007), 'Against Citizenship as a Predicate for Basic Rights', *Fordham Law Review* 75, 2541–8.

——(2009), 'English Lessons: A Comparative Analysis of UK and US Responses to Terrorism', *Current Legal Problems* 62(1), 136–67.

——(2009), 'Out of the Shadows: Preventive Detention, Suspected Terrorists, and War', *California Law Review* 97, 693–750.

——and Dempsey, J (2002), *Terrorism and the Constitution: Sacrificing Civil Liberties in the Name of National Security* (New York: W.W. Norton & Co.).

Colquhoun, P (1796), *Treatise on the Police of the Metropolis* (London: H. Fry).

Cooke, DJ and Michie, C (2011), 'Violence Risk Assessment: Challenging the Illusion of Certainty', in B McSherry and P Keyzer (eds.), *Dangerous People: Policy, Prediction, and Practice* (New York: Routledge), 147–61.

Cornelisse, G (2011), 'A new articulation of human rights, or why the European Court of Human Rights should think beyond Westphalian sovereignty', in M Dembour and T Kelly (eds.), *Are Human Rights for Migrants? Critical Reflections on the Status of Irregular Migrants in Europe and the United States* (Abingdon: Routledge), 99–119.

Cornford, A (2012), 'Criminalising Anti-Social Behaviour', *Criminal Law and Philosophy* 6, 1–19.

Corrado, ML (1996), 'Punishment and the Wild Beast of Prey: The Problem of Preventive Detention', *Journal of Criminal Law & Criminology* 86(3), 778–814.

Council of Europe (1988), *The Simplification of Criminal Justice* (Strasbourg: Council of Europe).

Council of Europe (2005), *Report by the Commissioner for Human Rights on his Visit to the United Kingdom, 4–12 November 2004* (Strasbourg: Council of Europe).

Crawford, A (1994), 'The Partnership Approach to Community Crime Prevention: Corporatism at the Local Level?', *Social and Legal Studies* 3(4), 497–518.

——(1998), *Crime Prevention and Community Safety: Politics, Policies, and Practices* (London: Longman).

——(2009), 'Governing through Anti-Social Behaviour: Regulatory Challenges to Criminal Justice', *British Journal of Criminology* 49, 810–31.

——and Evans, K (2012), 'Crime Prevention and Community Safety', in M Maguire, R Morgan, and R Reiner (eds.), *The Oxford Handbook of Criminology* 5th edn (Oxford: Oxford University Press), 769–805.

Dauvergne, C (2008), *Making People Illegal: What Globalization Means for Migration and Law* (Cambridge: Cambridge University Press).

Dawson, J (2010), 'Community Treatment Orders', in LO Gostin, et al. (eds.), *Principles of Mental Health Law and Policy* (Oxford: Oxford University Press), 513–54.

Demleitner, N (2003), 'Abusing State Power or Controlling Risk?: Sex Offender Commitment and Sicherungsverwahrung', *Fordham Urban Law Journal* 30, 1621–69.

——(2004), 'Misguided Prevention: The War on Terrorism as a War on Immigrant Offenders and Immigration Violators', *Criminal Law Bulletin* 40, 550–75.

Dennis, I (2012), 'Security, Risk and Preventive Orders', in GR Sullivan and I Dennis (eds.), *Seeking Security: Pre-empting the Commission of Criminal Harms* (Oxford: Hart Publishing), 169–92.

Department of Health (2008), *Mental Health Act Code of Practice*.

Dershowitz, A (2006), *Preemption: A Knife that Cuts both Ways* (New York: W.W. Norton).

Dinh, V (2002), 'Freedom and Security after September 11', *Harvard Journal of Law and Public Policy* 25, 399–406.

Dinwiddy, J (1989), *Bentham* (Oxford: Oxford University Press).

Dobrowolsky, A (2007), '(In)Security and Citizenship: Security, Im/migration and Shrinking Citizenship Regimes', *Theoretical Inquiries in Law* 8(2), 628–62.

Dodsworth, F (2007), 'Police and the Prevention of Crime: Commerce, Temptation and the Corruption of the Body Politic, from Fielding to Colquhoun', *British Journal of Criminology* 47(3), 439–54.

Doob, A and Webster, C (2003), 'Sentence Severity and Crime: Accepting the Null Hypothesis', in M Tonry (ed.), *Crime and Justice. A Review of Research* vol. 30 (Chicago: University of Chicago Press), 143–95.

Downes, D and Rock, P (2011), *Understanding Deviance* 6th edn (Oxford: Oxford University Press).

Drenkhahn, K, Morgenstern, C, and van Zyl Smit, D (2012), 'Preventive Detention in Germany in the Shadow of European Human Rights Law', *Criminal Law Review* 3, 167–87.

Dubber, MD (2005), *The Police Power: Patriarchy and the Foundations of American Government* (New York: Columbia University Press).

——(2005), 'The Possession Paradigm: The Special Part and the Police Model of the Criminal Process', in RA Duff and SP Green (eds.), *Defining Crimes: Essays on the Special Part of the Criminal Law* (Oxford: Oxford University Press), 91–118.

——(2013), 'Preventive Justice: The Quest for Principle', in A Ashworth, L Zedner, and P Tomlin (eds.), *Prevention and the Limits of the Criminal Law* (Oxford: Oxford University Press), 47–68.

——and Farmer, L (eds.) (2007), *Modern Histories of Crime and Punishment* (Stanford: Stanford University Press).

Duff, RA (1986), *Trials and Punishments* (Cambridge: Cambridge University Press).

——(1997), *Criminal Attempts* (Oxford: Oxford University Press).

——(1998), 'Dangerousness and Citizenship', in A Ashworth and M Wasik (eds.), *Fundamentals of Sentencing Theory* (Oxford: Clarendon Press), 141–64.

——(2001), *Punishment, Communication and Community* (Oxford: Oxford University Press).

——(2005), 'Criminalising Endangerment', in RA Duff, and Green, SP (ed.), *Defining Crimes: Essays on the Special Part of the Criminal Law* (Oxford: Oxford University Press), 43–64.

——(2007), *Answering for Crime: Responsibility and Liability in the Criminal Law* (Oxford: Hart Publishing).

——(2007), 'Crimes, Regulatory Offences and Criminal Trials', in H Müller-Dietz, H Egon Müller, and KL Kunz (eds.), *Festschrift für Heike Jung* (Baden-Baden: Nomos), 87–98.

——(2010), 'Perversions and Subversions of Criminal Law', in RA Duff et al.(eds.), *The Boundaries of the Criminal Law* (Oxford: Oxford University Press), 88–112.

——(2012), 'Risks, Culpability and Criminal Liability', in GR Sullivan and I Dennis (eds.), *Seeking Security: Pre-Empting the Commission of Criminal Harms* (Oxford: Hart Publishing), 121–42.

——(2013), 'Pre-Trial Detention and the Presumption of Innocence', in A Ashworth, L Zedner, and P Tomlin (eds.), *Prevention and the Limits of the Criminal Law* (Oxford: Oxford University Press), 115–32.

Dunn, J (1969), *The Political Thought of John Locke* (Cambridge: Cambridge University Press).

Dworkin, R (2003), 'Terror and the Attack on Civil Liberties', *The New York Review of Books* 50(17), 37–41.

Dyzenhaus, D (2001), 'The Permanence of the Temporary: Can Emergency Powers Be Normalized?', in R Daniels, P Macklem, and K Roach (eds.), *The Security of Freedom: Essays on Canada's Anti-Terrorism Bill* (Toronto: Toronto University Press), 21–37.

——(2013), 'Preventive Justice and the Rule-of-Law Project', in A Ashworth, L Zedner, and P Tomlin (eds.), *Prevention and the Limits of the Criminal Law* (Oxford: Oxford University Press), 91–114.

Eastman, N (1999), 'Public health psychiatry or crime prevention', *British Medical Journal* 318, 549–51.

——(2005), 'The psychiatrist, courts and sentencing: the impact of extended sentencing on the ethical framework of forensic psychiatry', *The Psychiatrist* 29, 73–7.

——and Peay, J (eds.) (1999), *Law without Enforcement: Integrating Mental Health and Justice* (Oxford: Hart Publishing).

Edwards, A and Hughes, G (2009), 'The Preventive Turn and the Promotion of Safer Communities in England and Wales', in A Crawford (ed.), *Crime Prevention Policies in Comparative Perspective* (Cullompton: Willan Publishing), 62–85.

Edwards, J (2010), 'Justice Denied: the Criminal Law and the Ouster of the Criminal Courts', *Oxford Journal of Legal Studies* 30, 725–48.

Emmerson, B, Ashworth, A, and Macdonald, A (2012), *Human Rights and Criminal Justice* 3rd edn (London: Sweet & Maxwell).

Endicott, T (2011), *Administrative Law* 2nd edn (Oxford: Oxford University Press).

Engelmann, SG (2003), ' "Indirect Legislation": Bentham's Liberal Government', *Polity* 35, 369–88.

Epstein, R and Mitchell, B (2009), 'Indeterminate Imprisonment for Public Protection and the Impact of the 2008 Reforms', *Criminal Law and Justice Weekly*. Available at <http://www.criminallawandjustice.co.uk/features/Indeterminate-Imprisonment-Public-Protection-and-Impact-2008-Reforms>.

Equality and Diversity Forum (2008), *Response to 'The Path to Citizenship: The Next Steps in Reforming the Immigration System'* (London: Equality and Diversity Forum).

Ericson, R (2006), 'Ten Uncertainties of Risk-Management Approaches to Security', *Canadian Journal of Criminology and Criminal Justice* 48(3), 345–57.

——(2007), *Crime in an Insecure World* (Cambridge: Polity).

Farmer, L (2006), 'The Jurisprudence of Security: The Police Power and the Criminal Law', in MD Dubber and M Valverde (eds.), *The New Police Science: the Police Power in Domestic and International Perspective* (Stanford CA: Stanford University Press), 145–67.

Farrington, DP (2002), 'Developmental Criminology and Risk-Focused Prevention', in M Maguire, R Morgan, and R Reiner (eds.), *The Oxford Handbook of Criminology* 3rd edn (Oxford: Oxford University Press), 657–701.

Fazel, S and Danesh, J (2002), 'Serious Mental Disorder in 23,000 Prisoners', *The Lancet* 359, 545–50.

——and Grann, M (2006), 'The Population Impact of Severe Mental Illness on Violent Crime', *American Journal of Psychiatry* 163, 1397–403.

Feeley, M (2004), 'Actuarial Justice and the Modern State', in G Bruinsma, H Elffers, and J de Keijser (eds.), *Punishment, Places, and Perpetrators: Developments in Criminology and Criminal Justice Research* (Devon, Cullompton: Willan Publishing), 62–77.

——and Simon, J (1992), 'The New Penology: Notes on the Emerging Strategy of Corrections and its Implications', *Criminology* 30(4), 449–74.

——and——(1994), 'Actuarial Justice: The Emerging New Criminal Law', in D Nelken (ed.), *The Futures of Criminology* (London: Sage), 173–201.

Feinberg, J (1984), *Harm to Others* (New York: Oxford University Press).

Feldman, D (2008), 'Deprivation of liberty in anti-terrorism law', *Cambridge Law Journal* 67(1), 4–8.

Feldman, N (2002), 'Choices of Law, Choices of War', *Harvard Journal of Law and Public Policy* 25(2), 457–85.

Felson, M (2002), *Crime and Everyday Life* 3rd edn (London: Sage).

——and Clarke, RV (1997), 'The Ethics of Situational Crime Prevention', in G Newman and R Clarke (eds.), *Rational Choice and Situational Crime Prevention* (Aldershot: Dartmouth), 197–218.

——and——(1998), *Opportunity Makes the Thief: Practical theory for crime prevention. Police Research Series No. 98* (London: Home Office).

Fennell, P (2010), 'Review of the Lawfulness of Detention in the Courts and Mental Health Tribunals', in LO Gostin, et al. (eds.), *Principles of Mental Health Law and Policy* (Oxford: Oxford University Press), 557–642.

Fennell, P (2010), 'Mental Disability and the Sentencing Decision', in LO Gostin, et al. (eds.), *Principles of Mental Health Law and Policy* (Oxford: Oxford University Press), 777–802.

——(2010), 'The Statutory Definition of Mental Disorder and the Availability of Appropriate Treatment', in LO Gostin, et al. (eds.), *Principles of Mental Health Law and Policy* (Oxford: Oxford University Press), 71–102.

——(2011), *Mental Health: Law and Practice* 2nd edn (Bristol: Jordan Publishing).

Fenwick, H (2002), 'The Anti-Terrorism, Crime and Security Act 2001: A Proportionate Response to 11 September?', *Modern Law Review* 65(5), 724–62.

Ferzan, KK (2011), 'Inchoate Crimes at the Prevention/Punishment Divide', *San Diego Law Review* 48(4), 1273–97.

——(forthcoming), 'Preventive Justice and the Presumption of Innocence', *Criminal Law and Philosophy* available Online First at http://link.springer.com/article/10.1007%2Fs11572-013-9275-0#page-1.

Fielding, J (1755), *A Plan for Preventing Robberies within Twenty Miles of London with an Account of the Rise and Establishment of the Real Thieftakers* (London: A. Millar).

——(1758), *An Account of the Origin and Effects of a Police Set on Foot by His Grace the Duke of Newcastle, in the Year 1753* (London: A. Millar).

Fisher, E (2002), 'Precaution, Precaution Everywhere: Developing a "Common Understanding" of the Precautionary Principle in the European Community', *Maastricht Journal of European and Comparative Law* 9(1), 7–28.

Floud, J (1982), 'Dangerousness and Criminal Justice', *British Journal of Criminology* 22, 213–28.

——and Young, W (1981), *Dangerousness and Criminal Justice* (London: Heinemann).

Foucault, M (1979), *Discipline and Punish: The Birth of the Prison* (Harmondsworth, Middlesex: Peregrine).

Freeden, M (1978), *The New Liberalism: An Ideology of Social Reform* (Oxford: Oxford University Press).

Fuller, LL (1964), *The Morality of Law* (New Haven: Yale University Press).

Gable, L and Gostin, LO (2010), 'Human Rights of Persons with Mental Disabilities: the European Convention on Human Rights', in LO Gostin, et al. (eds.), *Principles of Mental Health Law and Policy* (Oxford: Oxford University Press), 103–66.

Gainotti, S, et al. (2008), 'Ethical Models underpinning Responses to Threats to Public Health: a Comparison of Approaches to Communicable Disease Control in Europe', *Bioethics* 22, 466–76.

Gans, J, et al. (2011), *Criminal Process and Human Rights* (Sydney: Federation Press).

Gardner, J (2006), 'What security is there against arbitrary government?', *The London Review of Books* 28(5), 1–9.

——and Shute, S (2000), 'The Wrongness of Rape', in J Horder (ed.), *Oxford Essays in Jurisprudence* (Oxford: Oxford University Press), 193–217.

Garland, D (1985), *Punishment and Welfare: A History of Penal Strategies* (London: Gower).

——(1996), 'The Limits of the Sovereign State: Strategies of Crime Control in Contemporary Society', *British Journal of Criminology* 36(4), 445–71.

——(2000), 'Ideas, Institutions and Situational Crime Prevention', in A von Hirsch, D Garland, and A Wakefield (eds.), *Ethical and Social Perspectives on Situational Crime Prevention* (Oxford: Hart Publishing), 1–16.

——(2001), *The Culture of Control: Crime and Social Order in Contemporary Society* (Oxford: Oxford University Press).

Gearty, C (2005), 'Human Rights in an Age of Counter-Terrorism: Injurious, Irrelevant or Indispensable?', *Current Legal Problems* 58, 25–46.

Giddens, A (2002), *Where Now for New Labour?* (Cambridge: Polity).

Gledhill, K (2011), 'Preventive Sentences and Orders: The Challenges of Due Process', *Journal of Commonwealth Criminal Law,* 1(1), 78–104.

——(2012), *Defending Mentally Disordered Persons* (London: LAG Education and Service Trust).

Glover, R (2012), 'The Uncertain Blue Line—Police Cordons and the Common Law', *Criminal Law Review*, 245–60.

Goldsmith, A (2007), 'Preparation for Terrorism: Catastrophic Risk and Precautionary Criminal Law', in A Lynch, E Macdonald, and G Williams (eds.), *Law and Liberty in the War on Terror* (Annandale, NSW: The Federation Press), 59–74.

Goodey, J (2002), 'Whose Insecurity? Organised crime, its victims and the EU', in A Crawford (ed.), *Crime and Insecurity: The Governance of Safety in Europe* (Cullompton: Willan Publishing), 135–58.

Gostin, LO (2000), *Public Health Law* (Berkeley: University of California Press).

——, et al. (2002), 'The Model State Emergency Powers Act: Planning for and Response to Bioterrorism and Naturally Occurring Infectious Diseases', *Journal of the American Medical Association* 288, 622–8.

Gray, J and Smith, GW (1991), 'Introduction', in J Gray and GW Smith (eds.), *On Liberty in Focus* (London: Routledge).

Griffith, EEH (1997), 'Ethics in Forensic Psychiatry: a cultural response to Stone and Appelbaum', *Journal of the American Academy of Psychiatry and the Law* 26, 171–84.

Gross, O and Ní Aoláin, F (2006), *Law in Times of Crisis: Emergency Powers in Theory and Practice* (Cambridge: Cambridge University Press).

Gunn, J (2000), 'Future directions for treatment in forensic psychiatry', *British Journal of Psychiatry* 176, 332–38.

Günther, K (2013), 'Responsibility to Protect and Preventive Justice', in A Ashworth, L Zedner, and P Tomlin (eds.), *Prevention and the Limits of the Criminal Law* (Oxford: Oxford University Press), 69–90.

Haggerty, K (2003), 'From Risk to Precaution: The Rationalities of Personal Crime Prevention', in R Ericson and A Doyle (eds.), *Risk and Morality* (Toronto: University of Toronto Press), 193–214.

Hale, B (2010), *Mental Health Law* 5th edn (London: Sweet and Maxwell).

Hanson, RK and Howard, P (2010), 'Individual confidence intervals do not inform decision-makers about the accuracy of risk assessment evaluations', *Law and Human Behaviour* 34(4), 275–81.

Harcourt, B (1999), 'The Collapse of the Harm Principle', *The Journal of Criminal Law and Criminology* 90(1), 109–94.

——(2003), 'The Shaping of Chance: Actuarial Models and Criminal Profiling at the Turn of the Twenty-First Century', *The University of Chicago Law Review* 70(105), 105–28.

——(2007), *Against Prediction: Profiling, Policing, and Punishing in an Actuarial Age* (Chicago: University of Chicago Press).

——(2013), 'Punitive Preventive Justice: A Critique', in A Ashworth, L Zedner, and P Tomlin (eds.), *Prevention and the Limits of the Criminal Law* (Oxford: Oxford University Press), 232–72.

Hardy, K and Williams, G (2011), 'What is "Terrorism"? Assessing Domestic Legal Definitions', *UCLA Journal of International Law and Foreign Affairs* 16(1), 77–162.

Harel, A (2008), 'Why only the state may inflict criminal sanctions: the case against privately inflicted sanctions', *Legal Theory* 14, 113–33.

Harris, D, et al. (2009), *Harris, O'Boyle & Warbrick: Law of the European Convention on Human Rights* 2nd edn (Oxford: Oxford University Press).

Harris, GT, Rice, ME, and Quinsey, VL (2008), 'Shall evidence-based risk assessment be abandoned?', *The British Journal of Psychiatry* 192, 154.

Harrison, K (2011), *Dangerousness, Risk and the Governance of Serious Sexual and Violent Offenders* (Abingdon: Routledge).

Hart, HLA (1965), *The Morality of Criminal Law: Two Lectures* (Jerusalem: Hebrew University).

——(1968), *Punishment and Responsibility* (Oxford: Oxford University Press).

——(2008), *Punishment and Responsibility*, ed. J Gardner (Oxford: Oxford University Press).

Hart, SD, Michie, C, and Cooke, DJ (2007), 'Precision of actuarial risk assessment instruments: Evaluating the "margins of error" of group v. individual predictions of violence', *Journal of Psychiatry* 190, 60–5.

Hayek, FA (1960), *The Constitution of Liberty* (Chicago: Chicago University Press).

Hayter, T (2004), *Open Borders: The Case against Immigration Controls* (London: Pluto Press).

Hebenton, B and Seddon, T (2009), 'From Dangerousness to Precaution: Managing Sexual and Violent Offenders in an Insecure and Uncertain Age', *British Journal of Criminology* 49, 343–62.

Heilbrun, K (1997), 'Prediction versus management models relevant to risk assessment: the importance of legal decision-making context' , *Law and Human Behaviour* 21, 347–59.

Her Majesty's Inspectorate of Constabulary (2013), *Stop and Search Powers: Are the Police using them Effectively and Fairly?* (London: HMSO).

HM Government (2011), *Prevent Strategy* Cm 8092 (London: HMSO).

HM Government (2011), *Review of Counter-Terrorism and Security Powers Review Findings and Recommendations* Cm 8004 (London: HMSO).

HM Government (2011), *Review of Counter-Terrorism and Security Powers: Summary of Responses to the Consultation* Cm 8005 (London: HMSO).

HM Government (2012), *Channel: Protecting vulnerable people from being drawn into terrorism. A guide for local partnerships* (London: HMSO).

HM Government (2013), *The Coalition Together in the National Interest* (London: HMSO).

HM Inspectorate of Prisons (2012), *Remand Prisoners: a Thematic Review* (London: HMIP).

Hobbes, T (2008, 1651) *Leviathan* (Oxford: Oxford University Press).

Hodgson, J and Tadros, V (2013), 'The Impossibility of Defining Terrorism', *New Criminal Law Review* 16(3), 494–526.

Hoffman, S and Macdonald, S (2010), 'Should ASBOs Be Civilized?', *Criminal Law Review* 6, 457–73.

Home Office (1997), *Life Licences: Reconviction and Recall by the End of 1995: England and Wales* (London: HMSO).

Home Office (2005), *Controlling Our Borders: Making Migration Work for Britain. Five-Year Strategy for Asylum and Immigration* (London: HMSO).

Home Office (2006), *New Powers against Organised and Financial Crime* Cm 6875 (London: HMSO).

Home Office (2010), *Protecting Our Border, Protecting the Public. The UK Border Agency's Five-Year Strategy for Enforcing our Immigration Rules and Addressing Immigration and Cross-Border Crime* (London: HMSO).

Home Office (2011), *Control of Immigration Quarterly Statistical Summary First Quarter 2011* (London: HMSO).

Home Office (2011), *UKBA Business Plan 2011–2015* (London: HMSO).

Home Office (2012), *Code of Practice (England, Wales and Scotland) for the Exercise of Stop and Search Powers under Section 43 and 43A of the Terrorism Act 2000, and the Authorisation and Exercise of Stop and Search Powers Relating to Section 47A and Schedule 6B to the Terrorism Act 2000* (London: HMSO).

Home Office (2012), *Operation of Police Powers under the Terrorism Act* (HOSB 11/12) (London: HMSO).

Home Office (2013), *Statistics on Football-Related Arrests and Banning Order, Season 2011–12* (London: HMSO).

Hood, R and Shute, S (2000), *Parole Decision-Making: Weighing the Risk to the Public* (London: Home Office).

——and——(2000), *The Parole System at Work: Home Office Research Study No. 202* (London: HMSO).

——and——(2002), *Reconviction Rates of Serious Sex Offenders and Assessments of Their Risk* Research Findings 164 (London: HMSO).

Horder, J (2012), 'Harmless Wrongdoing and the Anticipatory Perspective on Criminalisation', in GR Sullivan and I Dennis (eds.), *Seeking Security: Pre-empting the Commission of Criminal Harms* (Oxford: Hart Publishing), 79–102.

——(2012b), 'Criminal Attempt, the Rule of Law, and Accountability in Criminal Law', in L Zedner and JV Roberts (eds.), *Principles and Values in Criminal Law and Criminal Justice* (Oxford: Oxford University Press), 37–50.

House of Commons (1818), *The Third Report from the Select Committee on the Police of the Metropolis* (London: House of Commons).

House of Commons Home Affairs Committee (2013), *The Draft Anti-Social Behaviour Bill: Pre-Legislative Scrutiny* (London: House of Commons).

House of Commons Justice Committee, (2008), *Towards Effective Sentencing* (HC 184–I).

Hudson, B (2006), 'Punishing Monsters, Judging Aliens: Justice at the Borders of Community', *Australian & New Zealand Journal of Criminology* 39(2), 232–47.

Hughes, G (1998), *Understanding Crime Prevention: Social Control, Risk and Late Modernity* (Buckingham: Open University Press).

Hunt, A (2007), 'Criminal Prohibitions on Direct and Indirect Encouragement of Terrorism', *Criminal Law Review*, 441–58.

——(forthcoming), 'From control orders to TPIMs: variations on a number of themes in British legal responses to terrorism', *Crime, Law and Social Change*. Available at SSRN: <http://ssrn.com/abstract=2235805>.

Husak, D (2008), *Overcriminalization: The Limits of the Criminal Law* (Oxford: Oxford University Press).

——(2011), 'Lifting the Cloak: Preventive Detention as Punishment', *San Diego Law Review* 48, 1173–204.

——(2013), 'Preventive Detention as Punishment? Some Possible Obstacles'', in A Ashworth, L Zedner, and P Tomlin (eds.), *Prevention and the Limits of the Criminal Law* (Oxford: Oxford University Press), 178–93.

Huysmans, J (2006), *The Politics of Insecurity: Fear, Migration and Asylum in the EU* (London: Routledge).

——and Buonfino, A (2008), 'Politics of Exception and Unease: Immigration, Asylum and Terrorism in Parliamentary Debates in the UK', *Political Studies* 56(4), 766–88.

Ignatieff, M (1978), *A Just Measure of Pain: The Penitentiary in the Industrial Revolution 1750–1850* (London: Macmillan).

——(2004), *The Lesser Evil: Political Ethics in an Age of Terror* (Edinburgh: Edinburgh University Press).

Innes, M., et al. (2007), *Hearts and Minds and Eyes and Ears: Reducing Radicalisation Risks through Reassurance Oriented Policing:* (Cardiff: Cardiff University).

Ip, J (2013), 'Sunset Clauses and Counterterrorism Legislation', *Public Law*, 74–99.

——2013, 'The reform of counterterrorism stop and search after Gillan v United Kingdom', *Human Rights Law Review*, 13(4), 729–60.

Jackson, JD and Summers, SJ (2012), *The Internationalisation of Criminal Evidence* (Cambridge: Cambridge University Press).

Janus, ES (2000), 'Civil commitment as social control', in M Brown and J Pratt (eds.), *Dangerous Offenders: Punishment and Social Order* (London: Routledge), 71–90.

——(2004), 'The Preventive State, Terrorists and Sexual Predators: Countering the Threat of a New Outsider Jurisprudence', *Criminal Law Bulletin* 40, 576–98.

——(2006), *Failure to Protect: America's Sexual Predator Laws and the Rise of the Preventive State* (Ithaca: Cornell University Press).

Jareborg, N (ed.) (1988), *Essays in Criminal Law* (Sweden: Iustus Forlag).

Johnstone, L (2011), 'Assessing and Managing Violent Youth: Implications for Sentencing', in B McSherry and P Keyzer (eds.), *Dangerous Offenders: Policy, Prediction, and Practice* (New York: Routledge), 123–45.

Joint Committee on Human Rights (2009), *Demonstrating Respect for Rights? A Human Rights Approach to Policing Protest* (HC 320–1).

Joint Committee on Human Rights (2010), *Counter-Terrorism Policy and Human Rights (Sixteenth Report): Annual Renewal of Control Orders Legislation* (HL Paper 64, HC 395).

Joint Committee on Human Rights (2012), *Draft Enhanced Terrorism Prevention and Investigation Measures Bill* (London: HMSO).

Judicial Studies Board (2007), *Anti-Social Behaviour Orders: A Guide for the Judiciary* 3rd edn (London: JSB).

Justice (2009), *Secret Evidence* (London: Justice).

Kaufman, E (2013), 'Hubs and Spokes: The Transformation of the British Prison', in KF Aas and M Bosworth (eds.), *The Borders of Punishment: Migration, Citizenship, and Social Exclusion* (Oxford: Oxford University Press), 166–82.

Kavanagh, A (2010), 'Special Advocates, Control Orders and the Right to a Fair Trial', *Modern Law Review* 63(5), 836–57.

Kemshall, H (2003), *Understanding Risk in Criminal Justice* (Maidenhead: Open University Press).

——(2008), *Understanding the Community Management of High Risk Offenders* (Maidenhead: Open University Press).

——(2011), 'Crime and risk: Contested territory for risk theorising', *International Journal of Law, Crime and Justice* 39(4), 218–29.

——and Maguire, M (2001), 'Public protection, partnership and risk penality: The multi-agency risk management of sexual and violent offenders', *Punishment and Society* 3(2), 237–64.

King, P (2000), *Crime, Justice and Discretion in England 1740–1820* (Oxford: Oxford University Press).

Knowles, D (2010), *Political Obligation: A Critical Introduction* (Abingdon: Routledge).

Krasmann, S (2007), 'The enemy on the border: Critique of a programme in favour of a preventive state', *Punishment and Society* 9(3), 301–18.

Labour Party (1995), *A Quiet Life: Tough Action on Criminal Neighbours* (London: Labour Party).

Lacey, N (1988), *State Punishment: Political Principles and Community Values* (London: Routledge).

——(2001), 'In Search of the Responsible Subject: History, Philosophy and Social Sciences in Criminal Law Theory', *Modern Law Review* 64(3), 350–71.

Lamond, G (2000), 'The Coerciveness of Law', *Oxford Journal of Legal Studies* 20, 39–62.

Law Commission (2007), *Conspiracy and Attempts*, Consultation Paper No 183 (London: Law Commission).

Law Commission (2010), *Criminal Law in Regulatory Contexts*, Consultation Paper No 195 (London: Law Commission).

Law Commission (2013), 'Criminal Liability: Insanity and Automatism, a Discussion Paper'.

Lazarus, L (2012), 'Positive Obligations and Criminal justice: Duties to Protect or Coerce?', in L Zedner and JV Roberts (eds.), *Principles and Values in Criminal Law and Criminal Justice: Essays in Honour of Andrew Ashworth* (Oxford: Oxford University Press), 135–55.

—— (2012), 'The Right to Security—Securing Rights or Securitizing Rights', in R Dickinson, et al. (eds.), *Examining Critical Perspectives on Human Rights* (Cambridge: Cambridge University Press), 87–106.

Leader-Elliott, I (2011), 'Framing preparatory inchoate offences in the Criminal Code', *Criminal Law Journal* 35, 80–97.

Leng, R, Taylor, R, and Wasik, M (1998), *Blackstone's Guide to the Crime and Disorder Act 1998* (London: Blackstone).

Liberty (2008), *Liberty's Evidence to the Joint Committee on Human Rights Call for Evidence on the Draft Legislative Programme 2008–09* (London: Liberty).

—— (2013), *Committee Stage Briefing on the Anti-Social Behaviour, Crime and Policing Bill in the House of Commons* (London: Liberty).

Lidz, C, Mulvey, E, and Gardner, W (1993), 'The accuracy of predictions of violence to others', *Journal of the American Medical Association* 269(8), 1007–11.

Lippke, RL (2007), *Rethinking Imprisonment* (Oxford: Oxford University Press).

—— (2008), 'No Easy Way Out: Dangerous Offenders and Preventive Detention', *Law and Philosophy* 27(4), 383–414.

—— (2011), *The Ethics of Plea Bargaining* (Oxford: Oxford University Press).

Loader, I and Walker, N (2005), 'Necessary Virtues: The Legitimate Place of the State in the Production of Security', in B Dupont and J Wood (eds.), *Democracy, Society and the Governance of Security* (Cambridge: Cambridge University Press), 165–95.

—— and —— (2011), *Civilizing Security* (Cambridge: Cambridge University Press).

Locke, J (1690), *Two Treatises of Government* (Cambridge: Cambridge University Press, 1988).

Logan, C (2011), 'Managing High-Risk Personality Disordered Offenders', in B McSherry and P Keyzer (eds.), *Dangerous People: Policy, Prediciton, and Practice* (New York: Routledge), 233–47.

Lomell, HM (2012), 'Punishing the Uncommitted Crime: Prevention, Preemption, Precaution and the Transformation of the Criminal Law', in B Hudson and S Ugelvik (eds.), *Justice and Security in the 21st Century: Risks, Rights and the Rule of Law* (London: Routledge), 83–100.

Loughnan, A (2008–2009), 'Legislation We Had to Have: The Crimes (Criminal Organisations Control) Act 2009 (NSW)', *Current Issues in Criminal Justice* 20, 457–65.

Lowe, V (2005), '"Clear and Present Danger": Responses to Terrorism', *International and Comparative Law Quarterly* 54, 185–96.

Luban, D (2005), 'Eight Fallacies about Liberty and Security', in RA Wilson (ed.), *Human Rights in the War on Terror* (Cambridge: Cambridge University Press), 242–57.

Lynch, A, Macdonald, E, and Williams, G (eds.) (2007), *Law and Liberty in the War on Terror* (Sydney: The Federation Press).

Lynch, M (1998), 'Waste Managers? The New Penology, Crime Fighting and Parole Agent Identity', *Law and Society Review* 32, 839–69.

MacCormick, N (2005), *Rhetoric and the Rule of Law: A Theory of Legal Reasoning* (Oxford: Oxford University Press).

Macdonald, K (2011), *Review of Counter-Terrorism and Security Powers* Cm 8003 (London: HMSO).

Macdonald, S (2006), 'The Principle of Composite Sentencing: its Centrality to, and Implications for, the ASBO', *Criminal Law Review*, 791–808.

——(2007), 'ASBOs and Control Orders: Two Recurring Themes, Two Apparent Contradictions', *Parliamentary Affairs* 60(4), 601–24.

Mackay, RD (2010), 'Mental Disability at the Time of the Trial', in LO Gostin, et al. (eds.), *Principles of Mental Health Law and Policy* (Oxford: Oxford University Press), 757–76.

——(2010), 'Mental Disability at the Time of the Offence', in LO Gostin, et al. (eds.), *Principles of Mental Health Law and Policy* (Oxford: Oxford University Press), 721–56.

——(2010), 'Transfer to Hospital', in LO Gostin, et al. (eds.), *Principles of Mental Health Law and Policy* (Oxford: Oxford University Press), 803–20.

Macklem, A (2001), 'Borderline Security', in RJ Daniels, P Macklem, and K Roach (eds.), *The Security of Freedom* (Toronto: University of Toronto Press), 383–404.

Martin, R (2006), 'The Exercise of Public Health Powers in Cases of Infectious Disease: Human Rights Implications', *Medical Law Review* 14, 132–43.

Matravers, M (2013), 'On Preventive Justice', in A Ashworth, L Zedner, and P Tomlin (eds.), *Prevention and the Limits of the Criminal Law* (Oxford: Oxford University Press), 235–51.

Maurutto, P and Hannah-Moffat, K (2006), 'Assembling Risk and the Restructuring of Penal Control', *British Journal of Criminology* 46, 438–54.

Mawby, RC and Gisby, W (2009), 'Crime fears in an expanding European Union: Just another moral panic?', *The Howard Journal of Criminal Justice* 48(1), 37–51.

Mazerolle, LG and Roehl, J (1998), *Civil Remedies and Crime Prevention* (Cullompton, Devon: Willan Publishing).

McCulloch, J and Carlton, B (2006), 'Preempting Justice: Suppression of Financing of Terrorism and the "War on Terror"', *Current Issues in Criminal Justice* 17(3), 397–412.

McDonald, S (2007), 'Involuntary Detention and the Separation of Judicial Power', *Federal Law Review* 35, 25–79.

McLeod, AM (2012), 'The US Criminal-Immigration Convergence and its Possible Undoing', *American Criminal Law Review* 49, 105–78.

McLeod, R, Sweeting, A, and Evans, R (2010), *Improving the Structure and Content of Psychiatric Reports for Sentencing: Research to Develop Good Practice Guidance* (London: Ministry of Justice).

McMullen, J (1998), 'The Arresting Eye: Discourse, Surveillance and Disciplinary Administration in Early English Police Thinking', *Social and Legal Studies* 7(1), 97–128.

McSherry, B (2004), 'Terrorism Offences in the Criminal Code: Broadening the Boundaries of Australian Criminal Laws', *University of New South Wales Law Journal* 27, 354–72.

——(2006), 'Sex, Drugs and "Evil" Souls: the Growing Reliance on Preventive Detention Regimes', *Monash University Law Review* 32(2), 237–74.

——(2009), 'Expanding the Boundaries of Inchoate Crimes: The Growing Reliance on Preparatory Offences', in B McSherry, A Norrie, and S Bronitt (eds.), *Regulating Deviance: The Redirection of Criminalisation and the Futures of Criminal Law* (Oxford: Hart Publishing), 141–64.

——and Keyzer, P (2009), *Sex Offenders and Preventive Detention: Politics, Policy and Practice* (Sydney: Federation Press).

——and——(2011), '"Dangerous" People: An Overview', in B McSherry and P Keyzer (eds.), *Dangerous People: Policy, Prediction, and Practice* (New York: Routledge), 3–12.

Mead, D (2009), 'Of Kettles, Cordons and Crowd Control', *European Human Rights Law Review*, 376–94.

——(2010), *The New Law of Peaceful Protest* (Oxford: Hart Publishing).

Melia, MC (2011), 'Terrorism and Criminal Law: The Dream of Prevention, the Nightmare of the Rule of Law', *New Criminal Law Review* 14(1), 108–22.

Meyerson, D (2007), 'Why Courts Should not Balance Rights', *Melbourne University Law Review*, 873–903.

Mill, JS (1859, 1979), *On Liberty* (Harmondsworth, Middlesex: Penguin).

Miller, GH (2008), 'Alan Stone and the Ethics of Forensic Psychiatry: An Overview', *Journal of the American Academy of Psychiatry and the Law* 36(2), 191–4.

Miller, T (2003), 'Citizenship & Severity. Recent Immigration Reforms and the New Penology', *Georgetown Immigration Law Journal* 17, 611–66.

——(2005), 'Blurring the Boundaries between Immigration and Crime Control after September 11th', *Boston College Third World Law Journal* 25, 81–124.

Ministry of Justice (2010), *Breaking the Cycle: Effective Punishment, Rehabilitation and Sentencing of Offenders* Cm 7972 (London: Ministry of Justice).

Ministry of Justice (2010), *Statistics on Race and the Criminal Justice System 2010* (London: Ministry of Justice).

Ministry of Justice (2011), *Anti-Social Behaviour Order Statistics England and Wales 2011* (London: Ministry of Justice).

Ministry of Justice (2012), *Anti-Social Behaviour Order Statistics England and Wales 2011* (London: Ministry of Justice).

Ministry of Justice (2012), *Court Statistics* (London: Ministry of Justice).

Ministry of Justice (2012), *Criminal Justice Statistics* (London: Ministry of Justice).

Ministry of Justice (2012), *MAPPA Guidance 2012. Version 4* (London: Ministry of Justice).

Ministry of Justice (2012), *Multi-Agency Public Protection Arrangements, Annual Report 2011–12* (London: Ministry of Justice).

Ministry of Justice (2012), *Statistics on Race and the Criminal Justice System 2010* (London: Ministry of Justice).

Monahan, J (2001), *Rethinking Risk Assessment: The MacArthur Study of Mental Disorder and Violence* (New York: Oxford University Press).

Monahan, J, et al. (2005), 'An actuarial model of violence risk assessment for persons with mental disorders', *Psychiatric Services* 56, 810–15.

Moore, M (2010), *Placing Blame: A Theory of the Criminal Law* (Oxford: Oxford University Press).

Moore, MS (2009), 'The Moral Worth of Retribution', in A von Hirsch, A Ashworth, and J Roberts (eds.), *Principled Sentencing: Readings on Theory and Policy* 3rd edn (Oxford: Hart Publishing), 110–14.

Morse, S (2007), 'The Non-Problem of Free Will in Forensic Psychiatry and Psychology', *Behavioral Sciences & the Law* 25, 203–20.

Morse, SJ (1998), 'Fear of Danger, Flight from Culpability', *Psychology, Public Policy, And Law* 4, 250–67.

——(1999), 'Neither Desert nor Disease', *Legal Theory* 5, 265–309.

——(2011), 'Protecting Liberty and Autonomy: Desert/Disease Jurisprudence', *San Diego Law Review* 48(4), 1077–125.

Mossman, D and Sellke, T (2007), 'Avoiding errors about "margins of error"', *British Journal of Psychiatry* 191, 561–2.

Murphy, C (2012), *EU Counter-Terrorism Law: Pre-Emption and the Rule of Law* (Oxford: Hart Publishing).

Neocleous, M (2000), 'Social Police and the Mechanisms of Prevention: Patrick Colquhoun and the Condition of Poverty', *British Journal of Criminology* 40(4), 710–26.

——(2006), 'Theoretical Foundations of the "New Police Science"', in MD Dubber and M Valverde (eds.), *The New Police Science: The Police Power in Domestic and International Governance* (Stanford: Stanford University Press), 17–41.

——(2008), *Critique of Security* (Edinburgh: Edinburgh University Press).

Neumann, P (2010), *Prisons and Terrorism: Radicalisation and De-radicalisation in 15 Countries* (London: ICSR).

ni Raifeartaigh, U (1997), 'Reconciling Bail Law with the Presumption of Innocence', *Oxford Journal of Legal Studies* 17(1), 1–21.

Nickel, JW (2013), 'Restraining Orders, Liberty and Due Process', in A Ashworth, L Zedner, and P Tomlin (eds.), *Prevention and the Limits of the Criminal Law* (Oxford: Oxford University Press), 156–77.

Nozick, R (1974), *Anarchy, State and Utopia* (Oxford: Blackwell).

Ogletree, C and Sarat, A (2013), *Life without Parole: America's New Death Penalty?* (New York: New York University Press).

Ohana, D (2006), 'Responding to Acts Preparatory to the Commission of a Crime: Criminalization or Prevention', *Criminal Justice Ethics*, Summer/Fall, 23–39.

——(2007), 'Desert and Punishment for Acts Preparatory to the Commission of a Crime', *Canadian Journal of Law & Jurisprudence* 20, 113–42.

——(2010), 'Trust, Distrust and Reassurance: Diversion and Preventive Orders Through the Prism of *Feindstrafrecht*', *The Modern Law Review* 73(5), 721–51.

O'Malley, P (1996), 'Risk and Responsibility', in A Barry, T Osborne, and N Rose (eds.), *Foucault and Political Reason: Liberalism, Neo-Liberalism and Rationalities of Government* (London: UCL Press), 189–207.

——(2004), *Risk, Uncertainty and Government* (London: The Glasshouse Press).

——(2009), 'Jeremy Bentham', *University of Sydney Law School, Legal Studies Papers*, 9/10 September.

——(ed.), (1998), *Crime and the Risk Society* (Aldershot: Ashgate).

——and Hutchinson, S (2007), 'Reinventing Prevention: Why did "Crime Prevention" Develop So Late?', *British Journal of Criminology* 47(3), 373–89.

Ormerod, D (2007), 'The Fraud Act 2006—Criminalising Lying?', *Criminal Law Review*, 193–219.

——Choo, A, and Easter, R (2010), 'The "Witness Anonymity" and "Investigation Anonymity" Provisions', *Criminal Law Review*, 368–88.

Osborne, D and Gaebler, T (1992), *Reinventing Government: How the Entrepreneurial Spirit is Transforming the Public Sector* (New York: Penguin).

Padfield, N (2002), *Beyond the Tariff: Human Rights and the Release of Life Sentence Prisoners* (Cullompton: Willan Publishing).

——(2005), 'Back door sentencing: is recall to prison a penal process?', *Cambridge Law Journal* 64, 276–9.

——(2008), *Text and Materials on the Criminal Justice Process* (Oxford: Oxford University Press).

——and Liebling, A (2000), *An Exploration of Decision-Making at Discretionary Lifer Panels* (London: Home Office).

——and Maruna, S (2006), 'The revolving door at the prison gate: Exploring the dramatic increase in recalls to prison', *Criminology and Criminal Justice* 6(3), 329–52.

——Morgan, R, and Maguire, M (2012), 'Out of Court, Out of Sight? Criminal Sanctions and Non-Judicial Decision-Making', in M Maguire, R Morgan, and R Reiner (eds.), *The Oxford Handbook of Criminology* 5th edn (Oxford: Oxford University Press), 955–85.

Parmet, WE (2008), 'J.S. Mill and the American Law of Quarantine', *Public Health Ethics* 1(3), 210–22.

Peay, J (1989), *Tribunals on Trial* (Oxford: Clarendon Press).

——(2011), *Mental Health and Crime* (Abingdon: Routledge).

——(2012), 'Mentally Disordered Offenders, Mental Health and Crime', in M Maguire, R Morgan, and R Reiner (eds.), *The Oxford Handbook of Criminology* 5th edn (Oxford: Oxford University Press), 426–49.

Perkins, E (2003), *Decision-Making in Mental Health Review Tribunals* (London: Policy Studies Institute).

Player, E, et al. (2010), 'Remanded in Custody: an Analysis of Recent Trends in England and Wales', *The Howard Journal of Criminal Justice* 49, 231–51.

Pratt, J (2007), *Penal Populism* (London: Routledge).

Prison Reform Trust (2010), *Unjust Deserts: Imprisonment for Public Protection* (London: PRT).

Prison Reform Trust (November 2012), *Bromley Briefings Prison Factfile*.

Quirk, H, Seddon, T, and Smith, G (eds.) (2010), *Regulation and Criminal Justice: Innovations in Policy and Research* (Cambridge: Cambridge University Press).

Radzinowicz, L (1956), *A History of English Criminal Law and its Administration from 1750. Volume 3* (London: Steven & Sons Limited).

——and Hood, R (1986), *The Emergence of Penal Policy in Victorian and Edwardian England* (Oxford: Oxford University Press).

Rafter, N (2011), 'Origins of Criminology', in M Bosworth and C Hoyle (eds.), *What is Criminology?* (Oxford: Oxford University Press), 143–56.

Ramsay, P (2009), 'The Theory of Vulnerable Autonomy and the Legitimacy of Civil Preventative Orders', in B McSherry, A Norrie, and S Bronitt (eds.), *Regulating Deviance: The Redirection of Criminalisation and the Futures of Criminal Law* (Oxford: Hart Publishing), 141–64.

——(2012), 'Imprisonment under the Precautionary Principle', in GR Sullivan and I Dennis (eds.), *Seeking Security: Pre-Empting the Commission of Criminal Harms* (Oxford: Hart Publishing), 193–218.

——(2012), *The Insecurity State: Vulnerable Autonomy and the Right to Security in the Criminal Law* (Oxford: Oxford University Press).

——(2012), 'Preparation Offences, Security Interests and Political Freedom', in RA Duff, et al. (eds.), *The Structures of the Criminal Law* (Oxford: Oxford University Press), 203–28.

——(2013), 'Democratic Limits to Preventive Criminal Law', in A Ashworth, L Zedner, and P Tomlin (eds.), *Prevention and the Limits of the Criminal Law* (Oxford: Oxford University Press), 213–34.

Rawlings, P (2003), 'Policing before the Police', in T Newburn (ed.), *Handbook of Policing* (Cullompton, Devon: Willan Publishing), 47–71.

Rawls, J (1973), *A Theory of Justice* (Oxford: Oxford University Press).

Raynor, P (2012), 'Community Penalties: Probation, and Offender Management', in M Maguire, R Morgan, and R Reiner (eds.), *The Oxford Handbook of Criminology* 5th edn (Oxford: Oxford University Press), 928–54.

Raz, J (1977), 'The Rule of Law and its Virtue', *Law Quarterly Review* 93, 195–211.

Reynolds, E (1998), *Before the Bobbies: The Night Watch and Police Reform in Metropolitan London 1720–1830* (Palo Alto, CA: Stanford University Press).

Richards, EP (1989), 'The Jurisprudence of Prevention: the right of societal self-defense against dangerous individuals', *Hastings Constitutional Law Quarterly* 16, 329–92.

Richardson Committee (1999), *Review of the Mental Health Act 1983: Report of the Expert Committee*.

Richardson, G (2012), 'Mental Disabilities and the Law: from Substitute to Supported Decision-Making', *Current Legal Problems* 65, 333–54.

——and Machin, D (2000), 'Judicial Review and Tribunal Decision-Making: A Study of Mental Health Review Tribunals', *Public Law*, 494–514.

——and Thorold, O (1999), 'Law as a Rights Protector: Assessing the Mental Health Act 1983', in N Eastman and J Peay (eds.), *Law without Enforcement* (Oxford: Hart Publishing), 109–32.

Roach, K (2004), 'The World Wide Expansion of Anti-Terrorism Laws after 11 September 2001', *Studi Senesi*, CXVI (III Serie, LIII-Fasc. 3), 487–527.

——(2011), *The 9/11 Effect: Comparative Counter-Terrorism* (Cambridge: Cambridge University Press).

Robinson, PH (2001), 'Punishing Dangerousness: Cloaking Preventive Detention as Criminal Justice', *Harvard Law Review* 114(5), 1429–56.

Rogers, J (2008), 'The Codification of Attempts and the Case for "Preparation"', *Criminal Law Review*, 937–54.

Rose, D (2004), *Guantanamo: America's War on Human Rights* (London: Faber & Faber).

Rose, N (2000), 'Government and Control', *British Journal of Criminology Special Issue: Criminology and Social Theory* 40, 321–39.

Rudolph, C (2003), 'Globalization and Security: Migration and Evolving Conceptions of Security in Statecraft and Scholarship', *Security Studies* 13(1), 1–32.

Rutherford, A (1988), 'Boundaries of English Penal Police', *Oxford Journal of Legal Studies* 8(1), 132–41.

Ryan, A (2011), 'Hobbes' political philosophy', in T Sorell (ed.), *The Cambridge Companion to Hobbes* (Cambridge: Cambridge University Press), 208–45.

Sanders, A, Young, R, and Burton, M (2010), *Criminal Justice* 4th edn (Oxford: Oxford University Press).

Schauer, F (2013), 'The Ubiquity of Prevention', in A Ashworth, L Zedner, and P Tomlin (eds.), *Prevention and the Limits of the Criminal Law* (Oxford: Oxford University Press), 10–22.

Scottish Risk Management (2011), *Framework for Risk Assessment, Management and Evaluation: Frame* (Paisley: Scottish Risk Management).

Seddon, T (2008), 'Dangerous Liaisons: Personality Disorder and the Politics of Risk', *Theoretical Criminology* 10, 301–17.

Semple, J (1993), *Bentham's Prison: A Study of the Panopticon Penitentiary* (Oxford: Oxford University Press).

Sentencing Council (2011), *Assault: Definitive Guideline* (London: Sentencing Council).

Shapiro, M (1981), *Courts—A Comparative and Political Analysis* (Chicago: University of Chicago Press).

Sharpe, JA (1990), *Judicial Punishment in England* (London: Faber & Faber).

Sigworth, EM and Wyke, TJ (1980), 'A Study of Victorian Prostitution and Venereal Disease', in M Vicnius (ed.), *Suffer and Be Still. Women in the Victorian Age* (London: Methuen & Co. Ltd), 77–99.

Simester, AP (2012), 'Prophylactic Crimes', in GR Sullivan and I Dennis (eds.), *Seeking Security: Pre-Empting the Commission of Criminal Harms* (Oxford: Hart Publishing), 59–78.

——and von Hirsch, A (2006), 'Regulating Offensive Conduct through Two-Step Prohibitions', in A von Hirsch and AP Simester (eds.), *Incivilities: Regulating Offensive Behaviour* (Oxford: Hart Publishing), 173–94.

——and von Hirsch, A (2011), *Crimes, Harms and Wrongs: On the Principles of Criminalization* (Oxford: Hart Publishing).

——et al. (2010), *Simester and Sullivan's Criminal Law* 4th edn (Oxford: Hart Publishing).

Simon, J (2005), 'Reversal of Fortune: The Resurgence of Individual Risk Assessment in Criminal Justice', *Annual Review of Law and Social Science* 1, 397–421.

Simpson, AWB (1992), *In the Highest Degree Odious: Detention without Trial in Wartime Britain* (Oxford: Oxford University Press).

Skeem, J and Monahan, J (2011), 'Current directions in violence risk assessment', *Current Directions in Psychological Science* 21(1), 38–42.

Sklansky, DA (2012), 'Crime, Immigration, and Ad Hoc Instrumentalism', *New Criminal Law Review* 15(2), 157–223.

Slobogin, C (2003), 'A Jurisprudence of Dangerousness', *Northwestern University Law Review* 98(1), 1–62.

——(2011), 'Prevention as the Primary Goal of Sentencing: The Modern Case for Indeterminate Dispositions in Criminal Cases', *San Diego Law Review* 48, 1127–71.

Smilansky, S (1994), 'The Time to Punish', *Analysis* 54(1), 50–3.

Smith, A (1978), *Lectures on Jurisprudence* (Oxford: Oxford University Press).

Solivetti, L (2005), 'Who Is Afraid of Migration and Crime?', *The Howard Journal of Criminal Justice* 44(3), 322–5.

Spalek, B and Zahra McDonald, L (2011), *Preventing Religio-Political Extremism Amongst Muslim Youth: A Study Exploring Police–Community Partnership* (Birmingham: University of Birmingham).

Stanton-Ife, J (2012), 'Preventive Detention at the Margins of Autonomy', in GR Sullivan and I Dennis (eds.), *Seeking Security* (Oxford: Hart Publishing), 143–68.

Steiker, C (1998), 'The Limits of the Preventive State', *Journal of Criminal Law and Criminology* 88, 771–808.

——(2013), 'Proportionality as a Limit on Preventive Justice: Promises and Pitfalls', in A Ashworth, L Zedner, and P Tomlin (eds.), *Prevention and the Limits of the Criminal Law* (Oxford: Oxford University Press), 194–213.

Stone, A (2008), 'The Ethical Boundaries of Forensic Psychiatry: A View from the Ivory Tower', *Journal of the American Academy of Psychiatry and the Law* 36(2), 167–74.

Stumpf, J (2007), 'The Crimmigration Crisis: Immigrants, Crime and Sovereign Power', *Lewis & Clark Law School Legal Research Paper Series* Paper No. 2007–2, 1–44.

——(2011), 'Doing Time: Crimmigration Law and the Perils of Haste', *UCLA Law Review* 58, 1705–48.

Styles, J (1987), 'The Emergence of the Police', *British Journal of Criminology* 27(1), 15–22.

Sullivan, GR (2012), 'The Hard Treatment of Innocent Persons in State Responses to the Threat of Large Scale, and Imminent Terrorist Violence: Examining the Legal Constraints', in GR Sullivan and I Dennis (eds.), *Seeking Security: Pre-Empting the Commission of Criminal Harms* (Oxford: Hart Publishing), 293–322.

Sunstein, C (2005), *Laws of Fear: Beyond the Precautionary Principle* (Cambridge: Cambridge University Press).

Tadros, V (2007), 'Justice and Terrorism', *New Criminal Law Review* 10(4), 658–89.

——(2007), 'Rethinking the presumption of innocence', *Criminal Law and Philosophy* 1, 193–213.

——(2013), 'Controlling Risk', in A Ashworth, L Zedner, and P Tomlin (eds.), *Prevention and the Limits of the Criminal Law* (Oxford: Oxford University Press), 133–55.

——and Hodgson, J (2009), 'How to Make a Terrorist Out of Nothing', *Modern Law Review* 72(6), 984–98.

Tasioulas, J (2006), 'Punishment and Repentance', *Philosophy* 81, 279–322.

The Law Commission (1994), 'Binding Over', *Law Com No. 222* (London: The Law Commission).

The Law Commission (2009), *The Admissibility of Expert Evidence in Criminal Proceedings in England and Wales* (London: The Law Commission).

The Parole Board for England and Wales (2012), *Guidance to Members on LAPSO*.

The Parole Board for England and Wales (2013), *Annual Report and Accounts 2012/13 HC346* (London: The Stationery Office).

Thomas, PA (2003), 'Emergency and Anti-Terrorist Powers 9/11: USA and UK', *Fordham International Law Journal* 26(4), 1193–233.

Thompson, SG (2002), 'The White-Collar Police Force: "Duty to Report" Statutes in Criminal Law Theory', *William and Mary Bill of Rights Journal* 11, 3–65.

Thomson, L (2011), 'The Role of Forensic Mental Health Services in Managing High-Risk Offenders: Functioning or Failing?', in B McSherry and P Keyzer (eds.), *Dangerous People: Policy, Prediction and Practice* (Abingdon: Routledge), 165–82.

Thorburn, M (2010), 'Reinventing the Nightwatchman State', *University of Toronto Law Journal* 60, 425–43.

——(2011), 'The Constitution of Criminal Law; Justifications, Policing and the State's Fiduciary Duties', *Criminal Law and Philosophy* 5, 259–76.

Titmuss, RM (1958), *Essays on the Welfare State* (London: Allen & Unwin).

Tomkins, A (2010), 'National security and the role of the court: a changed landscape?', *Law Quarterly Review* 126, 543–67.

——(2011), 'National Security and the Due Process of Law', *Current Legal Problems* 64(1), 215–53.

Tribe, L and Gudridge, P (2004), 'The Anti-Emergency Constitution', *Yale Law Journal* 113(8), 1801–70.

Tulich, T (2012), 'A View Inside the Preventive State: Reflections on a Decade of Anti-Terror Law', *Griffith Law Review* 21(1), 209–44.

Urbinati, N and Zakaras, A (2007), 'Introduction', in N Urbinati and A Zakaras (eds.), *J.S. Mill's Political Thought: A Bicentennial Reassessment* (Cambridge: Cambridge University Press), 1–7.

Vess, J (2005), 'Preventive Detention versus Civil Commitment: Alternative Policies for Public Protection in New Zealand and California', *Psychiatry, Psychology and Law* 12(2), 357–66.

von Hirsch, A and Ashworth, A (2005), *Proportionate Sentencing: Exploring the Principles* (Oxford: Oxford University Press).

——and Jareborg, N (1991), 'Gauging Criminal Harm: A Living-Standard Analysis', *Oxford Journal of Legal Studies*, 11, 1–38.

——and Wasik, M (1997), 'Civil Disqualifications Attending Conviction: A Suggested Conceptual Framework', *Cambridge Law Journal* 56, 559–626.

——et al. (1999), *Criminal Deterrence and Sentence Severity: An Analysis of Recent Research* (Oxford: Hart Publishing).

Waldron, J (2003), 'Security and Liberty: The Image of Balance', *Journal of Political Philosophy* 11(2), 191–210.

——(2007), 'Mill on Liberty and the Contagious Diseases Act', in N Urbinati and A Zakaras (eds.), *J.S. Mill's Political Thought: A Bicentennial Reassessment* (Cambridge: Cambridge University Press), 11–42.

——(2010), *Torture, Terror and Trade-Offs: Philosophy for the White House* (Oxford: Oxford University Press).

Walen, A (2011), 'A Punitive Precondition for Preventive Detention: Lost Status as a Foundation for a Lost Immunity', *San Diego Law Review* 48, 1229–72.

——(2011), 'A Unified Theory of Detention', *Maryland Law Review* 70(4), 871–938.

Walker, C (2005), 'Prisoners of "War all the time"', *European Human Rights Law Review* 1, 50–74.

——(2007), 'Keeping control of terrorists without losing control of constitutionalism', *Stanford Law Review* 59(5), 1395–464.

——(2007), 'The Treatment of Foreign Terror Suspects', *Modern Law Review* 70(3), 427–57.

——(2009), *Blackstone's Guide to the Anti-Terrorism Legislation* (Oxford: Oxford University Press).

——and Horne, A (2012), 'The Terrorism Prevention and Investigations Measures Act 2011: One Thing but not much the Other?', *Criminal Law Review* 6, 421–38.

Walker, N (1972), *Sentencing in a Rational Society* (Harmondsworth: Allen Lane).

——(1996), 'Ethical and Other Problems', in N Walker (ed.), *Dangerous People* (London: Blackstone), 1–12.

——(1997), 'Harms, Probabilities and Precautions', *Oxford Journal of Legal Studies* 17(4), 611–20.

Wallerstein, S (2012), 'On the Legitimacy of Imposing Direct and Indirect Obligations to Disclose Information on Non-Suspects', in GR Sullivan and I Dennis (eds.), *Seeking Security* (Oxford: Hart Publishing), 37–58.

Wandall, R (2006), 'Actuarial risk assessment. The loss of recognition of the individual offender', *Law, Probability and Risk* 5, 175–200.

Wasik, M (2012), 'The Test for Dangerousness', in GR Sullivan and I Dennis (eds.), *Seeking Security: Pre-Empting the Commission of Criminal Harms* (Oxford: Hart Publishing), 243–64.

Weait, M (2007), *Intimacy and Responsibility: The Criminalization of HIV Transmission* (London: Routledge-Cavendish).

Weber, L (2011), ' "It sounds like they shouldn't be here": immigration checks on the streets of Sydney', *Policing and Society* 21(4), 456–67.

——and Bowling, B (2004), 'Policing Migration: A Framework for Investigating the Regulation of Global Mobility', *Policing & Society* 14, 195–212.

Wells, C (1997), 'Stalking: The Criminal Response', *Criminal Law Review*, 463–70.

Westen, P (2011), 'The ontological problem of "risk" and "endangerment" in criminal law', in RA Duff and SP Green (eds.), *Philosophical Foundations of Criminal Law* (Oxford: Oxford University Press), 304–27.

Wilson, W (2013), 'Participating in Crime: Some Thoughts on the Retribution/Prevention Dichotomy in Preparation for Crime and How to Deal with it', in A Reed and M Bohlander (eds.), *Participation in Crime* (Farnham: Ashgate), 115–41.

Wishnie, M (2012), ' Immigration Law and the Proportionality Requirement', *UC Irvine Law Review* 2, 415–52.

World Health Assembly (2005), *International Health Regulations* 2nd edn (Geneva: World Health Organization).

Zedner, L (1991), *Women, Crime, and Custody in Victorian England* (Oxford: Oxford University Press).

——(2005), 'Securing liberty in the face of terror: reflections from criminal justice', *Journal of Law and Society* 32(4), 507–33.

——(2006), 'Policing before and after the Police: the historical antecedents of contemporary crime control', *British Journal of Criminology* 46(1), 78–96.

——(2006), 'Opportunity makes the thief-taker: the influence of economic analysis on crime control', in T Newburn and P Rock (eds.), *The Politics of Crime Control* (Oxford: Oxford University Press), 147–72.

——(2007), 'Seeking Security by Eroding Rights: The Side-Stepping of Due Process', in B Goold and L Lazarus (eds.), *Security and Human Rights* (Oxford: Hart Publishing), 257–76.

——(2007), 'Preventive justice or pre-punishment? The case of control orders', *Current Legal Problems* 59, 174–203.

——(2009), 'Fixing the Future? The pre-emptive turn in criminal justice', in S Bronitt, B McSherry, and A Norrie (eds.), *Regulating Deviance: The Redirection of Criminalisation and the Futures of Criminal Law* (Oxford: Hart Publishing).

——(2009), *Security* (London: Routledge), 35–58.

——(2010), 'Security, the State and the Citizen: the changing architecture of crime control', *New Criminal Law Review* 13(2), 379–403.

——(2012), 'Erring on the side of safety: Risk assessment, expert knowledge, and the criminal court', in GR Sullivan and I Dennis (eds.), *Seeking Security: Pre-Empting the Commission of Criminal Harms* (Oxford: Hart Publishing), 221–41.

——(2014), 'Terrorizing Criminal Law', *Criminal Law and Philosophy*, 8(1), 99–121.

Index

Introductory Note: References such as "178–9" indicate (not necessarily continuous) discussion of a topic across a range of pages. Wherever possible in the case of topics with many references, these have either been divided into sub-topics or only the most significant discussions of the topic are listed. Because the entire work is about 'preventive justice', the use of this term and certain others which occur constantly throughout the book as entry points has been minimized. Information will be found under the corresponding detailed topics.